The Undeserving Rich

American Beliefs about Inequality, Opportunity, and Redistribution

It is widely assumed that Americans care little about income inequality, believe opportunities abound, admire the rich, and dislike redistributive policies. Leslie McCall contends that such assumptions are based on incomplete survey data and economic conditions of the past rather than present. In fact, Americans have desired less inequality for decades, and McCall's book explains why. Americans become most concerned about inequality in times of inequitable growth, when they view the rich as prospering while opportunities for good jobs, fair pay, and high-quality education are restricted for everyone else. As a result, they tend to favor policies to expand opportunity and redistribute earnings in the workplace, reducing inequality in the market rather than redistributing income after the fact with tax and spending policies. This book resolves the paradox of how Americans can at times express little enthusiasm for welfare state policies and still yearn for a more equitable society, and forwards a new model of preferences about income inequality rooted in labor market opportunities rather than welfare state policies.

Leslie McCall is Professor of Sociology and Political Science, as well as Faculty Fellow at the Institute for Policy Research, at Northwestern University. She is the author of *Complex Inequality: Gender, Class, and Race in the New Economy* (2001). Her work on economic inequality has been published in the *American Sociological Review*, *Annual Review of Sociology*, *Demography*, *Economic Geography*, *Perspectives on Politics*, *Signs*, and *Socio-Economic Review*, as well as in several edited volumes.

The Undeserving Rich

*American Beliefs about Inequality, Opportunity,
and Redistribution*

LESLIE McCALL

Northwestern University

CAMBRIDGE
UNIVERSITY PRESS

CAMBRIDGE
UNIVERSITY PRESS

32 Avenue of the Americas, New York NY 10013-2473, USA

Cambridge University Press is part of the University of Cambridge.

It furthers the University's mission by disseminating knowledge in the pursuit of education, learning, and research at the highest international levels of excellence.

www.cambridge.org
Information on this title: www.cambridge.org/9781107699823

First published 2013
Reprinted 2013

A catalog record for this publication is available from the British Library.

Library of Congress Cataloging in Publication data
McCall, Leslie, 1964– author.
The undeserving rich : American beliefs about inequality, opportunity, and redistribution / Leslie McCall, Northwestern University.
  pages cm
Includes bibliographical references and index.
ISBN 978-1-107-02723-7 (hardback) – ISBN 978-1-107-69982-3 (paperback)
  1. Income distribution – United States. 2. Equality – United States. 3. United States – Economic conditions. I. Title.
HC110.I5M374 2013
339.2´20973–dc23   2012037611

ISBN 978-1-107-02723-7 Hardback
ISBN 978-1-107-69982-3 Paperback

Contents

Tables and Figures

Tables

Figures

Preface and Acknowledgments

Despite the title, this book is not about bashing the rich. When I first started studying how Americans think about economic inequality, in the late 1990s, and happened upon this title midway through the following decade, it was uncommon to put the rich at the center of analysis. They attracted little of the attention that was routinely showered on the poor. But the notion that the rich are worthy of detached investigation and informed criticism, like the poor, is becoming more acceptable. This does not mean, however, that we ought to fall into the same trap that often plagues the study of the "undeserving poor." Singling out any group often leads to a pathologizing of that group, and this tends to obscure how the group fits into the rest of society. This book is about how the rich fit into Americans' understanding of inequality and opportunity, in ways that characterize the rich as both productive and unproductive members of society, and thus both deserving and undeserving of their riches.

A central thesis of this book, which seems at once more plausible today than it did when I first began to formulate it, and yet still contrary to ingrained notions of the American dream, is that beliefs about economic inequality are shaped by views about the rich and not the poor (who are more central to beliefs about poverty). Not long ago, when attention was more heavily focused on the poor, poverty, and welfare, the escalation of economic inequality had yet to be fully recognized. Income inequality was an issue that was little discussed, and was often lumped in with discussions of poverty and the redistributive policies that alleviate poverty, such as welfare and progressive taxes. Additionally, in the pioneering days of research by labor economists on rising wage inequality in the 1990s, inequality was posed primarily as a divide between those with and without

xi

a college degree, or between U.S. workers and the new working classes of the developing world, a divide exacerbated by globalization.

From this vantage point, it is remarkable to observe how dramatically attention has shifted from issues concerning the poor and poverty to those concerning the rich and inequality. Much of this is a consequence of new research on the concentration of earnings in the top fractiles of the distribution, as well as to events such as the financial crisis, the Great Recession, and especially the Occupy Wall Street movement (although, as I discuss in Chapter 2, the negative spotlight on the rich was surprisingly bright in much of the 1980s and 1990s). But with this new emphasis on the rich, I wonder whether the pendulum has swung too far in the other direction, particularly with the expanded ranks of the unemployed and insecure in the Great Recession. Here again is where I hope that an analysis of inequality will center on how the rich fit into the larger society – the chasm between the rich and the poor, the rich and the middle class – rather than the rich alone.

How do Americans think about the interconnectedness of these groups? The deserving and the undeserving rich, as I define these concepts in this book, refer mainly to the contributions that the rich make (or do not make) to the broader economic prosperity of the nation, as compared to the contribution that everyone else makes (or does not make) to the broader economic prosperity of the nation. Thus this book is not about the political capture of democracy by the rich, or about how the rich get an easy ride in life or stack the deck more and more in their children's favor in the educational system and labor market, or about how Americans "feel" about the rich (e.g., whether they admire or envy them), although these are all extremely important topics addressed by a number of brilliant books published over the past several years that sit prominently on my bookshelf.

Instead, what I examine are views about the structure of income and the economy, and what I find is a kind of coherence among many Americans in their views of the rich and inequality that may be surprising to most readers. This coherence is counterintuitive in light of widespread assumptions that Americans "vote against their economic self-interest." But it is also counterintuitive in light of opposing arguments, that Americans are capable of calibrating the political and economic direction of the country by zeroing in on a few accessible and vital economic indicators such as unemployment and inflation rates, or lean in a direction that is generally in their economic self-interest yet distorted by lack of information and the incapacity to form effective economic and political organizations.

The coherence that I find suggests that Americans are both more and less clued in than any of these views suggest. On the one hand, I show that many Americans are attuned to the distributional nature of growth, not to growth alone, becoming more critical of inequality as recessions turn into recoveries that are perceived as benefiting the rich at the expense of the rest of Americans. And the media, far from posing solely as an apologist for the rich and rising inequality, often document the tilt of inequitable growth toward the rich, and did so especially in the recovery from the early 1990s' recession. My analysis of public opinion and media data go only to 2010, however, just a year into the most recent recovery. The Occupy Wall Street movement came after I concluded my study, two years into the recovery, which is consistent with the timing of the peak of media attention to rising inequality in the mid-1990s when expectations were frustrated by the first "jobless" recovery on historical record. When new public opinion data from the 2012 General Social Survey become available, a return to peak-level concerns about inequality is expected, and would be consistent with both the pattern in the 1990s that I uncover and with what is likely to have been a deluge of negative coverage of inequality in the wake of the Occupy movements.

On the other hand, Americans are somewhat in the dark as to how to address the problem of inequality, although I would attribute this more to a lack of political leadership than to ignorance. Traditional redistributive policies championed by liberals are not necessarily transparent in their link to the underlying concerns that Americans have about inequality, which is that it restricts the scope of economic growth by limiting opportunities for good jobs with fair pay for Americans up *and* down the ladder. Greater labor market opportunities are the ultimate goal. But how to achieve this is not clearly articulated by politicians and other elites, and what social scientists do advocate along these lines is not always straightforward to implement. In this book, I highlight education, jobs, and fair pay, rather than progressive taxes and other government social policies, as the outcomes that those Americans increasingly concerned about inequality wish to see. This is what I find in this book, but this does not mean that progressive taxes and social policy are unpopular or incapable of enhancing opportunity, only that this case needs to be made more clearly or forcefully, as has been accomplished in several successful ballot measures to raise taxes on the rich at the state level.

Perhaps most important from a scholarly perspective, current surveys do not allow us to dig deeper into views about the full spectrum of economic, labor market, and educational policies that would create an equal opportunity society. This is because of our surveys' legacy of asking more about social rights from the government than about economic rights from employers. Both new policy ideas and new survey questions are sorely needed to better capture and implement the popular will for a more equitable economy.

This project dates to the late 1990s, when I was in the final stages of completing my book on differences in patterns of earnings inequality by education, gender, and race. When I was asked about my research by a new acquaintance, I usually turned the question around and asked whether he or she had heard anything about the rise in economic inequality. Even if people knew about the issue, I sensed that it was of little consequence or interest to them. Most of the time, eyes glazed over in response to my question, and I tried not to take it personally. Ever since then, I have been interested in how people think about inequality. It has been a very long journey and I am indebted to many people and institutions, although I alone take responsibility for the shortcomings that remain.

I wrote my first proposal on the subject of attitudes about income inequality to the Carnegie Foundation Fellowship Program in 2000. My first thanks therefore go to Patricia Roos, Dean of Social Sciences at Rutgers University, where I was an assistant professor at the time, to nominate me for the fellowship program. She was also a tremendously supportive colleague throughout my time at Rutgers, as were my wonderful colleagues in Women's and Gender Studies and at the Center for the Critical Analysis of Contemporary Culture, where I spent a year as a Fellow. I was a finalist for the Carnegie fellowship, but in the end, Carnegie teamed up with the Russell Sage Foundation (RSF) to support working groups around the country to investigate the consequences of rising inequality.

Although I was not at any of the universities in which such working groups were formed, I was fortunate enough to join the group at Princeton University. At that time, I was familiar with the economics, geography, and demographics of earnings inequality but knew little about the politics of income inequality. I am especially grateful to Larry Bartels for his advice and encouragement during this period, to Paul DiMaggio for introducing me to the virtues of the General Social Survey, and to Bruce

Western and Michael Hout (as part of the Berkeley working group) for helping in numerous ways during these years to smooth my transition into this new area of research. I later spent a stimulating year (2008–2009) as a visiting scholar at the Princeton University Center for the Study of Democratic Politics (CSDP), where I benefited from CSDP seminar participants, conversations with Marty Gilens and Devah Pager, and research assistance from Meredith Sadin.

I might not have had the opportunity to become involved in these groups if I had not been a visiting scholar at the Russell Sage Foundation when I first started thinking about beliefs about inequality. During the 2000–2001 academic year at RSF, I met several people whose research, generosity, and conversations led me in new directions related to this project, especially John Mollenkopf, also a visiting scholar that year, and David Callahan, co-founder of Demos: A Network for Ideas and Action. I became a Senior Fellow at Demos during the 2001–2002 academic year, which enabled me to begin working full time with data on attitudes about income inequality. Julian Brash, then a graduate student at the CUNY Graduate Center, was the research assistant who helped get this project off the ground. RSF also supported the research with a small grant, which marked the beginning of Lane Kenworthy's involvement. Lane's expertise as a political sociologist was essential as I was just getting acquainted with the field. I have relied heavily on Lane's renowned good sense and clear thinking ever since. His collaborations on two articles, one of which is included in an updated version in Chapter 5, are integral contributions to this book.

I moved to Northwestern University in 2005 and was immediately welcomed into the (truly) interdisciplinary community that is the Institute for Policy Research (IPR). Through IPR I was able to continue to have contact with political scientists and to meet social scientists from other disciplines long interested in the study of beliefs about economic justice. Fay Lomax Cook was not only the incomparable director of IPR but also a leading expert in public opinion research herself. She created a vibrant interdisciplinary space for social scientists of all kinds to flourish. More specifically, she and other members of the political science community at Northwestern, especially Ben Page, were unusually generous in attending talks, reading drafts of chapters, and providing feedback. IPR also supported the research assistance of Derek Burke, a superb graduate student in sociology, in the final year of writing.

I want to single out my IPR colleagues Jamie Druckman and Jennifer Anne Richeson. I consulted Jamie on everything from the content analysis of media coverage, which I undertook without any idea of how challenging and labor-intensive it would be, to my book proposal. Even now he is an indispensable resource as Jenn, a social psychologist, and I embark on our new research project to extend the media analysis in the book and to experimentally study the book's theoretical framework (a project also supported by the Russell Sage Foundation). Jenn was an equally extraordinary source of information and advice given her discipline's long-standing expertise in beliefs about meritocracy and a just world. To Jamie and Jenn, your brilliance and integrity embody the very best of academia; my initial work would never have grown into this book without your advice, support, and friendship.

There are several others at Northwestern (past and present) who enabled me to move forward on this project at several critical junctures. Although no longer at Northwestern, Jeff Manza was a major reason I moved there. I sought his counsel early in this project and continue to do so. Most crucially, he originally raised the idea with me to replicate the GSS questions on inequality in the 2008 survey, which then led to additional replications in 2010 and 2012, and to my membership on the General Social Survey Board, where I have learned a tremendous amount about survey research from the best in the field (special thanks go to board member Andy Gelman for his engagement with and insights into many aspects of my research). I am grateful to the GSS board for accepting my proposals to replicate questions in the 2008 and 2010 surveys, to the National Science Foundation for providing the funding for these replications, and particularly to Patricia White at NSF. I also want to acknowledge Northwestern University for its generous provision of research funds through the AT&T Fellowship. These funds supported a talented team of undergraduates, whose contribution to the coding of newsweekly articles was both conceptual and empirical. I thank Julie Davis and Andre Nickow, and especially Elyze Krumholz, Eric Peterson, and Jordan Fein. Last but not least, my colleagues in the Sociology Department afforded me the much needed space and time to develop this interdisciplinary project.

Soon after this project evolved and expanded into a book-length study, it was reviewed by a couple of presses. I want to thank all the anonymous reviewers, as their careful reading and constructive comments significantly strengthened the book. Michele Lamont generously read the manuscript at this time and fundamentally reshaped my methodological orientation by pointing out the cultural sociology in its pages and broadening its reach. I am probably not as successful at this as I would like to be, but to the extent that I bridge qualitative and quantitative orientations to the study of inequality, I have Michele to thank. I also appreciate the many pieces of advice small and large from my editors at Cambridge University Press, Eric Crahan and Robert Dreesen. Thanks finally to my production coordinator Ken Karpinski and especially to my copy editor Alison Anderson for coming to my rescue at the last minute.

In addition to the considerable amount of behind-the-scenes support I received along the road from start to finish, I presented my research at numerous universities, institutes, and conferences, where I engaged in countless conversations with colleagues and graduate students around the country and the world, which forced me to understand better my topic and audience, sharpen my analyses, and hone my argument. I know from these encounters that there are many superb graduate students working on these issues; they will be shaping the future of this field for years to come.

The very last of the institutions to have a hand in the writing of this book, and in particular the writing of this preface and the final copyediting of the manuscript, is the Institut d'Études Politiques de Paris, or Sciences Po, where I was lucky enough to have a visiting position for a month, thanks to Marco Oberti, Alain Chenu, and Lincoln Quillian. Every time I cringed at going back to copyediting or tweaking a figure, and ruminated over other finishing touches, I reminded myself of where I was and hoped that I could give something that is a fraction as valuable back to my colleagues at Sciences Po, who graciously exposed me to the excellent French scholarship on this topic. For this, I am particularly grateful to Marie Duru-Bellat and Nonna Mayer.

As is probably obvious by now, this book did not come about in a smooth, orderly, or timely fashion. Throughout the ups and downs, I relied on my friends and family to keep my spirits up and my mind distracted by our many adventures. Each one of them was essential in their own way (and heard more about the book than they ever wanted to): Adam, Carolyn, Dylan, Catherine, Tareque, Danni, Dave, Devah, Johnny, Margarita, Niamh, Billy, Nicole, Amy, Mark, Monica, Greg, Cecilia, Patricia, Nick, Alex, Casey, Lexi, Athena, Natasha, and Mitt. I dedicate this book to my parents who in the last few years created a comforting and supportive space for me to work on completing it despite our rather different views on its subject matter.

Introduction

Thinking about Income Inequality

In the past decade, one sensational event after another has been connected in some way to rising economic inequality. Most recently, the Occupy Wall Street movement catapulted the issue into our living rooms. Not only did the protesters demand greater economic and social equality for the bottom ninety-nine against the top one "percenters," but they coined a new set of class categories in the process and dramatically altered the focus of the 2012 Presidential campaign. Almost a decade ago, when I began research on American beliefs about rising inequality, the scandals surrounding Enron were making front-page news, with the pension funds of workers and retirees evaporating into thin air as the coffers of executives mysteriously survived.

In between Enron and Occupy Wall Street, there is no shortage of occasions to reflect on the state of income inequality in the United States – the Bush tax cuts of 2001 and 2003, the outsourcing of middle-class jobs to Ireland and India in 2004, Hurricane Katrina in 2005, the Great Recession in 2007, and the financial crisis in 2008. At each turn in the road, reporters and commentators concerned about rising income inequality but dismayed by the lack of political attention given to the issue declared that finally it would be taken seriously. And this says nothing of the events prior to the 2000s, several of which pointed the finger at rising inequality just as vehemently, as I show in Chapter 2 in my analysis of media coverage.

Yet nothing has changed. Income inequality continues its rise to heights unfathomable just a few generations ago. The late public intellectual and eminent Harvard sociologist Daniel Bell wrote in 1973 that earnings inequality "will be one of the most vexing questions in a post-industrial society." He said this even as he calculated the existing differences in pay between "the head of a corporation and a common laborer" to be "30:1," a paltry disparity by today's standards in which the figure hovers in the hundreds to one. Equally astonishing, for reasons I detail later in the book, Bell wrote about these disparities in pay as a matter of equal opportunity and economic efficiency. He feared that the vaunted status of the United States as the land of opportunity and economic abundance could be in jeopardy if extreme disparities went unchecked as "economic decisions become politicized and the market replaced by social decisions." An "unjust meritocracy" would ensue in which "distinctions [are] invidious and demean those below" while "those at the top convert their authority positions into large, discrepant material and social advantages over others." All this he wrote while criticizing affirmative action in higher education and the workplace on the grounds that it too violated the principle of equal opportunity. Thus Bell's deliberate, and as we will see unique, description of inequality of rewards as integral to the structure of opportunity was not the position of a strident liberal.[1]

How then did we end up here from there, especially given all that has transpired in the intervening decades to insinuate economic inequality into American society? One of the most resounding answers from the halls of academia to the corridors of the Capital to the press rooms of the media is that Americans really do not care much about income inequality. Counter to Bell, Americans dwell resolutely, if not always happily, in the land of opportunity, a territory far removed from the land of inequality. The rich reap the rewards they deserve for being smart, working hard, and producing prosperity for the rest of us. Meanwhile, the poor get what they deserve for not availing themselves of the opportunities the United States lavishes on all who are willing to persevere through thick and thin to bequeath a better life to their children. Known as the American dream, this set of beliefs is trotted out to explain why Americans go along with the massive gulf in earnings between the top and the bottom, as well as why they fail to demand more from government to ease their economic insecurities when inevitably they arise. According to the American dream, the solution is within our grasp if only we try harder. If my neighbor can move up, then so can I.[2]

So stated, the American dream is both a genuine article of faith and an embarrassingly easy target to poke holes in. This chimeral aspect of the American dream is the reason it appears nowhere in the title of this book, in the titles of the chapters, or in most of the text. It is obfuscating as both popular ideology and theoretical construct.[3] Yet

I open with it because its familiarity to lay and expert observer alike helps translate the three-headed, two-layered conundrum at the center of this book into a straightforward question: why do "we" (commentators) think that Americans believe that opportunity is available, inequality is okay, and redistribution is bad, despite a good deal of evidence to the contrary? The three heads refer to beliefs about opportunity, inequality, and redistribution, and the two layers to "our" opinions of what Americans think about these issues on the one hand, and to Americans' actual beliefs about them on the other. On what basis do experts and everyday observers assert that Americans believe in the American dream? And how does this accord with what Americans *really* believe? Finally, why does this matter for answering the questions of how we got from there (Bell's era of small ratios between executive and worker pay) to here (our era of gargantuan ratios) without much apparent resistance, until the Occupy Wall Street movement, and where we might be headed in the future?

First, where did the idea that Americans do not care about income inequality come from? The reality about *this part* of the American dream is that there have been scant data upon which to evaluate how widely it is held or why it is held at all. This is true not only for beliefs about income inequality but for the question of whether adherence to the dream is impervious to transformations in the structure of opportunity, inequality, and redistribution.

This is not for lack of trying. Scholars have gone to ingenious lengths to ascertain how Americans are adapting to high levels of inequality. They have studied everything from self-reported levels of happiness to support for progressive tax policy and partisan political leanings. And what they find appears to accord with the American dream: Americans are not responding to escalating inequality in the way that we might expect if they were disturbed by it; they are not becoming less happy, more supportive of progressive taxes, and more liberal. To explain these findings, scholars often make the contrast between Americans' unflinching faith in hard work as the surest route to success and Europeans' proclivity to say that luck is more important for getting ahead in life. Americans, unlike Europeans, are inoculated against anxieties about inequality by their belief in the possibility of upward mobility. Also influential are the ideas that Americans are unaware of the scale of inequality or they are duped into having great admiration for the rich and thinking that someday they too will be rich. This wishful thinking drives antipathy to heavily redistributive policies as well as to the undeserving poor.[4]

In short, the scholarly record shines on many surfaces related to the American dream, but it actually skirts the issue of beliefs specifically about income inequality. This shortcoming is almost entirely a result of the paucity of public opinion data directly on income inequality, as well as on the social groups such as the rich that are potentially implicated in beliefs about inequality. By contrast, there are plenty of data on the social issues that predate rising income inequality and that predominated in public policy debates during the proliferation of modern public opinion polling in the 1970s and 1980s: welfare, poverty, racial and gender inequality, and equal rights and opportunities for the poor, minorities, and women.[5]

Although I build on the many excellent studies alluded to above, and especially on the most in-depth investigations of beliefs about inequality conducted prior to the era of rising income inequality, I refocus the lens.[6] I place explicit beliefs about income inequality, from the data that *are* available on the topic, in the center of the analysis without losing sight of their crucial relationship to beliefs about opportunity and redistribution. In fact, I began this project looking *only* at beliefs about inequality in order to avoid inferring them from beliefs about opportunity and redistribution, as is so often done out of necessity. Only after some time did I realize how interdependent the three views were, that understanding beliefs about inequality required engagement with beliefs about opportunity and redistribution. As important: with opportunity at the heart of the American dream, it too begins to take on an altogether different hue when held up to the light of beliefs about inequality. Thus the bigger picture of what "we" think about what Americans think changes as a consequence of widening the view.

The second way that I try to alter our approach to understanding how Americans think about inequality involves, in some respects, a narrowing, rather than a broadening, of the field of vision. By this I mean that I focus on the U.S. case alone. There is no denying that some of the most convincing conclusions about American beliefs about opportunity and redistribution to date come from cross-national comparisons. Certainly, for instance, Americans appear both more optimistic about their chances for upward mobility through hard work and less supportive of redistributive policies than Europeans do.[7]

But one can also gain comparative leverage by studying changes in beliefs over time and differences among individuals *within* a country. Indeed, the American Political Science Association's Task Force on Inequality concluded that "studying changes [over time] in political behavior and public opinion is essential to evaluate the impact of rising economic inequality."[8] This approach can furthermore help weaken the grip that static ideas of American exceptionalism continue to have on our theoretical frameworks and popular discourses. In Chapter 3, I analyze the only available time series of data directly on income inequality, stretching over two decades from 1987 to 2010. As a complement to the public opinion data, in Chapter 2 I explore media coverage of inequality and social class in every year from 1980 to 2010. This enables me to situate changing beliefs about inequality within the context of the major economic events related to rising inequality that I mentioned in the opening paragraph. Media discourses also provide a window into how economic phenomena other than the business cycle help shape American perceptions of fairness and public policy on economic issues.

If we change the way we go about studying American beliefs about inequality, opportunity, and redistribution in these ways, how does that change the story we tell about what Americans think? Far from not caring about income inequality, the small number of questions that do exist on this topic reveal a substantial share of Americans that have long desired less inequality, and sometimes much less. This is something that specialists in the field have been documenting since at least the 1970s.

On the lower end of estimates, 41 percent of Americans said in 1980 that they desired "more equality than there is now" or "complete equality of income"; 41 percent disagreed in 1987 that "all in all, economic differences in this country are justified"; 55 percent agreed in 1987 that "personal income should not be determined just by one's worth. Rather, everyone should get what they need to provide a decent life for their family"; and between 38 percent and 58 percent from 1987 to 2010 disagreed that "large differences in income are necessary for America's prosperity."

On the upper end of estimates, 60 percent agreed in 1987 that "it would be better for everyone if the distribution of wealth in this country were more equal"; between 71 percent and 86 percent from the 1970s to the present said that heads of corporations are overpaid; between 58 percent and 77 percent from 1987 to 2010 agreed that "income differences in America are too large"; and between 66 percent and 83 percent desire a gap in pay between executives and unskilled workers that is lower by 20 percent or more than what they think the gap is (which is much lower than the actual gap). I can confidently say that no question has been asked of Americans in which the responses fall outside this range of opposition to inequality.[9] Even more recent questions in the American National Election Studies that provide information about the

actual level of income inequality elicit desires for less inequality within
the range described here, suggesting that lack of information does not
inhibit opposition to inequality.[10]

Although these data are not widely known, few among those who are
familiar with them dispute the contention that many if not most Americans are dissatisfied with the degree of income inequality in their country.
And as I said earlier, this is not a finding of recent vintage; it goes at least as
far back as the halcyon days, at least as regards levels of income inequality, of the 1970s. What is in dispute are the strength and consistency of
these attitudes, the extent to which Americans comprehend the trajectory
and scale of trends in inequality over time, and their consequences and
policy implications (although one could say this of just about any political
attitude). But with so much deflection from the issue of income inequality
in the broader discourse and in existing social surveys and public opinion
polls, these debates are still inchoate. They continue to beat around the
bush of *whether* Americans know and care about rising income inequality. In this book, I examine these questions too, but I extend the inquiry to
what would appear to be a pivotal question that nevertheless is obscured
by both present and long-standing debates. This is the question of exactly
why Americans might be concerned about income inequality. Asking the
"why" question sidesteps the polarized debates about whether Americans
care or not and instead seeks to determine the parameters under which
they do and do not care.

There are, of course, many potential explanations for why income
inequality would matter to Americans. They may be concerned about
their own financial situation if their earnings have declined in relative or
even absolute terms, and realize that they would be better off with more
redistribution, as suggested by median voter theories. They may be concerned about matters of procedural justice, whether opportunities and
rewards are distributed fairly to those at the bottom, middle, and top,
as discussed by numerous psychological studies. They may be concerned
about the adverse effect of income inequality on other social spheres,
such as crime, politics, education, residential segregation, or health care,
as documented by scholars across the social sciences. They may have
fuzzy norms of fairness in which some level of distance between the rich
or poor and everyone else is seen as unsavory, as alluded to by theories of class resentment and envy of the rich. They may be concerned
about those who are in need through no fault of their own, as suggested
by theories of humanitarianism, reciprocity, and deservingness. Or they
may fear that income inequality has adverse effects on the economy itself,
not just for themselves but for all Americans, as debated by economists

who study the relationship between economic growth and income inequality.[11]

Ideally we would possess data on each of these propositions and the policy solutions associated with them. However, no such data exist. In this book, I examine as many of them as possible with the most comprehensive data available on public opinion about inequality, opportunity, and redistribution. My data come mainly from the General Social Survey but also from the American National Election Studies. In Chapter 1, I mine the historical and theoretical record as well, going as far back as the nineteenth century, to ascertain the social conditions under which the reigning assumptions about American beliefs regarding inequality, opportunity, and redistribution became crystallized. I conclude from a wide range of evidence that concerns about income inequality are best understood as fears of narrowing opportunities. Although this argument draws from several of the aforementioned perspectives, in particular studies of the relationship between economic growth and income inequality, its inspiration comes from a somewhat surprising source: previous research on attitudes about racial and gender inequality.

One of the less-appreciated observations made by James Kluegal and Elliot Smith in their definitive study of beliefs about inequality in the early 1980s was that Americans appeared to become more intolerant of racial and gender inequality in the 1970s and 1980s as their awareness of the issues was informed and ignited by the civil rights movement. From my perspective, the most interesting aspect of this dynamic was that even though Americans generally favored equality of opportunity over equality of outcomes for minorities and women, much of the *evidence* for whether opportunities were unequal rested on whether *outcomes* were unequal. Unequal pay or unequal educational attainment between racial and gender groups functioned as signals of unequal opportunities. James Coleman in "The Coleman Report" and John Roemer in *Equal Opportunity*, among others, went farther in the public policy arena. They sought to measure, and thereby define, unequal opportunities as unequal outcomes.[12] The intuition was that restrictions of opportunities are often difficult to observe whereas inequalities of outcomes are less so, and yet these represent the cumulative effect of differential opportunities over time. It was exactly this substitution of equal outcomes for equal opportunities that unnerved Bell and provoked his opposition to affirmative action on the grounds that it overreached the public mandate for equal opportunity.

If not born in this cauldron, the misleading opposition between opportunity and outcomes at the root of the American dream (i.e., that

Americans care about the former and not the latter) was at least fortified, as I discuss in more detail in Chapter 1. Yet when applied to the issue of class inequality, Bell endorses the interdependence of outcomes and opportunities in his formulation of an "unjust meritocracy" described in the introduction to this chapter. Unfortunately, this approach has never been fully adapted to the study of inequalities of opportunity and outcomes related to class, even by Bell. Doing so requires a better conceptualization of what opportunity and inequality represent within the context of income inequality (as opposed to in the context of racial and gender inequality).

With regard to opportunity, for example, in Chapter 4 I develop five "tropes" of what equal opportunity means to Americans. These tropes go well beyond the role of individual hard work in getting ahead, which I refer to as the "bootstraps" opportunity trope. I define the availability of jobs, the assurance of fair pay, and the equal treatment of individuals from different class backgrounds as central but distinct elements of a full-opportunity society. I term these the "rising tide," "just deserts," and "equal treatment" opportunity tropes. With these examples, I illustrate how Americans have a much more encompassing understanding of what opportunity means, and how it can be unfairly restricted, than is commonly thought. Similarly, in Chapters 3 and 4, I expand on the conceptualization of income inequality to include views about the rich and, in Chapter 5, on the conceptualization of redistribution to include views about the kind of labor market redistribution, such as a fair distribution of pay in a "just meritocracy," that would result in greater work opportunities for ordinary Americans.

With this broader conceptualization in mind, I turn the predominant explanation of why Americans *do not* care about income inequality on its head. Instead of inferring from their belief that opportunity is widely available that Americans do not care about income inequality, I contend that Americans can construe income inequality as itself a restriction of economic opportunity. This occurs when everyone does not appear to be benefiting from economic growth or suffering from economic troubles. When the rich stand out as unscathed by economic turmoil, for example, they are potentially deemed undeserving for two reasons: they are prospering when others are not (a violation of norms of fairness), and their own poor stewardship of the economy may be a cause of the turmoil (a violation of "just deserts" opportunity if their compensation remains stratospheric, and a violation of "rising tide" opportunity if inequality adversely affects economic growth).

In this view, it is not how the rich attained their position that is unsettling, which is a matter of intergenerational immobility ("equal treatment" opportunity), but rather what they did with their position, which is a matter of "just deserts" and "rising tide" opportunity. Moreover, it is the *equitable distribution* of income that is desired rather than simply the *growth* of income. This means that the rich can be perceived as undeserving even during expansions in the business cycle, as I demonstrate in Chapters 3 and 4. This approach builds on but also significantly modifies influential theories that link political attitudes to the rhythms of the business cycle and other macroeconomic indicators.[13]

If at times Americans believe that income inequality restricts economic opportunity, it follows that those with such concerns would seek policies that expand opportunities rather than redistribute income through the tax system as a response to their concerns. This is because it is distortions in the private sector allocation of opportunity and rewards precipitated by income inequality that are most distressing. Americans care about their own economic livelihood, to be sure, but they see it as linked to the economic health and equity of the economy overall. This kind of sociotropic orientation is found in studies of voting behavior as well, in which assessments of the national economy are more influential in the choice of candidates and parties than assessments of personal finances.[14] Consequently, the causes of restrictions of opportunity that have to do with excessive income inequality, such as distortions in pay at the top or the use of unfair social advantages in getting ahead, become causes for action in expanding opportunity. Policies plainly associated with producing equitable economic opportunity are favored, whereas government redistribution – the focus of nearly all previous scholarship on the politics of income inequality – is not. This is not because government redistribution does not affect growth and opportunity, but because it is not *associated* with creating growth and opportunity.[15] When it is, such as when it is linked to shoring up access to education that enhances economic opportunities, it should be met with higher approval.[16] Thus my approach is discerning: it does not group the usual suspects of popular social policies all under the same umbrella of policies that expand opportunity and reduce inequality.

Despite the focus on income inequality, then, all three of the social norms of inequality, opportunity, and redistribution are central to the story told in this book. Each is reconceptualized as having multiple dimensions that reach beyond current definitions and that are more consistent with the new era of rising inequality, as well as with prior eras (in theory, as I argue in Chapter 1). These dimensions are then brought together in a framework that theoretically identifies the mechanisms that bind them together. The connections that underlie these mechanisms, in turn, are examined empirically to avoid to the extent possible drawing inferences across a long chain of beliefs. The upshot is that Americans turn out to be much more critical and coherent in their views than anyone would have predicted, including those who have usefully argued, in different forms, for the complexity, ambivalence, and inconsistency of American beliefs, the lack of information about the issue, or the priority of other issues that are more pressing and concrete, such as economic insecurity.[17] In short, this book aims to replace the dominant narrative of American tolerance for inequality with a coherent alternative that also incorporates American beliefs about opportunity and redistribution.

The Un/Deserving Rich

With sufficient prima facie evidence in hand that a significant share of Americans care about income inequality, my primary purpose in this book, as I said previously, is to transition to thinking carefully about why Americans have the views they do and the implications of this for politics and public policy. I outlined a number of alternative explanations and then offered the view that I have come to hold in the process of conducting the research for this book. But it is worth expanding on some of the alternative explanations further and then sketching a more precise account of the perspective that I develop and organize around the concept of the "undeserving rich."

The explanation perhaps most often associated with criticisms of inequality is that those from advantaged backgrounds are given preferential treatment in education and the labor market by dint of the better preparation their parents' money can often, though not always, buy. This is the problem of the unequal starting gate, and it is the justifiable focus of much social science research on the lack of social mobility from one generation to the next. To the extent that the playing field can be leveled, particularly for children in their access to quality education, a genuine meritocracy will flourish. This is *the* definition of equal opportunity (a level playing field as measured by intergenerational mobility) that is said to justify inequalities in outcomes as both fair and economically functional, allocating talent more efficiently than a system that squanders the talents of the disadvantaged.[18] As a normative matter, most everybody is on board with this depiction of both the problem of inequality and its solution, although putting the solution into practice is often a different and more contentious matter.

This approach has an unintended consequence, however. It tends to focus attention only on the starting gate because it assumes that any resulting distribution of outcomes is fair if the starting gate is equal. Inequities in the allocation of pay, another avenue through which opportunity can be derailed, are brushed over or not even contemplated as a problematic aspect of inequality. But both Bell in his "unjust meritocracy" and the ironic originator of the term "meritocracy," Michael Young, recognized that the distribution of rewards can itself lead to the corruption of a meritocracy even if everyone is sorted correctly according to their talents. In his 1958 classic dystopian novel, *The Rise of Meritocracy*, Young tells the story of greedy technocratic elites hoarding resources and crushing the souls of the meritless masses. Ultimately this behavior is dysfunctional for the economy as well as for society.

The "undeserving rich" is a conceptual intervention that follows from Young and Bell and identifies the actors that are involved in the making of an unjust, and inefficient, meritocracy. It is meant to include unfair inequalities not only in preparation and access but in pay. Pay disparities are unfair when earnings exceed the contribution and performance of those in the driver's seat of the economy, those who are seen as economic leaders and are expected to deliver economic prosperity for all. Conversely, pay disparities are also unfair when earnings fall short of the contribution and need of hardworking Americans farther down the ladder. The "deserving rich," by contrast, corresponds to a scenario in which the rich are extolled for their ingenuity and contribution to equitable growth. Under these conditions, the *amount* of inequality in pay between those at the top and bottom is not the primary consideration; the tolerable level of inequality is any level that is compatible with widespread opportunities for a good job with fair pay for most workers. Thus another common explanation of beliefs about inequality – that they reflect abstract considerations of fairness pertaining to the absolute level of inequality – matters less than practical considerations about the availability of opportunities, in the broadest sense of the term, and the role of the rich in securing or subverting those opportunities.[19]

I trace in Chapter 1 the relationship between the reality and perception of inequality and opportunity across iconic eras of U.S. history, identifying the occasions when equitable growth fostered a virtuous harmony of moderate inequality and expanding opportunity that was historically specific, yet underwrote transhistorical theories of Americans' indifference to inequality. Writing about economic attitudes in *The Affluent Society* in the late 1950s, for instance, John Kenneth Galbraith opined that "few things are more evident in modern social history than the decline of interest in inequality as an economic issue . . . [and] in one way or another [the decline is] related to the fact of increasing production."[20] To Galbraith, this was not a cause for celebration but a call to arms to reverse the "social imbalance" between private wealth and public restraint in social spending. Like Bell, Galbraith saw high levels of inequality even in an era of historically low levels, another sign that context matters at least as much as absolute levels in shaping norms about inequality. Galbraith also observed changes in attitudes about inequality and their origins. A massive increase in well-being, spurred by "increasing aggregate output," had displaced "redistribution or even the reduction of inequality" as a social demand, he complained.

I adopt Galbraith's general logic in this book, but prefer to use the label "redistribution" more flexibly so that equitable growth in the private sector and the labor market represents a different but no less potent form of redistribution in the public mind than do progressive taxation and social spending. By this definition, concerns about inequality in an era of inequitable growth or contraction, as in the 1980s and subsequent decades, would prompt demands for greater labor market redistribution through cuts in pay at the top, job growth, and fair pay, for example, rather than for taxing the rich, unless progressive taxation is transparently linked to a fairer *economy* as well as a fairer *society*.[21] This should be the response if Galbraith's logic regarding beliefs about inequality is applied to the conditions of inequitable growth in the "New Gilded Age." The prevailing assumption that Americans are tolerant or indifferent to inequality is therefore a relic of a bygone era, a postwar paradise that Galbraith attempted to demystify. Although we cannot expect American beliefs to change on a dime with the onset of the New Gilded Age, my purpose here is to integrate historical conditions into our theoretical models of American beliefs and to use these insights to better understand how such beliefs evolve over time, and particularly in our day and age.[22]

In the same vein, then, that scholars have connected perceptions of the poor to Americans' tolerance for poverty and social policies related to poverty, I argue that perceptions of the rich are connected to Americans' tolerance for and social policies related to inequality. The frame of the "undeserving rich" is derived from the concept of the "undeserving poor," which describes public antipathy toward the poor under particular conditions and the resulting implications for redistributive policy preferences (i.e., if the poor are not hardworking or belong to a subordinate minority group, they are undeserving of welfare).[23] In an analogous fashion, the "undeserving rich" describes public antipathy toward the rich under particular conditions and the resulting implications for redistributive policy preferences. Beyond this analogy, however, the framework I develop in this book erects a stricter analytical separation between inequality and poverty than is common in the literature. This separation is necessary in the new era of inequality in order to put important but under-scrutinized and under-theorized social groups under the microscope, such as the rich, and to avoid questionable assumptions about how Americans think about inequality in ways similar to how they think about poverty.

Method

But how realistic is it to attribute such a seemingly sophisticated outlook to ordinary Americans? Readers well-versed in political science debates on citizen competence may be skeptical. According to some, the best we can expect is for Americans to tune into the big issues of the day and digest elite messages with little information and a (sometimes large) dose of partisan bias that taps into a more general ideological orientation. Because it is often presumed that income inequality is an issue of little salience, and is complex and obscured by elite interests and maneuvers, American ignorance should only be accentuated in this territory. For instance, Larry Bartels' *Unequal Democracy*, one of the most important books of our time, posits that low- and middle-income Americans engage in "unenlightened self-interest" and "myopia" in their support of inequality-enhancing policies, such as the Bush tax cuts, and inequality-promoting parties, such as the Republicans. He found that even those who comprehend that income inequality is much larger than in the past and proclaim it a "bad thing" are no more likely than others to oppose tax cuts for the rich. If Americans cannot square their opposition to rising income inequality with tax cuts for the rich, how can we expect them to adopt the gestalt of the undeserving rich?[24]

From the very start of this project in the early 2000s, I was sympathetic to this possibility. My intuition was that neither the trend toward rising income inequality nor its connection with redistributive tax policy was particularly transparent to the American public. As Americans we are not routinely schooled in the virtues of redistributive politics, either as I described them under the "undeserving rich" rubric or as they are described by conventional welfare state models in which the median voter follows his or her self-interest in endorsing income redistribution. Instead, either there is a void in media and political discourses on these matters – although it is much less of a void than commonly assumed, as I show in Chapter 2 – or redistribution is vilified as antigrowth.[25]

My conjecture is much the same when it comes to discourses of hard work and luck. These concepts purportedly draw the line between Americans and Europeans in beliefs about inequality and redistribution, but the concepts are not articulated with equal force on both sides of the Atlantic. As economists Alesina, Glaeser, and Benabou, among others, argue, beliefs about luck and hard work are themselves endogenous to society.[26] They are what need to be explained rather than what should be doing the explaining. Consequently, in an American culture with almost no ideology or folklore of luck, as far as I can ascertain, we should not expect luck's complicated implications for social policy to orient beliefs about distributive justice.[27] Bartels' findings and skepticism are justifiable in this context, as is his attribution of much of the blame for American "ignorance" and American inequality to political elites.

All this may be true while nonetheless a quite different sort of question remains apropos: has American culture nourished other interpretations of unfairness in economic matters, and other avenues of distributive justice? And how would we know if it did? In trying to answer this question, my goal is to fully excavate, to the extent possible with available data, beliefs in and around the single issue domain of income inequality. This is a more modest objective than resolving long-standing debates about American political competence. In the end, beliefs about inequality do manifest more opposition and coherence than the prevailing theories of tolerance and ignorance predict, but the main lesson I draw from this is that our theoretical models specifically about beliefs about income inequality need to be revised, and not that Americans are fully and always competent or that partisan and material biases are irrelevant. An accumulation of studies with similar conclusions on different issues may contribute to these broader debates about the consistency of American political beliefs, but as important, I think, is the development of methodological approaches that open-mindedly explore fine-grained structures of belief in circumscribed issue domains. These in turn may lead to new theoretical models in these domains as well as to insights into broader theories of political knowledge.[28]

The methodological approach I pursue in this book is aimed at this level of analysis. On the one hand, my approach follows standard protocol in survey research by analyzing available questions in well-respected nationally representative social surveys. I am especially indebted to the social scientists who had the foresight to design the Social Inequality Modules of the International Social Survey Program beginning in 1987 and to replicate them in 1992, 1996, and 2000. In 2008 and 2010, I was involved enough in the analysis of these items to request that they be included, and to obtain support from the General Social Survey Board and the National Science Foundation to do so. My rationale was that the questions about income inequality on the Social Inequality Modules were the only ones that were repeated over time, asked specifically about multiple dimensions of income inequality, and did not conflate the issue of inequality with government policies (i.e., did not include language about the government's role in reducing income inequality).

These questions presented a unique opportunity to examine American beliefs about income inequality in a historic era of rising inequality. In conjunction with the General Social Survey's (GSS) core battery of questions about social spending priorities and a few additional questions in both the GSS core and the Social Inequality Modules about opportunities to get ahead, these data also enabled an investigation of the implications of beliefs about inequality for social policy preferences, as well as the role that beliefs about hard work and upward mobility play in this relationship. The GSS data permitted, in short, an investigation of the three-headed conundrum stated at the outset of this chapter: whether Americans do indeed think that opportunities are available, inequality is okay, and redistribution is bad despite what appears to be prima facie evidence to the contrary.

On the other hand, my investigation of these questions led in a number of surprising directions. The emphasis of the book on answering the "why" question, based in significant degree on leveraging changes over time in beliefs, necessitated a methodological stance more akin to that of qualitative researchers in comparative historical and cultural sociology than of quantitative researchers in survey research.[29] Because of the relatively small number of time points of attitudinal data (6 years from 1987 to 2010), in Chapter 3 I use qualitative methods of comparison and contrast among concurrent macro-level trends to rule out alternative explanations of changes in beliefs over time (e.g., do beliefs about income inequality follow the trend in the business cycle, actual levels of income inequality, political party dynamics, media coverage, etc.?). Chapter 2 also incorporates a thick description of the cultural and historical context of discourses of class and inequality in a detailed content analysis of media coverage of these topics over the last three decades. Finally,

Chapter 1 provides a theoretical probing of the meaning of and relationship among the concepts of inequality, opportunity, and redistribution over the past two centuries and across the disciplines of social science. In short, the survey analysis is situated within a broader historical, cultural, and theoretical framework rooted in real-world dynamics and historical conjunctures in a single society regarding a single constellation of issues long central to American culture.

Although I found that attention to the macro institutional and cultural context of income inequality in the United States was essential to interpreting why Americans care about inequality, it is my hope that these explanations will function in turn as hypotheses for future research. In particular, it will be valuable to subject these hypotheses to stricter causal tests than is possible with existing survey data; this can be done through experimental research, for instance. New questions and instruments ought to be designed that accord better with the nature of beliefs about inequality in American culture that I propose in this book. I discuss the possibilities for further causal as well as cultural and survey analysis in the concluding chapter, where I map out a new research agenda for research on beliefs about income inequality, economic opportunity, and social and economic policy.

Focusing on the "why" question also required a somewhat different approach to survey research than is common in much of social science research on attitudes, beliefs, and values. On the one hand, best practice in social psychology typically entails working with multi-item scales that have robust reliability properties derived from psychometric testing. Social psychologists are admirably precise in their articulation of both concepts and individual-level mechanisms and how these are and should be operationalized in laboratory experiments. The large and impressive literature on meritocratic beliefs in a just world and other justice beliefs is a testament to the scientific value and payoff of this approach.[30] On the other hand, best practice in the more macro-level studies of political beliefs in political science focuses less on mechanisms in concept-specific domains. Yet, like psychology, these studies entail bundling multiple items into broader issue categories (e.g., economic and cultural values or political ideology and partisanship) and tracing them over time and space to arrive at powerful stories of aggregate swings in mass political preferences. Similarly, with respect to voting preferences, a few aggregate indicators carry the preponderance of weight, such as the state of the national economy and the party of incumbents.[31]

By comparison to the venerable traditions of research in social psychology and political science, the survey questions at my disposal are rich in combining questions about beliefs in all three areas of interest in this project – income inequality, economic opportunity, and redistribution – but they are relatively few and varied within each area, and were not custom designed to answer the questions about mechanisms across areas that I put to them. In some respects, this gives me greater confidence in the validity of the findings I do uncover than if I had inadvertently tipped the scales in my favor in the design of questions. But it also means that my approach must of necessity combine deductive reasoning about mechanisms with inductive analyses of the items that are available to me. Ultimately, the interpretive approach I adopt in analyzing single items and the interrelationships among them will be judged by its potential to illuminate beliefs about income inequality in the real world of rising inequality. Thus my goal is to fuse the social psychologist's careful attention to concepts and mechanisms and the political scientist's careful attention to real world, macro dynamics. Perhaps the middle ground I chart is not surprising given my training in sociology.

Finally, all of these methodological considerations lead me to revisit the second layer of questions that underlies this study, the layer that asks how we come to know what we say we know about American beliefs toward income inequality. I am as engaged with this question as I am with the question of what Americans themselves say about income inequality, in dialogue as much with academic and popular discourses of inequality and opportunity as with the attitudes of individual Americans. This book examines how we came to hold the theories and discourses we do, as well as the nuances of beliefs among Americans.

My primary goal, then, is to reduce the considerable arc of inference that now exists between what we say Americans believe and the instruments we use to draw such conclusions. I do this by taking both theoretical models of lay perceptions of the social world and lay perceptions themselves and calibrating them to historical conditions and a wider range of data and evidence than is typically considered in studies of beliefs about income inequality.[32] The moment we inhabit now, with Occupy Wall Street and its sister movements having already galvanized worldwide attention to the issue of income inequality, is as much a part of the history and context I unearth and unravel in this book as is the post–World War II period of equitable growth, and the period of rising income inequality that began in the 1970s and 1980s. I hope the

narrative I develop about how Americans think about inequality, opportunity, and redistribution helps put events such as Occupy Wall Street
in long-term perspective, informed by and contiguous with long-held
desires for abundant and equitably distributed opportunity, and consequently with whatever level of income inequality that is compatible with
this elementary but profound American demand.[33]

Organization of the Book

The book proceeds in Chapter 1 to examine the historical and theoretical development of what I refer to as the three main perspectives on
American beliefs about income inequality: the tolerance, ignorance, and
ambivalence perspectives. I pull together the disparate strands of research
in economics, sociology, political science, history, and social psychology
into these three perspectives and show how each perspective articulates or
assumes a particular relationship to beliefs about opportunity and redistribution, as well as to historical conditions. The alternative framework
presented above and in greater detail in the next chapter draws on all three
perspectives to craft an approach that is adaptable to multiple historical
conditions, and most important, goes "beyond the opposition between
inequality and opportunity" (as the title of the next chapter puts it).

The following four chapters consist of empirical analyses of the different components of the theoretical framework developed in Chapter 1.
In the first empirical chapter, Chapter 2, I provide a systematic analysis
of media coverage of social class and income inequality in the top three
newsweeklies (*Newsweek*, *TIME*, and *U.S. News and World Report*) in
every year from 1980 to 2010. The analysis reveals the "cultural supply side" of discourses of social class and income inequality in the United
States, showing for the first time the point when rising inequality emerged
as a new social reality (in the early 1990s), how it was portrayed as a
new social problem, and why it followed a nonlinear pattern, ebbing and
flowing over three decades when income inequality itself continued to
grow.[34] Contrary to expectations, news articles traversed a complex and
varied terrain and were often nuanced in alluding to the problematic ways
in which income inequality functioned as a restraint on opportunity for
the middle class as the economy expanded for those at the top but not
for the rest of Americans.

The following three chapters examine public opinion about income
inequality (Chapter 3), economic opportunity (Chapter 4), and redistribution and other social policy preferences (Chapter 5). Chapter 3 focuses

exclusively on beliefs about income inequality, changes in these beliefs over time, and alternative explanations of these changes over time. The analysis shows that concerns about income inequality grew over the period of rising income inequality, contrary to arguments about the development of more permissive social norms.[35] But it also shows that concerns grew in a nonlinear pattern, contrary to the reasonable expectation that outrage should erupt with the rise in inequality itself.[36] In order to answer the "why" question by accounting for changes over time in beliefs, the chapter examines compositional shifts in a wide range of factors, such as education, income, demographic characteristics, and political orientation, as well as changes in the intensity of beliefs among different groups. As mentioned earlier in this chapter, it also examines aggregate trends in actual income inequality, real median wages, unemployment, consumer confidence, and electoral dynamics. After considerable testing, I conclude that the trend in beliefs is most consistent with trends in media coverage of the issue, which peaks at the same time as widespread and mainstream opposition to income inequality in the early and mid-1990s, even relative to the recent period of financial crisis and Great Recession (according to the latest available survey data, which is in 2008 and 2010).

Chapter 4 then takes up the relationship between beliefs about economic opportunity and beliefs about income inequality directly, as this relationship is implied by the trend in opposition to income inequality (Chapter 3), the content of media coverage (Chapter 2), and the historical and theoretical development of beliefs about income inequality (Chapter 1). I develop several new ways of defining what equal opportunity means to Americans and then show how Americans draw coherent and logical connections between particular violations of equal opportunity and corresponding problems with income inequality. To take just one example, an overwhelming majority of Americans will say that hard work matters more than luck or help from others in getting ahead, but these beliefs have *little to no* bearing on beliefs about income inequality, belying a nearly universal arc of inference from faith in hard work to tolerance of inequality attributed to Americans. What is more, based on rarely used data, I find that a substantial minority of Americans say that social advantages, such as knowing the right people and having educated parents, *are* important factors in getting ahead, and that these beliefs *do* lead to more critical attitudes toward income inequality. Few commentators acknowledge that Americans make such connections, however, and thus believe that research ought to focus on showing how social mobility has stalled in recent decades rather than how income inequality has increased. This chapter shows that Americans grasp that the two go hand in hand and no such choice is necessary, or even preferable.

The political consequences of these and other findings are then explored in Chapter 5, where I take up the direct relationship between beliefs about income inequality and a wide spectrum of social policy preferences. Increasing concerns about income inequality in the 1990s, for example, were not accompanied by increasing support for assistance to the poor and for progressive taxation. Instead, they were accompanied by preferences for more spending on education, a policy domain associated centrally with expanding opportunities. Even support for other policies that are often associated with expanding opportunities or limiting inequality, such as health care and social security, did not rise in tandem with concerns about income inequality. Moreover, Chapter 4 showed that Americans object to social advantages in getting ahead by the well-off and the well-connected, as well as to overpaying executives and underpaying workers. Importantly, Americans view these distortions in compensation as limiting access to good jobs and fair pay for Americans as a whole. This chapter therefore reconceptualizes policy preferences related to income inequality in terms of curbing the excesses of the undeserving rich and expanding the opportunities of deserving workers. Americans appear to desire opportunities for education and redistribution in the labor market more than government redistribution (conventionally understood) as a way to counteract rising inequality.

This book relies upon existing data sources to formulate a new perspective on how Americans think about inequality, opportunity, and redistribution. Although existing data sources were sufficient for this purpose, and even help to validate the findings by the very fact that they were not constructed with this perspective in mind, the findings of this book suggest that there may be better ways to divine American attitudes on these topics. The concluding chapter summarizes the main findings; discusses the recent shift toward identifying values, beliefs, and social norms as important factors in the policy-formation process; and proposes a new agenda for studying beliefs related to these central tenets of American culture. This will point the way forward as more surveys seek to include questions related to income inequality, a movement that is already underway, and more students of cultural, historical, and comparative social science seek to resolve the many puzzles that remain with in-depth qualitative and contextual analysis.

I

Beyond the Opposition between Opportunity and Inequality

Theories of American Beliefs about Inequality from the Nineteenth Century to the Present

When economists first began documenting the rise in inequality in the 1980s and 1990s, they naturally placed economic solutions at the top of the list of remedies for what was then considered a predominantly economic problem. Based on their assessment of the causes of rising inequality, economists advocated everything from raising the minimum wage and stemming union decline to curtailing immigration and trade with low-wage countries. Increasing the human capital of the nation was – and still is – an especially favored solution. Yet despite convincing research and a few policy successes, little has been done to reduce inequality in any substantial way. By the early 2000s, this fact prompted a political turn in the debate over inequality. Politics began to figure more prominently as both cause and solution.[1] In fact, a rapidly expanding stream of research by some of the nation's leading political scientists is interrogating anew the centuries-old question of how political and economic inequality are intertwined.

Very much in its early stages, political research on rising income inequality is already covering a broader swath of topics than just a few years ago. But one of the central topics in this discussion has not changed much. It concerns the long-standing question of why the United States does so little to redistribute income despite its high level of market inequality. One might answer this question in a number of different ways, but a common reply is that Americans care only about opportunity and not about inequality, preventing significant redistributive policies from seeing the light of day. Although scholars increasingly greet this claim with a skeptical eye, it nevertheless remains deep-seated. It also signals the salient role that public sentiment plays in the politics of income inequality.

To one degree or another, American beliefs about income inequality, economic opportunity, and government redistribution are implicated in much of the recent research and public discourse on the causes and consequences of rising economic inequality.

Despite this, the most in-depth studies of American beliefs about inequality and inequality-related issues were actually conducted in the 1960s, 1970s, and 1980s, prior to the era of rising inequality. This fact may be of little concern in itself, because in most respects these studies have stood the test of time with flying colors. Indeed, the prevailing theoretical perspective on American beliefs about income inequality among scholars, what I refer to as the "ambivalence" perspective, is rooted in these brilliantly nuanced studies. Still, contending perspectives do exist, especially across disciplinary lines. And even among proponents of the ambivalence perspective today, there is little consensus regarding the exact nature of contemporary public opinion on income inequality.

In a related vein, no research past or present has sought to explain American attitudes about income inequality as a dynamic process or to develop a general theory of changes in beliefs that would help shed light on the current era of rising inequality. For many, beliefs about inequality are best understood as an unquestioned staple of American culture, part and parcel of an American dream ideology that has endured through the ages. For others, there is clear evidence of a shift in attitudes but less clarity in how or why the shift took place. For instance, some scholars contend, reasonably, that inequality has risen to such transparent and immoral heights that even otherwise-tolerant Americans object to it. But this raises as many questions as it answers. What defines an excessive and immoral level of inequality? What is the tipping point, and when and why did it occur? For still other observers, inequality is so complex a political and economic matter that it is unlikely that ordinary Americans understand much about it. More critical is what elites think and do about inequality. From this view, changes occur, but they are top-down and cater to the affluent. Even here, we are only in the opening rounds of discovery and debate about how exactly this illuminates the U.S. predicament.

There is no doubt truth in each of these perspectives, and it would be foolish to reject any of them in full when they have so many good points in their respective corners. My objective therefore is to come at these topics from an altogether different standpoint: to treat American beliefs about income inequality as contextually specific with the potential to vary across historical and social conditions. Although many social scientists share this uncontroversial and even taken-for-granted proposition about most things, it has yet to be incorporated into contemporary understandings of rising income inequality. I do this while at the same time drawing out the hidden dynamics of theories about egalitarian beliefs developed in the previous era of declining income inequality. I articulate how these theories appear to have been shaped crucially by their own historical moment, thus circumscribing some of their potential applicability to the present.

I begin with a description of the widely agreed-upon theory of how Americans think about economic inequality *in principle*. Going by various names, this is the ideology of the American dream, the American ethos, the American creed, American exceptionalism, or just plain economic individualism.[2] I also provide a reading of this ideology's historical and social foundations because they are still widely referenced in accounts of American beliefs and yet can often be misleading. This is especially true in the account that I refer to as the "tolerance" perspective, in which Americans are said to be accepting of high levels of inequality. This is one of the three main accounts of Americans' beliefs about economic inequality *in practice* that I describe in this chapter. The other two are the "ambivalence" and "ignorance" perspectives, both alluded to above. I consider how each of these three perspectives grapples with how egalitarian beliefs ought to respond to changes in economic and social conditions. In the latter part of the chapter, I focus in particular on the ambivalence perspective because of its more explicit engagement with the potential for contextual factors to alter beliefs about inequality. I situate this perspective within postwar America and the transformations of the 1970s and beyond that led to rising income inequality, showing how this perspective comports more with the former than the latter period.

Throughout the chapter, the discussion builds upon previous theories in sociology, political science, economics, social psychology, and history, and yet suggests a different framework for understanding beliefs in the era of rising inequality. A static conceptualization of ambivalence as a tension between believing in America as the land of opportunity on the one hand and objecting to extreme disparities in economic well-being on the other hand is substituted for a more dynamic and historicized conceptualization in which beliefs about economic opportunity and income inequality are interdependent rather than counterposed, with the precise nature of their interdependence shifting over time. The notion of ambivalence therefore plays a less central role in the new framework than in current theories, and American beliefs emerge as more coherent than previously imagined.

Theories of Beliefs about Inequality

There are many richly detailed observational studies of beliefs about inequality, as well as a large and established field of experimental research on distributive justice. Much of this literature is based on original surveys and/or semi-structured interviews conducted at a single point in time. Changes over time are sometimes discussed but usually only for a limited number of items repeated from earlier surveys.[3] These studies are a gold mine, but unfortunately they largely predate the era of rising inequality. Moreover, questions about inequality – or at least the kind of "rich versus poor" inequality on the rise since the 1970s – are surprisingly few in the proliferation of public opinion polls over the past couple of decades. Until very recently, most social surveys and opinion polls focused instead on attitudes about other dimensions and domains of inequality, such as racial and gender inequality, poverty, equal opportunity, and government policies aimed at reducing inequality.[4]

Why do we see such a gap in the social survey and public opinion literature on beliefs about income inequality? Most likely, it can be chalked up to the timing of trends in income inequality. Earnings and income inequality were not considered an important social problem until relatively recently. Few people outside of academic and policy circles knew about rising inequality, and researchers were divided until the early 1990s over both its magnitude and persistence.[5] The distributional ramifications of long-term transformations toward a postindustrial economy were not fully appreciated until the 1990s either, perhaps because of their isolation at first to particular regions of the country and sectors of the economy.[6] The social issues that did dominate public discourse were those that emerged from the social policies and movements of the 1960s and 1970s, in particular the antipoverty and civil rights movements and the backlashes they subsequently spawned.

Nevertheless, the findings and insights from earlier research on inequality ring true today in several important respects. Because the research record was thin at that time, scholars took a remarkably comprehensive approach to the topic of inequality. They investigated everything from fundamental orientations toward capitalism, socialism, and democracy to perceptions of fairness in interactions among workers, family members, friends, and strangers. Fortunately, there was considerable agreement in the findings and interpretations across the studies, at least concerning beliefs about inequality as they were measured at that time. I describe these areas of agreement briefly in the next section; my emphasis in the rest of the chapter turns then to the less-noted areas of disagreement. These include disagreements in orientations toward social and historical change in 1980s-era studies in sociology and political science, in theoretical frameworks stemming from other traditions and disciplines (such as economics and history), and in more recent research emerging from renewed interest in the topic across the social science disciplines.

Beliefs in Principle: The Multiple Spheres Approach

It is impossible to overstate the volume of writing on American economic and political ideologies concerning the broad and noble idea of equality. In modern times, this is especially true of the fervent scholarly activity on this topic in the period preceding the rise in income inequality. Following the tumultuous movements of the 1960s, scholars were understandably preoccupied with questions of racial and gender inequality and poverty. In order to get a better handle on how greater equality might be achieved, however, such scholars inquired into the workings of the major social institutions of American society – capitalism and democracy – that would need to accommodate the new demands for equality. As it happened, existing beliefs about the economy and politics were also shaken up by other momentous forces occurring at roughly the same time, such as the oil crisis, Watergate, stagflation, and increasing global economic competition. The potential for deep systemic transformation was contemplated seriously at least by some, and this intuition must have had a hand in prompting the expansive studies of economic and political beliefs at that time.[7]

No doubt to the surprise of scholars, what these studies actually found was that the liberal tradition of free markets and limited government, what we call conservative ideology today, was largely affirmed in survey after survey of the American public. In one of the first and most influential studies, Lloyd Free and Hadley Cantril devised a five-question scale of beliefs concerning "the proper sphere and role of government and the nature and functioning of the American socioeconomic system." They found that Americans leaned slightly in the conservative direction with respect to the role of government but were "more pronouncedly conservative" in their notions of economic freedom and responsibility. This latter conclusion came from responses to two questions about an individual's responsibility to manage his or her own economic affairs. Between three-quarters and four-fifths of Americans agreed that "any able-bodied person who really wants to work in this country can find a job and earn a living" and "we should rely more on individual initiative and not so much on governmental welfare programs." Together with responses to three additional questions about the government's role in "local matters" and "regulating business," Free and Cantril surmised that about half of Americans are conservative in their ideological orientation (considering government's role and economic responsibility together), and another third are moderate. Liberals are a distinct minority.[8]

Free and Cantril did not broach the subject of equality head on, but the conservative ideology they articulated would of necessity chip away at that other famous strain in American thought and society: egalitarianism. To examine egalitarian beliefs more explicitly, and to parse out their relation to conservative ideology, the concept of separate social spheres was widely deployed in the literature following Free and Cantril's 1967 treatise. The idea was that equality could mean different things in different spheres; that although "almost all Americans claim the label of egalitarianism, they differ on what equality means," and "to be egalitarian in one way may require being inegalitarian in another."[9] According to one influential rendition in Jennifer Hochschild's *What is Fair?*, Americans apply different principles of distributive justice to different domains of society. The principle of equality is applied to the political and social realms, and the principle of differentiation is applied to the economic realm. In the former realm, all individuals are to be treated with equal respect under the law, in politics, and in social interactions in a forthright rejection of feudal and aristocratic traditions. These are the familiar refrains of America's vaunted egalitarianism proclaimed so famously (and cited so widely) by the luminary of nineteenth-century history and social thought, Alexis de Toqueville.[10]

Whereas the principle of equality prevailed in the political and social realms, the economic sphere was governed by the belief that individuals differed in their economic worth and ought therefore to differ in their rewards as well. As long as opportunities are open to all and no one is restrained from scaling his or her true heights, the principle of equality of opportunity in the economic sphere is upheld. Under these conditions, unequal rewards are given in proportion to unequal contributions and considered the "just deserts" of a free market. Such a reward system also benefits society at large by spurring individuals to succeed and fostering innovation and prosperity.[11] Conversely, government interference short-circuits the virtues of free enterprise and harms both individual achievers and society at large. As Mary and Robert Jackman argue, "the dominant achievement ideology permeates Americans' way of thinking sufficiently to submerge the issue of equality itself and to rephrase the political debate more in terms of equality of opportunity."[12]

Yet these same studies also tell us that, however firmly Americans adhere to the principle of unequal rewards, they do not embrace it whole-heartedly and often blur the boundaries between spheres. This can be seen most transparently in the striving for greater equality, status, and meaning outside of work – in moral values, social and family circles, consumption habits, and political causes. Fulfillment in these other arenas of life has value in and of itself, but it also helps to offset ethical misgivings or material hardships associated with economic inequality.[13] Americans often take this impulse a step further by applying principles of political and social equality to matters of economic security. For instance, majorities tend to support policies that provide a minimum degree of equality in material well-being among all Americans so that basic needs for food, shelter, health, safety, and even a job are met.[14] Put a little differently, the dictates of a free market economy may be considered liberating, func-tional, and even fair, while at the same time the resulting distribution of rewards is more unequal than Americans can stomach, more than they think is befitting of a affluent and democratic nation. In this event, they turn to the government for relief.

The reach of egalitarianism into the economic sphere is thus circum-scribed yet still more expansive than typically assumed. On the one hand, the economic sphere is conceptually sealed off from government inter-vention, leaving legitimate debate about social policy and redistribution to hinge on special cases of individuals or groups worthy of government support. This conjures up an image of piecemeal change, with the process of inclusion over time limited to a weak version of T. H. Marshall's civil, political, and social rights advancing in fits and starts to encompass more individuals and more rights as time goes on. Social rights are granted, but they are designed to infringe as little as possible on the private sector and to eschew dependency on government assistance. This makes formal polit-ical inclusion in the guise of political rights a more feasible and palatable option than substantive economic justice.[15] On the other hand, although Americans express antigovernment and pro–free market sentiments as "ideological conservatives" in principle, they support social programs as "operational liberals" in practice. Indeed, nearly half (46 percent) of Free and Cantril's ideological conservatives *simultaneously* endorsed a wide range of social policies, so that in total operational liberals accounted for almost two-thirds of Americans in their study.[16]

In sum, any understanding of beliefs about economic inequality must take as a baseline view the principle of differentiation in the economic sphere, in which unequal financial rewards are perceived as acceptable, functional, and even fair; individuals undertake primary responsibility for their own livelihood; and government is restrained from involving itself too aggressively in economic affairs. But it is only a baseline. The inclination to invalidate equality of condition in the economic domain but to pursue it in other domains of social and political life is a common explanation of the lack of forceful opposition to high levels of inequality, one that does not imply that Americans are unmoved by disparities in material well-being.

Historical Foundations of Beliefs in Principle: The Tolerance Perspective

Popular support for social programs that help the needy can be justified on the basis of core humanitarian or egalitarian values that require the fulfillment of basic needs in a society that has the wherewithal to do so, but acceptance of inequality in the *market* is premised on what is potentially a more radical belief: equality of opportunity. Although few in America think that incomes should be completely equal, taking this option off the table, nearly nine in ten believe that "our society should do whatever is necessary to make sure that everyone has an equal opportunity to succeed." As Larry Bartels sardonically notes, if these responses were taken at face value, they would "imply an astounding level of public support for what would have to be a very radical program of social transformation," including everything from eliminating inherited wealth and local school funding to leveling the social and economic advantages of "intelligence, physical attractiveness, and freakish athletic skills." Although Bartels admits that this is probably not what Americans have in mind, he nevertheless believes that responses such as these provide "a striking testament to the force of 'equal opportunity' in American culture."[17]

So just how radical is the demand for equal opportunity? Is it even real, in the sense of having been born of a history of opportunities for upward mobility spread widely enough to have become a legitimate basis for unequal rewards? Or is the entire notion a mirage, espoused by those who have already won the race and rigged the rules in favor of their family, friends, and associates? These questions reflect the range of debate over the social, economic, and political foundations of American ideologies of equality. On the one side are those who cling to these ideologies as authentic expressions of a unique and enviable American experience.[18]

On the other are those who see them as emblematic of the interests of elites who maneuver politically and stealthily to prevail over popular aspirations for greater equality. In the middle are those who see both factors at work, from inspiring vistas of opportunity to advantages tilted unjustly toward the affluent and advantaged. This tension in turn creates the grounds for changes in perceptions of inequality and increasing expectations for greater inclusion.

I have deliberately stacked the deck in favor of the middle ground, not only because it is consistent with my own orientation in this book toward understanding variation and change in the American experience – dislodging the static image of an archetypical American individualist – but also because it is consistent with the new historiography of American exceptionalism. Historians (across the social sciences) are the ultimate arbiters of the extent to which social conditions have been consistent with ideologies of equality and opportunity in the United States, and whether these conditions varied over time or across otherwise similar nations. And if there is any consensus at all among historians, it is that scholars have tended to overstate the "liberal consensus" and resulting lack of economic conflict in American history, as promulgated first by Alexis de Toqueville and then later by Louis Hartz and Seymour Martin Lipset, among many others. The historian Thomas Haskell advocates instead a "postexceptionalist" perspective in which neither exceptionalism nor antiexceptionalism is proffered in advance, so that the "the particularities of different times and different nations" become the center of analysis.[19]

In this reading, liberalism in both its free market and antigovernment forms is but one of several influential traditions in American history and society. Republican and religious traditions of self-government among relative economic equals represent a second compelling approach, and what Rogers Smith terms "ascriptive hierarchy" and Carole Pateman and Charles Mills "the domination contract" a third.[20] These "multiple traditions" begin to bring ideologies of American equality and opportunity down to earth without jettisoning the factors that did indeed foster beliefs of rugged individualism. Thus religious freedom, a natural rights invective against aristocratic privilege, a system of checks on centralized or European-style "despotic" government, an early franchise to white men regardless of economic station, rapid industrialization, and a fertile and expansive frontier must be balanced against slavery, genocidal expropriation of Native American and Mexican lands, exclusion of women from the rights of citizenship for over half of the country's history, an "ethos of civic virtue and economic regulation for the public good" derived from republicanism and Protestantism, farm populism, labor strife, and the state's extensive legal and institutional power.[21] This contrast bespeaks both a tension between ideal and reality and a challenge to the very notion that the liberal ideal was ever capable of singularly representing the American tradition.

With the theoretical perspective of multiple traditions in hand, it is possible to examine the narrower question of whether hopes of economic opportunity were nurtured by economic conditions during early eras of American history while keeping in mind the pitfalls of transhistorical and whitewashed assumptions of American liberal individualism. To some economists, such as Alberto Alesina and Edward Glaeser, the United States is indeed exceptional, but only in thought and not in material reality. These economists argue that despite similar economic foundations in their countries, Americans and Europeans diverge in their economic and political beliefs because they have been indoctrinated by different forces. Americans have been indoctrinated by economic and political elites to believe that effort is fairly rewarded and government redistribution is unnecessary. Europeans have been swayed by powerful socialist and labor movements to believe that luck determines the class into which one is born and likely to stay, necessitating a compensatory system of social support. Although beliefs about redistribution on the two sides of the Atlantic are central to legitimating and reinforcing divergent welfare regimes, they are the outcome of *political* rather than economic developments that stretch far back in history.[22]

To other economists, however, continental differences in economic conditions were in fact once quite substantial and most likely helped to lay the groundwork for at least the initial construction of ideologies of equal opportunity. Economists in this camp are at odds as to how the ideological dynamic unfolded, but they all take nineteenth-century European social theorists at their word in describing a richer, more economically free and mobile America as compared to Europe.[23] More recent accounts along these lines are beholden to the empirical evidence marshaled by the economist Joseph Ferrie and his colleagues. They assembled census data on the occupations of white native-born sons and fathers in Great Britain and the United States at three time points from the mid-1800s to the late-1900s and calculated rates of intergenerational mobility in each era, controlling for differences in the occupational structure. Their findings confirmed the conventional wisdom, but only in part. They found the United States to be significantly more fluid than Great Britain in the mid-nineteenth century, but the two converge over time as Great Britain becomes more mobile and the United States less so.[24] Sociologists had previously documented the growing convergence of the twentieth century but not the divergence and subsequent convergence of the nineteenth century.[25]

Ferrie also assesses the causes of differences across time and place, examining such central factors as expanding education and geographic mobility. As is well known, the United States was an early provider of universal public education, which offered an accessible route to upward mobility. Ferrie is careful to add, however, that Britain caught up to the United States in its public provision of education during the latter part of the nineteenth century. He further speculates that even though educational opportunities continued to expand in the United States, educational inequality – as a result of uneven financing across regions – may have widened as well, "resulting in fewer opportunities for progressive redistribution through the provision of greater educational resources to those whose parents could least afford to directly invest in their children." Rates of internal migration were also much greater in mid-to-late nineteenth century United States than in both contemporaneous Britain and twentieth-century United States. Ferrie argues that this is less a story of frontier-induced mobility than one of uneven regional growth.[26]

Economists take this evidence and argue that *contemporary* differences in American and European attitudes about social mobility are derived from these historical differences and affect preferences for redistributive policies to this day. Ferrie acknowledges the arguments of Alesina and colleagues that "the image of the United States as a place where mobility remains the norm ... undermine support for a fiscal regime of higher taxes and higher transfers like that seen in Europe." But based on his findings, Ferrie suggests that "the vastly different public perceptions of mobility prospects and corresponding policy differences today might be more a legacy of historical experience than a reflection of current circumstances."[27] Likewise, in an earlier and influential piece, Thomas Piketty cites Lipset's explanation of differences in the political outlooks of American and European workers as stemming from "varying historical experiences ... [which seem] much more important than slight variations in [contemporary] rates of mobility."[28] These historical experiences are the basis upon which individuals learn about the positive return to effort and the negative "incentive costs of redistribution," which are also reflected in the social mobility experiences of friends and family members. These signals feed into policy preferences that are aligned more with imperfect information about past patterns of social mobility than with more proximate information about current income and mobility prospects.

Finally, for economists Roland Benabou and Jean Tirole, historical conditions play a critical role in establishing different American and European belief systems as well. But, in their version of history, what was most consequential was that "the initial generations who settled in America were self-selected to have a low disutility for effort" or a "religious background that made effort-promoting beliefs particularly desirable." Another influential factor reiterated here is the "availability of free [*sic*] land," which they argue was more likely to have shaped "initial views on opportunity and social mobility . . . rather than to facilitate control of the masses by the wealthy" as Alesina and his colleagues argue in their "top-down" model of indoctrination.[29] These historical conditions led to diametrically opposed American and European equilibria. The former is "characterized by a high prevalence of just-world beliefs and a relatively laissez-faire public policy" and the latter by "more pessimism and a more extensive welfare state."[30] Here "just-world beliefs" refer to an optimistic view of how effort is rewarded and a skeptical view of the need for a social safety net.[31] In contrast to Piketty's model of imperfect information, Benabou and Tirole embed their "bottom-up" model in the psychological dispositions demanded of individuals who cannot depend on the government for economic support. Optimism is thus adaptive in its potential to motivate effort in an insecure economic environment. As important, the American equilibrium leads to greater productivity and higher income in the aggregate, although at the cost of more poverty.[32]

This last set of implications of the Benabou and Tirole model should not be underestimated. Reasonable people may disagree over comparable measures of social mobility across countries and historical eras, or over whether European social theorists were blinkered or overly sanguine in their perceptions of U.S. economic egalitarianism. But if we loosen the definition of opportunity to include the average standard of living of a nation, even Alesina and Glaeser acknowledge that "there is certainly some objective truth to the view that America has been a land of opportunity, not in the sense that Americans are all that more mobile, but just in the sense that Americans both today and historically have been richer than Europeans."[33] They are skeptical that this is an aspect of the environment that could alter the lived experiences of opportunity and redistribution, but others are not as inclined to do so. As we will see below, the economic abundance of the post–World War II era may have been a decisive element in the reemergence of views of American economic exceptionalism at that time.

I have relied mainly on economists to narrate the historical record of equality of opportunity in nineteenth-century America. As economists, they are uniquely qualified to do so, particularly in an era so laden with rhetoric and devoid of modern attitudinal data. Their work also centrally and richly engages questions of ideologies of equality, and therefore cuts to the heart of the matter we are concerned with. Their verdict largely concurs with contemporaneous European observers, contemporary popular impressions, and a formidable strain in American scholarship that identifies Americans as "ideological conservatives," in Free and Cantril's words. But contrary to many other social scientists, Free and Cantril included, economists are much more likely to oppose an undifferentiated American economic individualism to a hegemonic European social democracy, despite genuine efforts to recognize heterogeneity among individuals within nations, to allude to the presence and importance of struggle on both continents, and to cite several sociologists and political scientists who find a less tidy resolution of beliefs. Moreover, these accounts are frozen in the nineteenth century, with either economic conditions or political institutions of that era capable of determining the entire course of twentieth-century beliefs.[34] This is despite insightful attempts to recognize the potential impact of "shocks" that could spell the unraveling of American and European equilibria, such as the Great Depression and World War II.[35]

In the following sections, I examine the continuities and controversies in understanding American beliefs about inequality, opportunity, and redistribution in the twentieth century. My emphasis will remain on the social conditions that undergird or belie such beliefs. Fast-forwarding to the second half of the twentieth century, I return to the most in-depth studies of American attitudes about inequality and the "ambivalence" perspective redolent in those studies. One form of ambivalence was already apparent in the discussion earlier in the chapter of beliefs in principle: Free and Cantril's contrast between conservative economic ideologies and support for liberal government policies. But there is another version of ambivalence that we have yet to consider. This is ambivalence between the principle and practice of inequality *within the economic sphere itself.*

In the discussion earlier in the chapter, it was the concept of separate economic, social, and political spheres that allowed for unpalatable economic differences to be mitigated by social relations and political action, but this conceptualization says nothing of addressing concerns about the fairness of differences in *market* outcomes themselves. In theory, such outcomes are assumed to be legitimate in a society of equal opportunity. Although we have seen that this assumption has some basis in historical reality, it is not the entire story of the nation's history. Similarly, the "tolerance" perspective claims that Americans are optimistic about economic opportunity and tolerant of income inequality. However, it does so without probing into perceptions of economic inequality itself, or even more deeply into perceptions of economic opportunity. In the next sections, I move the discussion not only into the twentieth century but into the territory of beliefs directly about income inequality and equal opportunity in practice, and into the more nuanced perspective of ambivalence.

Beliefs about Inequality in Practice, I: Ambivalence in the Postwar Period

The gulf between reality and ideal produces ambivalence about equality not only in the confrontation between economic and political life but also within each domain. For example, despite the American commitment to the ideal of equal opportunity, tolerance of economic inequality is by no means universal in this country...the narrowing of the ideal-real gap may entail bringing economic reality into line with the economic ideal of equal opportunity.[36]

Once we exit the world of the American dream, and the tolerance perspective that it implies, we enter a world of beliefs that are much less pristine than the ideals of equal opportunity and just deserts portray. In espousing equality of opportunity and rejecting strict equality of outcomes, Americans unwittingly employ a relatively accessible measurement of opportunity (equality) and a more vague measurement of outcomes (inequality). This vagueness stems from the fact that inequality of outcomes can theoretically have no limit even though Americans seem to prefer moderate over extreme levels. The point that I wish to emphasize here is that there are important consequences of this vagueness for gauging beliefs about inequality. Inequalities of outcomes are abstractions for most people, and all the more so because of this vagueness; therefore, such disparities are challenging to perceive with any precision. For this reason, Americans are not typically asked about "how much inequality exists" or "how much inequality is fair," but rather are presented with a variety of less-direct questions that elicit a wider spectrum of attitudes about inequality than we have thus far encountered.

In arguably the most extensive representative survey of beliefs about inequality ever fielded in the United States, James Kluegal and Elliot

Smith found that beliefs about economic inequality in principle often collide with beliefs about economic inequality in practice. Perhaps their most innovative evidence comes from a split-ballot experiment in which individuals are asked whether their family would be better off if income inequality were reduced.[37] Half of the respondents were asked this question before a battery of eleven other questions about the virtues and vices of income inequality, and half after. These other questions asked whether incomes should be more equal because everyone's needs are similar and their contributions equally important; whether greater equality would reduce societal conflict, motivation to work, investment in the economy by the rich, or individual freedoms; and whether it was even possible to equalize incomes in view of fundamental differences in human nature. Because these questions would prime survey respondents about the general advantages and disadvantages of inequality, Kluegal and Smith wanted to know whether the inclination to think in a self-interested way about inequality would be altered by such priming. They found that priming did indeed make a difference: 42 percent of the respondents who were primed agreed that their family would be better off, whereas a much larger 62 percent of those who were not primed agreed. On net the virtues of inequality were apparently more persuasive than the vices, but nonetheless, two-fifths to three-fifths would prefer (assuming self-interest) a world with *less* inequality.

When Americans are asked more directly about whether they prefer more or less inequality, the same range of replies is given. For example, about half of the respondents think there should be "about the present level of income equality," whereas 38 percent would opt for "more equality than there is now" and another 3 percent for "complete equality of income."[38] Similarly, in a 1987 pilot of the American National Election Studies, in which questions about equality of outcomes were temporarily added to a now well-known battery of questions about equality of rights and opportunities, 41 percent disagreed that "all in all, economic differences in this country are justified"; 60 percent agreed that "it would be better for everyone if the distribution of wealth in this country were more equal"; and 55 percent agreed that "personal income should not be determined just by one's worth. Rather, everyone should get what they need to provide a decent life for their family."[39] Need-based considerations also tempered achievement-based ones in a survey conducted in the late 1970s. Asked whether "people with more ability would earn higher salaries under a fair economic system," 78 percent agreed, while only 15 percent "declined to choose" and 7 percent thought earnings should be equal. By contrast, when asked whether a "person's wages should depend on how much he needs to live decently," only 45 percent disagreed and said instead that "the importance of his job" was of foremost concern, 20 percent agreed, and 35 percent declined to choose.[40]

Much of the existing literature that finds Americans to be tolerant of inequality also emphasizes the bad rap heaped on the poor, but this literature largely neglects American beliefs about the rich or assumes that Americans extol rather than resent the rich. Kluegal and Smith, however, asked a full battery of questions about why "there are rich people" in addition to the more typical battery of questions about the poor. They also investigated whether rich, middle-class, and low-income folks were fairly rewarded for their work by asking whether the earnings of a representative set of occupations were too much, too little, or about right "for the contribution that they make to society."

Here again a more complex picture can be gleaned from the attempt to probe more deeply into the fairness of inequality. For example, among the three most important reasons usually given for why there are rich people in the United States, two involve individual characteristics (personal drive/willingness to take risks and hard work/initiative) but one involves social advantages (money inherited from families). Of the next two most important reasons, one involves individual characteristics (great ability/talent) and the other involves social advantages (political influence).[41] With respect to occupational pay, the most emphatic reactions were to the earnings of those at the very top of the ladder – owners and executives of large corporations, professional athletes, movie stars and top entertainers, and medical doctors. For these occupations, 69 to 78 percent of respondents thought the pay was too much. On the other end, the occupations that were most likely to be deemed underpaid were lower-level white-collar workers, teachers in elementary and high schools, and nonunionized factory workers.[42] In a separate study, Sidney Verba and Gary Orren make the observation that evaluations of top (executive), blue-collar (auto worker), and low-end (elevator operator) jobs are the most likely to be politicized as measured by their stronger associations with ideological beliefs in comparison to evaluations of other occupations.[43]

More recent and in-depth studies by Michelle Lamont confirm that the rich are not held in uncritically high regard by Americans lower down the ladder. Even though everyone would understandably like to bask in the material security and advantages of having a lucrative job, the rich are often seen as morally inferior to the middle class.[44] Moreover, whereas it is often reasoned that Americans go easy on the rich because they think unrealistically that someday they too will be rich, polls reveal instead a rather accurate appraisal of the low chances of becoming rich. When asked in a Gallup poll "how likely it is that you will ever be rich," 67 percent said that it was "not very likely" or "not at all likely" in 1990 and 72 percent responded in this way in 2012. Social psychologists are coming to similar conclusions about the ambivalence that Americans feel toward the affluent. The economically successful are regarded as competent and deserving on the one hand and cold and calculating on the other.[45]

Despite evidence of a more critical stance toward inequality and the rich than is often assumed, however, the most comprehensive studies on beliefs about inequality in the 1980s are still replete with references to the ambivalence of American attitudes about inequality and inequality-related issues, and this ambivalence must be accounted for. Americans are skeptical of the availability of true equality of opportunity and disapprove of existing levels of inequality, yet support for the free market in principle is strong. The rich deserve to be well compensated for their hard work and contributions to society, yet many of them are overpaid. Why this ambivalence? As many have written, some of it may be due to the inherent tension between liberty and equality, capitalism and democracy. True equality of opportunity can produce vastly unequal rewards between those who succeed and those who do not, even if by legitimate means. Any realistic level of inequality can then circumscribe equality of opportunity in subsequent generations as the playing field becomes tilted toward the well-off. Only a radically equal starting gate could counter the adverse effect of unequal rewards on equal opportunities across generations. This is why so much research on inequality focuses on intergenerational patterns of social mobility, and the extent to which inequalities in family income produce inequalities in the educational and economic attainment of children.

Yet there is another, less noted tension in these studies as well. It concerns the question of whether there is an ideal or acceptable level of inequality of rewards, *even if the positions themselves are attained through open and competitive procedures.* For example, in discussing income gaps between "the head of a corporation and a common laborer, between a professor at the top of the scale and an instructor," Daniel Bell worried that the rationale for these gaps would be "one of the most vexing questions in post-industrial society." In raising the question, even the relatively cautious Bell hoped to guard against the evolution of an "unjust meritocracy...which makes these distinctions invidious and demeans those below."[46] Here a fluid and flourishing market society in which the pursuit of self-interest redounds to the benefit of all, and all are oriented toward increasing economic productivity, is derailed. Rewards and productivity become distorted or decoupled, and norms of freedom become meaningless for those locked in desperate conditions. This was the dystopic version of meritocracy that Michael Young conjured up in his seminal *The Rise of Meritocracy*. But even before then, this dystopic vision was a common trope of the Gilded Age in the late nineteenth century, when the United States changed from "an agrarian, small-scale, and relatively egalitarian society to a nation of corporate capitalism, huge institutions, and vast differences in wealth." In fact, the heroes of Horatio Alger's stories during this period were not rich capitalists, as commonly assumed, but those who escaped the misery of factory life to achieve a respectable middle-class existence.[47]

Surprisingly absent in contemporary debates about inequality is a serious reckoning with this possibility, a theory of exactly *when* and *why* inequality of rewards is perceived as excessive or otherwise becomes contested. The ambivalence perspective gives us a nuanced framework, but it offers only a snapshot of beliefs and does not illuminate when self-interest or concerns about need, deservingness, and fairness are activated in real historical time. To be sure, the contentious history of struggles over equality is often recounted in impressive detail, but then we end up back where we began, with the balancing act (or stalemate) of ambivalence firmly entrenched in the American consciousness. But is ambivalence the modus operandi or just one state among many? When exactly are the scales tipped, and what turns up or down the volume of opposition?

For insight into these questions, I look once again to the social and historical conditions under which beliefs about inequality are formed, this time in the more recent past, and in the next section in the current period of rising inequality. Despite the mostly static nature of the data on beliefs about inequality in the 1970s and 1980s, scholars writing at this time could not help but speculate about the possibilities for change. In so doing, they began to plant the seeds for a more dynamic conceptualization of ambivalence that helps us to discern when the scales of opposition and acquiescence might be tipped in one direction or the other.

Kluegal and Smith offer the most detailed analysis of "potential challenges" to "dominant ideology" beliefs, which is the term they use to describe Hochschild's principle of acceptable differentiation in the economic sphere. They discuss two sources of such challenges: (1) individual experiences of inequality, and (2) social liberalism arising from objections to poverty and racial and gender inequality that had been given "increased attention" during the two decades prior to their 1980 study.[48]

Although adherence to the dominant ideology is virtually universal, they argue that social and political characteristics affect the extent of ambivalence about it. For example, blacks, women, and low-income individuals are more likely to perceive structural barriers to economic opportunity and to support redistributive policies even though they are no less likely to justify inequality of outcomes in principle.[49] Of greater interest, however, is Kluegal and Smith's notion that wider social transformations and socioeconomic conditions present challenges to the dominant ideology. Whereas gender and racial inequalities and poverty are the structural challenges that occupy center stage in the milieu of the 1970s and 1980s, also mentioned are the inflation and unemployment of that period as a potential new challenge on the horizon. These conditions could limit perceptions of opportunity and dispose Americans toward a more structural interpretation of unequal outcomes as opposed to one rooted in individual responsibility and just deserts.

Several other scholars recorded significant shifts in attitudes – or the potential for them – during this period as well. Jennifer Hochschild argued that "[i]t does not seem farfetched to see the 1940s, 1950s, and 1960s as an era of expansion and optimism, and to see the 1970s as an era of slowing down and of increasing pessimism. That leaves the 1980s poised for an explosion of anger and demands for change among those left behind earlier."[50] Similarly, writing in 1985, Robert Bellah and colleagues make an impassioned plea for attending to the deeper communal needs of society "now that economic growth is faltering and the moral ecology on which we have tacitly depended is in disarray."[51] Finally, Herbert McCloskey and John Zaller report a massive turnabout in attitudes toward business in which "levels of public confidence were higher in the more prosperous decade of the 1960s. As late as 1968, for example, 70 percent of the public expressed confidence that 'business tries to strike a fair balance between profits and the interests of the public,' compared with only 15 percent in 1977."[52] Seymour Martin Lipset and William Schneider wrote that these shifts had a basis in reality, citing Three Mile Island, Love Canal, the oil crisis, and stagflation.[53]

Both the speculation and data discussed above suggest that the perceived fairness and prosperity of the market economy are important factors in the formation of beliefs about inequality *even when income inequality itself is not transparently increasing* (as it was not in the 1970s). Remarkably, affirmative responses to the Louis Harris poll about whether the "rich are getting richer and the poor are getting poorer" increased by 10 percentage points over the 1970s, from 67 percent in 1971 to

77 percent in 1977, even though there was no evidence of rising income inequality per se. What were typically considered barriers to *equal opportunity*, however, were everywhere to be seen, with increased attention to poverty, unemployment, rising costs of living, and racial and gender gaps in occupations and earnings. In pondering the "future of capitalism," McCloskey and Zaller argued that it would depend on capitalism's "effectiveness in producing and equitably distributing the goods and services Americans expect."[54]

According to these criteria, there seems to be little disagreement about the effectiveness of capitalism in the pre-1970s era, and much more in the era that follows. For perceptions of inequality, what distinguishes these two periods? Why was there so much speculation in the 1980s about changes in future beliefs about inequality before there was any evidence of rising income inequality? After describing the social conditions of the postwar period, including new historical research that tempers the consensus view of a liberal capital-labor accord, I examine the social conditions of the last three decades and incorporate perspectives from scholars writing in the 1990s and 2000s as well.

Economic growth and unemployment are perhaps the most straightforward and visible indicators of economic conditions for the American public, but there is no a priori reason why abundant growth, a high standard of living, and low unemployment should be associated with equality of opportunity, equitable outcomes, or the virtues of capitalism (as opposed to the wise hand of government). Do Americans view these conditions as interconnected, and if so, how and why?

Beginning with the relationship between economic growth and the private economy, there is a large body of economic, comparative, and historical research on the role that prosperity in the post–World War II period in the United States played in fostering an image of unfettered economic abundance.[55] I use the word "image" deliberately but cautiously. On the one hand, the image is only an image: not only was wartime and postwar military government spending a boon to the economy, the U.S. welfare state was much larger than assumed, once "hidden" tax-subsidized contributions to employers for the provision of health and pension benefits are taken into account.[56] On the other hand, the image is real in conveying the veritable strength of corporate America in the immediate postwar period, both absolutely and relative to war-torn Europe. This strength was a key factor in winning the privatization of benefits against a strong liberal-labor-consumerist coalition pushing for greater government protections against unemployment, inflation, illness, and old age. A primarily employer-based system of benefits provision, or welfare capitalism, was eventually institutionalized even though it represented a radically boiled-down version of labor's and consumer groups' demands.[57]

If the image and reality of economic abundance and social benefits came to be associated with the postwar private economy, what about its association with equality and opportunity? During the immediate postwar decades, many plausible indicators of equality and opportunity moved in tandem with each other and with economic growth in a single juggernaut. Jobs, incomes, and benefits all expanded to create what John Kenneth Galbraith at the time called a "mountainous rise in well-being," one that was relatively evenly distributed across the population thanks to the strong wage-equalizing influences of wartime wage and price controls, unions and collective bargaining, the minimum wage, and equity norms in large corporations.[58] According to a historian of the period, Lisabeth Cohen, "[f]aith in the mass consumption postwar economy came to mean much more than the ready availability of goods to buy. Rather, it stood for an elaborate, integrated ideal of economic abundance and democratic political freedom, both *equitably distributed*, that became almost a national civil religion from the late 1940s into the 1970s."[59]

The "social compact" between capital and labor was a central element of this zeitgeist, but there was much more to it than this. In time, the economy came to be heralded as fair and efficient in principle as well as the source of redistributive norms in practice for those both inside and outside of the collective bargaining orbit.[60] Major conflicts continued to exist – from who could get a foot in the door to who reaped the most rewards once inside – but visible (in terms of consumption) and real (in terms of the distribution of national income) gains were made by families throughout the income distribution.[61] The key exceptions were glaring – African Americans and women – but these exceptions tended to be laid at the feet of a discriminatory society. They were not considered evidence first and foremost of an inherently unequal market economy but were seen as a distortion in which white men were unfairly concentrated in the best jobs.[62] These injustices notwithstanding, I refer to the combination of growth and redistribution in the labor market as perceived *equitable growth* or what others call *shared prosperity*.[63] Thus one of the essential features of the postwar equitable growth paradigm was that redistribution became associated with the fruits of economic prosperity rather than with government tax-and-transfer policy.

This did not mean that the state had no visible role whatsoever in facilitating equitable growth, only that this role would be more indirect than outright income redistribution. Consider the example of regulatory policy. Writing in the early 1980s about the "confidence gap" in business, labor, and government, Lipset and Schneider concluded from numerous polls that "Americans clearly believe that business should be pressured to change its ways in the interest of consumers and workers. Hence, they repeatedly approve of regulations to reduce specific evils . . . [while rejecting] an excess of regulation."[64] Regulation of business without onerous government interference was a brilliant way to simultaneously meet citizen demands for fiscal conservatism, greater economic and consumer justice, and individual responsibility. This was true even throughout the 1950s and 1960s, prior to the tax revolts beginning in the 1970s.[65] In fact, historians increasingly trace popular support for economic regulation to combat high prices and low wages, as well as other business infractions, as a central component of *liberal* economic citizenship stretching from the late-nineteenth century to the present. The power and cohesiveness of the most radical of these political coalitions waxed and waned over time, with their denouement by the end of the 1950s, but active engagement with the state over issues of economic regulation goes at least as far back as the Progressive Era.[66]

Equitable growth in the private sector, aided by government regulation and fiscal restraint, was therefore the backdrop against which the ambivalence perspective emerged in the inequality scholarship of the 1970s and 1980s. Although scholars argued that the new economic turbulence of their times would transform attitudes about inequality, and had already documented inclinations in a more oppositional vein, they were impressed above all else by acquiescence to the status quo. They saw the scales tipped unequivocally in favor of the dominant American dream ideology. And the scales were indeed so tipped, but these studies came at the tail end of a period of extended equitable growth.

Writing about economic attitudes in *The Affluent Society* in the late 1950s, John Kenneth Galbraith opined that "few things are more evident in modern social history than the decline of interest in inequality as an economic issue . . . [and] in one way or another [the decline is] related to the fact of increasing production."[67] To Galbraith, this was not a cause for celebration but a call to arms to reverse the "social imbalance" between private wealth and public restraint in social spending. Momentum did shift in this direction in the 1960s as a result of antipoverty and civil rights activism, but income inequality was but one of a constellation of injustices receiving increased attention. Galbraith himself saw the reduction of poverty as far more urgent than the reduction of inequality, and he was not alone. A few scholars writing on beliefs about income inequality in the 1980s did comment on the high level of income inequality at that time, even before inequality began to rise, but these were relatively isolated remarks in the literature.[68]

With the ambivalence perspective understood within this historical context, we can return to the broader theoretical question of how the reality and perception of income inequality are related to one another and what this portends for beliefs in the era of rising inequality. As we have seen, equitable growth during the postwar decades was a fusion of expanding opportunity and declining inequality, at least across social class, making it impossible to separate the extent to which perceptions of expanding opportunities or declining inequality supported ideologies of economic individualism. Most likely both were at work. What we can say is that it was a broad and popular understanding of the restriction of *opportunity* (the definition of which I discuss in much greater detail in Chapter 4) in the form of slowing growth, rising unemployment, entrenched poverty, and enduring racial and gender disparities, that was projected by scholars at the time to swing the pendulum of beliefs about *inequality* in a more oppositional direction. It was not widening income inequality as such, which had yet to rear its head, nor was it a narrow definition of limited opportunity as either intergenerational immobility or economic recession.

In fact, when forms of economic inequality were invoked, their primary purpose was to pinpoint violations of equal opportunity. Entrenched and racialized poverty, and racial and gender gaps in pay, were forms of economic inequality that were deployed as indicators of restricted opportunities. For example, unequal outcomes for children in schools and for equally qualified individuals in the labor market were offered as hard evidence of opportunities denied. Conversely, creation of greater equality of outcomes was a procedure to equalize opportunities, as in affirmative action. This was not uncontroversial, of course. It led to a rancorous debate over whether (un)equal outcomes should be the yardstick of (un)equal opportunities in both education and the labor market. In *The Coming of Post-industrial Society*, Daniel Bell wrote passionately against the conflation of equality of outcomes with equality of opportunity. Conservative politicians similarly sought to discredit the use of outcomes as either indicators of or solutions to the problem of unequal opportunity. The war between an equal opportunity and an equal outcome approach arose most vociferously in regard to issues of racial and gender equality, but unfortunately it also colored the way we conversed about other dimensions of economic opportunity and inequality.[69]

In sum, although debates beginning sometime in the 1960s and 1970s drove a conceptual wedge between equal opportunities and equitable outcomes in policy and academic discourses, the social reality of equitable growth in the postwar period was that the two went hand in hand, as they had appeared to do before the rise of the Gilded Age in the nineteenth century as well. Americans may have seen widespread economic opportunity as the preferred source of more equitable outcomes, and may have prioritized equalizing opportunities to equalizing outcomes on procedural grounds, but there is little evidence that they pitted equal opportunity against equitable outcomes as competing goals, caring only about the former and not the latter.

Both the ambivalence and tolerance perspectives help to reinforce this opposition by failing to fully historicize and contextualize beliefs or to recognize the symbiosis of equal opportunities and equitable outcomes in both social reality and social thought. Scholars of these perspectives are of course keenly aware of how unequal outcomes can restrict opportunities, but often this relationship is conceptualized mainly in terms of the prevailing definition of opportunity as intergenerational mobility. Moreover, this kind of relational thinking is rarely attributed to ordinary Americans. Multilayered images of restricted opportunities and unequal outcomes – such as inequitable growth and Bell's "unjust meritocracy" – are left undeveloped. Yet these are the very possibilities that the future held in store.

Beliefs about Inequality in Practice, II: Ignorance in the Era of Rising Inequality

What has happened since the rupture of the 1970s mentioned by Hochschild, Kluegal and Smith, and Cohen, among many others? As is now well known, productivity and median earnings diverged as an expanding economy no longer boosted earnings across the distribution as had been the norm in the 1940s through the 1960s.[70] Until the late 1990s, employment grew but with less vigor than in the postwar decades, and real earnings actually fell or stagnated for the majority of men and a minority of women. Racial minorities and white women were more formally incorporated into the economy and made great strides, but discrimination continued, inequality within groups increased, and poverty leveled off. The economic boom of the late 1990s *did* lift most boats, but it did so fantastically for some and modestly for others. Prosperity in terms of high productivity, employment, and growth rates returned but the towering levels of inequality erected over the 1980s and early 1990s to heights not seen since before World War II were left mostly intact. When the economy faltered again in the 2000s, as it inevitably would, for the first time median family income failed to grow in real terms over a business cycle. Remarkably, the poverty rate is as high today as it was in 1965. Unlike the 1940s through the 1960s, this was growth but not equal growth.[71] Did Americans perceive it as inequitable as well as unequal? Did they care?

My detailed empirical analysis of these questions – including media coverage and public opinion on income inequality – appears in the next four chapters, so my aim in the rest of this chapter is twofold. First, I consider how others have answered these questions over the past couple of decades in which rising income inequality became an issue of significant concern among scholars and other policy and political elites and activists. This discussion will be relatively brief, as only a handful of scholars and public opinion experts have explicitly examined this topic, and most concur with the "tolerance" or "ambivalence" perspectives described above. I highlight new variations on these positions and then focus on one perspective that has gained prominence: the view that Americans are largely uninformed about the issue of income inequality. I refer to this as the "ignorance" perspective. My second aim is to compare these responses to the theoretical framework that I have been developing to interpret beliefs about income inequality, economic opportunity, and redistribution. This framework draws on previous work, but it differs in its more explicit embrace of the context dependence of beliefs and in its thesis that Americans view equitable outcomes and opportunities as interconnected rather than alternative goals.

In our times, the predominant view among most observers – economists, social psychologists, journalists, and some political scientists – remains that Americans are tolerant of income inequality. To several proponents of this view, the basic fairness and prosperity of the U.S. economy was never in doubt during the structural shifts and hardships of the 1970s, 1980s, and 1990s. The payoffs to skill-biased technological change, in the form of more highly skilled jobs, greater productivity, and lasting prosperity, more than offset its dislocations. To be sure, those in low-skill jobs were hurt, but unemployment was relatively low (in the 1990s), and higher education became more widely available. Lipset concludes from such data that "stories of America's post-1970 economic decline have clearly been exaggerated," and the "leaner and meaner" restructuring of the American economy has led to a "rebirth of America's competitive standing" and "more improvements in occupational status than declines."[72]

It is noteworthy that Lipset wrote this prior to the economic boom of the late 1990s and amid negative media coverage of inequality, to which Lipset was in part responding in his defense of American exceptionalism.[73] After the boom began, mainstream media coverage subsided and concerns about inequality were deemed out of order in the wake of renewed prosperity.[74] Thus Lipset deploys an encompassing definition of opportunity that goes beyond measures of intergenerational mobility to argue that the American dream writ large was never seriously imperiled by rising inequality. He also implicitly recognizes the interdependence of inequality and opportunity, with inequality defanged by advances in economic competitiveness and human capital attainment, even as he explicitly reiterates the opposition between Americans caring about opportunity and not inequality.

The only other prominent public opinion experts who weighed in early on this subject came to the same conclusion, and they and Lipset were commonly cited in studies by economists on the subject. For instance, in a widely circulated study of the impact of inequality on levels of happiness across countries, economists Alesina, DiTella, and MacCulloch concluded that "[c]ountries differ greatly in the degree of income inequality that they tolerate... Americans are willing to tolerate quite large disparities in wealth as long as they perceive that wealth is the result of effort and that everyone can make it if enough effort and talent is devoted to the task."[75] In drawing this conclusion, Alesina and colleagues relied on the only study at that time of attitudes toward income inequality to be published after inequality began to rise. Unfortunately, because of the paucity of data directly on inequality, the study surveys attitudes mainly about opportunity and redistribution rather than inequality.

Despite this, the authors of the study, noted public opinion experts Everett Ladd and Karlyn Bowman, wrote that "there is some ambivalence about wealth in the United States but no particular resentment... Americans tolerate great differences in wealth if they believe that opportunity is broadly present."[76] Bowman later argued in an op-ed that "there's little evidence that rising income inequality ever captured the public's imagination."[77] There is a growing literature on trends in intergenerational mobility motivated in part by this view. Researchers are asking whether social mobility *is* greater in the United States than elsewhere, justifying the alleged acquiescence to inequality among Americans. Most scholars come to the conclusion that mobility is *not* greater in the United States and then struggle to explain why Americans are so optimistic.[78]

From the vantage point of trying to understand beliefs about income inequality, what is perhaps most notable about these studies, together with their kindred spirits in the tolerance literature discussed earlier, is that despite the appeal and sophistication of their theoretical frameworks, there is almost no empirical evidence marshaled specifically on beliefs about income inequality to buttress claims of tolerance. Those that do delve into such data resurface with a more nuanced and ambivalent view consistent with past interpretations. For example, Benjamin Page and Lawrence Jacobs return convincingly to the territory explored by Free and Cantril forty years ago and show that little has changed: Americans are conservative in espousing free enterprise and limited government but liberal in desiring needed social programs.[79] Yet, curiously, this and other studies falling under the big tent of the ambivalence perspective differ quite substantially in their assessment of how much Americans know about income inequality, how much they care about it, and how much they are willing to do about it.

The biggest point of disagreement surrounds the question of how much Americans really understand about the economics of income inequality and the politics of income redistribution. According to Page and Jacobs, a majority of Americans is aware that income inequality increased, wants to see less of it, and is willing to hike progressive taxes to shore up popular social programs such as education and health care.[80] In his monumental book *Unequal Democracy*, however, Larry Bartels tests the ice to see just how deep American progressive public opinion runs. For the first time, Bartels examines whether knowledge and norms about income inequality *directly* affect support for redistributive policies (i.e., taxes) rather than inferring such a relationship from separate responses to questions first about inequality and then later about social policy. Surprisingly, he finds that they largely do not, and are distorted by partisan leanings when they do.

This leads Bartels to conclude that abstract facts and values have little influence on policy preferences and even less on responses to real-life policy proposals such as the George W. Bush tax cuts he studies. Drawing from John Zaller's theories of elite influences on public opinion, Bartels contends that the progression from facts and values to policy preferences is a minefield dominated by partisan elites. An uninformed public is simply outgunned and incapable of acting in its rational interest despite declared support for liberal policies on many a social survey.[81] Although the power of elite partisan politics to determine economic outcomes and sway individual beliefs receives the lion's share of attention in Bartels' account, deep psychological factors that reinforce the status quo also enter his story, and these overdetermine the uninformed citizen. Thus, Bartels starts off unequivocally in the ambivalence camp, aware that Americans have complex and contradictory views that include a significant dose of egalitarianism.[82] But then he veers more persistently toward an insurgent view that I refer to as the "ignorance" perspective.

Several not-altogether-compatible positions veer in this same direction. As mentioned in an earlier section, in the work of Benabou and Tirole, for instance, the tendency for ordinary people to believe (erroneously) in a just world is said to help them navigate an insecure economic environment; such beliefs nurture the incentives needed to keep up the good fight. In the more psychological version presented by Bartels, who cites the influential work of political psychologist John Jost, beliefs in a just world protect against the potential anxiety-inducing experience of living in a capricious world. In the absence of major societal disruptions and shocks, tolerant beliefs are locked in not because they are what people genuinely believe after careful deliberation, but because they are psychically functional.[83] Bartels acknowledges that Americans can have consistently egalitarian views, and indeed argues elsewhere in the book that low-income and high-income voters do have different, economically aligned preferences. This may be an inconsistency in his argument, or it may be that the influence of political partisanship and biased information varies across issues. Those issues involving outright income redistribution may prompt elites to become more obstructive, leaving the public stuck between a rock and a hard place, begging for crumbs. Whatever the reason, ultimately he is not sanguine that citizen preferences mean much given broader political and psychological forces.[84]

Also consistent with the ignorance perspective, but in contrast to both Bartels and proponents of the just-world thesis, is the argument that the public would protest if only it was better informed of the extremes of income inequality in the nation today. These scholars differentiate themselves from the "tolerance" perspective by confirming that Americans do indeed prefer less inequality than exists, and they differentiate themselves from the "ambivalence" perspective by having fewer qualms about taking policy preferences at face value. They believe the crux of the matter is not that Americans are satisfied with high levels of inequality or too conflicted to form coherent opinions on the issue, but that they "drastically underestimate" how much inequality exists, a tendency well known from research dating back to the 1980s and 1990s.[85]

For example, in a recent and widely publicized article, Michael Norton and Daniel Ariely find that families in the top fifth of the income distribution are estimated by respondents to take in "only" 59 percent of national income when in reality they rake in 80 percent.[86] Norton and Ariely believe that this lack of information has significant immobilizing consequences. And, they may indeed be right that there is some line in the sand across which inequality is excessive enough to incite protest, and that this line is between the upper fifth holding 59 and 80 percent of national income. But one could just as reasonably argue that an adequate degree of information about levels of inequality already exists (i.e., that the top fifth owns three times its share of national income).[87] It is therefore unclear whether the updating of facts alone would prevail against the headwinds of elite manipulation, partisanship, and psychological orientations toward the status quo catalogued by Bartels and others. Jacob Hacker and Paul Pierson, who also decry Americans' lack of information, thus pinpoint the media and strong progressive organizations as the solution not only to popular ignorance but to political powerlessness.[88]

Where, then, does the preponderance of evidence lie in assessing beliefs about income inequality in the era of rising inequality – in the tolerance, ambivalence, or ignorance camp? If you were looking to hedge your bet, you might put your money on the ambivalence perspective, as it mixes ignorance and opposition with a large dose of tolerance. The least parsimonious option, ambivalence may nevertheless portray the most accurate interpretation that we have of American beliefs about income inequality. The evidence is not yet in on this question, however, for three reasons that I have mentioned at various points in this chapter.

First, although a few studies make a compelling argument that the scales have recently tipped in an oppositional direction, no one has yet shown whether changes in public opinion are correlated with changes in either income inequality or knowledge of income inequality. Taking a page from the ignorance perspective, why should we believe that knowledge and opinion responded so transparently to rising inequality? Indeed, one recent study shows that the trend in income inequality corresponds to an increase in conservative mass policy preferences, an unexpected result if Americans knew about and opposed rising inequality.[89] Second, in the urgency to establish what Americans know and do not know in a politically contentious atmosphere of heightened inequality, somehow the question has gone unasked of *why* Americans would care about income inequality in the first place. Even if there is some point at which inequality becomes "too extreme," what determines that point? And what does that imply about how Americans think inequality should be addressed? Finally, and related, very little effort has been made to study beliefs directly about income inequality and then to connect such beliefs systematically to beliefs about opportunity and social policy.[90]

The Un/Deserving Rich

I have argued in previous sections that the lore of American tolerance for inequality cannot be shorn from its social and historical context. I suggest the same for the emerging sentiment that Americans are dissatisfied with their nation's growing level of inequality. As many studies show, Americans have more critical attitudes about economic inequality than implied by the tolerance perspective. But even though such attitudes appear to have spread in recent decades, they were readily apparent in the 1970s and 1980s before inequality began to escalate. Moreover, rising inequality is not the only feature of the current era that distinguishes it from past eras, and therefore it may not be the only factor driving a more oppositional stance toward income inequality. In fact, virtually all observers in the tolerance and ambivalence camps alike agree that other features of eras past and present – most notably their structures of opportunity – are pivotal in shaping beliefs about inequality and assessing the consequences of inequality (in a tolerant direction). What we are missing, then, is an understanding of how structures of inequality and opportunity interact to produce contexts of opposition as well as the more familiar contexts of tolerance and ambivalence.

In the eras of American history that define the legacy of tolerance for inequality, both opportunity and equality flourished in the form of equitable growth for the core (white, male) citizens of the nation. In the postwar era, equitable growth was fueled by economic expansion in the private sector and kept in service of ordinary Americans by a host of wage- and income-equalizing institutions and the regulation of business. As a whole, these institutions did not bear the imprint of popular government tax and transfer policies, even if progressive taxation was one of their hidden pillars. Rather, the appetite for government spending was met surreptitiously by expanding revenues generated "automatically" by robust economic growth, which reaped all the credit for the fruits of redistribution.[91] The implications of this history for how Americans think about equal opportunity and equitable outcomes is, I suggest, that they think about them holistically as the twin products of the kind of economic prosperity they came to desire and expect, and which once embedded was slow to dislodge as a symbol of redistribution.[92] If this view is correct, then the alternative view that extreme levels of inequality per se are what violate norms of fairness and incite demands for government redistribution focuses too exclusively on inequality of outcomes, whereas the reigning view that Americans care only about opportunity and not inequality focuses too narrowly on opportunity.

Fortunately, as discussed above, we have several precedents for jointly conceptualizing opportunity and inequality in a manner that illuminates oppositional as well as tolerant beliefs about income inequality. First, Kluegal and Smith's "challenges to the dominant ideology" were infused with liberal critiques of poverty, racial and gender inequality, and rising unemployment in the 1960s and 1970s. These (and other accounts) were all posed broadly as problems of opportunity as much as problems of inequality, and all preceded any indication of rising income inequality.[93] Second, unequal outcomes by race and gender routinely function as indicators of unequal opportunities in both the law and educational policy. This is especially the case when unequal opportunities are more challenging to observe than unequal outcomes, as is often the situation in the study of economic opportunity and income inequality as well. And, third, Daniel Bell introduced the notion of an "unjust meritocracy" in which distorted disparities in rewards between the top and bottom discourage those below and jeopardize the productive functioning of a meritocratic economy.[94]

I introduce the term "the undeserving rich" to signal a similar dynamic, in which unfairness as a normative concern converts into unfairness as a practical problem. This occurs not only when disparities offend sensibilities but when they restrict opportunities for making an honest living. This is where a zero-sum metaphor is apropos, as excesses at the top can appear to have (and actually have) both direct and indirect negative consequences for the economic well-being of workers all the way down the ladder.[95] Thus the undeserving rich are those who are implicated in producing a form of inequality that is perceived to either symbolize or directly contribute to limited opportunities. By contrast, the deserving rich are the celebrated shepherds of equitable growth.

The idea of the undeserving rich also helps to identify a mechanism by which beliefs about income inequality are linked to knowledge about inequality and to policy preferences. First, as in the case of gender and racial inequality, it is one of the great frustrations of law and social science alike that unfair class barriers to economic opportunity are challenging to observe in action. Yet, it is plausible to infer them from unequal outcomes among social class groups (as is done when unequal outcomes among racial and gender groups are used to infer unequal opportunities among such groups). This suggests that relevant and visible social groups such as the rich will shape knowledge about income inequality and its consequences for economic opportunity. Several studies have already alluded to the role that perceptions of the rich may play in fostering beliefs about inequality, and I explore this role in greater detail in subsequent chapters.[96]

Second, the concept of the undeserving rich implies a particular set of policy prescriptions rather than a smorgasbord of liberal entitlements. The concept, as I employ it, construes the rich as undeserving not because they are envied or resented or disliked for psychological or moral reasons (although all of these dynamics may be at play), or because they attained their positions unfairly through social connections, but because their riches are not always commensurate with their perceived contributions to the common good.[97] By implication, the solution is not to punish the rich by expropriating their income but to redirect their attention and resources toward lifting all boats. This would entail regulating business, creating good jobs, and redistributing earnings in the *labor market* as much as redistributing income in order to enhance opportunity-creating programs such as education. In short, the concept of the undeserving rich is useful in identifying social actors who are perceived to part of the problem of inequality but who also ought to be an active part of the solution.[98]

In the remainder of the book, I apply this theoretical framework to beliefs about income inequality (Chapter 3), economic opportunity (Chapter 4), and social policy (Chapter 5) during the era of rising income inequality in the United States. Although this chapter has identified the main constellation of beliefs associated with each of several eras of American history, the rest of the book will nevertheless not treat the era of rising income inequality as an undifferentiated period of inequitable growth hitched to a single configuration of beliefs. It will attempt instead to capitalize on the substantial degree of variation in economic and political conditions from the 1980s to the present to test the framework against alternative explanations of beliefs about income inequality and related issues and to chart how beliefs evolved over time. Before I analyze beliefs, however, I begin in the next chapter with the central question raised by the ignorance perspective: how much can we expect Americans to know about income inequality? For this, I analyze media coverage of the issue from 1980 to 2010.

2

The Emergence of a New Social Issue

Media Coverage of Economic Inequality and Social Class in the United States, 1980–2010

The claim that Americans do not care about income inequality, and indeed the claim that they do, rests on a critical assumption: that they know enough about the issue to form an opinion about it. It is a tricky business to determine exactly how much information is enough to develop sensible ideas about an issue, but we can get a rough idea by comparing income inequality to issues that have a longer history of scrutiny by survey researchers. The premier example here is the state of the national economy. On this issue we expect Americans to have strong opinions, but we also expect them to have opinions that bear at least some resemblance to factual information, such as the unemployment or inflation rate. Not only are these statistics relatively easy to interpret, they are routinely reported by the news media as they rise and fall over the course of a business cycle.[1] By contrast, we are wary of asking for opinions about the complicated details of specific legislation regarding tax policies or financial regulation. For these issues, the degree of economic literacy required to be politically engaged is generally quite a bit higher.[2]

A set of issues that falls somewhere between these extremes is racial and gender inequality. On the one hand, Americans have biases when it comes to these topics, and their grasp of the underlying racial demographics of the United States is distorted. Yet, on the other hand, their opinions about policies related to racial and gender equality are likely to be informed by a vague sense that there has been considerable progress over the long run even as a lingering level of inequality remains. This is not a sanguine view of Americans' knowledge of racial and gender inequality, but a rather low bar given that gender and especially race relations might be regarded as front and center topics in American society.[3] With this low bar in mind, we can ask whether Americans know at least as much about income inequality as they do about racial and gender inequality. At a minimum, is it plausible to assume that Americans are aware that something has changed over the past couple of decades?

To answer this question, in an ideal world, we would have asked Americans about income inequality long ago and followed up periodically over the years. We can get a glimpse of what this might have produced from the popular and oft-repeated Harris poll about whether "the rich get richer and the poor get poorer." When this question was first asked in 1966, only 45 percent of respondents agreed. Then something dramatic happened over the late 1960s and early 1970s, and by 1973 a majority of Americans agreed with the statement. Since that time, the range has fluctuated between 65 and 83 percent, as if rising inequality is simply a normal state of affairs.[4] A factual question introduced by Larry Bartels in the 2002 American National Election Studies provoked a similar response: 74 percent agreed that "differences in income between rich people and poor people... are larger than 20 years ago."[5] When the question was replicated in 2004 and 2008, the share increased to 81 and 79 percent, respectively. These numbers are comfortably in the range of the Harris poll. At first blush, they do not evoke a great deal of confidence in Americans' awareness of rising income inequality.

We can quibble over the wording of these questions and whether it is possible to infer much of anything from them, but the broader point is that we have little public opinion information on which to assess Americans' *knowledge* of income inequality.[6] One reason for this may be that, like financial regulation, tax policy, and other arcane policy issues, income inequality is too complex for ordinary Americans to fathom. It has stumped generations of economists and other social scientists seeking to understand its sources and consequences, and the cognitive difficulties surrounding the issue are evidently among the reasons that survey researchers have rarely designed questions on the topic. [7] As two experienced scholars of public opinion put it, "pollsters appear to have concluded, correctly in our view, that buzzwords such as *economic inequality* – common in political discussions – do not convey much to most Americans."[8]

A more sophisticated lay understanding of economic inequality might also be impeded by other cognitive challenges. For example, to a lay and expert audience alike, the social groups to which income inequality refers are ill defined (e.g., who's in the middle class?), and there is potentially no limit to the number of such groups (e.g., poor, lower class, working class, middle class, upper middle class, upper class, rich, affluent).[9] The metrics of income inequality are also less transparent than the metrics of either unemployment or racial and gender inequality. The unemployment rate is a comprehensible number fluctuating within a small range. Although contested, gender and racial inequality can at least be compared against the legal norm of zero discrimination embraced by nearly all Americans. This implies that a racial or gender disparity of any size could potentially be deemed unfair. By contrast, Americans do not favor complete equality of income, leaving us with no norm against which to compare how much income inequality is too much.[10] In fact there is no reason to expect opposition to be greater, and to have a greater impact on politics and policy, when executives make 500 times the average pay of their workers as opposed to 100 times.[11]

Yet, although the prima facie case against the informed American appears strong, survey and especially qualitative data provide fairly compelling evidence that people are capable, even astute, observers of class distinctions. The work of Pierre Bourdieu, Michele Lamont, and Alfred Young, among others, reveals that individuals are more attuned to hierarchies of class than we are accustomed to thinking. Class distinctions are filtered through discourses of moral, cultural, and especially socioeconomic differentiation, some national in scope and others specific to the social environment of particular social classes and racial groups.[12] At a conference on "How Class Works" at New York University in 2006, journalists from the *New York Times*, *The News Hour*, and *Harper's* shared similar observations. One wrote that "Americans are obsessed with class, and although they might not always use that word, they possess a highly sophisticated and refined vocabulary for discussing it."[13] This is compatible with survey research on perceptions of the occupational order, in which individuals provide remarkably consistent results when asked to rank occupations by prestige and earnings.[14] Moreover, many policies affecting earnings and income inequality are stock elements of American political culture, such as the minimum wage, unemployment compensation, welfare, and taxes.

Perhaps, then, what Americans *can* know about income inequality is a function not of cognitive ability alone, but of what political scientists call "frames in communication" and what Michele Lamont calls the "cultural supply side." Lamont defines the cultural supply side as the "cultural repertoires, traditions, and narratives that individuals have access to," such as the educational system and the mass media.[15] Included as well are the political traditions and social institutions of a nation. The excellent research done to date on the culture of class in contemporary America has focused more on perceptions of class in everyday life than on the cultural supply side. In the former, the emphasis is on the "social psychological side" or the "reception" of cultural notions of class, although not simply as a one-way street.[16] The supply side has not been entirely ignored, of course, as it is a time-honored tradition to write on the distinctiveness of American institutions – such as an "open" frontier, early universal education, the absence of a feudal past, and the political weakness of labor – in shaping the ideology of the American dream.[17] But one is hard-pressed to find empirical research on the production of a mass public discourse of class and class inequality, certainly during the era of rising income inequality. This may be because scholars think such a discourse simply does not exist, as the ideological and institutional character of the United States has always seemed antithetical to it.[18] As plausible as this hypothesis may sound, we can nevertheless ask whether the emergence of a new social reality in rising inequality has the capacity to alter the national dialogue.

Two kinds of empirical evidence that can help answer this question are political rhetoric and news media coverage. Each is frequently used to assess the *potential* extent and character of public knowledge about a particular subject. In this chapter, I focus on the news media as arguably the main conduit through which political messages are filtered and consumed. Media coverage includes topics that fall outside the purview of politics narrowly construed as well.[19] Many salient political, economic, and cultural issues are covered extensively, including welfare, government spending, health care, downsizing, and abortion, to name just a few. Such issues are framed by the chatter of politicians and other elite actors seeking to influence public opinion toward a particular viewpoint.[20] Public interest is also presumed to play some role in setting the agenda of coverage: in part because of an assumed lack of interest among the public, the salience of income inequality is not taken to be on par with these other issues. In fact, those familiar with trends in income inequality probably consider coverage to be episodic at best, and put some of the blame for this on a willfully distracted public.[21] If the public are *unaware* of a new social trend, however, how can we be sure they are uninterested in it? Declarations that Americans do or do not care about rising income inequality may therefore be unwarranted unless there is some other source of widely available information on the subject – personal experience and social networks perhaps – or if we assume that rising inequality is simply everywhere to behold.[22]

Without denying the play of these other potential sources of information, or the influence of public interest itself on media coverage, the main purpose of this chapter is to examine whether in fact there has been a political and media blackout of the topic of income inequality. As those who speak of the complexity of the issue can attest, along with those well-versed in the media analysis of other cultural objects and contentious political issues, this task is more daunting than first appears. The challenge lies in defining the scope of the topic if the intuition is correct that rising inequality receives little coverage, or if its discovery as a new social issue emerged episodically over time.[23] To compensate for this lack of direction from the actual media, we may want to cast a wide net and include topics that bear both directly and indirectly on inequality and yet are not necessarily discussed in this exact light. Examples include reporting on cuts in social programs for the poor or taxes on the rich without any mention of how these policy shifts affect income inequality. There may also be stories about concession bargaining between employers and unions, the squeezing of the middle class, excessive CEO pay, or the increasing distance between the spectacularly rich and the merely rich, all failing to go the extra yard in drawing out the implications for trends in income inequality.

As these examples make clear, income inequality encompasses a wide spectrum of policy domains and images of the class structure. Inequality is shaped not only by a whole host of government programs but by the wage-setting practices of private employers and broader economic and demographic changes. In this respect, it does not resemble the study of a single policy issue, such as welfare or health care, or a singular view of the class structure, such as the rich versus the poor. Income inequality involves different groups in different ways at different times. The topic is best thought of as a meta-issue, with a galaxy of causes, consequences, forms, values, and policy solutions affiliated with it.[24] The next sections acknowledge this complexity while at the same time bringing order to it. Income inequality is a complex topic to be sure, but I show that media coverage does not make it impossible for ordinary Americans to comprehend. Indeed, it is not uncommon for journalists to spin a remarkably coherent narrative of inequality that is at odds with American-dream ideology.

After developing a framework for identifying how income inequality and class disparities are portrayed by the media, the following sections describe the trend in coverage and the content of coverage from 1980 to 2010. (This is the same period as that for which attitudinal data about income inequality are available from the General Social Survey, and the trend in public opinion about inequality is examined in the following chapters.) The main results from the media analysis over this period reveal a pattern of coverage concentrated at some points more than others in a trajectory that does not mimic the more or less linear upward trend in actual income inequality. Equally important, the coverage varies in substance, with the spotlight shifting from implicit to explicit coverage and from a focus on one social group to another, with particular emphasis on the rich and the middle class. Coverage also varies in the degree to which it is cast in a positive or negative light or as a central topic of political debate. Overall, the nature of coverage suggests that although American consumers of the media are exposed to factual information about levels and trends in income inequality, it is more likely that they absorb a whole package of ideas about the economy and politics that influences not only how the issue is comprehended and connected to social policy, but also how the media read public interest and consequently decide to cover the issue.[25]

This approach to the role of media coverage in influencing public opinion also reinforces the point made earlier about the difficulties of interpreting metrics of income inequality and the need to look beyond the reporting of facts and figures. We know that a majority of Americans desire less inequality than currently exists despite significantly underestimating how much that is.[26] We can infer from this that two kinds of information about income inequality are potentially important in explaining why concerns flare up. First, there may be a national consensus about a truly excessive level of inequality that would trigger heightened concerns among greater numbers of Americans if only they knew about it. As mentioned above, we have no research telling us what that magical level of excessive income inequality is. But if we assume we have reached it, this perspective implies that factual knowledge would be the most transformative kind of knowledge.

Second, it may be that some other aspect of the context of inequality is likely to provoke a response in one direction or another. It is a matter not necessarily of updating facts and figures, but one of articulating a compelling reason for why the issue is worth attention. In this instance, the information provided is of a consequential rather than factual nature. To paraphrase one of the journalists who spoke at the NYU conference mentioned above, it may be more important to know how the game is being played, who the winners and losers are, and what they are winning and losing, than to know the final score.[27] Ultimately, this is a question of why Americans *do* care about the issue of income inequality, not why they *should* care about it. I take this question up again and more directly in terms of public opinion (and not knowledge of the issue) in future chapters. Here I examine those aspects of the game that the media considered newsworthy over the period in which income inequality was rising sharply to heights unseen since the 1920s.

Defining Media Coverage of Income Inequality

Just as public opinion about rising income inequality will depend on awareness of it, so too will reporting. When did awareness of this social issue emerge among journalists? To answer this question, we first need to understand how the record of research on the topic evolved over time. As we will see later in the chapter, the earliest debates about income inequality seeped into the media as researchers began to notice the increase in the 1980s. Because earnings are the main component of income, and earnings disparities appeared to be rising in the 1980s, researchers focused at the outset more on the widening disparity in hourly *earnings* between high-skilled and low-skilled workers in the *labor market* than on disparities in *incomes* between rich and poor *families*. This focus on disparities in labor-market earnings also meant that economists were inclined to locate the causes of rising inequality in the private rather than the public sector. For a long time, the only public policy that academic researchers examined closely as a possible source of rising earnings inequality was the minimum wage. Most labor economists claimed that the more important causes were rooted in fundamental technological changes that increased the relative demand for high-skilled workers, although others countered that changes in wage-setting institutions such as unions were just as consequential.[28]

In the early 1980s, then, research on inequality was much less varied than it is now. Moreover, the real flood of academic studies was still some years away. Even when academic research flourished in the 1990s, rising inequality was still considered principally an affair of the private sector economy. Remarkably, the role of tax policies in affecting top incomes did not emerge as a focal part of the academic story until the early 2000s, when new "facts" about income inequality became available. Freshly mined data from income tax records provided reliable information as never before about incomes at the very top of the distribution.[29] The role of changing family structures in altering levels of income inequality among households also took off as a research topic in the late 1990s and early 2000s.[30] Finally, as described in Chapter 1, only in the last decade has the study of the distinctly political origins of rising inequality captured the attention of political scientists.

Thus to the extent that media coverage of the fact of rising inequality is dependent on the discovery of this fact by experts, we should expect coverage to roughly trace the trajectory of academic knowledge as it evolved from heated debates over its very existence in the 1980s to the panoply of perspectives that surround the issue today. Although the world of journalism is far more independent than this formulation suggests, even journalists who are ahead of the academic curve turn to experts to inform and shape their ideas. We will find important examples that violate this simple model, but it offers a useful first approximation of the expected changes over time in the content of media coverage concerning income inequality.

With this model in mind, I develop four analytical distinctions to define the content of media coverage about income inequality.[31] A summary of these distinctions is provided in Table 2.1. Three of the four are already apparent in the brief historical account of academic knowledge given above. The first is the distinction between inequality in labor-market earnings and inequality in total income including capital and government income, or, if one prefers, between forms of inequality associated with private sector dynamics and those associated with the family or welfare state dynamics. This distinction is useful for many reasons. First, if coverage is tilted toward one form of inequality as opposed to another, this could color or "prime" how Americans think about the issue. For example, the slant of coverage could affect whether Americans see inequality as propelled mainly by economic, social, or political forces. Second, this distinction ensures that coverage of income inequality includes and distinguishes among news articles with widely varying content. Awareness of both government and private sector sources of inequality also wards against limiting the field of analysis to a single form of economic inequality that may be dominant in scholarly or political circles at any given point in time. Indeed, content analysis seeks to determine empirically if and when different forms and dimensions of inequality predominate in media coverage.

The second analytical distinction concerns the causes and policy solutions associated with income inequality. These can be broken down into government and private variants as well, but here we are interested in going beyond the identification of descriptive trends to examine the multiple and potentially conflicting causes and policy solutions associated with

TABLE 2.1. *Defining Media Coverage of Economic Inequality*

---

(1) **Type of inequality**
   (a) Labor-market inequality, unaffected directly by government taxes and transfer programs.
   (b) Total-income inequality, including the contribution of family formation patterns and government taxes and transfer programs.
(2) **Causes and policy solutions associated with inequality**
   (a) Multiple causes of labor market inequality include skill-biased technological change, globalization, immigration, and declines in wage setting institutions and social norms, and associated policy solutions.
   (b) Multiple causes of total income inequality include declines in social spending on low-income individuals and families (e.g., unemployment benefits and means-tested programs) and declines in progressive taxation, and associated policy solutions.
(3) **Social class groups**
   (a) Categories of workers (typically large groupings) identified in economics literature on rising earnings and income inequality, including skill groups, union workers, minimum wage workers, immigrants, executives, and the rich and wealthy (with incomes from both labor and capital).
   (b) Categories of individuals (typically large groupings) identified in broader literature on inequality, in popular culture, and by social program receipt, including the poor, unemployed, middle class, blue-collar workers, and white-collar workers.
(4) **Relational or comparative language connecting social class groups**
   (a) *Explicit* comparisons or relations among two or more hierarchically ordered social class groups, including relational language such as inequalities, gaps, differences, disparities, and divides, or comparative language such as winners, losers, primary beneficiaries, etc.
   (b) Presence of two or more hierarchically ordered social class groups without explicit comparative or relational language among them but with *implicit* reference to different and unequal economic circumstances or redistributive processes.

---

inequality within each sector. In the private sector, for example, changes having to do with shifts in the supply of and demand for skilled labor are a leading explanation of rising wage inequality. This set of explanations implies that educational policies are the most likely to ameliorate inequality. As mentioned above, however, other explanations are often taken to be equally important, such as globalization and the decline of wage-setting norms and institutions.[32] When income inequality is discussed in relation to government policies, the line between descriptive trends and causal factors is more difficult to discern, especially when redistributive public policies are at issue. For example, a *descriptive* report of a change in the tax code that alters the income distribution is simultaneously a report of the *cause* of a change in income inequality (i.e., tax policy). Once again, which of these causes and associated policy solutions are covered can affect how individuals are primed to think about the significance of inequality or how it should be addressed.

Whereas the first two analytical distinctions presented in Table 2.1 define the general subject matter of coverage related to income inequality, the third and fourth distinctions seek to operationalize it. The third distinction identifies the social groups implicated in different forms or measures of income inequality. This is fundamental to *the definition of inequality as a gap, difference, or disparity among groups or individuals in an economically hierarchical relation to one another*. Social group distinctions of this sort are extremely challenging to codify. There are both conceptual and practical reasons why this is the case. Conceptually, my first cues about how to define the relevant social groups in the analysis of rising income inequality came from economic studies, even though these studies are less precise than more general theories of class structure for defining social class categories. With some important exceptions, the economics literature led the way in documenting the trend of rising inequality and thus in shaping public discourse.[33] Consistent with that literature, I employ gradational and status-based definitions of class groups, focusing in particular on the categories most frequently studied by labor economists, such as high-skilled and low-skilled workers, workers with mean or median earnings, unionized workers, and groups located at the extreme right tail of the income distribution, such as high-paid executives and professionals.

There were several more practical considerations that led to the inclusion of social class categories that ordinary people commonly use to process information about inequality. First, some groups rarely discussed in economic studies of rising inequality nevertheless resonate with the public and are central in the literature on inequality outside labor economics. These include the middle class, the poor, the unemployed, and both blue- and white-collar workers. Typically, economic studies of rising wage and earnings inequality include only the employed, avoid imprecise terms such as "the middle class" and "white-collar workers," and do not examine poverty and the poor.[34] This is not to say that these groups are irrelevant to the study of rising inequality. Both the poor and the unemployed are crucial to studies of household and family income inequality, for example. In such studies, factors beyond hourly wage rates are examined as explanations of rising income inequality, such as the rise in single-mother families and the generosity of unemployment benefits.[35] The "middle class" too is a term that was referenced early on by authors outside the field of labor economics. The influential anthropologist Katherine Newman, for example, wrote clairvoyantly in the late 1980s and early 1990s about the "declining fortunes" of the middle class.[36] Because of these different ways of discussing inequality, there may be some definitions of social groups that are less common in economics than they are in popular parlance, and these need to be taken into account in the analysis.

The fourth and final analytical distinction that is necessary in defining and operationalizing coverage of income inequality concerns comparisons and relationships among social groups. The definition given a moment ago states that inequality is "a gap, difference, or disparity among groups or individuals in an economically hierarchical relation to one another." The initial, and in retrospect naïve, objective of this analysis was to identify articles about the fact of rising gaps, differences, and disparities in earnings, income, and wealth. But we found only a limited number of articles that fit this criterion, and soon our main objective mushroomed into a broader set of objectives. Articles falling under the new umbrella were those that mentioned two or more hierarchically ordered social groups (as defined under the third analytical distinction) in which unequal economic circumstances or changes in circumstances were implicitly or explicitly stated. In essence, this amounted to introducing a continuum of media coverage based on the degree to which comparative or relational language is used in reference to social class groups.

As one travels from one end of this continuum to the other, the representation of income inequality obviously becomes less or more precise. Where precision is greatest, we have *explicit* mentions of the fact of rising income inequality, in which two or more hierarchically ordered groups are conjoined in comparative or relational language (e.g., there is mention of a gap/disparity/difference in wages, earnings, income, or wealth between two groups located at different parts of the distribution). On the other end of the continuum are discussions of two hierarchically ordered groups but without an explicit comparison (e.g., trends in wages at the bottom and the top mentioned at different points in the article). Readers could nevertheless infer that one group is doing well while the other is not, leading to a recognition of inequality or changes in inequality. This I consider an *implicit* mention of inequality.

In the middle of this continuum are government policies that affect the income distribution through taxes and transfers (e.g., unemployment benefits, welfare, progressive taxes). The comparative gain or loss to a particular social group may be either implicit or explicit. For example, the unadorned reporting in a news story of cuts in government spending on social programs for the needy alludes to a comparison among social groups, where only one group at the bottom suffers cutbacks. All else being equal, these cuts will lead to an increase in inequality, but this implication may not be stated directly in the coverage. This process could be made more transparent, however, with the addition of explicit comparative language about the relative status or change in status of different groups (e.g., "the deepest cuts in government spending are for social programs serving the needy"). The implications for income inequality need not be mentioned directly in either scenario for readers to draw conclusions about it. This is because government redistributive programs are already understood as relational in the sense of inherently producing winners and losers unequally situated across the distribution. In coding, however, we will note whether the mention is explicit or implicit.

In sum, our core subject matter is stated in its most abstract form in the first distinction of Table 2.1, and in its most practical form in the third and fourth distinctions. Taking the definition of hierarchical social class groups given in the third distinction, coverage of inequality is defined operationally as falling along the continuum from 4a to 4b. The causes and policy solutions associated with inequality stated in 2a and 2b are not essential in defining coverage of income inequality. These may or may not be present, but because they figure in our theoretical interest in the topic, I have included them here as well.

News Media Coverage of Income Inequality

Following previous studies by Martin Gilens and Paul Kellstedt, among others, a team of students and I used the *Readers' Guide to Periodical Abstracts* to search for articles on income inequality from 1980 to 2010 in the three major American newsweeklies of *Newsweek*, *TIME*, and *U.S. News & World Report* (*USNWR*).[37] The *Readers' Guide* provides subject terms for each article, and this predefined list of hundreds of subject terms served as our introduction to the data. The good news is that the list included subject terms corresponding directly to the types of inequality described in sections 1a and 1b of Table 2.1, such as "income inequality" and "wage differentials." The bad news is that these subject terms yielded only a small number of articles. This was not due to a shortage of coverage alone. Several other factors were at play: subject terms were not included in the list during part of the time period (e.g., "income inequality"), were included but not often used to describe relevant subject matter (e.g., "wage differentials"), or were included but used to describe irrelevant subject matter (e.g., "wage differentials" often referred to gender wage gaps). In total, we gathered only fifty articles on these two subjects and seven more on "equality" and "meritocracy" over the thirty-one-year period of our study, after excluding nineteen irrelevant articles.[38] By this measure we would indeed conclude that there had been a media blackout on income inequality.

Despite these limitations in how the articles were catalogued, this original sample of articles nonetheless furnishes us with the first piece of evidence of when income inequality came into being as a named subject. The subject term "income inequality" did not appear on the scene until 1988 when it was used to define the subject matter of an article in *USNWR* titled "Dreams, Myths and Realities" by columnist Mortimer Zuckerman. No other article appeared with this subject term in the 1980s in any of the three newsweeklies, even though the term was evidently in circulation in the *Readers' Guide* by the late 1980s. Equally interesting is that this lone article is incisive, meeting the criteria that define explicit coverage of income inequality set forth in section 4a of Table 2.1. This is a clue that the issue must have already been kicking around for a while, and in fact Zuckerman lets on that his article was inspired by a piece in the *Atlantic Monthly* a month earlier by one of the pioneering journalists on the subject, Thomas Edsall.[39] Both articles use data from the Congressional Budget Office to "stunningly document the growing inequality in American life... [in which] most of our citizens have not benefited from recent U.S. prosperity." Zuckerman touches on many of the contextual factors associated with rising income inequality, including factors having to do with both the government and private sectors, as described in sections 2a and 2b of Table 2.1. The article is vague about how these pieces fit together, but that is not its purpose, which is to cast the issue of income inequality as a threat to the American dream of shared prosperity and to put this rendering of the issue squarely on the agenda of the 1988 presidential election for both parties.[40]

In the original batch of fifty-seven articles produced by the four subject terms listed above, only three additional articles appeared in the 1980s with relevant subject terms other than "income inequality." One of these is as explicitly about income inequality as the Zuckerman article is, another is implicitly about income inequality as described in section 4b of Table 2.1, and the third was ultimately deemed irrelevant.[41] The two relevant articles appear in 1984 and 1985 in *USNWR* with the subject term "wage differentials."[42] The subject of the 1984 article is given away by its title: "Is Middle Class Really Doomed to Shrivel Away?" This article decries a "small group of academics" for falsely sounding the alarm bell on the shrinking middle class. According to the journalist, these academics argue that "new high-technology industries offer fewer middle-income jobs and pay most workers less than do the old smokestack industries." The bulk of the article then refutes the notion that America is becoming a "land of haves and have-nots . . . a view now coming under fire by many economists," several of whom are quoted in the article. That debates over the imperiled middle class were afoot at this time among elites in academic, journalistic, and public policy circles is corroborated by other sources.[43] The article fulfills the criteria in 4a of Table 2.1 by focusing explicitly on rising earnings inequality and the purported causes of rising earnings inequality in the private sector, as described in sections 1a and 2a.

The article appearing in 1985, by contrast, is a prime example of a story falling on the implicit end of the continuum described in section 4b of Table 2.1. This article, "Two-Tier Pay Stirs Backlash among Workers," describes a new two-tier system instituted by employers to cut labor costs in unionized industries during the 1982 recession. New workers were hired at a lower rate than existing workers performing the same job. Direct comparisons of earnings between new and old hires were made, but the workers resided in the same broad social class of blue-collar workers, and therefore the criterion involving hierarchically ordered groups was not met (see sections 3a and 3b). Nonetheless, the article mentions conflicts between unions and employers over the new wage-setting policy, and this brings a higher social class group into the mix (i.e., employers). Union–employer bargaining over wages, like government social programs and taxes, also connotes to readers a process of redistribution (i.e., of earnings). Because this and other articles akin to it rarely discuss the compensation of employers or managers directly, however, we are left with only implicit references to distributive conflicts, and no explicit mention of inequality between social class groups. As we will see later, this means that the large volume of coverage of union–employer disputes in the 1980s covers the issue of rising inequality mostly in implicit rather than explicit terms.

Although the three relevant articles in the 1980s offer perfect illustrations of the continuum of coverage identified in sections 4a and 4b of Table 2.1, and index broader debates occurring in other publications and venues at that time, it stands to reason that they represent only a small portion of relevant coverage in the 1980s. In particular, one of the major categories of articles on income inequality described in sections 1b and 2b concerns redistributive public policies, yet we have no examples of this in the original batch from the 1980s. Anyone familiar with this era knows that the news was replete with stories of Reagan's tax policies, many of which make explicit mention of disproportionate benefits or gains flowing to one social class group or another and thus fulfilling the criteria listed in section 4a of Table 2.1. These articles are missing from our first batch of fifty-seven articles because they did not have the appropriate subject terms ("income inequality," "wage differentials," "equality," or "meritocracy"). Instead they had terms such as "income taxes" or simply "incomes" or "taxation." Reporting on subsequent tax policies in the 1990s and 2000s also omitted subject terms referring to inequality even though they typically offer accessible depictions of changes in the income distribution.

In the remainder of this chapter, I present the full results from the original batch of articles, and then describe two other methods of selecting and coding articles to compensate for the limitations in the original method. The other two methods cast a wider net of subject terms and thus introduce additional subject matter in two different ways. The first replicates the original procedure by deductively selecting subject terms from the predefined list provided by the *Readers' Guide*. Subject terms associated with social class groups were selected in order to locate articles that discuss class disparities without necessarily raising the issue of rising income inequality head on. An additional search was conducted for subject terms associated with employment conditions. These data function as a standard against which to size up trends in the coverage of economic inequality. They also serve as a substantive indicator of job insecurity, which has increased alongside income inequality and may contribute to feelings of economic anxiety and injustice.[44] Because our focus is on a small number of theoretically derived subject terms, these articles were not coded for content. They are discussed as measures of trends in the overall volume of coverage over time and in the content of coverage as defined by individual subject terms on inequality, social class (e.g., "rich" and "middle class"), and employment conditions (e.g., "downsizing" and "outsourcing"). Corroborating evidence from other sources is also presented.

Next we use the method employed by Martin Gilens in *Why Americans Hate Welfare* to adjust for the noncomparability of subject terms over time.[45] We expand the population of articles to include all those that have at least one of the subject terms found in the original population of relevant articles on income inequality. Because there were multiple subject terms per article, including "incomes," "taxes," the "middle class," and so on, thousands of articles were obtained in this way. We then took a random sample and hand coded them into the categories described in sections 4a and 4b of Table 2.1. I discuss these methods in further detail in the appendices to this chapter. As in other sections, my main discussion in the text revolves around the question of whether, when, and how the issue of income inequality was covered by the media. With the articles collected by this third and more comprehensive method, my first priority is to establish the trend in coverage of income inequality, and my second is to identify the content of coverage in terms of its degree of explicitness, its focus on government policy or private sector dynamics, and ultimately its understanding of *why* the issue of income inequality is worthy of media attention.[46]

Articles with Subject Terms on Economic Inequality, Social Class, and Job Insecurity

Although there were only three relevant hits in the 1980s, inequality became a new subject of media coverage in the first half of the 1990s (see the first panel of Figure 2.1). The interval from 1992 to 1996 produced several consecutive years of multi-article coverage. Coverage then subsided until nearly a decade later when the same pattern as in the early to middle 1990s materialized over the 2004 to 2009 period. Each wave consisted of the same peak number of articles in a given year (five), occurring in 1995, 1996, 2006, and 2009. The issue of inequality was covered as much in the 1990s, then, as it was during a period in the 2000s when conditions seemed riper than ever with a deep recession and financial crisis heating up during and after a popular presidential election. Thus income inequality appears to have been equally significant as the fact of it was discovered and disseminated more widely in the early and middle 1990s than it had been previously. Despite a growing economy in the mid-1990s, anxiety and resentment was palpable in titles such as "Bridging the Bitter Incomes Divide" (May 30, 1994), "The New World of Paychecks" (May 6, 1995), and "Crumbs for the Majority" (February 26, 1996), all in *USNWR*.

Evidence from other sources lends credence to this impression. In 1995, noted *Washington Post* journalist Steven Pearlstein asserted that the issue of inequality had become politically salient, indeed central, without breaching the partisan divide:

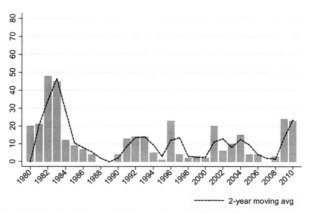

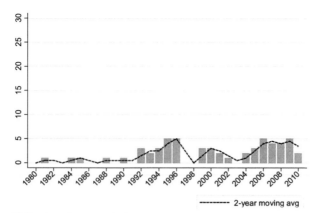

(1) Number of articles with inequality subject terms (4 terms).

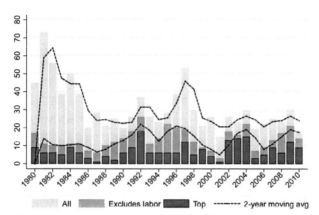

(2) Number of articles with class subject terms (15 terms).

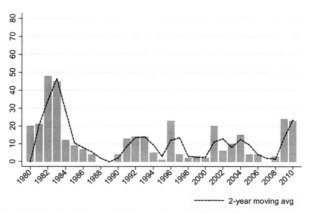

(3) Number of articles with job insecurity subject terms (5 terms).

FIGURE 2.1. Number of newsweekly articles from *Time*, *Newsweek*, and *USNWR* with subject terms on themes of economic inequality, social class, and job insecurity, 1980 to 2010. See Appendix A for subject terms on economic inequality and Table 2.2 for subject terms on social class and job insecurity. *Source:* Readers' Guide to Periodical Abstracts.

[T]he income gap between rich and poor has become the central issue in American politics, and the party that figures out what to do about it – or makes the right noises about it – will dominate American politics. That was the message from the left and the right, Democrat and Republican, politician and pollster, economist and financier at a forum on inequality held yesterday on Capital Hill.[47]

Although Patrick Buchanan's visibility in the Republican primaries that same year spread the message of growing economic insecurity and inequality, aiming "his rhetoric at top executives such as Robert E. Allen, the head of AT&T, who received huge salaries while laying off thousands of workers," coverage was broader than any one candidate.[48] For instance, a short study on attitudes toward inequality, published in 1997, opened with examples in the mid-1990s of the media's "bombardment of stories about fabulous salaries and extravagant lifestyles." This occurred as the economy for ordinary Americans seemed to be heading nowhere in what was the first "jobless" recovery of the postwar period.[49]

Although income inequality breaks into the news again around the turn of the century after a short dip in the late 1990s, there is little sense of urgency. One article reports that "the gap between rich and poor has actually narrowed slightly for the first time since the 1970s." The author nevertheless proceeds to line up the reasons for why the rich getting much richer is still a problem even if the plight of those at the bottom is improving.[50] In another article entitled "Indifferent to Inequality," the columnist Robert Samuelson argued not only that inequality was less important than poverty, but that poverty is caused by social problems unrelated to inequality. He added that Americans were indifferent to the likes of Bill Gates, and that the "massive social experiment" of inequality was accompanied by "a phenomenal [economic] expansion." Tellingly, by this stage in the coverage, Samuelson could bemoan the "long running debate over rising economic inequality in America . . . one of those fashionable bugaboos that, for the past 15 years or so, commentators, politicians, and scholars have proclaimed as one of the nation's gravest problems."[51] Similarly downplaying the issue of inequality, Dinesh D'Souza wrote in an editorial in *USA Today* that:

We are right to be troubled by such extremes [in inequality]. *But an excessive focus on inequality carries the presumption that the explosion of affluence we are experiencing is cause for mourning, when in fact it is cause for celebration:* the United States has extended to millions of ordinary people the avenues of freedom and personal fulfillment previously available only to the aristocratic few . . . we should understand that inequality is the inevitable byproduct of a growing and prospering economy. In our zeal to improve the conditions of the less well-off, we should not imperil the engine of economic growth that lifts all of us, rich and poor alike, to a higher standard of living."[52]

In the late 1990s, the reputations of CEOs and high-tech America were aglow, not yet tarnished by the bursting of the stock market bubble and the Enron-spawned corporate scandals of the early 2000s.[53]

Interestingly, the relative lull in direct coverage of income inequality (i.e., in articles with inequality subject terms) persists through the corporate scandals until the second wave of multi-article, multiyear coverage emerges in 2004–2009. The scandals were not covered principally as issues of income inequality but addressed executive malfeasance and outrageous pay, a subject that I capture with an expanded list of subject terms below.[54] Coverage of income inequality resumes in anticipation of the presidential election of 2004 but settles on no single topic in subsequent years. The Bush tax cuts for the wealthy figure more consistently than do other subjects, but the broader terrain is diffuse, including such topics as the outsourcing of white-collar jobs, the rising cost of living relative to pay for the middle class and even upper class (e.g., for health care, education, mortgages, and raising a family), the economic downturn and its disproportionate effect on different groups (e.g., the young and minorities), excessive pay among executives responsible for the financial crisis, and "the end of upward mobility" (the title of a 2009 article). By now, a nontrivial portion of coverage is the prerogative of elite columnists who have either spent years on the beat or are academic experts. For instance, nearly two decades after his article debuted in 1988 with a subject term of "income inequality," Mortimer Zuckerman penned one-quarter of the articles in the late 2000s wave of relevant coverage.[55]

It is tempting to assume that this store of experience translated into a more finely honed message about inequality, but the essence of the message seems to have remained remarkably consistent. Whereas *Newsweek* columnist Samuelson downplayed the topic in sunny 2000, he is wringing his hands in 2006 as he revisits the theme found in earlier coverage in which inequality is believed to "threaten America's *social compact*, which depends on a *shared sense of well-being*." Instead of the broad-based wealth that Americans desire, for the deserving rich as well as the deserving poor, Samuelson finds only "trickle-up economics, with most benefits flowing to the top."[56] In another piece in 2007, he projects that "economic inequality could become a political flash point [in 2008], because the income gains at the top seem so outsized and gains elsewhere are so choppy. The very uncertainty means that, even amid great prosperity, Americans feel anxious."[57] Sounding similar notes in 2006, Zuckerman wrote that:

The fabled equal-opportunity U.S. society is now hostage to a gathering of circumstances that must be addressed, for the sake of social justice, and to obtain the greatest benefits from the talents of U.S. citizens...We are robbing the poor to enrich the rich. *This is not to say that the rich aren't entitled to the fruits of their hard work, talent, risk-taking, and innovation,* but *the rewards for high achievers shouldn't be inconsistent with an economy that helps the average American family.* And certainly the government shouldn't be exacerbating the differences in income between the rich and the nonrich.

As he does on a regular basis, Zuckerman proposes to remedy all this with increased spending on education and, post-Bush tax cuts, greater progressivity in the tax code.[58]

Samuelson's idea of a "social compact" based on a "shared sense of well-being" invokes the notion of communal responsibility for achieving the American dream. Both he and Zuckerman imagine the dream in peril if only the rich prosper and government stokes the imbalance and injustice with regressive taxes. Although these editorials *imply* that opportunity for all depends not simply on individual hard work but on the responsible behavior of the rich, one of the first articles on inequality to appear in 2008 makes this pitch directly. It was written in January, and it is helpful to recall that unemployment levels were relatively low at this point, the recession had not been officially called, and the collapse of Bear Stearns was still a few months away. Thus the article is less serious than one might expect. Indeed, it is a tongue-and-cheek letter "To the Rich, from America" by Daniel Gross at *Newsweek*. He is pleading with the rich to live up to their end of the bargain after Americans have given them all that they could ever want in tax cuts and even "looked the other way at the gaucherie of extreme consumption, spawned by the greatest concentration of wealth since the 1920s." It is worth quoting at length:

All we've asked in return is that you do a couple things you're really good at: *spend and invest that money close to home. Hire us,* and keep the cash registers ringing, the asset managers managing and all the service providers providing the many services you so richly deserve...*Generally speaking you've lived up to your end of the bargain...but lately, worrisome signs indicate that...you may not be acting in the national interest.* America's private-equity firms are plowing into India, China, Asia and Latin America, and private bankers are urging clients to drop the home bias . . . But your country needs you now, more than ever. *And after all we've done for you, it's the least you can do.*[59]

In other parts of the article, Gross cites statistics on the stagnant incomes and growing indebtedness of the middle class as a point of comparison to the vast fortunes of the rich.

As the tumultuous years of 2008 and 2009 unfold, the litany of urgent issues lengthens and yet – or perhaps as a consequence – the connections to income inequality wear thinner than one might expect. On the one hand, the themes of Wall Street greed and irresponsibility, rising unemployment, economic anxiety, pessimism about upward mobility, and cuts in essential services are all given their due. In a couple of instances, mentions of the potential fallout for Obama's ability to hold onto his young, minority, and educated constituents launch the articles into more partisan territory, but this is not an overarching theme.[60] On the other hand, the fact of rising income inequality is mentioned with only as much regularity as in other peak years in the 1990s. Moreover, as I show later, coverage is less frequent by some measures and is as likely to be implicit as explicit.[61] One article even discusses new research depicting rising income inequality as a function of growing upward mobility. The author, Zuckerman once again, asserts this as the reason that Americans do not make political hay of rising inequality.[62] At the end of our period, then, articles directly on income inequality are trenchant and wide-ranging but no more so than in the first wave of coverage in the 1990s. They do not reach a crescendo with the financial crisis and Great Recession as many would have expected (or at least not until the Occupy Wall Street movement bursts on the scene in the fall of 2011).

To gain additional perspective on this and other stretches of years, I shifted the search criteria from the fact of income inequality to the topic of social class. We encounter many more articles here, as shown in the second panel of Figure 2.1 (note the expanded scale of the y-axis). The subjects for this second search include those referring to broad social class groups or relations between such groups (e.g., "class conflict"). I experimented with various lists of subject terms to ensure that I was capturing the appropriate subject matter.[63] As it turns out, many more subject terms describe the upper end of the class structure than the lower end. For example, there are subject terms for "millionaires" and "billionaires" but shockingly not for "lower class" and "working class."[64] That said, "labor" and its affiliate terms such as "labor unions" and "collective labor agreements" more than make up for this lacuna. Unfortunately, the labor category also seeps unhelpfully into the separate topic of employment conditions. I therefore present the results for social class with and without labor-related articles. Finally, because I wanted to construct a portrait of class and class inequality unhinged from that of poverty and the poor, which are too often lumped together with inequality, I omitted subject terms referring to the poor. The final list includes the following fifteen subject terms: elites, big business, executives/salaries, the rich, the overclass, the upper classes, avarice, white collar workers, the middle classes, blue-collar workers, skilled labor, the minimum wage, labor, social classes, and class conflict.[65]

The trend in coverage of social class groups is presented in the second panel of Figure 2.1. The top trend line and the top of the light gray bars include all articles in this category. The second trend line and the top of the darker gray bars exclude articles with labor in the subject term. The distribution of subject terms pooled over the entire period is presented on the left side of Table 2.2. I begin with a discussion of articles excluding labor.

Coverage of social class groups was not insubstantial in the 1980s (excluding labor), but it climbed to new heights in the first half of the 1990s just as coverage of inequality did. This was particularly true in 1992, when the tally of articles was the highest of any year (26). Nearly three-quarters of these articles centered on groups at the top of the ladder: executives/salaries (11), the rich (4), and elites (3), which are displayed together in the bottom range of black bars. Articles on the middle class (5) also made a significant showing at this time, but these are not shown separately in Figure 2.1. Subject terms referring to the top strata were by far the most popular throughout the three decades as well, accounting for over half of the articles collected under the social class theme, while the middle classes contributed another fifth. To a much larger degree than one might expect, then, the volume of coverage on class is dictated by the volume of coverage on the middle class and especially the rich. Much of this coverage is negative, so this finding is not a straightforward result of the middle- and upper-class bias of the mainstream media.[66]

After the early 1990s, coverage of the top end is concentrated again at various points in the remainder of the 1990s and then more so in the 2000s, whereas coverage of the middle classes is concentrated in the mid-1990s followed by the early 1990s and the late 2000s.[67] In the mid-1990s, coverage of the top makes up less than 50 percent of the total, with a greater emphasis on the middle class as well as a smattering

TABLE 2.2. *Distribution of Subject Terms in Articles on Themes of Social Class and Job Insecurity*

	No.	Pct.		No.	Pct.
I. Social Class Groups			**II. Job Insecurity**		
Executives/Salaries	91	21.8	Unemployment	224	62.2
Elites	22	5.3	Layoffs	101	28.1
Big Business	9	2.2	Corporations/Downsizing	4	1.1
Rich	108	25.9	Outsourcing	17	4.7
Overclass	3	0.7	Job Security	14	3.9
Upper Classes	5	1.2			
Avarice	11	2.6	Total	360	100.00
White-Collar Workers	19	4.6			
Middle Classes	75	18.0			
Blue-Collar Workers	13	3.1			
Skilled Labor	18	4.3			
Minimum Wage	26	6.2			
Social Classes	9	2.2			
Class Conflict	8	1.9			
Subtotal	417	100.0			
All but Labor	417	43.6			
Labor	539	56.4			
Total	956	100.0			

Note: Articles may appear more than once if they have more than one subject term in this list.
Source: Readers' Guide to Periodical Abstracts.

of articles on class conflict (which only occurs in the mid-1990s), the minimum wage, and blue-collar workers. There is little coverage in the late 1990s through the early 2000s of most topics. Coverage of the upper tier resumes in response to the corporate scandals of Enron, WorldCom, and Tyco; the excessive pay of executives such as Jack Welch of General Electric, Richard Grasso of the New York Stock Exchange, Conrad Black of Hollinger, and Michael Ovitz of Disney, to name a few; and the bias of George W. Bush's tax cuts toward the wealthy. A study of negative media coverage of CEO compensation similarly finds that such coverage is "highest in years 1991–1992, 1996, and 2002–2003."[68]

Although income inequality is not a subject term in any of these articles, it is the heart of the matter in many of them. This is especially true during the first spate of heightened coverage in the early and middle 1990s. There are several articles that are centrally on income inequality but have executives/salaries, the middle classes, and/or the rich as their subject terms. Here is a passage from the abstract of one article appearing in a special section on executive pay in *USNWR* in April 1992:

A special section examines the issue of executive pay. Outrage over high executive salaries is on the rise. During the Bush era, personal income for the average American has barely kept pace with inflation, but CEO pay has soared 23 percent to an average of $4.1 million at the nation's largest firms. CEO salaries have been attacked by shareholders, unemployed workers, presidential candidates, and Congress. Several firms have taken steps to address the problem... The CEO of United States Surgical presents his perspective on the issue, and a sidebar discusses the work of compensation consultant Graef Crystal.

Much like this one, articles on executive pay frequently juxtapose excessive pay at the top with statistics on either the stagnant pay of average Americans or the declining state of the economy, consumer confidence, or a particular sector or company. As an example of the latter, it was not uncommon for heightened competition with Japan in the automobile industry to be laid at the feet of excessive American executive pay.[69] Many also quote or cite academics and other experts and studies as this article does in referring to executive compensation expert Graef Crystal, whose 1991 book *In Search of Excess: The Overcompensation of American Executives* is a touchstone for news media coverage at this time.[70] Finally, coverage of these topics is largely in the negative direction in line with previous research on the negativity bias of news media coverage of political issues, and it is once again concerned with alerting *both* political parties to the issue.[71]

The melding of explicit references to both class and inequality begins in the early 1990s but continues into the mid-1990s when words such as "class," "class warfare," and "class conflict" make an appearance even in articles with only the middle class as the subject term. For example, in a March 1992, editorial in *TIME* titled "Double-Talk about 'Class,'" social critic and journalist Barbara Ehrenreich wrote that:

in their appeals to the middle class, the presidential contenders are breaking America's 200-year taboo on the mention of class... The politicians can be forgiven for mentioning class, however, because the issue became harder to ignore in the 1980s, when the rich got richer and the poor got poorer. Moreover, a middle size income started to have less purchasing power, with the result that people needed to be virtually rich if they wanted to be middle class in the old fashioned suburban sense.

Later, in 1996, "class conflict" emerges as the only subject term in a *Newsweek* article titled "Back to Class War?" by Meg Greenfield. She writes that:

[d]ownsizing and restructuring may make economic class warfare the future. Signs abound that large numbers of people in political groupings from right to left are ready for a new national heavy. The Soviet Union and its beastly commissars are no longer available for duty, and many white liberals seem to have finally found racial politics disappointing. *A substitute movement of some consequence can be seen forming around ill will toward the corporate executives, top-level managers, investment bankers, and other movers and shakers and deal makers in the flourishing new business universe.* The actions of some business and industry leaders, who ignore the human cost of technological upheaval, regard the layoff of thousands as a statistical rather than a real misfortune, and abdicate responsibility for the consequences of their business brilliance in the lives of their employees, can only fuel the cause.

Both of these articles self-consciously mark the crossing over of issues of class inequality into popular and bipartisan political discourse for the first time in the mid-1990s, nullifying taboos against a politics of class or superseding prior ideological divisions in American politics around communism and race.[72]

In sum, articles during the first half of the 1990s were not simply talking about economic swings and government policies that could have consequences for income inequality; they were embedding income inequality in the very fabric of the times. Journalists provided sophisticated commentaries, albeit frequently in the voices of experts, academics, and public intellectuals, but none of these were lone voices. Candidates in the 1992 and 1996 presidential elections such as Patrick Buchanan and Ross Perot injected the political discourse with concerns about American competitiveness and its potentially dire impact on the middle class even as the economy was well into its expansion phase. The media responded in a more or less bipartisan manner, dishing up a new and sobering reality that both parties would need to acknowledge and address because no less than the survival of the American dream was at stake. This degree of attention to the issue of income inequality would not be superseded even during the financial crisis and the Great Recession, although perhaps it was matched by the Occupy Wall Street movement, which is not covered in this analysis.

On the one hand, it is gratifying that coverage of income inequality and social class follow much the same trajectory (compare panels 1 and 2 of Figure 2.1). This solidifies our emerging sense of the introduction of income inequality as a social issue in the 1990s, and it affirms our intuition that coverage of income inequality should be interwoven with representations of social class disparities. On the other hand, validation of the *distinctiveness* of this trajectory would be gratifying as well. For this, I next turn to coverage of labor and then of employment conditions.

As shown by the light gray bars and the top trend line in the second panel of Figure 2.1, stories about labor do indeed march to the beat of a different drummer. These stories tower over all others in the early 1980s: 43 percent of the large number of articles on labor over the entire thirty-one–year period are written in the six-year stretch between 1980 and 1985, and over half of all articles on labor unions and collective labor agreements are written in this same six-year period. Consequently, the composition of labor-related articles in the early 1980s is skewed toward topics involving unions and collective bargaining, constituting nearly two-thirds of all labor articles from 1980 to 1985 and only about two-fifths thereafter. The news media chronicled labor disturbances in autos (Chrystler, GM), sports (Major League Baseball, National Football League), entertainment (Screen Actors Guild), steel (SWA), farm equipment (International Harvester, Caterpillar), mining (UMW), and of course airlines (PATCO). Although the subject terms "class conflict" and "class warfare" did not appear in the *Readers' Guide* at this time, the era was rife with labor conflict and concession bargaining. Income inequality was not an explicit point of contention as it was in the mid-1990s, but we know from labor economists and industrial relations specialists that these events were pivotal in its rise.[73]

The next and only other spike in coverage involving labor was more subdued and came in the mid-1990s. A good deal of this coverage was fixated on the story of alleged union corruption involving the insurgent leader of the Teamsters, Ron Carey, during his reelection campaign in 1996 (he was later exonerated). A number of more positive developments in the labor movement were covered as well, including the changing of the old guard at the AFL-CIO by the new SEIU president, John Sweeney, and the successful and widely publicized strike of part-time workers at UPS. Moreover, until his downfall, Ron Carey represented only one of many fresh faces in a new era of union activism bent on organizing new sectors of the economy as a way to staunch the fall in wages and benefits that was so much a part of rising income inequality. Here again, however, the fact of rising income inequality itself was seldom broached, and the salience of labor conflict, as evidenced by the volume of media coverage, was less than half of what it was in the early 1980s.

Surprisingly, even by today's standards, the early 1980s also stands out in its coverage of employment conditions. This trend is shown in the third panel of Figure 2.1 and the associated list and distribution of subject terms are presented in the right panel of Table 2.2. As one would expect, subjects such as "unemployment" and "layoffs" make up the lion's share of coverage of employment conditions over the entire three decades. But the number of articles with such newly coined subject terms as "downsizing" and "outsourcing" and even "job security" is not inconsequential: together they account for nearly a tenth of all articles. Moreover, coverage of these issues does not fall perfectly in line with coverage of unemployment, which hews more predictably to the business cycle. Instead, coverage of job insecurity overlaps to some degree with segments of the coverage of income inequality and social class.

In exploring these patterns in more detail, the first pattern to note is the influence of the business cycle on coverage of employment conditions throughout the three decades and especially in the early 1980s. The singular off-the-charts spike in the number of articles on this theme appears at this time. In these years of deep blue-collar recession, the media focused its attention almost exclusively on short-term unemployment, including both individual instances of job loss and mass layoffs. Although this emphasis persisted into the second phase of increased attention to employment conditions during and after the early 1990s recession, the sheer volume of articles on unemployment declined dramatically relative to the early 1980s. The same can be said of coverage during the third recessionary period in the early 2000s. Most likely this drop-off can be attributed to the lower unemployment rates in these recessions as compared to the so-called first Great Recession of the early 1980s, but this fails to explain the lower relative levels of coverage even in 2009 and 2010 during the second Great Recession.

The second pattern to note concerns a couple of unusual spikes in coverage during years not of economic recession but of economic expansion. In 1996, the number of articles on employment conditions exceeds the number in any of the recessionary years immediately preceding it. Twenty-three articles appear on the subjects of layoffs (14), job security (4), downsizing (3), outsourcing (1), and unemployment (1). A separate analysis of the *New York Times* and *Wall Street Journal* confirms that there was a sharp and isolated increase in coverage of downsizing in 1996.[74] The sudden and swift emergence of this issue meant that employment conditions were of greater salience in 1996 than in any other year except 1982 and 1983 and were on par with 2009 and 2010. The spike in 2004 (15 articles), by comparison, is more in keeping with the spikes in coverage of employment conditions in the early 1990s and early 2000s recessions. These articles are comprised of stories on the then new issue of outsourcing (9) as well as unemployment (5) and layoffs (1).

Americans were therefore contending with an unfamiliar and unsettling economic brew in both the mid-1990s and mid-2000s: a "jobless" recovery, a term formulated first to distinguish the early 1990s expansion from those coming before, and then later applied to the early 2000s expansion; heightened middle-class job insecurity from downsizing and outsourcing as the expansions unfolded; and an apparently flourishing elite, as we saw from earlier discussions of articles with subject terms referring to social class groups. The new economy seemed to involve sacrifice for white-collar workers as never before, and yet there were no signs of the economic revival to come later in the decade (in the 1990s) that might have justified the pain. And, today, the possibility of a silver lining from all that has occurred in the late 2000s is not in sight, although some kind of economic comeback for the majority of Americans is, we can only hope, inevitable.

In sum, the greater attention devoted to both inequality and inequality-related issues during the early and middle part of the 1990s is apparent. A jump in the number of stories on job insecurity, economic inequality, and/or social class occurred in 1992 and again in 1995 and 1996. Articles specifically on excessive executive pay and perks as an injustice in and of itself and as a drag on the economy peaked in the early 1990s amid mounting discontent about the economic downturn. The mid-1990s, by contrast, produced the only non-recessionary period between 1980 and 2010 when all of the issues we have considered align in a perfect storm of simultaneous coverage. By the end of the 1990s, coverage of all three topics subsides. Although coverage resurfaces in the late 2000s, and is embedded in the worst financial crisis since the Great Depression, the numbers tell us that it never exceeds the level of the mid-1990s. A closer reading also reveals a more diffuse subject matter that fails to coalesce as decisively around the connection between rising income inequality and threats to the American dream as was the case in the early and middle 1990s.

Articles on Inequality from an Expanded List of Subject Terms

As we have seen, articles on income inequality come in so many shapes and sizes that it is nearly impossible to maintain strict comparability in coverage over time with only a small set of subject terms. Moreover, subject coding by the *Readers' Guide* is not itself comparable over time, with new subject terms related to inequality introduced after the start of our time series in 1980.[75] We therefore employ a final method to cast the net as systematically as possible. As detailed in Appendix A, we collected all subject terms in the original population of relevant articles on inequality and defined this as our extended list of subject terms. The final list has sixty-three subject terms and encompasses many of the terms used above as well as many more general terms, such as "income" and "taxation," and more specific terms, such as "poor/statistics" and "foreign securities." The full extended list is provided in Appendix B. The population of articles containing at least one of these subject terms numbered in the many thousands, forcing us to take a random sample of articles stratified by year. All figures below are weighted to reflect sample selection criteria.

The variety of subject terms and the complexity of the subject matter also persuaded us to code articles by hand. Content coding by hand is a laborious process, but it enables a flexible approach to identifying and classifying subject matter that varies in content but not necessarily in theme. This flexibility is necessary under circumstances such as ours in which the subject of analysis is a new multifaceted social issue unfolding in real time in the real world. It is impossible under these exploratory conditions to deductively catalog the complete set of metaphors for inequality that could be invoked over a three-decade span of news coverage. To take just a couple of examples, the metaphor "Wall Street versus Main Street" spread wildly during the financial crisis in the late 2000s whereas stories about "union busting" were more germane in the early 1980s. Our unique coding scheme, applied to a large and disparate sample of articles, attempts to encompass this wide range of coverage and, in addition, to come to a better understanding of several gray areas of coverage. Unlike other comprehensive approaches to the study of media coverage, we assume neither that all of the articles from our search of subject terms are relevant nor that a preset list of phrases is definitive enough for use in a computer coding program. In our process of hand coding, we ultimately deemed irrelevant more than a third of the articles, with the rest divided into those that either explicitly or implicitly covered the topic of inequality or fell into two other related categories not discussed in this chapter.[76]

Although the results presented in Figure 2.2 confirm many of the features already discussed in Figure 2.1, they also introduce several new features of the coverage of economic inequality. The relatively small number of articles coded as directly on the subject of rising inequality is charted in the first panel of Figure 2.2, while the next two panels identify all articles falling into the explicit (including those in the first panel) and implicit

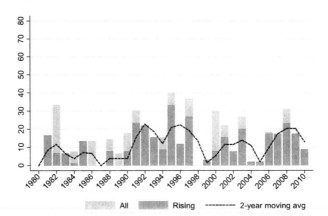

(1) Weighted number of inequality articles, using the most narrow definition.

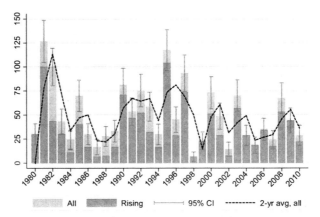

(2) Weighted number of inequality articles, all explicit.

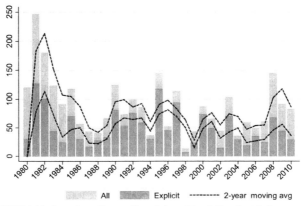

(3) Weighted number of inequality articles, all implicit and explicit.

FIGURE 2.2. Weighted number of newsweekly articles from *Time*, *Newsweek*, and *USNWR* on themes of economic inequality, 1980 to 2010. As described in Appendix A, content is coded from a random sample of articles with subject terms from the extended list in Appendix B. Numbers of articles in subcategories are nested in larger categories of articles. The 95 percent confidence interval is calculated from a saturated Poisson regression model with year dummies. *Source:* Readers' Guide to Periodical Abstracts.

categories described in sections 4a and 4b of Table 2.1. Similar to earlier patterns, the first multiyear surge in media coverage of rising inequality appears in the early and middle 1990s followed by a roller coaster of coverage thereafter. There is also the familiar mountain of coverage in the early 1980s on other inequality-related issues, many of which fall into the implicit category. In addition to these aspects of media coverage, however, stories about taxes enter the fray in greater numbers than in the foregoing analyses, owing to several tax-related subject terms now part of the search criteria. Equally notable, our coding of explicit and implicit articles gives no indication that time rendered a more refined and there-fore explicit treatment of the subject matter. To the contrary, explicit coverage peaked in the early 1980s and in the mid-1990s (see panel 2 of Figure 2.2).[77] To the extent that coverage expanded from the 1990s to the 2000s, it was because of an increase in implicit material (see panel 3 of Figure 2.2).

To get a better handle on the new material, I begin with news of inequality in the 1980s and proceed chronologically to the 1990s and 2000s. I briefly reiterate earlier patterns where they reappear but concen-trate on new topics and trends emerging from this much-larger sample of articles.

Although direct coverage of rising inequality in the 1980s is low, as shown in panel 1 of Figure 2.2, the volume of explicit and implicit articles on inequality is as high in the early 1980s as it is in the mid-1990s, as shown in panels 2 and 3. Unemployment is common in the articles of the early 1980s, as expected, although it is only one of sev-eral momentous topics on the docket. Because tax cuts topped Reagan's policy agenda, and these often went hand in hand with deficit-reducing slashes in social program expenditures, the news is saturated with stories of taxing and spending. What stands out above all else is the dizzying array of policy maneuvers pointing in all directions. This is particularly the case when Reagan is forced in his second and later years to raise taxes as the deficit fails to shrink and the economy refuses to rebound. Although the regressive elements of Reagan's tax deals are well known (e.g., increased payroll taxes and decreased top-end marginal tax rates), many progressive reforms were implemented in tandem, and the media covered them as such. For instance, tax brackets were indexed to infla-tion to help the middle class, and loopholes for corporations and the wealthy were eliminated with great fanfare (e.g., no more tax breaks for the "three martini lunch"). As a consequence, readers of the news were not fed a steady diet of tax reform beneficial only to the rich. Moreover, cuts to social programs were often portrayed in a one-sided manner as a bane to the unemployed and the poor as well as to minimum wage workers. The frenzy and novelty of policy transformations at this time resulted in much of the news coverage of inequality falling in the implicit category.[78]

As inflation and unemployment were wrested under control, major budget and tax reforms were passed, and economic recovery was set in motion, coverage of inequality-related subjects went into hiatus in the late 1980s. This is when we pick up the thin thread of articles directly on rising inequality, in which, perhaps with the perspective of time, the fact of rising inequality is increasingly written boldly on the wall. In the following decade, there are fewer articles overall than in the early 1980s if both implicit and explicit articles are combined (as in panel 3) but a greater share provide pointed commentary.

In an early example, we return to the same year in which an article was first tagged with the "income inequality" subject term, 1988. The subject term of this article is "U.S./Economic Policy," but it is another preelection plea to take growing middle-class economic anxiety seriously. The author argues that "many Reagan Democrats have been teetering on the edge of downward mobility throughout most of the lifestyles-of-the-rich-and-famous decade."[79] To document downward middle-class mobility, the journalist showcases the fact that median family income began to stagnate after 1973. Also during the late 1980s, several new books are published assessing the damage of a decade of regressive public policy and aggressive corporate restructuring. In some cases, authors are shoring up evidence for more speculative positions about the declining middle class that were advanced earlier in the decade and covered by the mainstream media at that time. Speculations are also put forward about whether Americans are aware of what is going on, with scholars taking opposing sides on the question.[80]

Taxes are resurrected in 1990 as a contentious issue during George H. W. Bush's presidency and the 1992 presidential election, and they are a mainstay of coverage of inequality-related topics in the mid-1990s.[81] In fact, media coverage of tax policy is as prevalent in 1995 as in 1981, the two peak years of explicit coverage of inequality (see panel 1 in Appendix C for the trend in explicit inequality articles on taxes). Concerns about the deficit and recession fuel debates about taxes in this period even though the recession is only half as deep as it was in the prior decade. However, worries about the long-term competitiveness of the U.S. economy and the ability of government to steer a more successful economic course in the future are at least as palpable as they were in the early 1980s.[82] Tax policy no longer shares equal billing with labor conflicts as it did in the early 1980s but is one of a plethora of issues. Executive pay is a major part of the storyline in the early 1990s, but by mid-decade there are as many stories that mention the poor (no doubt due to the vociferous debate over welfare reform), the middle class, and the rich more broadly. Stories that mention technological restructuring and global competition are small in number throughout the three decades but reach a peak in 1995 (as shown in panel 3 of Appendix C).[83] Thus the "it's the economy, stupid" slogan of Clinton's successful 1992 bid for the White House had considerable legs, preventing taxes from monopolizing center stage well into the mid-1990s.

Once income inequality had taken root as a social fact, it could have maintained at least a constant hum in news coverage and political debate, if not considerably more than that. This would seem to depend, however, on whether income inequality remains uncomfortably high or continues to be a symbol of social and economic ills and a threat to the American dream. Consistent with our earlier findings, coverage in this batch of articles declined from the mid-1990s, and then percolated up again in 2000, when coverage was not as predominantly about *rising* inequality as was the case in most other years (see panel 1 of Figure 2.2). In fact, overall levels of inequality as measured by the Gini coefficient did flatten out in the late 1990s and the ratio of the middle to the bottom declined. Still, some journalists continued to see harm in leaving pockets of the disadvantaged far behind in absolute terms, which could perhaps sow seeds of rebellion. Others wove inequality into a more general and anguish-filled narrative of what could happen if economic prosperity and budget surpluses fell victim to too much spending by Democrats or too much tax cutting by Republicans. Thus inequality is no longer hitched to an ailing economy but to fears of social isolation and resentment of the rich on the one hand and reckless triumphalism at America's unrivaled prosperity on the other.

Any number of events in the 2000s could have led to a flare-up in coverage of inequality, but interest was highest in 2003 and 2008 according to the analysis in Figure 2.2. Taxes, the rich, and the middle class were again prominent themes. For example, by the time President George W. Bush rolled out his proposal in early 2003 to cut taxes on dividends and capital gains to, as he said, jumpstart the stock market and stimulate the economy, his proclivity toward lightening the tax load disproportionately for the rich was no secret. If the increase in negative coverage of inequality is any indication, the tilt toward the rich was apparently less palatable in

2003 than during the first round of tax cutting in 2001. This is true for at least three reasons (all cited in stories in 2003): a multiyear jobless recovery putting unemployment back on the front burner; and projections of evaporating surpluses from the wars in Afghanistan and Iraq, and a run of corporate scandals, did the same for the deficit and hostility toward the rich, respectively. Despite this auspicious combination, none of the articles in 2003 focus on income inequality enough to warrant that label as a subject term (see panel 1 of Figure 2.1). The fact of rising income inequality played second fiddle to the fairness of the tax code, corporate malfeasance, and a humdrum economy. Rising income inequality was seen neither as the central ailment nor a central artery of that ailment.

The topic of income inequality raises its head for the last time in our time series in 2008, as shown in all three panels of Figure 2.2. On the one hand, we know from the discussion above that journalists were already warming up to the issue in 2006 and 2007. As the historic year of 2008 unfolds, the themes of greed, irresponsibility, and undeservingness become ubiquitous: "Wall Street" is contrasted scathingly to "Main Street," commercial banks and mortgage giants to ordinary homeowners, and federal bailouts to fiscal crises in the states. On the other hand, surprisingly, the topic of inequality is discussed in implicit as much as in explicit terms. The financial elite are blamed for the dismal state of the economy, to be sure, but when income inequality is confronted head on, it is also attributed to regressive tax policies, globalization, and skills mismatches. In December 2008, for instance, the *Newsweek* columnist Samuelson asserts that Obama can either save the economy or tend to social reform but he cannot have it both ways.[84] By contrast, in the early 1990s, excessive executive pay, stagnant wages, and a jobless recovery were almost perfectly aligned, so that fixing one meant fixing the other. The article to focus most thoughtfully on the issue of income inequality weighs one cause and solution against another and then concludes, emblematic of the time as well as the end of our journey through the newsweekly archives, that the income gap is "an issue that's been danced around for too long. It's time to address it."[85]

Why Is Inequality Covered?

The expectation that concerns about income inequality are a response to rising income inequality assumes that rising income inequality is known in some fashion to Americans. The role of "frames in communication," ideas, agenda setting, and the "cultural supply side" more generally have all received increased attention in recent years as scholars try to understand how individuals gather relevant information, form preferences, and make decisions.[86] Although there are many factors to consider, previous research is clear that media coverage is potentially critical in conveying political and economic information that both shapes and reflects citizen attitudes and behavior.[87] This seems especially important for issues whose visibility may be limited by their abstractness and complexity, lack of representation in mass-based membership organizations that can serve as conduits of information, and novelty.[88] Journalists convey information on such issues while at the same time targeting those issues that they think are congruent with public interest.

I therefore examined the extent to which inequality broke out of academic and policy circles and emerged as an issue worthy of popular attention, contrary to the widespread sense that there has been hardly any discussion of widening inequality at best and an ongoing drumbeat of American tolerance for inequality at worst. In fact, I found no shortage of material critical of inequality, even though I limited my search to the top three newsweeklies. But I also found two potential alternative hypotheses to be off the mark as well. First, income inequality was not discovered as a new social fact and then steadily covered with increasing frequency over the years as the trend itself continued upward and knowledge of it was gradually amassed among scholars. By no definition was coverage of income inequality greater at the end of our period in 2010 than at various points along the way. The trend in coverage was, in short, distinctly nonlinear.

Second, this nonlinear pattern did not track in any straightforward manner the dominant economic and political cycles of our times, such as the business or presidential election cycles. These cycles have much to commend them as explanations of economic and political behavior, and by no means were they irrelevant, but they were far from determinative. For instance, coverage was just as high, if not higher, during periods of economic expansion in the mid-1990s and mid-2000s as during periods of economic contraction in the early 1990s and early 2000s. Similarly, coverage was elevated *around* the presidential election season, but our analysis places that elevation sometimes a year before or a year after the election, and the triggering event could just as well have been a piece of policy legislation (e.g., Bush's second tax cut proposal in 2003) or an indicator of economic woes (e.g., jobless recovery and downsizing in 1996 or outsourcing in 2004) as the election itself. Furthermore, there was little activity around the 1988 presidential election. Finally, the

presidential election season does not come through in predicting the
content of coverage, which was more about rising inequality in 1992 and
1996 than in 2000. Still, a multivariate analysis including more detailed
data on economic and political conditions could reveal a systematic
pattern, and this is something future research should pursue.[89]

Until that time, what *does* appear to explain the nonlinear trend? Two
main factors stand out. First, economic and political trends resulting in
higher levels of income inequality must be laid bare in one way or another.
This means that the study and dissemination of those trends by academics
and other experts must first take place before the issue can gain a public hearing, and for the most part this process unfolds according to its
own rhythm. Although the trend of rising inequality was underway in
the 1980s, research by academics, the Census Bureau, and the Congressional Budget Office (CBO) generated more controversy than consensus.
The interpretive lens of "rising income inequality" was simply unavail-
able to journalists even though there was a treasure trove of coverage
of inequality-related topics, such as labor conflicts, reductions in social
programs, and regressive tax cuts. By contrast, news of economic events
such as excessive executive compensation in the early 1990s and downsizing in the mid-1990s were covered after considerable evidence about
the links between economic restructuring and rising income inequality
became available. In the 2000s, coverage of income inequality also incorporated new evidence about the concentration of income at the very
top of the distribution by the CBO, the Census Bureau, and academic
researchers, but this time the story never truly took off, even after the
financial crisis and Great Recession hit. Owing perhaps to the complexity
of the issue – its many causes, consequences, and forms, and the ongoing
lack of consensus regarding these – a number of frames coexisted and
diluted the message. The nature and extent of information diffusion and
consensus is thus the first factor driving coverage of income inequality.

Information does not ensure coverage, however. The second critical
factor therefore concerns *why* journalists decide to cover the issue when
they do. This is where the full content and context of coverage, rather
than the simple reporting of facts and figures, becomes decisive in the
quest to understand the parameters of public debate. Amid the extraordinary range of dimensions that a new meta-issue such as rising economic
inequality introduces, it is inevitable that some of those dimensions will
be deemed more worthy of coverage than others, by both the independent
judgment of journalists and the journalists' reading of public interest. The
content analysis reveals that the rich, the middle class, and the economic

relationship between them are potent elements of a recurring frame. In this frame, income inequality is not only an abstract statistic or indicator of "fairness" but a practical matter of how economic well-being is doled out.

Specifically, when income inequality has a *perceived impact on most Americans*, when it is indicted for harming the hardworking middle class, it gains legitimacy as a political issue and receives heightened coverage. Opportunity is held hostage by the irresponsible behavior of elites, and this puts the American dream in jeopardy. This putative harm to the middle class can surface at any time. It is not dependent on the business cycle or on any particular level of income inequality. In fact, one might infer from the time series of media coverage that economic downturns potentially detract from the issue unless inequality is implicated directly and centrally in the downturn, as appears to have been the case more in 1992 than in the post-2008 period (until the Occupy Wall Street movement emerges in 2011). In short, the rich can be seen as deserving under the glow of widely shared growth, as in the prosperous late 1990s, but the rich can also be taken to task for not living up to their end of the American bargain when good fortune only "trickles up" and not down. When that happens, hard work, individual responsibility, and the undeserving poor are not the only talk in town. Seemingly complex and un-American matters of equitable distribution steal the limelight.

Of greatest consequence in examining the news media, in the end, is the opening up of a new understanding of the American public discourse on inequality and class. It can no longer be taken for granted as a monolithic apology for the rich and ideologies of individualism any more than it can be considered a clarion call for economic equality. Over three decades, the issue of inequality surfaced repeatedly in largely critical and often bipartisan terms. This was particularly so in the 1990s, but some in the media industry also reached the point in the late 2000s when they were tiring of raising the issue for so many years without any action or resolution in sight. With the Occupy Wall Street movement having galvanized attention around the issue once again, perhaps even to heights unseen in the 1990s, it would be a mistake to think of this as the first instance of coverage and to shoot messages every which way about inequality's excessive level, its causes, consequences, and "proper" policy solutions. Rather than dissipate the message in this way, we can learn from past episodes of coverage that Americans neither uniformly resent nor idolize the rich but, as a matter of equity, ask only that they fulfill their obligations to the American people, creating opportunity for all and not just for themselves. In return, Americans are willing to give them hard work and a very long leash indeed.

Appendix A: Article Selection Methods

Articles on inequality were selected by searching the three newsweeklies of *TIME*, *Newsweek*, and *U.S. News and World Report* for articles with the subject terms "income inequality," "wage differentials," "equality," and "meritocracy." This search produced a list of fifty articles from 1980 to 2008. When articles from 2009 and 2010 were added in a subsequent stage of analysis, the list of relevant articles on inequality rose to fifty-seven. The original list of fifty articles was used to collect the extended list of subject terms, however, as the bulk of analysis took place prior to adding the two additional years of media coverage.

All subject terms in these fifty articles were collected to form the extended list of subject terms. We then eliminated terms referring to presidential candidates. These latter terms could lead us far from our subject matter and bias trends in favor of presidential election years (although this could be interesting to analyze in future research). Eliminating names such as Patrick Buchanan and Ross Perot is likely to lend a downward bias to coverage of income inequality during the period in which we witnessed the first concentration of explicit coverage of inequality in the early and mid-1990s. Note also that searches for each term turn up all subject terms that have that term embedded in it (e.g., the search for articles with "labor" as a subject term yields articles with subject terms such as "labor unions"). Our final list of included and excluded subject terms is provided in Appendix B.

The population of articles including any of the terms in the extended list in the years from 1980 to 2010 is 8,311. Articles with the inequality subject terms (i.e., the list of fifty-seven articles) were automatically included and thus had a 100 percent probability of inclusion. We took random 15 and 10 percent samples from the remaining articles stratified by year at three different stages of analysis. These articles are weighted to compensate for their lower probability of inclusion. The final sample includes 1,179 articles, or 14 percent of the population.

Each of the articles in the final sample was coded by a trained undergraduate coder (the detailed coding instructions are available upon request). The articles were coded into four main categories. The first category consisted of articles that were on the topic of inequality (i.e., income, wage, earnings, and wealth inequality and not gender or racial inequality).

The second category consisted of articles solely on employment and economic conditions, without any explicit mention of income, wages, earnings, wealth, etc. The third category consisted of articles that mentioned the financial well-being of a single social class group only rather than multiple, hierarchically ordered groups. The second and third categories isolate important economic changes occurring at the same time that economic inequality was rising, namely rising employment insecurity and declining or stagnant earnings for some groups and dramatic increases for other groups. With these categories, then, we sought to compare and contrast how the media covers different dimensions of the larger economic environment. The fourth category consisted of articles that were considered irrelevant. Aside from these four primary and mutually exclusive categories, there were many other secondary and overlapping categories, including references to specific social class groups and to the causes and policies associated with inequality.

Hand coding into categories was subjected to reliability tests during two different rounds in the analysis. In the first round, reliability tests were conducted on 15 percent of the coded articles at that point for the four primary categories and for a few of the secondary categories associated with these four main categories. These reliability tests are presented in the table below. Reliability was very high for the articles coded as relevant on the topic of inequality (.92) and for two of the secondary categories associated with this category: whether inequality was mentioned as rising (.92) or falling (1.0). Reliability was also acceptable for articles deemed irrelevant (.78). Reliabilities were lower for the two other main categories of relevant articles on employment conditions (.69) and the financial well-being of single groups (.56). Therefore, we eliminated the articles coded as irrelevant and we retained the articles coded as relevant on the topic of inequality. The latter are presented in the first panel of Figure 2.2; the trend line in this figure tracks all articles in this category, and the dark bars track articles coded as mentioning "rising" inequality.

The remaining articles in the other two primary categories were dissolved into a single category of "relevant, other." These articles were subjected to a second round of coding. It was at this stage that we developed the criteria stated in Table 2.1. As discussed above, distinction 4a is in practice composed of two subcategories: articles that mention the fact of inequality directly, and those that use explicit relational or comparative language involving two or more hierarchically ordered social class groups. Nearly all articles mentioning the fact of rising income inequality were netted in the first round of coding presented in the first panel of Figure 2.2. Consequently, in the second round, "explicit" refers mostly to articles in the second subcategory of 4a. All articles in the first and second rounds that meet the criteria in section 4a of Table 2.1 are shown in the second panel of Figure 2.2 while the "implicit" category of articles, which corresponds directly to the criteria listed in 4b of Table 2.1, is shown in the third panel. The top trend line in this panel traces all explicit and implicit articles in both rounds of coding, and the bottom line traces only the explicit articles. The reliability of coding an article according to any of the criteria in 4a or 4b in the second round is .85, whereas the reliability of the explicit/implicit distinction is .73.[90]

Coding Scheme: Reliability Tests on 1980–2008 Sample

	1st Round Reliability	2nd Round Reliability	N
First Round			
Irrelevant	0.78	NA	384
Relevant:			
A. Inequality	0.92	NA	97
Rising	0.92		
Falling	1.00		
Negative	0.75		
Positive	0.95		
B. Financial well-being for single group	0.56	NA	118
C. Economic/employment conditions	0.69	NA	213
D. Secondary categories			
Poor	0.80	NA	
Working class	0.46	NA	
Middle class	0.93	NA	
Rich	0.78	NA	
Taxes	0.84	NA	
Technology	0.68	NA	
Skills	0.61	NA	
Trade	0.79		
Total (first round)			812
Second Round			
Relevant (explicit and implicit inequality)		0.85	331
E. Explicit relational/ comparative language and multigroup		0.73	

Appendix B: Extended List of Search Terms

Affirmative Action
Affirmative action in education
Affluent market
Alternative minimum tax
American dream (philosophy)
Austin (Tex.)/Economic conditions
Budget/United States
Class conflict
Collective labor agreements
Computers and civilization
Computers and the poor
Computers/Study and teaching
Conservatism
Equality
Executives/Salaries
Family size
Foreign securities
Globalization
Income
Income inequality
Income inequality/Humor, satire, etc.
Income tax
Income tax/Deductions
Inflation (Finance)
Information technology/Economic aspects
Information technology/Social aspects
Inheritance tax
Investments, American
Labor
Labor/Education
Married couples/Economic conditions
Medical care/Costs
Meritocracy
Middle classes
Middle classes/Taxation
Minorities/Internet use
Nineteen hundred and eighties
Occupations

Appendix C: Additional Results

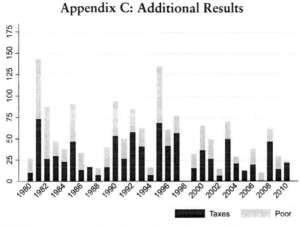

(1) Weighted number of articles mentioning taxes and the poor.

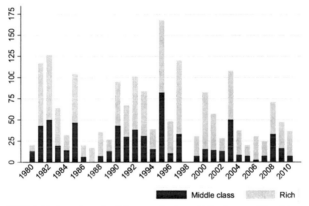

(2) Weighted number of articles mentioning middle class and the rich.

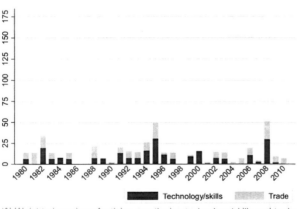

(3) Weighted number of articles mentioning technology/skills and trade

FIGURE C2.1. Weighted number of newsweekly articles from *Time*, *Newsweek*, and *USNWR* on various themes, 1980 to 2010. As described in Appendix A, content is hand coded from a random sample of articles with subject terms from the extended list of subject terms in Appendix B. Numbers of articles are stacked (i.e., not nested) and are not mutually exclusive. *Source:* Readers' Guide to Periodical Abstracts.

3

American Beliefs about Income Inequality

What, When, Who, and Why?

It is often said that Americans do not care about income inequality; if they did, they would be marching in the streets at its historic rise (well before 2011) and pressing for redistributive policies to reduce it. It is even suggested that a shift in social norms toward greater acceptance of inequality was a major factor contributing to the rise. Without public support, the argument goes, how could the egalitarian institutions of the post–World War II era – a period when tax rates on the rich were more than double what they are today, unions were strong, the minimum wage was high, and big employers provided ample benefits to their employees – have eroded to such a significant degree? Indeed, instead of worrying about rising inequality, Americans persist in believing in the importance of hard work in getting ahead, even as the distance needed to travel to the top gets longer by the day. Faith in the American dream of upward mobility appears, astonishingly, to be as strong as ever.[1]

Although such arguments ring true to our ears and conform to our conservative image of Americans as individualistic and antigovernment, they are not a very good barometer of beliefs about income inequality. The reason is fairly straightforward: such arguments are derived from surveys and theoretical models of beliefs about government redistribution and opportunities for upward mobility, not income inequality. Views about the related but distinct matters of redistribution and opportunity – such as lukewarm support for redistributive policies and optimism about the possibility of upward mobility – do imply that income inequality is of trifling concern to Americans. As shown in previous chapters, however, the handful of survey questions that ask directly about income inequality paint a rather different picture. In fact, most Americans prefer less inequality than they think exists, and sometimes much less. Moreover, as I show in this chapter and in much greater detail in the following chapter, Americans believe that opportunity is more restricted than the typical survey question lets on. Although recently scholars have done a better job of capturing American concerns about inequality and opportunity, there is still no agreement on what this really means. The literature has yet to tackle the key questions of exactly *what* Americans believe, *when* they believe it, and *why* they believe it. Indeed, it remains somewhat of a paradox that our convictions are so strong and our evidence so weak.[2]

In this chapter, I focus exclusively on beliefs about income inequality, drawing a strict separation between these beliefs and beliefs about redistribution and opportunity. Although the latter topics are important in coming to terms with how Americans think about inequality, they will be put aside for now and taken up in subsequent chapters once a clearer picture of sentiments toward income inequality emerges. To that end, I organize the discussion in this chapter around the standard questions of what, when, who, and why.

I begin with the seemingly simple question of *what* Americans think about income inequality. I discuss several dimensions of beliefs neglected in past research and yet germane to the period of rising inequality. For example, despite the phenomenal growth of incomes at the very top of the distribution, there has been scant discussion of how Americans associate income inequality with the fortunes of the rich.[3] In a similar vein, the relationship between economic growth and income inequality is a topic of major debate in economics but is considered perhaps too esoteric to broach with ordinary Americans.[4] By contrast, surveys in the 1970s and 1980s routinely inquired into how beliefs were shaped by perceptions of inequality as an incentive for innovation and growth, a line of inquiry I return to in this chapter.[5] I examine whether Americans think of income inequality as fueling or curbing economic growth, a debate that also surfaced in the media coverage of income inequality described in Chapter 2. These are some of the central questions in the study of attitudes about income inequality that are explored in this chapter.

I then proceed to more challenging questions, beginning with that of *when* Americans think what they do about income inequality. As I discussed in detail in Chapter 1, American beliefs about income inequality are typically assumed to be tolerant, static, and enduring, with perhaps only episodic swings during brief periods of reform or the slump of a business cycle. Recent scholarship suggests a more diverse array of possibilities, with some arguing that concerns about inequality grew as inequality itself climbed to new heights, and others arguing that norms of inequality grew more permissive with time, as noted above. Still others characterize Americans as largely ignorant of rising inequality. For the most part, these possibilities remain intriguing hypotheses, for neither stability nor change (nor ignorance) has been documented conclusively as of yet.[6] The six time points of survey data on attitudes about inequality examined in this chapter span much of the period of rising inequality, including the twenty-four years from 1987 to 2010, and therefore allow us for the first time to test hypotheses of change and stability in attitudes about inequality.

If American beliefs turn out to be less static and tolerant than is often assumed, a proposition for which I find considerable evidence below, a number of explanations of *why* Americans believe what they do can be assessed in a more rigorous manner than is possible when only a single cross-section of data is available. Can American beliefs be explained by the business or presidential election cycles, or the rise in inequality itself? If attitudes correspond to the actual trend in inequality, how do Americans know about the trend? Do attitudes instead follow media coverage of the issue, which differs from the trend in actual inequality, as documented in Chapter 2? Finally, as part of the *why* question, I examine *who* among Americans hold such beliefs. Do Americans think as one on the issue of income inequality, adhering in unison to the American dream as a national ideology? Or are shifts over time the result of growing polarization between income and partisan groups, in concert with increasing polarization in the income distribution and among political elites?[7]

In sum, even if Americans are said to care about income inequality, it is crucial to push farther into identifying exactly what they believe and why. Because this study takes place during a period of substantial economic, political, and social change, it capitalizes on a changing context to help illuminate in real historical time the underlying motivations of stated beliefs about income inequality. The ultimate aim is to open a much-needed window into how Americans think income inequality *specifically* should be treated as a social, economic, and political issue. This is an altogether different question from how they think other forms of inequality (e.g., access to education or health care) or economic hardship (e.g., poverty, old age) are to be treated, and a different question from how *we* think Americans *ought* to address problems of income inequality. Although it is impossible to generalize from this period to other periods, we can at least assess whether the New Gilded Age conforms to the expectations and assumptions we have developed about American beliefs toward income inequality.

We will find that it does not. Americans are surprisingly attuned to distributional outcomes, seeming to care more about the equitable nature of economic growth than economic growth per se. But despite this sensitivity to distributional concerns, there is no straightforward correspondence between either personal financial hardship or rising levels of inequality on the one hand and outrage over the widening chasm in incomes on the other. Nor are the politics of the issue as many political economists would predict, for there is little evidence of political polarization, and considerable evidence of mass beliefs shifting and evolving over time in a nonlinear fashion. These findings will be critical ingredients in understanding income inequality as a distinct social issue and in deciphering, in future chapters, the paths that connect beliefs about income inequality to preferences for expanding opportunities and redistributing incomes in a more just and fair manner.

What Do Americans Believe?

Arguably the best individual-level data on multiple dimensions of beliefs about income inequality replicated over time in the era of rising inequality come from the Social Inequality Modules of the General Social Survey (GSS) in 1987, 1996, 2000, 2008, and 2010, and the International Social Survey Program (ISSP) in 1992.[8] There are three relevant questions present in all six years:

Do you agree or disagree (with responses including strongly agree, agree, neither, disagree, and strongly disagree):

1. Differences in income in America are too large.
2. Inequality continues to exist because it benefits the rich and powerful.
3. Large differences in income are necessary for America's prosperity.

Agreement to the first two questions implies a lack of acceptance of inequality, whereas disagreement to the third question implies a lack of justification for inequality (this question is inverted so that agreement to all three questions indicates lack of tolerance for or justification of inequality). The range of responses from strong agreement to strong disagreement to these questions conveys the intensity of sentiments toward income inequality, which can also be used to gauge whether views about inequality are becoming polarized. As shorthand, I refer to these questions as the "too large," "benefits the rich," and "prosperity" questions, respectively. Although it would certainly be helpful to have additional and differently worded questions, these three are unique in their substantive focus on income inequality (with no reference to government intervention), replication over time during the period of rising inequality, attention to survey question bias, and coverage of multiple conceptual themes.[9]

Each of these characteristics is vital to analyzing beliefs about income inequality, especially over time, but particularly advantageous is the conceptual range of the three questions. One of the questions contains a straightforward query as to whether existing levels of income inequality are acceptable. The other two questions are more innovative in their allusions to the rich, a social group rarely studied or referenced in survey questions about income inequality. In the "benefits the rich" question, notions of fairness are invoked as the "rich and powerful" are expressly identified as a social group that both benefits from inequality and perpetuates it to its own advantage. The association of inequality with the rich is explicit in this question, but a further implication is that the rich *reproduce* inequality from one generation to the next at the expense of an equal starting gate for everyone else, an interpretation withstanding closer scrutiny in the next chapter. The "prosperity" question is less direct in its reference to the rich, but it nevertheless implies the possibility of becoming rich as a spur to succeed. Great wealth and power is the reward for hard work and talent, which in turn stimulates innovation, growth, and a prosperous society for all Americans. Thus we have two entry points into the investigation of whether Americans believe that the distribution of income benefits only those in the winners' circle or whether it is fair and functional for the nation as a whole.

Although these aspects of the questions are particularly helpful in a period of growing concentrations of income at the top, they share one significant shortcoming: they are not factual in nature, asking neither how much inequality exists nor whether it has risen or fallen over time. We are therefore unable to ascertain whether Americans knew about rising inequality. But no other dataset or public opinion poll contains this information, for two reasons. First, many survey researchers doubted whether factual questions were useful given the abstractness of the issue and the level of general misinformation in the population.[10] Second, factual questions have appeared in major surveys more recently as the issue gained traction, but only beginning in the early 2000s, too late to establish a

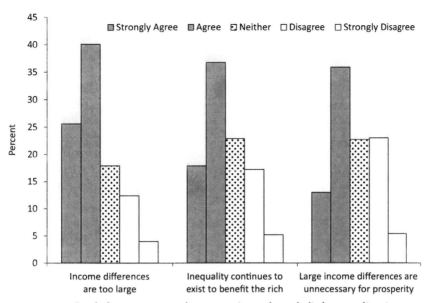

FIGURE 3.1. Pooled responses to three questions about beliefs regarding income inequality, 1987 to 2010. See Appendix Table A3.1 for question wording and response distributions by year. *Source:* 1987, 1996, 2000, 2008, 2010 General Social Survey and 1992 International Social Survey Program (weighted).

shift in knowledge from the 1970s when inequality was lower.[11] However, the time series of questions with the same wording across years in the GSS can help to identify whether American concerns are activated by changes in income inequality itself or by some other factor. If American attitudes toward inequality shift, this would suggest that there are conditions under which inequality is perceived as more or less acceptable, even if we cannot know for certain whether Americans' awareness of exact levels or changes in levels of inequality per se prompted such shifts. We return to these questions later in the chapter, including a review of the trend in media coverage (from Chapter 2) as an indicator of awareness of inequality.

We first take a brief look at what Americans think about income inequality for the period as a whole, shown in Figure 3.1. Responses to the three questions about income inequality leave little doubt that Americans are unsatisfied with the current state of affairs. The modal category for all three questions is agreement in the range of 36 to 40 percent: agreement that income differences are too large, inequality continues to exist because it benefits the rich and powerful, and large differences in income are unnecessary for prosperity. Because the modal response to the last

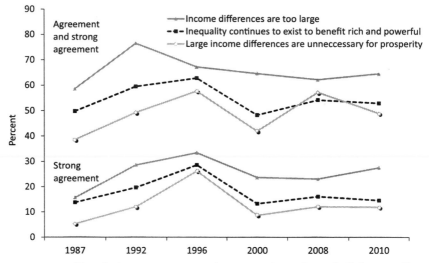

FIGURE 3.2. Trends in agreement to three questions about beliefs regarding income inequality, 1987 to 2010. See Appendix Table A3.1 for question wording and response distributions by year. *Source:* 1987, 1996, 2000, 2008, 2010 General Social Survey and 1992 International Social Survey Program (weighted).

question was originally "disagreement" that large differences in income are *necessary* for prosperity, the consistency of these results cannot be attributed solely to the tendency to agree to questions of this nature. Strong agreement to each question is also between 2.4 and 6.4 times larger than strong disagreement to the question (again, with strong agreement originally registered as strong disagreement for the "prosperity" question). Taken together, agreement and strong agreement ranges from 49 to 66 percent of all responses. Over the twenty-four–year period from 1987 to 2010, then, half to two-thirds of Americans accepted neither the current level of income inequality nor its stated rationale as a driver of economic prosperity that benefits all Americans and not just the rich and powerful.

Do American Beliefs Change over Time?

On average across years, sentiment regarding income inequality is not favorable, but this impression could be skewed by only one or two years of intense dissatisfaction. In most years, sentiment could be more neutral or even positive, in line with popular assumptions of a happily unequal America. As shown in Figure 3.2, agreement does range widely across years and questions, from 38 to 77 percent (combining strongly agree and agree responses) among the eighteen year-by-question combinations (three questions across six years). Despite this range, a 48 percent or greater share of respondents are in either agreement or strong agreement to the three questions in 16 of the 18 data points (4 of the 16 have between a 48 and 50 percent share). Agreement is also the modal category in all years, and typically by a long shot (see Appendix Table A3.1 for the full distribution of responses). Thus American concerns about income inequality fluctuate significantly, but they do so predominantly in the zone of disapproval.

Although the three questions are not asked in the same section of the survey, and their order varies across survey years, the shape of the fluctuations over time is nearly identical for two of the three and very similar for the third. There are three segments to the trend. The first and strongest is a large increase from the late 1980s to the 1990s in the share of respondents who agreed and especially strongly agreed to these questions. The percentage strongly agreeing that income differences are too large and continue to exist because they benefit the rich and powerful doubled from 16 to 33 and from 14 to 29, respectively, between 1987 and 1996. Even larger is the increase in those strongly agreeing that income differences are unnecessary for prosperity, which rose from 5 to 26 percent between 1987 and 1996. The mid-1990s is the peak in both strong agreement and total agreement for two of the three questions (the "benefits the rich" and "prosperity" questions). The peak in strong agreement is in 1996 for the "too large" question as well, but total agreement peaks earlier in 1992.

The second and third segments of the trend occur as concerns about inequality subside in the late 1990s and then either flatten out or stage a rebound at the end of the 2000s. For all three questions, strong agreement declines substantially from 1996 to 2000, and for this reason, total agreement decreases as well. There is an increase in agreement for all three questions, but it is less than the decline in strong agreement, and very small for two of the three questions. Although noteworthy, the drop in concerns about income inequality in 2000 does not fall below the baseline level in 1987; levels are much the same in 1987 and 2000 for two of the three questions ("prosperity" and "benefits the rich"). If we were to terminate the series in 2000, we would have a clear inverted U curve of concerns about income inequality. However, another uptick is apparent in the late 2000s. Strong agreement increases for all three questions from 2000 to 2010, as does total agreement for two of the three questions; for the third, total agreement stays the same. By the end of the twenty-four–year period, a larger share of Americans desires less income inequality than at the beginning of the period, but the difference is not as dramatic as it was in the 1990s. In short, concerns about inequality grew from 1987 to 2010, but not in a steadily upward direction as might be expected if mounting dissatisfaction simply corresponded to growing awareness and opposition to inequality as it escalated over the millennium decades.

But how much confidence should we have in these trends? Are they relatively minor, or the result of random noise? One important piece of evidence in answering these questions is that the puzzle of nonlinearity is not restricted to trends in agreement. Looking at the rest of the distribution of responses, we find the same pattern over time in strong *disagreement* to the questions, a measure of greater acceptance of income inequality (see again Appendix Table A3.1 for the full distribution of responses). Acceptance of inequality does not decrease as strong opposition peaks in 1996, as one would assume; rather, it increases as well. This is a sign of greater divergence in views about income inequality at the very moment that intense opposition is reaching its high-water mark, and it occurs for all three questions. Across all years, the highest level of strong disagreement occurred in 1996 accompanied by the highest level of strong agreement. The share of "neither" responses also dipped considerably in 1996 and was at or very near its lowest level for all three questions. Note that this nonlinear pattern of divergence implies that *mean* levels of opposition will be pulled more in the direction of tolerance than in other years, even though strong agreement was greatest in 1996, and at least three times as high as strong disagreement in that year. Nevertheless, average levels remain lowest (least tolerant) in 1996 for two of the three questions.[12]

The (1) distinctive distribution of attitudes toward inequality in 1996, (2) gradual increase in strong opposition for all three questions from 1987 to 1996, and (3) decline in strong opposition to all three questions in 2000 constitutes a trajectory and configuration of attitudes highly unlikely to be attributable to chance. In particular, the swell of opposition in the early and mid-1990s stands out as both a sign of significant shifts in beliefs about inequality over time and a puzzle that drives the rest of this chapter. Because "strong agreement" is the most internally valid and conservative measure of concerns about income inequality – excluding as it does the large number of those who may casually "agree" to the three questions – and because of the uneven pattern of polarization in responses across years that deflates mean levels of opposition in some years more than others, I focus on the trend in strong agreement over time. To be thorough, I will also refer at times to an analysis of an index of all three questions presented in Appendix Table A3.2, as well as to several other specifications and sensitivity analyses.[13] I turn now to a consideration of potential explanations of American concerns about income inequality over the twenty-four–year period from 1987 to 2010.

Why Do American Beliefs Change?

Although the nonlinear trend complicates the story of beliefs about income inequality, it has a scientific upside: it provides a unique trend line against which trends in other economic and political conditions can be compared. For example, if the business cycle affects beliefs about income inequality, beliefs should shift in the expected direction *at each inflection point* of the trend in unemployment, when the economy is expanding as well as when it is contracting. In addition to the business cycle, prior research pinpoints several other factors that may trigger a change in beliefs. These factors include economic or political phenomena that, like the business cycle, have well-defined trajectories over the period of rising inequality. In this section, two broad groups of factors are examined. I describe these briefly first and then in greater detail as the analyses unfold.

The first group is inspired by theoretical models in which particular political or economic segments of the population should be more inclined than other segments to oppose existing levels of inequality. Those individuals who identify as lower or working class, have below average education or income, or gravitate toward the liberal end of the political spectrum may feel especially aggrieved by rising inequality. If these groups expand or contract because of economic or political transformations, such as changes in the distribution of income or political partisanship, concerns about inequality may similarly expand or contract. The shift over time in concerns about inequality might therefore result from compositional shifts in the population: an increase or decrease in the size of certain groups relative to other groups that is significant enough to shift average opinion as well. Did compositional shifts take place in such a way as to explain both the ups and downs of American public opinion about income inequality? Or did they occur on a more minor scale, overtaken by countervailing tendencies among mainstream Americans? This first group of explanations is concerned, then, with the question of *who* cares about income inequality as a first cut at the question of *why* they care.

The second group of explanations is derived from theories of American exceptionalism and the American dream.[14] According to these well-known theories, Americans hold relatively undifferentiated attitudes toward inequality and, in comparative perspective, uniquely tolerant beliefs as well. Despite the universal appeal of American dream ideology, however, some more cautious observers acknowledge or even highlight an undertow of "ambivalence" in American attitudes. As I described in Chapter 1, among experts on the subject, this is perhaps the most widely held interpretation of American beliefs about income inequality. These same experts have also suggested that ambivalence can be provoked by conditions under which Americans as a whole are likely to disapprove of inequality.[15] I group these conditions into two categories: macroeconomic conditions (e.g., the business cycle) and norms of fairness related to income inequality itself. Such conditions, as I argued in earlier chapters, could dampen perceptions of widespread opportunity and dispose Americans to a more structural interpretation of unequal outcomes rather than one rooted in individual responsibility and just deserts. Each of these possibilities will require further definition, taken up in later sections. Because *who* cares about income inequality is an easier question to answer, I begin there.

Who Cares about Income Inequality?

The increase in opposition to inequality after the late 1980s could conceivably be due to an increase in the population share of one or more groups tending to dislike inequality, such as liberals or those with low incomes. In particular, it is often assumed that those situated at the bottom of the income distribution and most hurt by rising inequality will follow their self-interest and agitate for greater redistribution of income. To determine whether beliefs about inequality shifted over the 1987 to 2010 period because of these kinds of transformations, I estimate pooled cross-sectional binary logistic regression models with a set of year dummies and compositional covariates.[16] If shifts in composition fully or largely account for the shifts in attitudes, the dummy variable coefficients for 1992, 1996, 2000, 2008, and/or 2010 will shrink in size and no longer be statistically significant. We could then explain the trend in attitudes toward inequality in terms of group-specific experiences and ideologies. If the time trend is not accounted for by these shifts, we may infer that changes in opposition reflect more general, population-wide changes in attitudes.[17]

Compositional shifts in economic status, education, political orientation, and demographic factors are the most likely to induce attitudinal shifts. The first and perhaps most expected shift in attitudes would result from shifts in economic status. If large portions of the economy's growth go predominantly to those at the top end of the distribution, the incomes of those in the middle and below may stagnate or even decline. As many have shown, this has in fact occurred.[18] To the extent that workers associate trends in inequality with trends in their own compensation, self-interested opposition to the existing level of inequality may be higher among those who are falling relatively or absolutely behind.[19] If such groups comprise a growing share of the population, this will tilt the distribution of attitudes toward inequality in a more oppositional direction. After experimenting with several different measures and specifications of income, and finding little difference among them, I use a straightforward linear measure of family income. I also include a set of dummy variables for subjective class position, measured as lower, working, middle, and upper class.

A second potentially important compositional shift is in the educational makeup of the population. In addition to being a common indicator of economic status – the working class is frequently and increasingly defined as those without a college degree, for example – education can affect how individuals filter new information about changes in social and economic conditions.[20] Those with more schooling are generally less apt to blame rising inequality on individual deficiencies, such as low skills, and more inclined to perceive it as unfair. This may reflect a tendency toward social liberalism learned or accentuated in college, or it may reflect a tendency by those with access to more information to consider counter-hegemonic ideas and arguments about the economy and inequality.[21] Net of income, then, education may be positively associated with opposition to inequality. Educational attainment has risen over time, so this could perhaps be the cause of rising opposition to inequality.

The third compositional effect to consider is that of political orientation and ideology. Although previous research does not place a great deal of emphasis on political and ideological divisions in beliefs about inequality, I investigate them here because of a more recent interest in growing polarization in partisanship in the United States. Party orientation and political ideology are also important to consider because they often shape how information about politically salient issues and policy options is absorbed.[22] If liberals and/or Democrats increase their population share, this more liberal orientation might account for the increase over time in opposition to inequality. This may especially be the case in the election years of 1992, 1996, 2000, and 2008, when the Democratic presidential candidate won the popular vote. Alternatively,

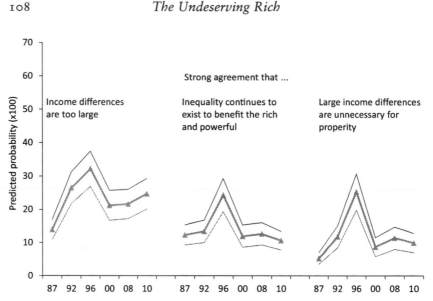

FIGURE 3.3. Adjusted trends in strong agreement to three questions about beliefs regarding income inequality, 1987 to 2010. Estimates are for a typical respondent net of controls for compositional shifts in a binary logistic regression model. Dashed line is 95 percent confidence interval. See Appendix for further details on the typical respondent, model specification, and question wording. *Source:* 1987, 1996, 2000, 2008, 2010 General Social Survey and 1992 International Social Survey Program.

a more conservative shift in the electorate might suggest that upward trends in opposition are less than they otherwise would be. Given heated debates over the extent and character of recent partisan realignments, especially among low income and non–college educated voters, I explore whether political orientation and ideology may have nonlinear effects by entering three dummy variables for party orientation and three for political ideology, as described further in the Appendix.[23]

Finally, a variety of demographic controls are included in all of the regression models presented below. These include age, age squared, gender, race, marital status, household size, presence of children, employment status, and region of the country. On the whole, these turn out to have little effect on the time trend and are not of strong substantive interest, so I do not discuss them further.[24]

The results of the compositional analysis are presented in Figure 3.3, which provides predicted probabilities of strong agreement for each year, after controlling for all of the factors mentioned above. To compare across years, the predicted levels of strong agreement are for a "typical" respondent with median, modal, or mean values on the independent variables depending on how they are measured.[25] The figure shows clearly that the trend in attitudes toward inequality is not explained by compositional shifts among economic, political, or demographic groups. The coefficients for the year dummies remain positive, statistically significant, and sizeable in magnitude. The predicted probability of strongly agreeing to the three questions for a typical respondent increased by a factor of 1.9, 1.1, and 2.3 from 1987 to 1992 for the "too large," "benefits the rich," and "prosperity" questions, respectively. From 1987 to 1996, the factor increases were considerably larger: 2.3, 2.0, and 3.9. Intense opposition to inequality was less likely in 2000 and 2008 than in 1996 but still significantly greater than in 1987 for two of the three questions. Thus the nonlinear trend in attitudes toward inequality is virtually unchanged by compositional shifts.[26]

Although the increase in opposition to inequality was broad-based, some groups were more or less likely than others to oppose inequality in all six years, and changes in the size of these groups do account for a small portion of the trend in opposition to inequality over the years of the study. By the same token, some explanations for the trend can be ruled out by the patterns of compositional shifts that did occur. Two findings in particular stand out.

First, taken as a whole, the indicators of economic status – family income, subjective social class, and education – have relatively weak and countervailing effects.[27] Although I experimented extensively with the functional form of both the income and education variables, neither was a consistently strong force in shaping beliefs about inequality across all years, all three questions, and all model specifications. Subjective social class is also uneven in its impact across years, mitigating concerns in some years by a shift toward higher class identities (as in 2010 relative to 1987) and amplifying concerns in other years by a shift toward lower class identities. For example, in 2008, the effects of an increase in mean income and a decrease in social class identification mostly cancel each other out, as higher incomes reduce concerns about inequality whereas lower class identities increase concerns.

A similar set of countervailing trends occurs with family income and education, affirming earlier suspicions that the two are not associated with opposition to inequality in precisely the same way. As expected, those with lower incomes are more likely to oppose inequality whereas those with higher incomes are more likely to embrace it. When education has its strongest impact, by contrast, those with more education are more likely to desire less inequality and to be skeptical of its usefulness in generating prosperity.[28] Thus education appears to reflect a socially liberal orientation toward inequality or access to specialized information, rather than objective economic status as such. Because of these differences in effects, increases in mean education and income over time tend to cancel each other out in their impact on attitudes about inequality.

Second, political ideology and partisanship are strongly and consistently associated with attitudes toward inequality in the expected directions: Democrats are significantly more inclined to oppose current levels of inequality than Republicans, and liberals are more inclined to do so than conservatives. But because the population became slightly less liberal and Democratic relative to 1987, particularly in the 1990s, shifts in ideological leanings were not conducive to the reactions we observe, and therefore the trend of increasing concerns becomes stronger when shifts in political ideology are accounted for (as shown in Appendix Tables A3.3 and A3.4). These results further suggest that increasing opposition to inequality was widespread, growing even in the face of a slight rightward ideological shift. In sum, a more educated population and one that at times expressed a lower class identity than in the late 1980s pushed beliefs in a more-critical direction, whereas rising incomes and more conservative politics pushed them in a more-tolerant direction.

Although the effects of income, education, and subjective social class were not robust across specifications, it is still possible that economically vulnerable groups dialed up their concerns about growing income inequality when the issue appears to have become more salient in the early and mid-1990s. That is, it could be that their *beliefs* changed more dramatically than their share of the population. This may be true of particular political and ideological groups as well, providing evidence of increasing political and ideological polarization over time. I look for such a shift in the intensity of concerns about inequality by examining changes in the size and significance of coefficients across years. This is measured by an interaction term between year and the factors that should affect beliefs about income inequality, which are the same ones explored in the compositional analysis: income, partisan identification, political ideology, education, and subjective social class. Figure 3.4 presents the factors for which I found a significant shift over time in their effect on the likelihood of respondents strongly agreeing that income differences are too large. The results are illustrated for the same typical respondent across years, as was done in Figure 3.3.

The shifts in beliefs over time presented in the figure reflect brief intervals of both polarization (by family income) and mainstream consensus

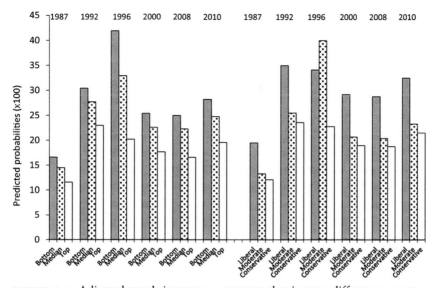

FIGURE 3.4. Adjusted trends in strong agreement that income differences are too large by income and political ideology, 1987 to 2010. Estimates are for a typical respondent net of controls for compositional shifts in a binary logistic regression model. Top is defined as 88th percentile; middle as 50th percentile; and bottom as 10th percentile. Ideological liberals and conservatives include multiple response categories. See Appendix for further details on the typical respondent, model specification, question wording, and variable definitions. *Source:* 1987, 1996, 2000, 2008, 2010 General Social Survey and 1992 International Social Survey Program.

(among moderates) occurring during the height of opposition to inequality in the mid-1990s. Beginning with the evidence of polarization, there are clear signs of a greater divergence in views between income groups at this time. Even though family income does not have a consistently strong effect across years on beliefs about inequality, it seems to make a significant difference during the height of intense opposition to inequality in the mid-1990s. The income effect becomes more negative in 1996 in predicting strong agreement to two of the three questions (the "too large" and "benefits the rich" questions), as well as in the index model. As indicated by the bars on the left side of Figure 3.4, this polarization was characterized by upper-income respondents objecting less to inequality in 1996 than they did in 1992, whereas respondents in the middle and at the bottom of the income distribution objected more (along with the average American).[29] Second, there is equally compelling evidence of growing mainstream skepticism of inequality in the early and especially middle part of the 1990s. As shown in the bars on the right side of Figure 3.4, moderates – accounting for some 40 percent of the sample – grew significantly more opposed to inequality in 1996. In fact, their opposition surpassed that of liberals: the share of moderates strongly agreeing that income differences are too large rose by 27 percentage points, from 13 to 40 percent, between 1987 and 1996, whereas it rose by only 14 percentage points for liberals, from 20 to 34 percent.[30]

In sum, the balance of evidence continues to point toward a unique concentration of concerns about income inequality among most Americans in the mid-1990s. This is illustrated by the unusual increase in opposition among moderates and confirmed by the ongoing significance of the time trend after the inclusion of compositional and behavioral controls. This is not to dismiss signs of polarization, however. Polarization among income groups is consistent with the spike in polarization in responses in 1996 that we observed in the earlier discussion of descriptive trends, where we found increases in strong agreement accompanied by increases in strong disagreement. In addition, polarization by family income is exactly what most political economy models would predict: a rational shift in preferences derived from one's position in the income distribution. Thus heightened concerns about inequality were widespread but by no means universal. This prompts the question of why polarization in views by income occurred in only one of the six years of our time series, not to mention the year of peak opposition. Those with a stake in rising inequality may have been reacting to the winds of change engulfing them if inequality was receiving both more attention and more negative attention from the press, as I showed in the previous chapter. I return to this possibility later in the discussion.

Macroeconomic Effects on Attitudinal Shifts

If the views of particular groups of Americans are not primarily responsible for the increase in concerns about income inequality in the early and middle 1990s, perhaps the shift in public opinion stems from a more general reason that cuts across social divides. If this is true, a leading candidate is the state of the national economy. In a review of public opinion on inequality, for example, Schlozman et al. write that "[a]ttitudes appear to vary somewhat with the business cycle.... Economic downturns tend to produce more egalitarian sentiments."[31] Similarly, one of the most influential theories of public opinion maintains that changes in policy preferences or "mood" are tethered to the rhythms of economic ups and downs. Even Americans who are expected to have little information or sophistication about economic matters stay abreast of the leading economic indicators. They lean more liberal when unemployment is high, favoring government action to mend the economy, and lean more conservative when inflation is high, favoring a brake on spending. Thus American views about income inequality, as for other policy-relevant issues, may move together across groups and in tandem with salient indicators of economic conditions.[32]

I evaluate this possibility in two ways. The first involves an analysis of another question from the GSS, and the second involves a comparison of the trend in beliefs about inequality with the trend in macroeconomic indicators such as the unemployment rate and the index of consumer sentiment. Because inflation has been relatively tame during the entire twenty-four–year period of this study, I do not examine it separately as an economic indicator, although it is likely to figure into responses to the GSS question that I do analyze.

This question asks whether "the way things are in America, people like me and my family have a good chance of improving our standard of living."[33] Nothing about the economic context is mentioned explicitly in the question, but it is probably safe to assume that the economic pulse of the nation contributes to a sense of either optimism or gloom about one's chances of moving up the ladder. This pulse would likely include the overall degree of joblessness and economic growth as well as the price of important consumption items such as a home or a college education for one's children. These items are central to living the American dream and yet may have become increasingly unaffordable over time even though inflation on average has been modest.[34] Thus this question is likely to capture reactions to both the consumption and production sides of the economy. Finally, we can view this question as a forward-looking measure of economic status, something that economists in particular argue is just as important in shaping beliefs about inequality and redistribution as current economic status.[35]

The responses to this question are shown in Figure 3.5, with the large markers indicating the years for which we have attitudinal data on income inequality. Although at any given point in time most Americans are optimistic about their chances for upward mobility, their degree of optimism fluctuates considerably throughout the 1990s and 2000s, and a substantial minority are pessimistic. On the one hand, nearly two-thirds of Americans on average either agree or strongly agree that "the way things are in America today, people like me and my family have a good chance of improving our standard of living." On the other hand, the proportion ranges from a little over half in 1992 to over three-quarters in 2000.

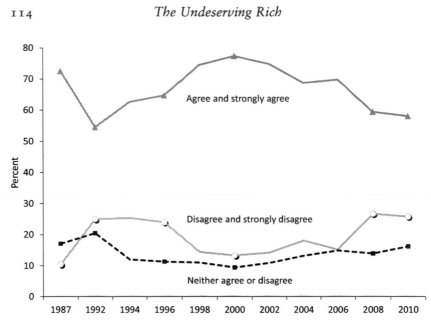

FIGURE 3.5. Trends in responses to a question about intragenerational upward mobility, 1987 to 2010. The wording of the question is: "The way things are in America, people like me and my family have a good chance of improving our standard of living – do you agree or disagree?" Markers indicate years of data on three questions about beliefs regarding income inequality. *Source:* 1972-2010 Cumulative File of the General Social Survey; 1987, 1996, 2000, 2008, 2010 General Social Survey; and 1992 International Social Survey Program (weighted).

Moreover, the share that strongly disagrees or disagrees is a quarter or more of Americans at four different time points. In fact, pessimism about future economic mobility increased during the same period that opposition to inequality did. The share of respondents strongly disagreeing or disagreeing more than doubled, from 10 percent in 1987 to 25 percent in 1992 and 24 percent in 1996; pessimism then declined to 13 percent in 2000 before peaking at 27 percent in 2008 and falling slightly to 24 percent in 2010. This roller coaster–like pattern seems to match at least some of the pattern of opposition to inequality. Does increasing pessimism about the future explain the rise in concerns about income inequality?

The two do appear to be quite strongly related to each other. Table 3.1 provides the average marginal effects of beliefs about upward mobility on beliefs about income inequality from the same models that produced Figure 3.3 (i.e., interaction effects are not included). The coefficients are negative, indicating that greater optimism results in a significantly lower

TABLE 3.1. *Adjusted Marginal Effects of Optimism about Intragenerational Upward Mobility on Three Questions about Beliefs Regarding Income Inequality, 1987 to 2010*

Strong Agreement that...	Income Differences are too Large	Inequality Continues to Exist to Benefit the Rich and Powerful	Large Income Differences are Unnecessary for Prosperity
Probability of strong agreement:[a]	.232	.140	.118
Average marginal effects:[b]			
Standard of living will improve[c]	−0.037 (.006)**	−0.038 (.005)**	−0.021 (.004)**

Notes: [a]For a typical respondent, who is female, white, married, employed, not living in the South, with one or more children; self-identifies as middle class, a Democrat or independent, and moderate; and has mean age, age squared, household size, education, family income, and year dummies. [b]Estimates are for a typical respondent from a binary logistic regression model with standard errors in parentheses. [c]Responses are 1=strongly disagree to 5=strongly agree. The within-sample mean is 3.6 and standard deviation is 1.04. See Figure 3.5 for question wording.

Source: 1987, 1996, 2000, 2008, 2010 General Social Survey and 1992 International Social Survey Program.

likelihood of strongly agreeing to each of the three questions about income inequality. For example, becoming more optimistic by only one point on a five-point scale decreases the likelihood of strongly agreeing that inequality is too large by about 16 percent (−.037/.232) and benefits the rich by about 27 percent (−.044/.14).

Moreover, returning to the analysis of compositional shifts discussed above (and presented in Appendix Table A3.4), we can see that part of the increase in the time trend of opposition to inequality is due to the increase in the share of mobility pessimists in the population. This is most evident in 1992, 2010, 2008, and 1996, in that order. In each of these years, as shown above in Figure 3.5, pessimism about upward mobility was at an elevated level. When this variable is entered into the compositional analysis, the year coefficients are significantly reduced, suggesting that the growth in mobility pessimism accounts for a substantial portion of the increase in opposition to inequality. However, the net time trend in opposition to inequality remains strong and significant.

If anything, by some measures the relationship between beliefs about upward mobility and income inequality appears no different or even weaker at the peaks of both opposition to income inequality (1996) and pessimism about upward mobility (2008). For example, concerns about income inequality did not intensify among mobility pessimists over the course of the 1990s, as they did, for instance, among moderates. Although the sense of pessimism was strong and significant in nearly all years as a predictor of all three questions about income inequality, the size of the effect in 1996 is not significantly different than in others years. Similarly, I explored whether beliefs about mobility and inequality were more highly correlated in 1996 than in other years after I controlled for factors that affect both kinds of beliefs (i.e., the compositional factors discussed above). The correlation was smallest in 2008 and 2010, followed by 1992 and 1996, the years in which concerns about both upward mobility and income inequality were greatest.[36] It is as though the two sentiments diverged at the very moments of their peak expressions.

Despite the inability of this particular question about social mobility to fully solve the puzzle of why beliefs about income inequality became so contested in the mid-1990s, we should not lose sight of the fact that it turned out to be a superior measure of economic well-being in helping to understand why Americans think about income inequality in the way they do. Whether we conceptualize it as a measure of optimism about the future or economic security in the present, it is the most important economic indicator of views of income inequality that we have encountered. This not only affirms the prominent place scholars give to social mobility and economic security as issues of paramount concern to Americans, it establishes income inequality as within their orbit. Rather than substituting one for the other, or prioritizing one over the other (i.e., equality of opportunity is a more important social norm than equality of outcomes), we must treat them as analytically distinct but related dimensions of beliefs about economic well-being in America, and better account for the various ways in which they interact with one another.

One step in that direction is to examine how beliefs about social mobility and income inequality correspond to trends in indicators of *actual* economic conditions. As we saw in Figure 3.5, there is an ebb and flow of optimism about living the American dream of upward mobility. This corresponded closely but not exactly to the trend in opposition to income inequality. What might distinguish the two series from each other? Thus far I have treated the mobility question as tapping an individual's sense of his or her *own* chances for upward mobility rather than a sense of opportunities for upward mobility *in society more generally*, which may track national economic conditions more tightly and offer a more pessimistic

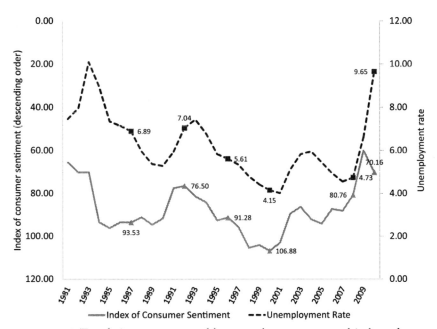

FIGURE 3.6. Trends in average monthly unemployment rate and index of consumer sentiment, April to March, 1981 to 2010. Markers indicate years of data on three questions about beliefs regarding income inequality. *Source:* Bureau of Labor Statistics and the University of Michigan Survey of Consumers.

view of the future (i.e., individuals tend to be more pessimistic about others than about themselves). Because the question is asking about "me and my family" and not society overall, my original interpretation is a plausible one, and the high levels of optimism suggest that individuals are indeed responding in this way. However, the question's reference to "*people like* me and my family" could prompt responses about opportunities more broadly, depending on the size and placement of one's reference group. This could in turn be closely tied to views about the national economy, helping to identify Americans' *perceptions* of the economy's ups and downs.

I therefore compare the trend in beliefs about upward mobility to the trend in unemployment and consumer sentiment, which is shown in Figure 3.6 (once again the triangle and square markers indicate the years of GSS attitudinal data on income inequality). The trend in unemployment and consumer sentiment is shown as a monthly average for the year prior to the typical period of data collection by the GSS. This way we can capture economic conditions leading right up to the time that the GSS is in the field.[37] Recall that mobility pessimism is high and comparable in size in 2008 (28 percent), 1992 (25 percent), and 1996 and 2010 (24 percent), and low and comparable in size in 1987 (11 percent) and 2000 (14 percent). Unemployment during our survey years is at its highest point by far in 2010 (9.65 percent), followed by 1992 (7.04) and 1987 (6.89). Unemployment is at its lowest point in 2000 (4.15) and 2008 (4.74), with 1996 (5.61) in between. The two series overlap to some degree in 1992 and 2010, signaling that high levels of unemployment are associated with high levels of pessimism about social mobility, and overlap again in 2000, when unemployment is low and optimism high.

Yet there are several discrepancies between the two series as well. First, pessimism about the future continues into 1994 and 1996 after unemployment rates begin to descend from their highs of the early 1990s (the recession ran from July 1990 to March 1991, but unemployment is a lagging indicator and did not peak until after the official notification of the recession's end). Feelings of economic insecurity about the future therefore persisted well after the recession, all the way into the mid-1990s. Second, and conversely, feelings of pronounced economic insecurity in 2008 *predated* the rise in unemployment during the latest recession, which officially began in December 2007 but was not announced until a year later. In other words, economic anxiety was high while the GSS was fielded in 2008 but before the recession was "called." Although this is not surprising given the considerable financial turmoil at the time – Bear Stearns collapsed in March 2008, and predictions of an impending recession were commonplace – it exposes the inadequacy of relying on business-cycle indicators alone in predicting perceptions of economic opportunity.

This discussion implies that beliefs about social mobility perform better than unemployment rates in tracking beliefs about income inequality, and indeed the discrepancies between trends in joblessness and beliefs about income inequality are substantial. First, if opposition to inequality was a result of poor macroeconomic performance, strong opposition should have been greatest by far in 2010 and higher in both 1987 and 1992 than in 1996, following the higher unemployment rates in those years relative to 1996. But that is not what we observe. Second, the unemployment rate cannot readily explain the nadir in opposition to inequality in 1987 relative to both 2000 and 2008, when unemployment was lower than in 1987. In particular, the year 2000 was one of the the most properous years in modern economic history and therefore should have led to the lowest level of concern about inequality in our data set, yet opposition to inequality is still greater in 2000 than in the beginning of our series in

1987. In sum, compared to what we would expect based on the business cycle, opposition to income inequality is lower in 1987 than it ought to be, and greater in 1996 and 2008 than it ought to be.

But perhaps we are looking in the wrong place, and it is consumer sentiment rather than macroeconomic performance that is the more proximate trigger of economic anxieties about the future and concerns about income inequality. As can be seen from a comparison of the two trends in Figure 3.6, the trend in consumer sentiment is similar but not identical to the trend in unemployment. The most notable difference is that consumer confidence is starting to slide in 2008 even though unemployment rates remain quite low. Consumer confidence is therefore more consistent with levels of anxiety about upward mobility and concerns about income inequality than joblessness rates are. Consumer confidence is also much lower in 1992 than in 1987 even though the unemployment rates are similar, which again is more consistent with greater economic anxiety and concerns about income inequality in 1992 relative to 1987. Still, 1996 remains in the middle of the pack of consumer sentiment, which is where its unemployment rate also sits. The degree of consumer sentiment in 1996 is more or less on par with that in 1987 and more confident than in 1992 and 2008, whereas beliefs about inequality are more critical.

In sum, although we do not have a long enough time series of beliefs about either social mobility or income inequality to more systematically test their association with indicators of macroeconomic performance and consumer confidence, the prima facie evidence suggests overwhelmingly that changes in both economic pessimism about future upward mobility and opposition to inequality cannot be attributed to the standard indicators of the business cycle. I provide additional evidence to this effect in the next chapter.

Effects of Inequality and the Media on Attitudinal Shifts
According to the evidence presented thus far, the shift in concerns about inequality cannot be fully or even mostly accounted for by changes in the composition of the population, the polarization of views among income and political groups, the business cycle, consumer sentiment, or optimism about upward mobility, although the latter comes the closest. I find that the trend in beliefs about income inequality is a trend of mass beliefs. Americans of all stripes viewed income inequality as more objectionable in the early and mid-1990s than at any other time between the late 1980s and 2010. Is there an explanation that can account for both the rise in concerns between the late 1980s and mid-1990s and the later decline

to levels that were still higher than in 1987? The final set of data that I harness to address this question is consistent with both increases and decreases in concerns about inequality during the era of rising inequality.

In this section I examine whether rising levels of income inequality may have themselves triggered heightened concerns. As the previous sections (and chapters) have shown, there are a number of reasons given for why Americans might care about income inequality, other than income inequality itself (e.g., the state of the national economy), as well as a number of reasons high levels of income inequality itself would be unwelcome.[38] Additionally, as discussed in the introduction to this chapter, several scholars have suggested that *more* permissive and tolerant social norms are one of the main reasons for the rise in income inequality in the United States.[39] Although these scholars may be referring primarily to the perspectives of politicians or affluent Americans, they may also be perplexed by the public's seeming lack of interest in the historic rise of income inequality (at least until the Occupy Wall Street movement in 2011). All of this is to say that the proposition that Americans may be both aware of changes in the distribution of income and capable of forming a critical opinion about it is by no means an obvious one.[40]

As I have now disproved many competing explanations, it is now time to explore the evidence in favor of the idea that Americans developed distinctively critical views about income inequality *as such* during the early and middle 1990s. My aim here is not to adjudicate among the wide range of reasons Americans would care about the issue, but to determine whether the trends we observe in actual levels of inequality and media coverage of inequality are consistent with the trend in concerns about inequality over the 1980s, 1990s, and 2000s. I provide a more elaborate test of some of these reasons in the following two chapters when I discuss the relationship between beliefs about income inequality and beliefs about economic opportunity and redistribution.

Numerous sources of data could be used to document the trend in wage inequality, earnings inequality, income inequality, or wealth inequality, to name just a few of the variants of economic inequality studied by social scientists. I begin with data from the Census Bureau. Over the full time period of this study, the Census measure of income inequality is probably the most commonly referenced in political discussions and debates and by journalists and scholars.[41] This is because information about inequality is disseminated by the Census Bureau in its annual Current Population Report on *Income, Poverty, and Health Insurance*, which is widely read by journalists covering economic issues. Because our objective is to

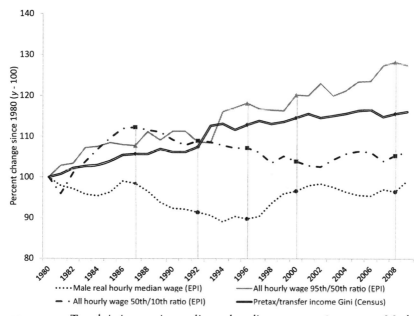

FIGURE 3.7. Trends in income inequality and median wages, 1980 to 2009. Markers indicate years of data on three questions about beliefs regarding income inequality. *Source:* Census Bureau Current Population Reports and the Economic Policy Institute (EPI).

examine the American public's response to changes in inequality, it makes sense to use this measure because this is the one with which they are most likely to be familiar.[42] Inequality is first measured with the Gini coefficient, which is the portion of total household income that would need to be redistributed from high-income households to low-income ones in order to have a completely equal distribution. The trends reported here are consistent with other widely used measures of inequality, and I also discuss alternative measures of inequality that follow different trajectories.[43]

Figure 3.7 shows the trend in income inequality from the beginning of its rise (1980) to the latest available year of data corresponding to our attitudinal data (2009). Once again the markers pinpoint the years for which there are attitudinal data on income inequality. Inequality, according to the Gini coefficient, increased between 1980 and the early 1990s, jumped between 1992 and 1993 because of a change in the Census Bureau's data collection methods, and then continued to increase in the late 1990s and the 2000s. Although not immediately apparent from the figure, the rate of increase was greater in the 1980s than in later years. This is generally true of other measures of inequality as well: all of them began to rise steeply in the 1970s and/or 1980s; most continued to rise for some part of the early to mid-1990s; then they followed different trajectories in the late 1990s. Some measures declined either throughout the 1990s or toward the late 1990s, such as the 50th/10th percentile ratio of hourly wages shown in Figure 3.7; others reached a plateau, such as the college/high school wage premium; and still others continued to increase steadily, such as the 95th/50th ratio of hourly wages, also shown in Figure 3.7. One of the most distinctive features of rising inequality is portrayed in Figure 3.7 as well: a decline in the median real hourly wages of men from 1980 to the latest year of available data in 2009. There is a notable fluctuation in this trend, however, with median real hourly male wages bottoming out in 1994. Does any part of these trends correspond to the trend in attitudes toward income inequality?

It is of course highly unlikely that most Americans have access to trend data on the complete set of measures of economic inequality. It is safe to assume, therefore, that Americans were unaware of the divergent trends in wages and inequality across different parts of the distribution documented in Figure 3.7. Instead, the most plausible hypothesis to derive from these data is that Americans were aware of the general trend toward increasing inequality or the general trend toward declining real wages (or both). Both of these trends are more likely to be newsworthy than any more-specific measure of income inequality targeted to one part of the distribution. And real wages are more readily accessible to Americans in the form of their own paychecks and consumption expenditures. I discuss the content of media coverage of income inequality and related issues in a moment (and in detail in the previous chapter), but here I want to reiterate the point that only two aspects of the trend in rising inequality are relatively uniform across measures and thus potentially accessible to the public: the rise in the 1980s and early 1990s and the continued high levels throughout the rest of the period.

In the most simplistic terms, then, income inequality rose and then did not decline. The period in the late 1990s when the feverish rise in overall income inequality finally broke also included the first sustained rise in real median earnings for men in a decade and a half. These two periods of the rise and then stabilization of income inequality correspond to the two periods in which concerns were growing until the mid-1990s and then declining at the end of the century to levels still above those in the late 1980s. Income inequality was leveling off but not returning to previous lows; thus attitudes could have remained elevated relative to the 1980s for this reason. If we are to confine ourselves to exact overlaps in trend lines, however, it is only the trend in median real hourly male wages that tracks attitudes about income inequality almost perfectly.

Among explanations considered thus far in this chapter, then, the continuing rise in inequality and the fall of men's real median wages up until the mid-1990s are the only ones that are consistent with the high-water mark of opposition to income inequality, and with a spike in pessimism about upward mobility. The increase in wages after this point is, furthermore, consistent with the decline in opposition and pessimism in the year 2000. Real male median wages began to decline again in the 2000s, also consistent with the rebound in concerns about income inequality and upward mobility.

Even if we assume minimal knowledge of trends in income inequality, however, there is still the question of how Americans acquired knowledge of these trends. For most, the main source of information about income inequality and average wages is likely to be media reports, although personal experience and networks could also supply the necessary clues at least about average compensation.[44] To supplement the data on trends in income inequality, I examined media coverage of economic inequality in the same years that trends in unemployment, consumer sentiment, income and wage inequality, and median wages are examined. Because the previous chapter provides an extensive analysis of media coverage, I present only a summary of the main findings here.[45]

As shown in Figure 3.8, the pattern of media coverage differs from the pattern of income inequality in important ways. The number of press stories dwindled to its lowest point in the late 1980s before the revival of coverage that overtakes the early and middle 1990s.[46] After the mid-1990s, media coverage of inequality drops off again as it did in the late 1980s. The trend of coverage presented in Figure 3.8 never returns to its previous peak, but it does pop up again toward the end of the 2000s. When other definitions of articles about inequality are used (as discussed in the previous chapter), there is also a blip in the calendar year 2000, though some of the increase is due to a more positive slant in tone.[47] Overall, coverage was higher in the 2000s than in the late 1980s.[48]

Thus there was little discussion of income inequality in the period for which we have attitudinal data on income inequality until the pronounced increase in the early and middle 1990s. After this point, the trend has another couple of peaks in the 2000s. The peaks and valleys after the mid-1990s run counter to the trend in actual income inequality, which according to most measures either remained at high levels or continued to increase. The peaks and valleys of media coverage after the

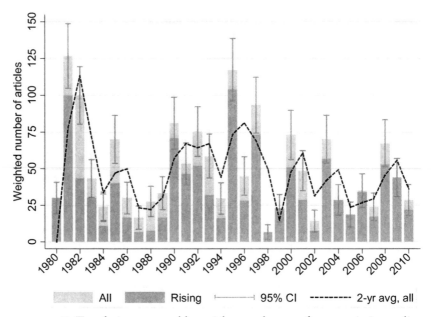

FIGURE 3.8. Trends in newsweekly articles on themes of economic inequality, April to March, 1981 to 2010. The 95 percent confidence intervals are based on a Poisson regression model. See the Appendices to Chapter 2 for further details on the coding of articles. *Source:* Readers Guide to Periodical Abstracts.

mid-1990s correspond more to the shifts over time in men's real median wages.

Given that both economic inequality and media coverage of economic inequality increased between 1987 and 1996, the increase in Americans' concerns about inequality over this period is consistent with an increase in concerns about the rise in inequality itself, as portrayed by the media. In later years, inequality continued to rise or remain at high levels but media coverage fluctuated, and at some points even became more positive, as in the year 2000. Public opposition to inequality declined after the mid-1990s, consistent with the decline in media coverage. But opposition to inequality remained higher than in 1987, consistent with higher levels of inequality and media coverage than in the late 1980s (as well as lower median male wages). Based on the in-depth content analysis of media coverage presented in the previous chapter, as well as the rest of the results from this chapter, I further consider in the next and concluding section the reasons media attention and public opinion about inequality rose and declined when they did.

The Un/Deserving Rich

Not only are levels of concern about income inequality high among Americans – half to two-thirds agree or strongly agree to the three questions about income inequality – but there is a clear trend toward greater concern about income inequality from the late 1980s (1987) to the mid-1990s (1996). Strong opposition doubled or quadrupled over this period. This was followed by a falloff in concern by the end of the 1990s (2000) and a resurgence in the late 2000s (2008 and 2010). For two of the three inequality questions, concern about inequality was still significantly greater throughout the 2000s than in 1987. This nonlinear trend is strong in the face of shifts in the income and education distributions, pessimism about upward mobility, the demographic composition of the population, the business cycle, consumer sentiment, and ideological orientations toward somewhat greater conservatism in the 1990s.[49] Concerns about inequality were widespread throughout the mainstream of America and peaked at a time when economic inequality was emerging as a distinct social and economic issue of national importance, as indicated by media coverage.

When taken together, the findings from previous sections paint a new picture of the context and character of opposition to inequality. The increase from 1992 to 1996 in strong agreement was much greater for the "prosperity" and "benefits the rich" questions than it was for the "too large" question. In particular, the increase for the "prosperity" question is much larger than for the other two questions, and yet bias toward opposition in the wording of this question is less than for the other two questions. This suggests that concern was more focused on the fairness and functionality of income inequality than on the level of inequality per se. The correlation of beliefs about inequality and opportunities for upward mobility are also no stronger in 1996, indicating that individual concerns about economic conditions and future opportunities gave way to more general "sociotropic" concerns about inequality and opportunity at a societal level. Even the greater degree of income polarization in responses to the questions in 1996, accompanied by a smaller showing of "neither" responses, suggests something unusual about this period. Amid a broad-based trend toward increasing opposition – intensifying among mainstream groups such as ideological moderates – those at the top with an economic stake in rising inequality reacted by defending its fairness. Importantly, there is no evidence that inequality had become an issue shaped by polarized elites, either in the public opinion data examined here or in the content analysis of media coverage examined in the previous chapter.[50]

It is especially noteworthy that at this time Americans did not appear to be conflating inequality with troubles in the economy. The high degree of intense opposition – as well as pessimism about upward mobility – occurred in a year in which macroeconomic indicators were actually better than in the two previous years of attitudinal data (i.e., 1987 and 1992). Despite the rosier economic outlook in the mid-1990s, the media analysis demonstrates that journalists and politicians were attuned to the issue of inequality. The message was that the economy was growing, but it was growing inequitably. This likely resulted in a general knowledge of the *consequences* of rising inequality for the economic well-being of the majority of Americans rather than a detailed knowledge of or concern with its *level*. Certainly, media coverage harped more on the consequences of rising inequality than on the fairness of inequality in and of itself. A space was opened up to question whether inequality was necessary for widespread prosperity or whether it unfairly benefited the rich at the expense of ordinary Americans in a zero-sum fashion, making the rich undeserving of their riches. Thus Americans were not misperceiving the economic fundamentals of the time but responding to the skewed nature of economic growth.[51]

By the end of the 1990s, much had changed. Economic conditions improved for the average American and for those at the bottom. Although the business cycle does not correspond exactly to the observed trend in opposition to income inequality, a broader notion of economic opportunity probably played an important role at this time as unemployment was at its lowest level since the late 1960s, some measures of inequality declined or leveled off, median male wages increased, and celebrations of the new high-tech economy and "charismatic CEO's" (i.e., the deserving rich) were ubiquitous.[52] The fruits of economic restructuring were finally "lifting all boats," even if some boats were lifted much higher than others. Perhaps not surprisingly, media coverage of *rising* inequality declined in the year 2000 despite its being a presidential election year and despite ongoing increases in the concentration of income at the top. In fact there were now a number of stories in which proponents championed the benefits (i.e., growth) of income inequality. Views of inequality bounced back to a more tolerant level as Americans maintained a desire for less inequality (more so than in 1987) but were not as concerned about the fairness or functionality of inequality as they had been earlier in the decade.[53]

We now know that the economic euphoria at the turn of the twenty-first century was short-lived. With two data points within just two years at the end of the 2000s, and many important events over the decade, we cannot say as much about present views of income inequality as we would like, but the lessons of the 1990s are instructive. On the one hand, income inequality continued to grow in the 2000s, pessimism about upward mobility was at a high point in our time series in 2008, unemployment was at its unambiguous high point in 2010, and consumer confidence was at its lowest level in 2010. Yet none of these led to higher opposition to inequality (relative to the previous peak in the mid-1990s).

On the other hand, a contentious political environment dovetailed with the severe economic recession, propelling a wide range of issues into the limelight. Inequality-related issues were getting renewed coverage by the media toward the end of the 2000s, but such coverage was no greater than in the early and middle 1990s. Most important, based on the findings from the 1990s, compositional shifts, recessionary periods, presidential elections, and economic anxiety about the future are not sufficient to produce intense concerns about inequality. Inequality must itself be implicated in the economic doldrums most Americans perceive either in their own lives or among the broader population, even, or perhaps especially, during periods of economic expansion when expectations for widespread recovery are primed. This did not occur in either 2008 or 2010, much to the surprise of many. Now that the issue is gaining more concentrated attention, as the recovery sputters and expectations rise much as in the mid-1990s, and the Occupy Wall Street movement catches up to long-standing public opposition to inequality, concerns may climb significantly again in 2012 (when the GSS fielded another round of the inequality questions).

Thus Americans care most about income inequality when it becomes a societal problem. Until now, social scientists have been unable to test this possibility. In earlier decades, income inequality was stable or even declining, and we had no consistent time series data on attitudes specifically about income inequality. At that time, the emphasis was on the ambivalence and inconsistency of beliefs about income inequality as compared to beliefs about opportunity and government redistribution, as I discussed in detail in Chapter 1. Desires for less income inequality seemed to sit uneasily, and weakly, alongside views of opportunity as widely available and limited support for government redistribution of income. Unfortunately, the tendency to focus only on these aspects of American public opinion persists strongly today.

Yet in the more recent period for which we have time series data, it is now possible to appreciate the historical specificity of this characterization of American beliefs. I evaluated beliefs about income inequality under quite different scenarios, yielding different views of Americans' concerns about inequality: relative concern when growth is perceived as inequitable, such as during the early and middle 1990s when the economy was expanding only for the affluent, and relative tolerance when growth is perceived as equitable, such as during the late 1980s and the late 1990s. Because growth was equitable in the postwar years up until the 1970s and, most likely, perceived to be equitable throughout the 1980s before the issue of rising inequality gained public attention, the dominant *theoretical* views of ambivalence and tolerance were consistent with distributive outcomes during a pivotal period of contemporary American history. This has probably had a lasting but misleading effect on our understanding of core American norms of equality. Much has changed, but whether the 1990s will ultimately be considered unique will depend not only on whether economic inequality continues to grow, which is likely, but on whether it gains the kind of critical attention about its negative consequences that it did during the early and middle 1990s, and appears to have gained in the last few years.

Appendix

Sample Definitions and Weights

The General Social Survey is a full probability, personal-interview survey of the United States population. Blacks were oversampled in 1987, and the oversampled cases were dropped from the analysis. All descriptive statistics reported in these chapters use weighted data (the GSS weighting variable *wtssall* for all years and the ISSP weighting variable *v176* for the 1992 data and *weight* for the 2010 panel data). The 2008 data consist of the cross-section sample only and not the panel sample. The 2010 sample is a re-interview of the 2008 cross-section.

Survey Question Bias

The questions are framed in two different ways so that agreement bias and measurement error do not run in the same direction for all three questions (the first two are toward opposition, the third toward tolerance of inequality). The focus on changes over time also minimizes bias because absolute levels of opposition/support are less important. Finally, the "too large" question is not asked in sequence with the "benefits the rich" and "prosperity" questions, limiting the problem of priming from one question to the next. In 1987, 1992, and 2000, the "benefits the rich" and "prosperity" questions are asked in sequence and in a prior section than the "too large" question. In 1996 and 2008, the questions are asked in the order presented in the text (i.e., "too large," "benefits the rich," and "prosperity") with one additional question on the government's role in reducing income differences inserted between the first question and the second and third questions. In 2010, the "too large" question appears in a section prior to the "benefits the rich" and "prosperity" questions.

Statistical Models of Descriptive Trends

For all three questions, 1996 has the greatest variance in responses. Polarization as measured by negative values of kurtosis (kurtosis value − 3) is greatest in 1996 for the "prosperity" and "too large" questions (although similar to levels of polarization in 1987 and 2010 for the "too large" question), and about the same in all years for the "benefits the rich" question. Heteroskedastic ordered logistic models also show that the residual standard deviation of responses is significantly greater in 1996 for all three questions (using the *oglm* command from Williams, 2006).

Binary logistic regressions with strong disagreement or strong agreement as the outcome (equal to 1) show that these responses are significantly greater in 1996 than in all other years for all three questions. When "neither" is the outcome, responses are significantly lower in 1996 than in all other years for the "prosperity" and "benefits the rich" questions. For the "too large" question, "neither" responses are lowest in both 1992 and 1996.

Ordered logistic regressions further show that opposition to inequality was significantly higher in 1996 than in all other years for the "prosperity" and "benefits the rich" questions. Because the "too large" question is affected by polarization of responses in 1996 to a greater degree than the other questions, the ordered logistic regression shows that opposition was highest in 1992, followed by 1996, although it is the reverse once the greater variance of responses in 1996 is controlled in a heteroskedastic ordered logistic model. The index regression shows peak levels of opposition in 1992 and 1996 that are equivalent and higher than in the other years.

Variables and Definitions

The covariates include all theoretically relevant variables that were available in all six years as well as demographic controls. Many other potentially relevant variables that are excluded in these analyses were not found to be associated with attitudes about income inequality (e.g., religion, job instability, union status, and mobility status relative to parents). Included variables are demographic characteristics (e.g., gender, race, age, age squared, family status, residential location, etc.), direct or objective economic status (i.e., education and family income), indirect or subjective economic status (i.e., subjective class identification and chances for upward mobility), and political orientation and ideology (i.e., partisan identification and political ideology). A list of all dependent and independent variables, along with descriptive statistics, is provided in Appendix Table A3.3.

Family income is top coded at different values across survey years by the GSS. The top code with the largest share of high-income respondents is in 1996, capturing 12.85 percent of the analysis sample. The other years were recoded to have top codes with similar shares of the high-income population. Analyses were run both with the consistent top codes and without them, and the results were similar.

Education is measured in ordinal fashion, with five categories ranging from less than high school to high school degree, some college, college degree, and postgraduate degree.

"Conservatives" includes slightly conservative, conservative, and strongly conservative; "Moderates" includes only moderates; and "Liberals" includes strong liberals, liberals, and slight liberals. Partisan differences were less straightforward to disaggregate given the ambiguous nature of the "other party" category. I experimented with several breakdowns and found the greatest overall parsimony with the following grouping: "Republican" includes strong Republicans, Republicans, and independents/near Republicans; "Democrats and Independents" includes independents, independents/near Democrats, and Democrats; "Strong Democrats and Other Party" includes only these two groups, as other party members tended to have beliefs similar to strong Democrats.

Analytic Models and the Typical Respondent

The preferred model is a binary logistic regression with "strongly agree" coded as one and all other responses coded as zero. The proportionate changes in responses over time vary for each of the five categories (strongly agree, agree, neither, disagree, and strongly disagree), suggesting that the parallel regressions assumption of an ordered logistic regression is too restrictive. This is the case with the effect of the time dummies on the outcome variables considered here (Long and Freese 2003; Williams 2006). I also estimated an OLS regression of an index that adds the full responses of the three inequality questions together. These results are provided in the Appendix Table A3.2.

To compare across years, the predicted levels of strong agreement are often presented for a "typical" respondent with median, modal, or mean values on the independent variables depending on how they are measured. The composition is fixed with median or modal values for categorical variables and means for ordinal variables: female, white, married, employed, not living in the South, self-identified as middle class, a Democrat or independent, moderate, with one or more children, and mean age, age squared, household size, education, and family income.

TABLE A3.1. *Marginal Distributions of Three Questions about Beliefs Regarding Income Inequality by Year, 1987 to 2010*

Questions		Percent Distribution (weighted)					
		1987	1992	1996	2000	2008	2010
Differences in	Strongly agree (1)	15.7	28.6	33.4	23.7	23.1	27.5
income in	Agree	42.8	47.9	33.8	40.9	39.1	37.1
America are	Neither	22.5	11.7	12.7	22.9	21.2	18.0
too large	Disagree	16.1	10.2	11.9	9.2	13.2	13.7
(INCGAP).	Strongly disagree (5)	2.9	1.7	8.2	3.4	3.4	3.8
	Mean	2.48	2.08	2.28	2.28	2.35	2.29
Large differences	Strongly agree (1)	5.3	12.1	26.2	8.7	12.1	11.9
in income are	Agree	33.3	37.2	31.5	33.3	45.1	37.1
unnecessary	Neither	29.5	23.9	13.0	29.7	19.2	21.8
for America's	Disagree	26.0	21.4	21.1	23.2	20.7	25.0
prosperity	Strongly disagree (5)	5.9	5.4	8.2	5.1	3.0	4.3
(INEQUAL5).*	Mean	2.94	2.71	2.53	2.83	2.57	2.73
Inequality	Strongly agree (1)	13.8	19.7	28.6	13.3	16.1	14.6
continues to	Agree	36.0	39.8	34.3	35.0	38.1	38.2
exist because it	Neither	27.0	18.1	14.3	28.6	22.2	27.5
benefits the	Disagree	19.3	18.3	14.2	18.0	18.1	15.9
rich and	Strongly disagree (5)	3.9	4.1	8.7	5.0	5.5	3.7
powerful	Mean	2.64	2.47	2.40	2.66	2.59	2.56
(INEQUAL3).							

* This question's wording was inverted so that strong agreement indicates opposition to inequality.
Source: 1987, 1996, 2000, 2008, 2010 General Social Survey and 1992 International Social Survey Program.

TABLE A3.2. *Linear Regression Effects on an Additive Index of Three Questions about Beliefs Regarding Income Inequality, 1987 to 2010*

	Three Question Index	
	Model 1	Model 2
Constant	1.400**	1.368**
	(0.180)	(0.180)
1992	0.369**	0.368**
	(0.052)	(0.052)
1996	0.404**	0.572**
	(0.052)	(0.098)
2000	0.195**	0.193**
	(0.055)	(0.054)
2008	0.248**	0.245**
	(0.051)	(0.051)
2010	0.225**	0.219**
	(0.051)	(0.051)
Family Income	−0.030**	−0.024**
	(0.006)	(0.006)
Education	0.086**	0.085**
	(0.014)	(0.014)
Other Demographic Controls	YES	YES
Subjective Class (Lower Class)		
Working Class	−0.084	−0.074
	(0.074)	(0.074)
Middle Class	−0.241**	−0.229**
	(0.077)	(0.077)
Upper Class	−0.418**	−0.402**
	(0.108)	(0.108)
Standard of Living Will Improve	−0.198**	−0.201**
(Strongly Disagree=1 to Strongly Agree=5)	(0.015)	(0.015)
Party Identification		
(Strong Democrats and Other Party)		
Democrats and Independents	−0.224**	−0.227**
	(0.044)	(0.044)
Republicans	−0.606**	−0.612**
	(0.049)	(0.049)
Ideology (Liberals)		
Moderates	−0.189**	−0.224**
	(0.040)	(0.042)
Conservatives	−0.465**	−0.462**
	(0.043)	(0.043)

	Three Question Index	
	Model 1	Model 2
Year Interactions		
Family Income * 1996		−0.048**
		(0.014)
Moderates * 1996		0.214*
		(0.089)
N	4,741	4,741
Adjusted *R*²	0.1759	0.1792

Notes: See Appendix text and Table A3.3 for variable definitions. Coefficients are unstandardized and standard errors are in parentheses. Probability levels are indicated by **$p <$ $= .01$; *$p < = .05$; †$p < = .10$.

Source: 1987, 1996, 2000, 2008, 2010 General Social Survey and 1992 International Social Survey Program.

TABLE A3.3. *Coding and Sample Means for Dependent and Independent Variables*

	1987	1992	1996	2000	2008	2010
Analysis Sample Means						
Three Question Index[a] (−3 to 3)	0.46	0.89	0.91	0.64	0.82	0.75
Too Large[b] (SA=1)	0.15	0.29	0.34	0.23	0.27	0.29
Benefits[b] (SA=1)	0.14	0.17	0.28	0.14	0.18	0.16
Prosperity[b] (SA=1)	0.06	0.14	0.29	0.10	0.14	0.13
Sex (Male=1, Female=2)	1.53	1.54	1.53	1.55	1.53	1.52
Race (White=1)	0.86	0.84	0.80	0.80	0.72	0.73
Age[c]	43.7	44.6	43.4	44.3	47.2	48.2
Marital Status (married=1)	0.58	0.59	0.52	0.50	0.49	0.51
HH Size	2.70	2.78	2.51	2.56	2.48	2.71
Children (any under 18 yrs=1)	0.39	0.42	0.39	0.37	0.33	0.34
South (=1)	0.32	0.29	0.33	0.35	0.36	0.35
Employed (=1)	0.68	0.66	0.70	0.67	0.64	0.61
Family Income (2008$/10⁴)	5.25	5.16	5.26	5.43	5.72	5.75

(continued)

The Undeserving Rich

TABLE A3.3 *(continued)*

	1987	1992	1996	2000	2008	2010
Education (1–5, LHS to COL+)	2.62	2.85	2.89	2.85	2.86	2.96
Lower Class	0.05	0.04	0.06	0.04	0.08	0.04
Working Class	0.42	0.40	0.44	0.45	0.49	0.35
Middle Class	0.49	0.54	0.46	0.46	0.40	0.53
Upper Class	0.04	0.02	0.04	0.05	0.04	0.08
Liberal[d]	0.30	0.24	0.24	0.27	0.28	0.29
Moderate[d]	0.37	0.35	0.40	0.37	0.38	0.35
Conservative[d]	0.33	0.41	0.36	0.36	0.34	0.36
Strong Democrat[e]	0.18	0.16	0.15	0.17	0.23	0.20
Democrat/Independent[e]	0.43	0.43	0.46	0.46	0.42	0.46
Republican[e]	0.39	0.41	0.39	0.38	0.35	0.34
Upward Mobility (1–5, 1=SD)[f]	3.80	3.38	3.56	3.85	3.43	3.45
N	1014	773	714	613	825	842

Notes: [a]The index is constructed as follows: responses to each inequality question are coded as 1 = strongly agree, 0.5 = agree, 0 = neither, −0.5 = disagree, and −1 = strongly disagree; the three question index was then calculated by adding the responses to all three inequality questions and ranges from −3 to +3. [b]Binary outcome variables for analysis with strong agreement = 1 and all other response categories = 0. [c]Age squared is also included in all regressions. [d]"Conservatives" includes slightly conservative, conservative, and strongly conservative; "Moderates" includes only moderates; and "Liberals" includes strong liberals, liberals, and slight liberals. [e]"Republican" includes strong Republicans, Republicans, and independents/near Republicans; "Democrats and Independents" includes independents, independents/near Democrats, and Democrats; "Strong Democrats and Other Party" includes strong Democrats and other party, [f]Upward mobility is based on a question about whether the standard of living of one's family will improve (GOODLIFE), with 1 = strongly disagree and 5 = strongly agree. See Figure 3.5 for question wording and response distributions.

Source: 1987, 1996, 2000, 2008, 2010 General Social Survey and 1992 International Social Survey Program.

TABLE A3.4. *Year Effects on Three Questions about Beliefs Regarding Income Inequality, 1987 to 2010*[a]

1987 (omitted)	1992	1996	2000	2008	2010
OLS regression of index of three inequality questions as outcome:[b]					
Year dummies (R^2=.02)	0.43	0.45	0.18	0.36	0.30
	(.056)	(.057)	(.059)	(.054)	(.054)
+ Demographics (R^2=.03)	0.42	0.43	0.16	0.32	0.27
+ Family income (R^2=.05)	0.42	0.44	0.18	0.36	0.30
+ Social class (R^2=.05)	0.43	0.43	0.18	0.33	0.32
+ Education (R^2=.06)	0.40	0.41	0.16	0.30	0.29
+ Politics (R^2=.15)	0.45	0.45	0.19	0.32	0.30
+ Mobility (R^2=.18)	0.37	0.40	0.19	0.25	0.23
	(.052)	(.052)	(.055)	(.051)	(.051)
OLS regression of index of three inequality questions as outcome (weighted):[b]					
Year dummies (R^2=.02)	0.43	0.44	0.11	0.30	0.25
	(.057)	(.063)	(.059)	(.059)	(.057)
+ Demographics (R^2=.03)	0.43	0.43	0.10	0.27	0.22
+ Family income (R^2=.05)	0.42	0.44	0.12	0.31	0.26
+ Social class (R^2=.05)	0.43	0.43	0.12	0.28	0.27
+ Education (R^2=.06)	0.41	0.41	0.10	0.26	0.25
+ Politics (R^2=.15)	0.44	0.45	0.13	0.28	0.27
+ Mobility (R^2=.18)	0.36	0.40	0.14	0.21	0.19
	(.054)	(.060)	(.056)	(.057)	(.054)
Y-standardized coefficients from binary logistic regression with strong agreement to the "too large" question as outcome:					
Year dummies (R^2=.02)	0.45	0.57	0.28	0.39	0.45
+ Demographics (R^2=.04)	0.44	0.56	0.25	0.32	0.37
+ Family income (R^2=.04)	0.43	0.56	0.27	0.35	0.40
+ Social class (R^2=.05)	0.45	0.56	0.27	0.32	0.41
+ Education (R^2=.05)	0.44	0.54	0.26	0.31	0.39
+ Politics (R^2=.08)	0.47	0.58	0.28	0.32	0.41
+ Mobility (R^2=.09)	0.42	0.55	0.28	0.27	0.36
Average marginal effects (discrete change from 1987) from binary logistic regression with strong agreement to the "too large" question as outcome:					
Year dummies (R^2=.02)	0.17	0.22	0.10	0.15	0.17
	(.026)	(.026)	(.028)	(.025)	(.025)
+ Demographics (R^2=.04)	0.17	0.22	0.09	0.12	0.14

(*continued*)

TABLE A3.4 (*continued*)

1987 (omitted)	1992	1996	2000	2008	2010
+ Family income (R^2=.04)	0.16	0.22	0.10	0.13	0.15
+ Social class (R^2=.05)	0.17	0.22	0.10	0.12	0.15
+ Education (R^2=.05)	0.16	0.21	0.09	0.11	0.15
+ Politics (R^2=.08)	0.18	0.22	0.10	0.12	0.15
+ Mobility (R^2=.09)	0.16	0.21	0.10	0.10	0.13
	(.025)	(.025)	(.026)	(.024)	(.024)

Average marginal effects from heteroskedastic ordered logistic regression with full response distribution to "too large" question as outcome:[c]

Year dummies (R^2=.01)	0.14	0.19	0.06	0.07	0.12
	(.015)	(.022)	(.016)	(.015)	(.018)
+ Demographics (R^2=.02)	0.13	0.19	0.06	0.06	0.10
+ Family income (R^2=.03)	0.13	0.19	0.06	0.07	0.11
+ Social class (R^2=.03)	0.13	0.18	0.06	0.06	0.12
+ Education (R^2=.03)	0.13	0.18	0.06	0.06	0.11
+ Politics (R^2=.05)	0.14	0.18	0.07	0.06	0.11
+ Mobility (R^2=.06)	0.13	0.17	0.07	0.05	0.09
	(.014)	(.020)	(.015)	(.014)	(.017)

Notes: [a]All variables are discussed in the Appendix and descriptive statistics are provided in Appendix Table A3.3. Standard errors are in parentheses. [b]Full range of responses to each of the three questions about beliefs regarding income inequality are coded from −1 to +1 and are added together to create the index, which ranges from −3 to +3. [c]Variance components of year dummies for 1996 and 2010 were significant and entered in the variance equation. Both also failed the Brant test of parallel slopes.
Source: 1987, 1996, 2000, 2008, 2010 General Social Survey and 1992 International Social Survey Program. N=4,741.

4

Why Do Americans Care about Income Inequality?

The Role of Opportunity

Americans are not satisfied with existing levels of income inequality, and their concerns have intensified since the 1980s. In trying to account for why Americans have these concerns and why they have grown, the previous chapter examined a number of explanations that social scientists think should be important. Political economists might expect, for example, that views about income inequality will be divided along income lines, with those at the bottom becoming increasingly angry about the growing concentration of income among the richest Americans. Political economists might also expect growing political polarization between Democrats and Republicans to fuel this anger, so that the rise and fall of concerns about inequality will mimic the rise and fall of Democratic politicians (especially presidents), who are the more likely advocates of reducing inequality. Finally, some may think that what Americans fundamentally care about is economic growth, so that when Americans express concerns about income inequality, they are really expressing concerns about the state of the national economy. Although I found some support for each of these compelling explanations, the evidence was relatively weak, and the trend in concerns about income inequality among the population as a whole remained strong.

This chapter explores an alternative explanation for why Americans care about income inequality: they view it as an indicator of unfairly restricted opportunities. On the one hand, this explanation appears obvious. It follows naturally from the theory that Americans (and their counterparts in many advanced industrial nations) accept inequality as long as opportunity is widely available. If Americans are dissatisfied with existing levels of inequality, it must be because they perceive cracks in the facade of equal opportunity.[1] On the other hand, most commentators and scholars find that, in fact, Americans retain a great deal of faith in the availability of opportunities to get ahead, even amid growing inequality.[2] Based on such findings, there might seem little reason to ponder whether, let alone why, Americans care about inequality. Moreover, even if a different sort of evidence could reveal a greater degree of skepticism about opportunity in America, it would not necessarily help in proving the hypothesis I explore in this chapter, namely, that concerns about inequality flare up not only from concerns about restricted opportunities but from concerns that *inequality itself is restricting opportunities.*

But perhaps the most important reason to explore these matters in greater detail is that there has been little empirical analysis of any persuasion on the connection between Americans' beliefs about economic inequality and their beliefs about economic opportunity. This is a consequence of several factors: a strong and understandable interest in cross-country comparative analysis, where researchers have been more intrigued by aggregate differences in support for redistribution across nations than in variation in beliefs *among* individual Americans;[3] the lack of data on beliefs about both income inequality and opportunity in the same surveys; and, related, a tendency to infer beliefs of one kind (e.g., about inequality) from beliefs of a different kind (e.g., about opportunity) when data are sparse, an inclination I discussed in Chapter 3. Because beliefs about inequality are so often inferred from beliefs about opportunity, I argued there for the need to examine beliefs about inequality on their own terms. Having done that, it is now time to consider the two sets of beliefs in concert.

I begin in the next section with a conceptual discussion of how Americans think about the meaning of equal opportunity. This conceptual discussion is necessary for two reasons. First, as John Roemer's lucid explication of equal opportunity makes clear, "opportunity is a vague thing."[4] For my purposes, then, it will be imperative to consider a wide range of common definitions of opportunity in order to determine whether beliefs about inequality are more attuned to some interpretations than to others. Although scholars have sought to probe deeper into American beliefs about inequality and opportunity before, they have tended to focus on the complexities stemming from beliefs about racial and gender discrimination.[5] I consider these, too, but extend the discussion to include unequal treatment according to family background, social connections, contributions to society, and job performance, among other possible sources and meanings of unequal opportunities. Because of this book's focus on income inequality, I devote greater attention to how opportunity is perceived to be allotted to individuals of different economic status rather than different racial, ethnic, gender, or national backgrounds, although these will come into play at times as well. Drawing from popular discourse and academic research alike, I describe five different versions or "tropes" of equal opportunity

Second, it is also important to conceptualize how beliefs about opportunity and inequality are related to one another rather than how they are opposed. For reasons I hope are obvious by now, I reach "beyond the opposition between opportunity and inequality" (as the title of Chapter 1 puts it) and do not assume that Americans care only about the former. At the same time, I do not assume that these concerns are always on the same footing. When faced with a forced choice between equalizing opportunity and equalizing outcomes, Americans will overwhelmingly favor the former.[6] But less appreciated is the fact that Americans view inequalities in outcomes as an impediment to equal opportunity. For example, although it is customary to think of concerns about income inequality as derived from prior assessments of opportunity (e.g., outcomes are unfair because of uneven access to education), I examine the possibility that Americans' views of income inequality function as a signal of unequal opportunities rather than a consequence of already formed beliefs about opportunity.[7] This possibility turns the conventional relationship between beliefs about inequality and opportunity on its head, and, I argue, is useful for understanding beliefs about unequal opportunities in both the labor market and the educational system.

After I elaborate further on this conceptual framework in the next section, the following sections follow an empirical strategy similar to the one pursued in Chapter 3. One of the key findings of that chapter was that pessimism about one's own chances of upward mobility – an indicator of general economic anxiety and economic opportunity – was powerfully associated with concerns about income inequality, but not fully consistent with changes in concerns about income inequality over time. This suggested that the peak of Americans' concerns about income inequality in the early and mid-1990s (1992 and 1996) was not attributable primarily to worries over one's own economic circumstances or the national economy (because peaks in mobility pessimism coincided more strongly with recessionary periods than did peaks in opposition to inequality). Building on the theoretical discussion and media analyses of earlier chapters, the most promising alternative hypothesis was that concerns about income inequality were related to concerns not about economic growth per se but about the *distributional* nature of economic growth, or the lack of expanding opportunities across the population as a whole.

This hypothesis is explored in much greater detail in this chapter by applying the method used in the previous chapter to a larger set of questions about perceptions of economic opportunity. I examine how strongly each is related to the same three attitudinal questions about income inequality that were the focus of Chapter 3. I then examine whether changes in perceptions of opportunity correspond to changes in perceptions of inequality. The results reveal a remarkably logical coupling of particular views about economic opportunity with particular views about income inequality, enabling a novel look into the black box of exactly why Americans care about inequality.

Five Tropes of Opportunity

As discussed in Chapter 1, the achievement of equality of opportunity is no simple matter. It requires the elimination of "birth, nepotism, patronage or any other criterion which allocates place, other than fair competition open equally to talent and ambition."[8] In this definition, allocation of "place" refers to the distribution of positions in the educational system and the labor market. Factors such as "birth" and "any other criterion" refer to anything that is arbitrary or beyond an individual's control, although some may want to insert "talent" into such a list as well. Academic researchers are painfully aware of how difficult (if not impossible) it is to achieve this idyllic state in practice, as well as the prior difficulty of agreeing upon the set of factors that create unfair advantages and disadvantages in the first place.[9]

In comparison to the complexity of these debates among philosophers and policy makers, views about opportunity among the public at large, as gleaned from social survey and public opinion data, are rudimentary. There is, however, much more than first meets the eye. In this section, I discuss five common tropes in public discourse that express relatively distinct versions or visions of equal opportunity. Although there is overlap among them, I present them first as separate ideas and later as interdependent concepts. I also consider how these tropes explicitly or implicitly incorporate the issue of income inequality, paying particular attention to how perceptions of opportunity and inequality influence each other. In the following empirical sections, I evaluate the public opinion record on indicators of beliefs about each of these tropes and income inequality.

TABLE 4.1. *Five Tropes of Opportunity*

Level playing field	Equal opportunities to prepare for the labor market, especially through education.
Bootstraps	The opportunity to "get ahead" in life through hard work and perseverance.
Rising tide	The availability of good jobs for all who seek them.
Equal treatment	Equal job opportunities (including pay) for individuals with equal qualifications, regardless of race, gender, class, or other characteristics unrelated to job performance.
Just deserts	Compensation commensurate with contribution and performance.

The first trope shown in Table 4.1 is the familiar "level playing field." In its most literal sense, the level playing field requires that all players be equally equipped in order for the game, and the outcome of the game, to be considered fair. If one team is equipped with outdated gear and the other with the latest gadgets, a victory by the better-equipped team would not be considered a victory by the better team. Figuratively, the trope of the level playing field defines equality as having an equal chance to prepare for and participate in the game of life.[10] More specifically, it typically refers to equality of educational opportunity, as education is widely viewed as the best preparation for economic success. Because education precedes employment, and information about educational quality is widespread (as almost everyone participates in the educational system), views about educational opportunity will tend to precede and shape views about the fairness of disparities in economic outcomes. Consequently, if Americans are concerned about inequality of outcomes, it may be because of their prior observation that everyone has not been given an equal shot at a good education.[11] This sequence of both "events" (educational attainment followed by labor market experience) and perceptions of those events describes the dominant conceptualization of how Americans think about opportunity and inequality, with beliefs about educational equality shaping beliefs about income inequality.

The second trope is the idea that opportunity is created by "pulling yourself up by your bootstraps." In a way, the "bootstraps" trope of hard work conquering adversity trumps all other tropes. It implies that economic success is possible against all odds, even against a tilted playing field, if one just works hard and perseveres. There are so many celebrated stories of Americans who have triumphed over trying circumstances, with

Supreme Court Justice Sonia Sotomayer a recent example, that it is virtually impossible *not* to subscribe in some measure to the notion that a strong work ethic will eventually pay off, commensurate with natural ability and talent. This implies that if American society is not perfectly open, it is open enough, or at least more open than anywhere else.[12] At a societal level, then, it is unlikely that Americans will ever find this form of opportunity, of hard work paying off, to be in serious jeopardy. At an individual level, however, one's own experience and that of family members and friends could lead to a sense of stalled upward mobility. If the obstacles to moving up the ladder appear unnecessary or unfair, even if their causes are unclear, Americans may question the legitimacy of disparities in outcomes. Here again, the sequence of events and perceptions of those events follows the dominant conceptualization of views about opportunity and inequality, with views about outcomes based on prior views about economic opportunity.

In contrast to the "bootstraps" trope, the next three tropes refer unambiguously to circumstances that are not within an individual's control and yet have significant consequences for the scope of opportunity in a society. The first is the "rising tide lifts all boats" trope. As discussed in Chapter 1, the historic abundance of work opportunities in the United States, from the western frontier to the era of mass production and the digital revolution, is one of the key reasons the United States is hailed as the land of opportunity. An ever-expanding economic pie generates opportunities for all who seek them, extinguishing sympathy for those who are unable to provide for themselves and their families. Given the centrality of economic prosperity to notions of opportunity, and the ready availability of information on the state of the economy through nonstop reporting on unemployment, inflation, the stock market, and so on, it is likely that Americans will be both aware of economic downturns and concerned about the consequent narrowing of economic opportunities.[13] Under the premise that the pain should be spread reasonably evenly among the population, and that effort yields less when jobs are scarce, these concerns could in turn reduce the willingness of Americans to tolerate large disparities in income (as was discussed in greater detail in Chapter 3). As others have noted, then, economic conditions can alter the public mood on a range of issues, among which I include inequality of outcomes.[14]

The fourth trope is the one of "equal treatment." Although this trope is of legalistic rather than popular origin, stemming from doctrines of antidiscrimination, it expresses the group-based definition of equal opportunity that often comes to mind when the term is uttered. Nowadays

Americans almost universally support the idea of equal treatment, in which individuals from different racial and ethnic groups, as well as men and women, must be accorded equal rights and afforded an equal chance to succeed in education, employment, and politics.[15] Although not enshrined in the letter of the law, Americans also regard preferential treatment and other advantages stemming from class background or social connections as a violation of the spirit of equal treatment. In essence, any circumstance in which someone is given an opportunity or an advantage (broadly defined to include an educational opportunity or a job, promotion, raise, bonus, or any other employment-related advancement) on the basis of a social characteristic inherently unrelated to merit is not in keeping with the principle of equal treatment.

In the particular realm of employment, equal treatment requires equal access to jobs and promotions for individuals of equal qualifications; it also includes equal pay for equal work. But because the sum of employment and compensation practices for every individual is difficult to observe in full, discrimination has often been defined in terms of unequal *group outcomes*, such as the underrepresentation of women and minorities in elite occupations, rather than unequal *individual treatment* with discriminatory intent. Although controversial and contested, group-based inequalities in outcomes are used as evidence or signals of inequalities in opportunity that occur earlier in the pipeline and constitute preferential treatment in training, testing, hiring, promotion, and compensation.[16] In this light, affirmative action can be understood as an equal opportunity policy whose proponents resorted to equalizing outcomes when equalizing treatment (via antidiscrimination procedures) proved ineffective.[17] Thus if Americans are concerned about visible disparities in outcomes, this may reflect a deeper concern that individuals who should be treated equally are not being so treated. This sequence of belief formation, with beliefs about outcomes preceding or coinciding with beliefs about opportunity, is the *reverse* of the sequence associated with the previous three tropes and with most conceptualizations of American beliefs about opportunity and inequality.

The fifth and final trope, "just deserts," presents a second example of how the line between beliefs about outcomes and opportunities can become blurred or the arrow reversed. Unlike the first four tropes, just deserts is a phrase that is not in common parlance; nevertheless, it refers to the familiar idea that "you get what you deserve." In the economic realm, just deserts defines fair economic rewards as those that are commensurate with performance and contribution, or to put it differently, with proven accomplishments rather than formal qualifications. In economist Amartya Sen's preferred version of meritocracy, for example, earnings function as an incentive to produce socially valued goods and are then contingent on having achieved that objective.[18] Although this may sound like an issue of inequality and not opportunity, it is plausible to think of it as both.

Take the example of unequal treatment in which an unqualified individual is hired for a job because he is an old family friend of the employer, the two having been raised by affluent parents living in the same upscale town. In the equal treatment context, a job opportunity for a qualified individual (perhaps from a low-income neighborhood) has been sacrificed, triggering a violation of equal treatment opportunity. Suppose now that the family friend performs badly on the job and yet is rewarded with a lavish bonus. In the just deserts context, the individual is undeserving of his pay *because of his poor performance* and not because of his use of social connections to secure his job. That is, a perceived injustice may have occurred even in the absence of knowledge of or concern about bias arising from social connections. In fact, perceptions of injustice may occur even if a person attains a job in an openly competitive manner. This example hints at a violation of equal opportunity in an additional sense: unmerited pay of this kind, in what Daniel Bell referred to as an "unjust meritocracy," could lead to distorted incentives and economic inefficiencies that adversely affect the job opportunities, pay, and morale of other employees and disadvantaged groups in the society more generally.[19] Violations of just deserts thus come into play at the other end of the job ladder too. If, for instance, an occupation is underpaid relative to its agreed-upon value, workers performing well in that occupation will be deprived of the financial rewards they deserve, and perhaps that the broader society believes they deserve as well.

These examples demonstrate that equal opportunity entails a system of fair pay as well as fair employment. And although the idea of fair pay is what distinguishes the just deserts paradigm, this paradigm also asserts that jobs and pay are interdependent (e.g., excessive pay at the top may constrain job and earnings opportunities for others down the line) or are jointly constitutive of equal opportunity (e.g., workers deserve a "good" job commensurate with skills as opposed to just "any" job). As one of the leading historians of the movement to gain equal employment opportunities for minorities and women, Nancy MacLean, writes, "the egalitarian vision of the early movements for inclusion survives most intact today among progressive labor activists, many of whom see the widening economic gap as the civil rights challenge of the new century."[20]

The Occupy Wall Street movement suggests that this sentiment is more widespread than MacLean may have imagined. Thus if Americans are concerned about disparities in outcomes, it may be because of a perception that distortions in the structure of pay propagate and reflect distortions in the structure of opportunity, again reversing the ingrained order of beliefs about opportunity and inequality.

Although each of these tropes has an independent logic, subsets of the five tropes are interdependent in a number of crucial respects as well. For example, Americans often think of meritocracy as a benign and noble philosophy fusing their ideals of opportunity and egalitarianism. But a closer look reveals its more limited scope and appeal. Using the terminology of the five tropes, a fully functioning meritocracy can be thought of as requiring a level playing field in education, equal treatment in employment, and just deserts in compensation, although the latter requirement often goes unacknowledged. Note that within this meritocratic apparatus, a person can succeed by deploying talent over effort. Effort is not irrelevant, but neither is it the linchpin: a high quotient of ability to effort can outproduce a high quotient of effort to ability.[21] The framework of meritocracy also does not require prosperity of the "rising tide lifts all boats" variety. A meritocracy demands only that merit, in terms of qualifications and contribution, determine outcomes; it says nothing of an abundance of jobs. Because it is unlikely that Americans would desire a society with only a few jobs going to only the brightest citizens, the predominant American view of opportunity is most likely one that extends well beyond meritocracy strictly defined.

This extension is necessary in order to include both "bootstraps" and "rising tide" opportunity as central components of the American definition of opportunity. Because such high regard is bestowed upon individuals who soar above their impoverished circumstances to succeed against all odds, the "bootstraps" trope is perhaps the quintessential trope of the land of opportunity. It prevails as a virtue even (or especially?) in a society that is not fully meritocratic.[22] Because the effect of individual economic initiative is greatly diminished in an environment of scarce material resources, the "rising tide" trope is either a close rival to the "bootstraps" trope or more likely its implicit condition. Americans are held responsible for their station in life precisely because job opportunities are perceived as plentiful. For these reasons, it is useful to think of the "rising tide" and "bootstraps" tropes as two sides of the same coin (demand and supply) and to distinguish them from the requirements of a meritocracy as it was originally defined. Which of these elements stirs the American psyche at any given moment, and in any given combination with the others, will shed considerable insight on the nature of beliefs about income inequality in America.

Finally, it is worth raising something that is often invoked in discussions of opportunity but which I have purposely avoided thus far: the issue of luck. Beliefs about hard work are routinely contrasted with beliefs about luck in getting ahead, with Americans emphasizing hard work and Europeans luck.[23] I do not discuss luck explicitly in any of the five tropes because, as far as I can discern, it is not a salient component of the American discourse of opportunity, which is perhaps why fewer Americans than Europeans select it as a response on public opinion surveys. In addition, research on attitudes about luck and hard work is concerned primarily with the impact of these attitudes on beliefs about redistribution, not directly on beliefs about inequality. In fact, beliefs about the role of luck are often regarded as the litmus test for whether a society believes that government should provide a strong social safety net. Although this is not my focus here, I do examine factors that are considered "beyond an individual's control" in several of the tropes ("rising tide," "equal treatment," and "just deserts") and their effects on beliefs about inequality. I suggest that luck may be masquerading under different, more vernacular guises. For this reason, beliefs about luck and examples of luck are included in the empirical analysis, although often in an indirect manner.

Beliefs about Opportunity and Inequality

Like the survey record on beliefs about income inequality, we lack comprehensive information on beliefs about opportunity, much less all five tropes of opportunity. Still, because this is not a heavily trodden field of research, there is considerably more data than I suspect most people are aware of, and the quality and coverage of topics is impressive. The most common questions on beliefs about opportunity are contained in well-known modules on egalitarianism, attitudes about racial and gender discrimination, and economic mobility.

On the topic of egalitarianism, for instance, Americans are routinely asked in the American National Election Studies (ANES) whether they support general egalitarian principles such as equal rights, equal treatment, and equal chances to succeed. Although these questions make no reference to particular social groups, such as the poor, rich, minorities, or women, other questions focus more explicitly on equal treatment opportunity, inquiring about the extent and causes of opportunities and inequalities among racial, ethnic, and gender groups.

Perhaps the most commonly cited questions about economic opportunity tend, not surprisingly, to be on bootstraps opportunity. Questions on this topic ask about the process of "getting ahead" through hard work. Other questions along these lines include references to getting ahead through education, family background, and knowing the right people, invoking aspects of the level playing field and equal treatment tropes of opportunity (and raising the specter of luck).

Asked less often are questions that bear directly on notions of just deserts and rising tide opportunity. One series of questions asks about how much individuals in a small group of occupations earn and how much they should earn, permitting an assessment of perceptions of fair pay and just deserts. It is also useful to explore responses to questions about sympathies toward specific groups, such as the poor and the rich, to understand whether such groups are considered deserving or undeserving.

Regarding the rising tide form of opportunity, there are few questions on the role economic growth plays in generating or constraining opportunity, with the exception of the question on income inequality and economic prosperity introduced in the previous chapter (e.g., "are large differences in income necessary for America's prosperity"), and examined further in this chapter. Views about the state of the economy and one's own personal financial situation in the ANES provide an additional vantage point into the impact of macroeconomic conditions on beliefs about income inequality.

The only trope that is not examined separately here is the level playing field. Because this trope has much in common with the equal treatment trope, it is touched upon in sections in this chapter on equal treatment opportunity, as well as in Chapter 5, when social policy preferences for educational reform are discussed in greater detail. More generally, I concentrate on opportunities in the labor market rather than in the educational system.

Bootstraps versus Equal Treatment Opportunity

Although the conceptual boundaries of the five tropes are often blurred in the empirical data, this presents something of an advantage in appraising the appeal of bootstraps opportunity relative to other concepts of opportunity. Perhaps the most frequently cited question on American beliefs about opportunity is a forced-choice question asking whether the "most important" reason that "people get ahead" is "their own hard work," "lucky breaks or help from other people," or both equally.[24] This question incorporates an explicit reference to hard work as well as to its importance relative to unequal treatment (i.e., help from others)

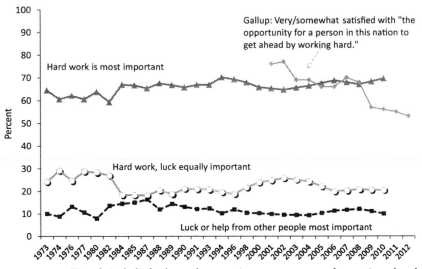

FIGURE 4.1. Trends in beliefs about the most important reason for getting ahead in life, 1973 to 2010. The wording of the question is: "Some people say that people get ahead by their own hard work; others say that lucky breaks or help from other people are more important. Which do you think is most important?" *Source:* 1972–2010 Cumulative File of the General Social Survey.

and luck. It has been asked as part of the core modules of the GSS since the survey's inception, providing a lengthy series of responses from the early 1970s to the present, and coinciding with all of the years in which the three questions about income inequality are asked. In a more limited number of years, a sequence of questions is available that includes separate items on the role of hard work, help from others, and various indicators of luck in the mobility process. I discuss the forced-choice item first and follow with a discussion of the extended battery of items.

The responses to the forced-choice question are charted in Figure 4.1 and show remarkable consistency across the twenty-four–year time period in which we have responses to questions about income inequality (1987 to 2010). From the late 1980s to the present, 65 to 70 percent of respondents said that hard work is the most important reason that people get ahead. The low point for the "hard work" option occurred before this time period, between the mid-1970s and 1982, when the percentage of responses hovered in the low 60s and dipped to 59 in 1982. It is tempting to conclude that the deep recession of 1982 was responsible for this slide in optimism, especially given another (much weaker) drop in 2002 on the heels of the 2001 recession. There is probably some truth

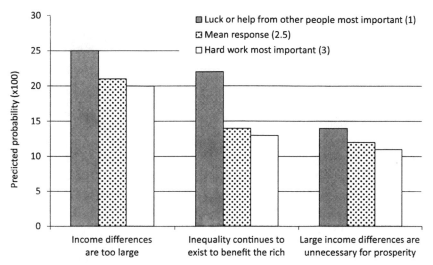

FIGURE 4.2. Adjusted effects of beliefs about getting ahead on strong agreement to three questions about beliefs regarding income inequality, 1987 to 2010. Estimates are for a typical respondent net of controls in a binary logistic regression model. See Appendix Table A4.1 for further details on the typical respondent and model specifications. *Source:* 1987, 1996, 2000, 2008, 2010 General Social Survey and 1992 International Social Survey Program.

to this conjecture, suggesting a positive association between an ebbing tide and pessimism about the payoffs of hard work. (In Chapter 3, we saw the same association between downturns in the economy and pessimism about upward mobility.) However, there was little change during the recessions of 1991 and 2008, and the changes that do occur are quite modest relative to the high degree of overall optimism about the importance of hard work in getting ahead.

On the face of it, this level of optimism and consistency does not bode well for explaining beliefs about inequality or changes in beliefs about inequality from the late 1980s to the late 2000s. This expectation is mostly, but not completely, borne out. As is apparent in Figure 4.2, there is a noticeable effect of beliefs about getting ahead on beliefs about income inequality, but the effects are weak for two of the outcomes, the "too large" and "prosperity" questions.[25] By comparison, the impact of optimism about upward mobility through improving one's own standard of living (shown in the previous chapter and in Appendix Table A4.1) is measured and distributed in much the same way as the "get ahead" variable, but it has both a consistently significant and larger effect across all three outcomes. A one-point decline in mobility optimism would increase strong agreement that income differences are too large by 4.1 percentage points, or a 20 percent increase above a typical level of strong agreement to this question, which is 21 percent. By contrast, a one-point decline in the belief that hard work is important for getting ahead would increase strong agreement by less than two-thirds as much, or 2.6 percentage points.

There is a striking exception to these generally weak effects, however. Beliefs about hard work in getting ahead have a considerably stronger impact on beliefs about the benefits of income inequality for the rich and powerful. A one-point decline in either mobility optimism or the power of hard work in getting ahead increases the extent of strong agreement to the "benefits" question by 4.6 or 4.1 percentage points, respectively. This is a 30 to 33 percent increase above a typical level of strong agreement to this question, which is 14 percent. As shown in Figure 4.2, a typical respondent who thinks that lucky breaks or help from others, rather than hard work, is the most important factor in getting ahead is much more likely to strongly agree that income inequality continues to exist because it benefits the rich and powerful (22 versus 13 percent). This is the average effect across years, but in 1996 the effect is magnified because of the more intense concern over inequality at that time. Nearly two-fifths (38 percent) of those typical respondents who thought that lucky breaks or help from others was the most important factor in getting ahead were in strong agreement about the role of the rich and powerful in perpetuating inequality. By contrast, about a quarter (24 percent) of those typical respondents who thought hard work was the most important factor in getting ahead were in strong agreement.

The strength of this particular relationship, coupled with weak relationships overall, offers mixed evidence of the role that beliefs about bootstraps opportunity play in shaping beliefs about income inequality. Because this may be a consequence of the forced-choice format of the "get ahead" question, these relationships are examined further with the extended battery of questions on the same topic available in a more limited number of years (1987, 1992, 2000, and/or 2010). Respondents were asked the importance of various factors in getting ahead in life and could decide for each one whether it was essential, very important, fairly important, not very important, or not important at all. The factors can be grouped into two broad categories corresponding to the two poles of the forced-choice question (i.e., hard work and luck/social connections).

In the first category, there is one question that asks specifically about the importance of hard work, and additional questions that ask about

TABLE 4.2. *Marginal Distributions of Questions about the Importance of Individual and Structural Factors in Getting Ahead*

Importance for Getting Ahead in Life...	Essential	Very Important	Fairly Important	Not Very Important	Not at all Important
Hard work	40.8%	50.9	7.3	1.0	0.1
Having a good education yourself	33.8	53.1	11.9	1.0	0.3
Ambition	40.8	49.3	8.7	0.9	0.2
Natural ability	11.2	45.1	38.1	5.2	0.5
Knowing the right people	10.0	33.9	42.1	11.7	2.3
Having well-educated parents	6.2	37.7	39.5	12.8	3.8
Coming from a wealthy family	3.9	18.4	30.0	32.2	15.5
A person's race	2.1	11.3	22.2	33.7	30.8

Notes: The wording of the question is (according to the 1987 questionnaire): "To begin, we have some questions about opportunities for getting ahead... Please show for each of these how important you think it is for getting ahead in life..."

Source: Social Inequality Modules of the 1987, 2000, 2010 General Social Survey and 1992 International Social Survey Program. Responses are weighted and pooled across available years, which vary depending on question.

other characteristics potentially within an individual's control, such as "having a good education yourself" and "ambition." In the second category, there are a number of questions that can be construed as examples of having "lucky breaks or help from others," such as "knowing the right people," "coming from a wealthy family," "having well educated parents," and "a person's race." An eighth factor, "natural ability," could be perceived as either an individual characteristic that legitimately confers rewards or a characteristic determined by luck, and thus I do not place it in either category a priori. In short, these eight factors span the divide between bootstraps and equal treatment opportunity.

Consistent with the large number of Americans who selected hard work in the forced-choice question, characteristics within an individual's control are the most likely to be deemed "essential" for getting ahead in life. As shown in the top rows of Table 4.2, 40.8 percent of respondents think that ambition and hard work are each essential, and 33.8 percent think that having a good education is essential. When responses in the "very important" category are added to those in the "essential" category, over 87 percent of Americans consider all three of these individual factors as a group to be of greatest significance for getting ahead in life. The core American belief in bootstraps opportunity is thus

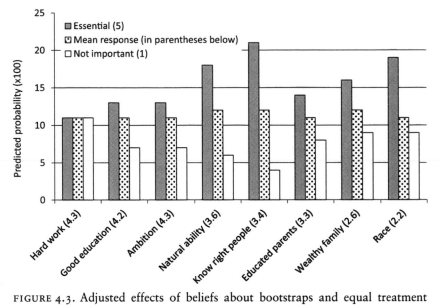

FIGURE 4.3. Adjusted effects of beliefs about bootstraps and equal treatment opportunity on strong agreement that inequality continues to exist to benefit the rich and powerful, 1987 to 2010. Estimates are for the typical respondent net of controls in separate binary logistic regressions for each dimension of opportunity as the independent variable. See Appendix Table A4.1 for further details on the typical respondent and model specifications. *Source:* Social Inequality Modules of the 1987, 2000, 2010 General Social Survey and 1992 International Social Survey Program.

strongly supported in these data, even more strongly than in the responses to the forced-choice question.

Although this is usually where the story ends, we have yet to reach the most important part for understanding beliefs about inequality. Perhaps because of the prevalence of bootstraps convictions, it turns out that beliefs about the importance of hard work and having a good education for getting ahead have *no discernible impact* whatsoever on beliefs about income inequality. As shown starkly in Figure 4.3 (and in Appendix Table A4.1), this is just as true for beliefs about the benefits of income inequality for the rich and powerful as it is for beliefs about whether income differences are too large and are unnecessary for prosperity (the results for these latter two questions are shown in Appendix Table A4.1). Thus support for the bootstraps notion of opportunity is certainly prevalent throughout the past four decades, but this widely recognized fact has little influence on beliefs about income inequality. As such, it is grossly misleading to cast it as an indicator of tolerant beliefs about income inequality, as is so often done.

In contrast, beliefs about income inequality *are* related to indirect indicators of the role of luck in getting ahead. Looking again at the results in Table 4.2, large minorities of Americans believe that, if not essential, "knowing the right people" and "having well educated parents" – potential violations of equal treatment and a level playing field – are central to getting ahead. When the "essential" and "very important" categories are combined, 44 percent of Americans consider each of these as important. The more direct question about social class background, whether "coming from a wealthy family" is important, receives much less support: only 22 percent of respondents ranked this as essential or very important. A person's race receives still less support, with only 13 percent ranking it as essential or very important. These lackluster responses no doubt reflect, at least in part, norms and biases against explicitly acknowledging the role of race and class in affecting life chances. As such, we can think of them as identifying the terms that Americans prefer to *avoid* in describing the role of luck and other structural barriers to opportunity in American society.

In contrast to individual factors such as hard work and a good education, each of the structural factors has a significant impact on beliefs about income inequality, with the strongest and most consistent effect coming from "knowing the right people."[26] Beliefs about the role of the rich and powerful in maintaining inequality are once again consistently implicated in these particular beliefs about equal treatment opportunity (see Figure 4.3 and Appendix Table A4.1), but so is the straightforward referendum on whether inequality is excessive. The perceived necessity of having the right family background and social connections in order to succeed in life leads to stronger agreement that income differences are too large. Notably, none of these "get ahead" factors have an effect on beliefs about the relationship between inequality and prosperity, something I discuss further in the concluding section of this chapter.

Based on these more detailed questions, the generally weak effects of the single (forced-choice) question about bootstraps opportunity on beliefs about inequality do not appear to be a fluke of question-wording format. In fact, those weak effects are only accentuated when respondents are permitted in separate questions to evaluate the importance of each potential cause of getting ahead. This is because American beliefs are multidimensional, with a bedrock foundation of individualism overlaid

TABLE 4.3. *Joint Distribution of Beliefs about Getting Ahead through Hard Work and Social Advantages*

Importance of Hard Work for Getting Ahead:	Essential/ Very Important	Fairly/Not Very/ Not at All Important
Importance of structural characteristics for getting ahead (knowing the right people, coming from a wealthy family, having well-educated parents, a person's race):		
Essential/very important	60.2	4.7
Fairly/not very/not at all important	31.5	3.6

Note: See Table 4.2 for question wording and response distributions.
Source: Social Inequality Modules of the 1987, 2000, 2010 General Social Survey and 1992 International Social Survey Program. Responses are weighted and pooled across available years, which vary depending on question.

with a layer of skepticism about whether the playing field is level in practice. As Table 4.3 shows, well over half of respondents (60.2 percent) believe that *both* hard work and at least one of the factors unrelated to individual initiative are essential or very important for getting ahead. Less than a third think that only hard work is essential or very important, and only 4.7 percent think that only nonindividual characteristics are essential or very important.

This multidimensionality, which has also been labeled inconsistency and ambivalence, and which I prefer to call the difference between principle and practice, has been studied extensively with respect to attitudes about racial inequality and social welfare policy but not, in the era of rising inequality, with regard to income inequality. In examining multiple dimensions of both opportunity and income inequality, we find a remarkably coherent association between beliefs about social advantages in getting ahead and the role of the rich and powerful in maintaining income inequality, and in turn with disapproval of the overall level of inequality.

Before turning to the question of whether growing concerns about social advantages in getting ahead may account for some of the growing concern about income inequality, there are two other factors associated with getting ahead that I have yet to discuss: ambition and natural ability. Although ambition is often thought of as a straightforward indicator of individual initiative, and natural ability a more complicated indicator of individual worth on the one hand and luck on the other, they were associated with beliefs about income inequality in the same way, as indicators of the perpetuation of social class advantages for the rich. Those who think that having ambition and natural ability are important are more likely to associate the benefits of income inequality with the rich and powerful. Those who find ambition important also think that current levels of income inequality are excessive. Again, neither of these is associated with thinking that inequality is necessary for prosperity. Although the finding for natural ability is somewhat expected – natural ability may legitimately be perceived as a function of luck and therefore as unfair – the negative slant of the findings for ambition are perhaps more surprising. Either Americans believe that ambition is unfairly inherited or cultivated in individuals from privileged backgrounds, or they classify it as a necessary but unsavory element of getting ahead, joining the ranks of the rich and powerful, and perpetuating a cycle of inequality. Both are perhaps consistent with evidence that Americans do not generally "like" or feel warmly toward the rich.[27]

Is it possible, then, that Americans thought that ambition, natural ability, and other indicators of luck were becoming more important in shaping opportunities to get ahead at the same time that they thought that the rich and powerful were playing a more important role in fostering income inequality? The most straightforward way to determine whether changes in beliefs about the role of hard work and social advantages in getting ahead were responsible for some of the changes in concerns about income inequality is to see whether such changes occurred, whether they occurred at the same time as changes in beliefs about income inequality, and whether they occurred in the expected direction. To that end, I focus on the forced-choice question because it is available for the most number of years.

We have already observed the flat line in Figure 4.1, reflecting very little change in beliefs about the perceived importance of hard work for getting ahead. In addition, and surprisingly, the estimates for each year reveal that the percentage of respondents who are placing their faith in hard work actually increased slightly over this period, from 65.4 in 1987 to 69.3 in 1996, 65.8 in 2000, 67.1 in 2008, and 69.6 in 2010. Meanwhile, strong agreement that inequality exists to benefit the rich and powerful grew in 1992 and peaked in 1996, but was only slightly larger at the end of the 2000s than in 1987. Thus concerns about hard work being thwarted by social advantages in getting ahead did not rise in tandem with concerns about income inequality. In fact, beliefs about bootstraps opportunity and income inequality favoring the rich were less interdependent in the mid-1990s than in other years.[28] Similarly, none of the trends in beliefs about income inequality were altered by changes in beliefs about the role of hard work, education, ambition, natural ability, knowing the right people, or parents' education, wealth, or race in getting ahead (although only a few years of responses are available for these questions).[29]

If anything, then, Americans became slightly more likely to support the bootstraps notion of opportunity in 1996 while at the same time they became more likely to express concerns about the unfairness of income inequality.[30] Increasing concerns about income inequality are not, therefore, explained by increasing skepticism about the payoffs of hard work and increasing concerns about the role of social advantages in getting ahead.

These findings have several important implications for understanding beliefs about income inequality. First, and most significant, beliefs about income inequality are commonly inferred from beliefs about bootstraps opportunity, yet we found little empirical basis for such an inference. Americans should not be cast as unconcerned about income inequality because of their seemingly unshakable confidence in the possibility (with unknown probability) of bootstraps opportunity. In fact, in tougher times, Americans may feel more pressure to rely on hard work as their only hope for achieving economic security. Even if they feel less optimistic about their chances for upward mobility, they may still profess an allegiance to the only way they know how to survive.[31]

Second, although the evidence of a relationship between beliefs about hard work in getting ahead and beliefs about income inequality is weak *in general*, the evidence that *was* uncovered of a relationship reveals an impulse to connect violations of both bootstraps and equal treatment opportunity to negative views of the rich. Those who believe that opportunity is heavily influenced by an individual's social advantages, especially by "knowing the right people," are more likely to associate the benefits of income inequality with elite social groups (i.e., the rich and powerful), and in a disapproving way, as they are also more likely to object to overall levels of income inequality. Such beliefs about social advantages in getting ahead may not have intensified and set fire to concerns about income inequality in the mid-1990s, as far as these data can tell, but they are a key component of those concerns at any given time, much like concerns about one's chances for upward mobility.

Third, and finally, the connections between beliefs about outcomes and opportunities discussed in this section are considerably more coherent than anyone would have expected. The unfairness of using social advantages in one generation to reproduce social advantages in the next generation is implied in the question about income inequality "continuing to exist because it benefits the rich and powerful," but it is not stated directly. It is only the particular coupling of this question with the questions on "getting ahead" that evokes public concerns about the transmission of inequality across generations. Moreover, these particular questions about getting ahead and income inequality are embedded in separate batteries of questions about opportunity and inequality, respectively, and yet they are the ones that stand out in relation to one another. There is therefore no reason to believe that the results in this section are a consequence of question ordering or priming. Instead, they suggest that a significant minority of Americans (and more if those who "agree" are added to those who "strongly agree" to the inequality questions) are crafting a coherent and positive connection between inequalities in opportunity and inequalities in outcomes that is consistent with the intergenerational reproduction of class.

Although my analyses modeled the effects of beliefs about bootstraps and equal treatment opportunity on beliefs about income inequality, we cannot adequately determine with the GSS data whether these particular perceptions of unequal opportunity precede, accompany, or follow perceptions of unfair outcomes. It is plausible, for instance, that the "end result" of social advantages in life, when a superstar is thrown into the spotlight and his or her background is thus revealed, is at least as visible to the general public as the progression of advantages enjoyed by the affluent throughout their early lives. Indeed, it is the end result of a Supreme Court Justice Sotomayor or a President Clinton that ratifies the notion of bootstraps opportunity and not the hard-won successes in the development of their individual careers, which are reported only in retrospect after fame sets in. Similarly, we may not have known about the poor grades of George W. Bush had he not assumed the presidency of the United States. In either the case of having overcome adversity or having capitalized on social class advantages, perceptions of outcomes often become precursors to perceptions of opportunities rather than the other way around.

Just Deserts Opportunity

Just deserts opportunity is distinguished from bootstraps and equal treatment opportunity by its emphasis on fair pay as the core component of equal opportunity. In this rendering, pay is pertinent to the definition of opportunity irrespective of whether jobs are acquired by hard work, talent, or preferential treatment. Although fair pay is defined as *pay* commensurate with performance and contribution, unfair pay may have consequences for *job* opportunities. Much like potential inefficiencies introduced by excessive pay compression, excessive pay inequality could result in distorted incentives, weakened firm performance, and sluggish economic growth of the rising tide variety. The various accounting, financial, and other corporate scandals of the past decade and a half perhaps illustrate this all too well. As discussed earlier in this chapter and in Chapter 1, an "unjust meritocracy" also has the potential to discourage and demean those at the bottom, as Young and Bell prophesied, spawning a downward spiral of lost opportunities.

The proposition that unfair and extreme inequalities in pay function as a signal of inequalities in opportunity has received surprisingly little scholarly attention. It cannot be too farfetched an idea, however, because journalists raised it in an almost taken-for-granted manner in times of public outrage over corporate scandals and excessive executive pay (as shown in Chapter 2). Fortunately, this proposition is implied in one of the main questions about income inequality in the GSS. The question of whether "large differences in income are necessary for America's prosperity" embeds the proposition that generous monetary rewards spur innovation and growth. If one disagrees with this proposition and concludes to the contrary that inequality is *not* necessary for prosperity, one is saying that a prosperous society is not predisposed to high levels of inequality. We may speculate further that inequality can itself be indicted for the role it plays in the various ways mentioned a moment ago in curtailing opportunities for good jobs and fair pay.

These interpretations of the relationship between perceptions of opportunity and income inequality are explored in this section. As mentioned in the Introduction and Chapter 1, large majorities of Americans think that occupations at the top are overpaid and those at the bottom are underpaid. This is a consistent finding across numerous studies with the unequivocal message that there is more inequality in pay than Americans believe is warranted. I examine the type of data upon which these studies are based and extend the inquiry to determine how closely perceptions of fair pay are related to more explicit judgments about income inequality. Although questions on perceptions of occupational pay are asked in only four of the six years in which questions on attitudes about income inequality are available, the four years span more than two decades of

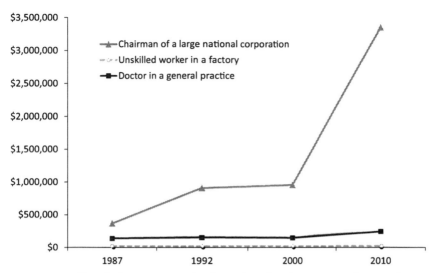

FIGURE 4.4. Trends in mean perceived earnings for three occupations, 1987 to 2010 (2000 $). See Table 4.4 for question wording and further information. *Source:* Social Inequality Modules of the 1987, 2000, 2010 General Social Survey and 1992 International Social Survey Program.

rising inequality (1987, 1992, 2000, and 2010). Over time comparisons are facilitated further by the inclusion of two occupations in all four years that cover opposite ends of the earnings distribution: executives ("chairman of a large national corporation") and unskilled workers ("unskilled worker in a factory").[32] Given this range, we can investigate whether beliefs about income inequality are shaped more by concerns about fair pay at the top or bottom.

Beginning with perceptions of changes in *pay* (rather than pay inequality), Americans appear to have been remarkably cognizant of the stagnation of earnings at the bottom and the skyrocketing of earnings at the very top. This is true especially for the periods between 1987 and 1992 and then again between 2000 and 2010. In the first period, the average perceived pay of executives rose by 148 percent and the average perceived pay of unskilled factory workers declined by 7 percent, as shown in Figure 4.4 and Table 4.4. By comparison, changes in perceived earnings were small from 1992 to 2000. Moreover, Americans distinguished trends in pay at the very top from those among "mere" professionals. The average perceived earnings of doctors ("doctor in a general practice") grew almost imperceptibly, from $136,883 in 1987 to $150,915 in 1992 and

TABLE 4.4. *Trends in Perceived and Desired Pay and Pay Ratios for Executives and Unskilled Workers, 1987 to 2010*

Year	Mean Perceived Pay (2000 $)		Mean Desired Pay/ Mean Perceived Pay	
	Executives	Unskilled	Executives	Unskilled
1987	$ 366,617	$20,591	0.54	1.14
1992	$ 909,483	$19,236	0.28	1.23
2000	$ 956,906	$20,129	0.35	1.31
2010	$3,350,051	$21,835	0.25	1.26

Year	Median ratio: 1) perceived pay inequality Executives/unskilled	2) desired pay inequality Executives/unskilled
1987	10.0	5.0
1992	15.0	5.3
2000	12.5	5.0
2010	30.0	6.7

Year	Median ratio: 1) desired pay/perceived pay		2) desired pay inequality/ perceived pay inequality Executives/unskilled
	Executives	Unskilled	
1987	0.70	1.11	0.60
1992	0.57	1.22	0.44
2000	0.67	1.25	0.50
2010	0.40	1.20	0.32

Notes: The wording of the question on perceived pay is (according to the 1987 questionnaire): "We would like to know what you think people in these jobs actually earn. Please write in how much you think they usually earn, each year, before taxes. Many people are not exactly sure about this but your best guess will be close enough. This may be difficult, but it is very important, so please try." The wording of the question on desired pay is: "Next, what do you think people in those jobs ought to be paid – how much do you think they should earn each year before taxes, regardless of what they actually get?" Executive pay is derived from questions about "the chairman of a large national corporation," and unskilled worker pay from questions about "an unskilled worker in a factory." Raw responses were obtained and then top coded to eliminate outliers (see the text for further details on top coding).
Source: Social Inequality Modules of the 1987, 2000, 2010 General Social Survey and 1992 International Social Survey Program.

$144,347 in 2000. These same patterns for unskilled workers and doctors are replicated in the 2000s, whereas the perceived earnings of executives soar by 250 percent from 2000 to 2010. Thus Americans had an impressive command of who was getting ahead and who was not in absolute terms, as well as how this may have shifted over the past two decades.[33]

At the same time, Americans increasingly believed that executives deserved much less than they earned, and skilled and unskilled workers

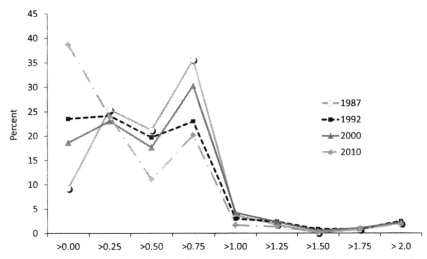

FIGURE 4.5. Trends in the ratio of desired to perceived pay of executives ("the chairman of a large national corporation"), 1987 to 2010. The *x*-axis indicates the range of the ratio (e.g., >0.75 indicates a ratio of greater than 0.75 and less than or equal to 1.00). See Table 4.4 for question wording and further information. *Source:* Social Inequality Modules of the 1987, 2000, 2010 General Social Survey and 1992 International Social Survey Program.

deserved more.[34] On average, unskilled workers were considered underpaid by 14 percent in 1987 and 26 percent in 2010, as shown in the far right column in the first panel of Table 4.4. There was also a marked increase in the share of Americans who said that unskilled workers should be earning more than they currently do. From 1992 forward, two-thirds of Americans believed that unskilled workers were shortchanged, up from 54 percent in 1987. (These results for unskilled workers are not shown.) By contrast, more Americans came to the conclusion that executives were overpaid, as shown in Figure 4.5. Those who thought executives should earn less than a quarter of what they earn rose from 9 percent of all respondents in 1987 to an astounding 39 percent in 2010. This was balanced out by many fewer Americans who thought executives deserved more or less what they earned, declining from over a third in 1987 to a fifth in 2010. Thus there is no evidence of a linear trend toward growing polarization in views of just executive pay, as suggested by previous research.[35]

Americans in growing numbers over the course of the 1990s and 2000s were therefore adducing a widening rift between what executives and ordinary workers deserved and what they earned, a clear violation of just deserts opportunity. A closer look reveals that these trends were driven by increases in the perceived pay of executives rather than decreases in what Americans thought executives ought to earn (labeled "desired" pay and pay inequality in Table 4.4). As shown in the second panel of Table 4.4, perceptions of the median pay ratio between executives and unskilled workers tripled from 10 to 30 – with executives making 10 and 30 times the earnings of unskilled workers according to the median estimate – between 1987 and 2010. The pay ratio between executives and unskilled workers desired by Americans rose as well, but only slightly and much less than the perceived pay ratio.

This increase in the desired level of pay inequality is curious and seems to contradict the evidence of growing concerns about income inequality presented in the previous chapter. However, it is most likely due to the imperfect attempts by individuals to calibrate, at least to some extent, their estimates of what executives should make to a wildly expanding estimate of what executives actually do make, even when these estimates vastly understate the true level of top-end pay (also remember that we are not asking for estimates from the same individuals over time, as in a panel study, or asking directly for estimates of relative pay between occupational groups).[36] As we will see in a moment, desired levels of pay inequality are much lower *relative to* perceived levels of pay inequality in all years, and are much lower in 2010 than they were in 1987. That is, in recent years Americans sought more of a reduction in pay inequality than they did a few decades ago.

Although the trend over the last two decades demonstrates a growing awareness of, and distaste for, earnings inequality, there is also a distinctly nonlinear pattern to these trends reminiscent of those found in the previous chapter: Americans found executives to be more deserving in 2000 than in either 1992 or 2010, although still less so than in the base year of 1987 (as shown in the third panel of Table 4.4). Similarly, the degree of desired pay inequality relative to the perceived level of pay inequality has changed significantly over time. Figure 4.6 and the third panel of Table 4.4 show the ratio of desired pay inequality to perceived pay inequality, with each form of inequality calculated as the ratio of executive to unskilled earnings.[37] The median level of inequality preferred by Americans in 1987 was three-fifths the level they thought existed at the time. This dropped to 44 percent in 1992, rose to 50 percent in 2000, and then fell precipitously to just 32 percent in 2010. The impression given by the full distribution in Figure 4.6 is similar to the one given by the median: a shift toward preferences for less inequality relative to

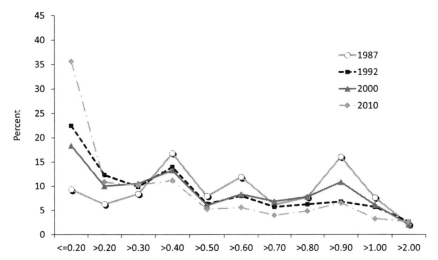

FIGURE 4.6. Trends in the ratio of desired pay inequality to perceived pay inequality, 1987 to 2010. The ratio is in pretax pay between executives ("the chairman of a large national corporation") and unskilled workers ("an unskilled worker in a factory"). The *x*-axis indicates the range of the ratio (e.g., >0.70 indicates a ratio of greater than 0.70 and less than or equal to 0.80). See Table 4.4 for question wording and further information. *Source:* Social Inequality Modules of the 1987, 2000, 2010 General Social Survey and 1992 International Social Survey Program.

perceived inequality in 1992, a shift back toward greater tolerance of inequality in 2000, and then a large increase in those preferring much less inequality in 2010, especially among those desiring less than 20 percent of what they perceive exists. Polarization also declines over the decades as more Americans prefer much lower levels of inequality, relative to what they think exists, in 2010 than in 1987.

Although these nonlinear trends in perceptions and preferences regarding pay inequality should be familiar from the last chapter – and are reassuring of the nonlinear trend in beliefs about income inequality found there – they are also distinctive in one crucial respect. On the one hand, the increase in desires for less *pay inequality* between 1987 and 1992 and then again between 2000 and 2010 is consistent with the increase in concerns about *income inequality* during these same periods, as is the greater tolerance for both kinds of inequality in 2000. On the other hand, desires for less pay inequality (relative to perceived levels of actual pay inequality) are at their unambiguous peak in 2010, whereas desires for less income inequality attain their peak in the early and middle 1990s.

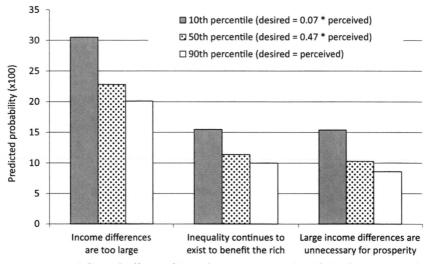

FIGURE 4.7. Adjusted effects of just deserts opportunity (desired pay inequality relative to perceived pay inequality) on strong agreement to three questions
about beliefs regarding income inequality, 1987 to 2010. Estimates are for a
typical respondent net of controls in binary logistic regression models shown in
Table 4.5. *Source:* Social Inequality Modules of the 1987, 2000, 2010 General
Social Survey and 1992 International Social Survey Program.

If opposition to (income) inequality was a straightforward by-product
of knowledge of (pay) inequality, should the heightened recognition and
disapproval of extreme disparities in pay that we see in 2010 not have
provoked a tidal wave of intolerance of income inequality? If not, why
not?

To answer these questions, we need to examine the relationship
between beliefs about pay inequality and beliefs about income inequality
directly, rather than assume that the two are either measures of the same
underlying construct of inequality or measures of completely separate
dynamics. We will see that the apparent eruption of awareness of rising
pay disparities in the late 2000s helps to explain rising concerns about
income inequality, but it is not the only, or even most consequential,
factor involved in understanding beliefs about income inequality.

First, unlike perceptions of bootstraps opportunity, perceptions of just
deserts opportunity do exert a strong overall impression on beliefs about
income inequality. Americans who desire a lower level of pay inequality than they estimate to exist are more likely to express concerns about
income inequality, resulting in the significant negative effects shown in
the first panel of Table 4.5 and illustrated in Figure 4.7. This is true for

TABLE 4.5. *Adjusted Marginal Effects of Beliefs about Occupational Pay Inequality on Three Questions about Beliefs Regarding Income Inequality, 1987 to 2010*

Strong Agreement that ...	Income Differences are too Large	Inequality Continues to Exist to Benefit the Rich and Powerful	Large Income Differences are Unnecessary for Prosperity
Probability of strong agreement:[a]	.190	.111	.091
(1) Average marginal effects of pay inequality (logged and standardized):[b]			
Desired pay inequality/ perceived pay inequality:			
Executives relative to unskilled workers[c]	−0.038 (0.007)**	−0.023 (0.006)**	−0.024 (0.006)**
Desired pay/ perceived pay:			
Unskilled workers	0.025 (0.007)**	0.010 (0.006)[†]	0.009 (0.006)
Executives	−0.033 (0.007)**	−0.021 (0.006)**	−0.023 (0.006)**
(2) Discrete change of time dummies:			
1992, without pay inequality variable	0.138 (0.025)**	0.011 (0.015)	0.076 (0.022)**
1992, with pay inequality variable	0.120 (0.024)**	0.003 (0.015)	0.063 (0.021)**
2000, without pay inequality variable	0.092 (0.027)**	−0.002 (0.017)	0.050 (0.023)*
2000, with pay inequality variable	0.077 (0.026)**	−0.008 (0.016)	0.040 (0.022)[†]
2010, without pay inequality variable	0.100 (0.024)**	−0.010 (0.014)	0.067 (0.021)**
2010, with pay inequality variable	0.066 (0.023)**	−0.027 (0.014)*	0.041 (0.019)*

Notes: [a]For a typical respondent, who is female, white, married, employed, and not living in the South; self-identifies as middle class, a Democrat or independent, and moderate; has mean age, age squared, household size, children, education, and family income; and has mean values on the year dummies. [b]Estimates are for a typical respondent from a binary logistic regression model with standard errors in parentheses. [c]Executives refer to "the chairman of a large corporation" and unskilled workers refer to "an unskilled worker in a factory." See Table 4.4 for question wording. $**p <= 0.01$; $*p <= 0.05$; $^{†}p <= 0.10$.
Source: Social Inequality Modules of the 1987, 2000, 2010 General Social Surveys and 1992 International Social Survey Program.

every year and for every outcome, although only the results for all years pooled together are given in the first panel of Table 4.5, and the results for 1992 are graphed in Figure 4.7. In 1992, the year with the highest level of concern about income inequality among the four years of data,

an otherwise typical respondent who was content with the perceived level
of pay inequality (i.e., desired pay inequality = perceived pay inequality)
had only an 8.6 percent chance of strongly agreeing with the statement
that inequality was unnecessary for prosperity. By contrast, an otherwise typical person who preferred a level of income inequality that was
less than a tenth of existing levels had a 15.4 percent chance of strongly
agreeing with this statement (recall that many more agreed with the statement). For the other two questions on income inequality, the likelihood
of strong agreement increases by 50 percent as satisfaction with existing
pay disparities sinks from the 90th (high satisfaction) to the 10th (low
satisfaction) percentile of the distribution.

Second, the effects of beliefs about fair pay on *changes* in beliefs about
income inequality are substantial. The results are presented in the second panel of Table 4.5. In the period from 1987 to 1992, there was an
increase in the share of Americans who strongly agreed (of about 7.6
percentage points on average) that the nation can prosper without large
differences in income, with about 17 percent of this increase due to an
increase between 1987 and 1992 in the share of individuals who preferred less pay inequality.[38] In the period from 1987 to 2010, when the
increase in desires for less pay inequality was more pronounced, 39 percent of the increase in strong agreement that inequality was unnecessary
for prosperity was accounted for by the shift in preferences toward less
pay inequality. The growing discrepancy between desired and perceived
pay inequality over time also accounts for some of the increase in strong
agreement that income differences are too large, with the impact again
much more salient in the period from 1987 to 2010 (accounting for 34
percent of the increase in strong agreement that income differences are
too large versus 13 percent in the period from 1987 to 1992). Overall,
then, we observe less of an increase over time in concerns about income
inequality once perceptions of occupational pay disparities are recognized, and this is especially so over the full span of our time series from
the late 1980s to the late 2000s.[39]

Yet, however much rising awareness of pay disparities may have
prompted a flare-up in concerns about income inequality in 2010, it was
not enough to surpass the degree of dissatisfaction with income inequality
in the early 1990s. What does this suggest about the influence of knowledge on norms of inequality? In additional analyses, I included perceived
pay disparities (as shown in the first column of the second panel of Table
4.4) as a crude measure of factual knowledge about inequality. As discussed in Chapter 1, it is often argued by those who believe Americans

are largely ignorant (rather than tolerant) of inequality that if only Americans knew how extreme inequality is, they would object to it in greater numbers. The measure of perceived pay disparities should give us an idea of how much estimates of inequality shape opposition to inequality.[40] I found that this variable was much less strongly (and sometimes insignificantly) associated with strong agreement to all three inequality questions than the measure of desired pay inequality relative to perceived pay inequality (the latter measure is shown in Table 4.5).[41] This is consistent with the findings of the previous chapter, which, together with this section's findings, suggest that awareness of inequality was accurate and critical enough in the 1990s to underwrite elevated concerns about inequality given the propitious environment at that time (as I also discuss in Chapter 2).

We have seen that Americans are dissatisfied with pay disparities, that this dissatisfaction grew dramatically over the 2000s, and that this growth explains a substantial portion of the growing dissatisfaction with income inequality. Finally, we would also like to know whether these developments reflect objections to unfair pay at the bottom of the occupational ladder or at the top. Beyond our interest in understanding the nature of American beliefs about economic fairness, the answer to this question has obvious implications for public policy, to be discussed in later chapters.

The additional results in the first panel of Table 4.5 present convincing evidence that it is concerns about unfair pay at the top that strike a chord with Americans. The more Americans think executives are overpaid, the more likely they are to strongly agree that income differences are too large, exist to benefit the rich and powerful, and are unnecessary for prosperity. Moreover, beliefs about the fairness of executive pay are as salient as desired levels of pay inequality in their impact on beliefs about income inequality. Whether Americans viewed excessive executive pay as a *cause* of economic malaise or simply an injustice in times of economic hardship for many Americans is impossible to determine, but certainly the former interpretation was entertained by journalists (see Chapter 2). Either way, perceptions of the deservingness of executives were bound up more tightly than perceptions of the deservingness of workers with concerns about income inequality.[42]

We have found throughout this section, in sum, that views about just deserts opportunity are intermeshed with views about income inequality. Unlike in the previous section, beliefs about opportunity here have a strong and consistent impact on beliefs about the relationship between income inequality and economic prosperity. Although an analogous pattern emerged in the previous section between views about violations of equal treatment opportunity and views about the rich and powerful in maintaining income inequality, it was somewhat more natural to grasp that relationship than this one between pay disparities and prosperity. As argued in the last section, the idea that social group advantages in getting ahead would contribute to social group capacities for perpetuating income inequality, and vice versa, is a coherent proposition about intergenerational immobility. By contrast, pay disparities are typically conceptualized as measures of inequality and not of economic prosperity, despite a venerable tradition of economic research on the relationship between income inequality and economic growth. Likewise, preferences for less pay inequality are typically construed as norms of fairness, conferring no information about perceptions of macroeconomic conditions. Extreme *levels* of inequality should be all that is necessary to provoke outrage over inequality.

But provided that prosperity is considered a central component of opportunity (i.e., "rising tide" opportunity), pay disparities may indeed function as signals of opportunity because of the motivational role they are intended to play in a meritocratic society bent on maximal levels of technological change and economic growth. To be sure, norms of fairness are violated by excessive pay at the top and insufficient pay at the bottom, but an "unjust meritocracy" also reflects distorted economic incentives that have potentially adverse economic consequences for the nation at large by restricting opportunities for good jobs at good wages for all but the most successful (at least according to the public). Conversely, Americans ought to be more accepting of exorbitant executive pay when the rising tide is "lifting all boats." Executives will be seen as justly rewarded for their beneficial stewardship of the economy, as was the case when concerns about inequality subsided in the boom years at the end of the 1990s. In short, just deserts are not merely a norm of fairness, nor are they simply a matter of individual opportunity in the form of rewards for individual merit. They are also a requirement for maintaining a virtuous and prosperous society for all Americans.

Rising Tide Opportunity
In perceiving a connection between fair pay and economic prosperity, Americans are making a more general connection between income inequality and rising tide opportunity. They are differentiating between a rising tide for the well-off and a rising tide that lifts all boats. They are expressing a preference for equitable growth over growth only for

growth's sake. This was also apparent in the findings from the previous chapter. Americans did not temper their concerns about income inequality between 1992 and 1996 when the economy began to recover from the early 1990s' recession. In fact, their concerns intensified during the jobless expansion of the mid-1990s. Only once the economy took off for the bottom as well as for the top at the end of the 1990s did concerns about income inequality subside. Concerns about income inequality are not simply dressed-up concerns about an imperiled economy; they are concerns about the democratic nature of economic growth.

In this section, I explore this subtle but significant point using data from sources other than the GSS, namely the American National Election Studies (ANES). Although the GSS has a superior time series of questions on income inequality, with the question on prosperity particularly apropos, the ANES has superior questions on perceptions of economic conditions. These questions allow us to examine whether perceptions of economic conditions mimic the trajectory of actual economic conditions (e.g., as measured by the unemployment rate), and whether and how perceptions of economic conditions are associated with beliefs about income inequality. Even if macroeconomic indicators are rebounding in an objective sense, Americans may not be convinced, and they may conflate their (erroneous?) subjective concerns about the economy with their concerns about income inequality. In other words, it is often asserted that what Americans are really festering about is the economy and not income inequality per se. We therefore want to be certain that it is income inequality that they object to rather than general economic malaise.

To measure perceptions of economic conditions, the ANES has a set of questions about how much better or worse off the national economy has become over the past year, as well as how much better or worse off the respondent is financially. These questions are frequently used by political scientists to distinguish between "pocketbook" voting based on individual finances and "sociotropic" voting based on national conditions. They are thus repeated as part of the ANES core modules throughout the time period of the 1980s, 1990s, and 2000s.[43] To measure beliefs about income inequality, the ANES has a special module of questions in 2002 and 2004 and a more limited replication of the module in 2008. Although this small number of years is not ideal, the module of questions on inequality is unique in providing insight into whether Americans knew about rising inequality (whether "the difference in incomes between rich people and poor people in the United States today is larger, smaller, or about the same as it was 20 years ago") and what they thought about it (whether it

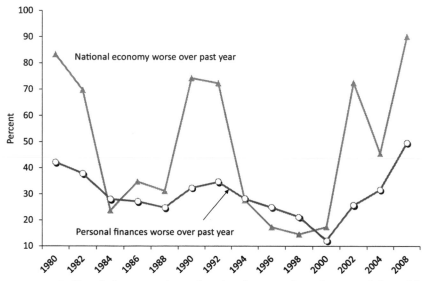

FIGURE 4.8. Trends in perceptions of national economic and personal financial conditions, 1980 to 2008. The wording of the questions is: "Would you say that over the past year the nation's economy has gotten better, stayed about the same or gotten worse?" and "We are interested in how people are getting along financially these days. Would you say that you and your family living here are better off or worse off financially than you were a year ago?" *Source:* 1948–2004 Cumulative File and 2008 American National Election Studies.

was a "good thing, a bad thing" or they had not "thought about it").[44] At least for these three years, we can assess the extent to which perceptions of personal and national economic conditions are conditioning opinions about income inequality. We examine this question after first determining how closely subjective perceptions of personal finances and national economic conditions overlap with objective indicators.

The data show resoundingly that subjective perceptions overlap very closely with objective conditions. As seen in Figure 4.8, Americans had a much sunnier outlook as the economic expansion of the 1990s wore on. In the twenty-nine–year period from 1980 to 2008, the third and fourth highest shares of Americans who thought that the economy was worse than a year ago appear in 1990 and 1992. These are the bookend years of the 1990–1991 recession, in which 74 and 72 percent of respondents characterized the economy as having "gotten worse" over the past year. By 1996, 1998, and 2000, however, perceptions had changed dramatically: the lowest shares of Americans over the period (15 and 17 percent) thought worse of the national economy relative to the previous year. These figures are more than 50 percentage points lower than the highs earlier in the decade. Because Americans are almost always more optimistic about their own financial situation than about the financial situation of others, the swings are not as exaggerated on this dimension. Still, they show the same pattern of pessimism at the dawn of the 1990s (35 percent saying their own financial situation in 1992 was worse than a year ago) followed by increasing optimism as the decade progressed (25 percent in 1996 and 12 percent in 2000).

Thus Americans were not misperceiving objective economic conditions, making them out to be more dismal than they actually were, at the same time that their concerns about income inequality grew. They were as optimistic on this score during the middle 1990s as they had been at almost any other time between 1980 and 2008.

Even though we have only two years of complete data on *both* beliefs about income inequality and perceptions of economic conditions in the ANES, we see almost exactly the same pattern as we saw in the previous chapter, in which concerns about inequality failed to dissolve as the economy began its recovery. In a helpful coincidence, the two years of ANES data differ in objective economic conditions and perceptions of those conditions. For instance, by the end of 2002 when the first questions on income inequality were asked, the economy had already passed into its second year of recovery, yet the official announcement of the end of the recession came, as is usually the case, much later in July 2003.[45] Unemployment, a lagging indicator, was declining at the end of 2002 but it was still a half–percentage point larger than two years later (5.9 percent in late 2002 versus 5.4 percent in late 2004) when questions about inequality were repeated. In turn, the share of Americans who thought the national economy was worse than a year ago was over 1.5 times higher in 2002 as in 2004 (72 percent versus 45 percent).[46] A stark change of this magnitude in perceptions of the economy over such a short period should have at least some impact on concerns about income inequality if such concerns are motivated by macroeconomic conditions narrowly construed. However, we find the opposite: concerns about income inequality actually increase from 2002 to 2004. The share believing income inequality to be higher and a bad thing rose from 41.3 percent in 2002 to 47.6 percent in 2004.[47]

This increase in concerns about income inequality was small but it nonetheless symbolizes the distinctiveness of such concerns relative to those about economic growth and prosperity, or rising tide opportunity. This difference is clear not only in the relative stability of beliefs about

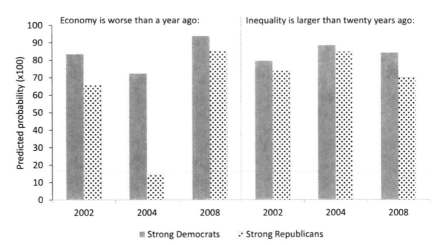

FIGURE 4.9. Adjusted effects of party identification on perceptions of the national economy and income inequality. Estimates are from ordered probit regression models including education, party ideology, partisan identification, and year; controls are set to midpoint values (see text for further details). See Figure 4.8 for the wording of the question about the national economy. The wording of the question about inequality is: "Do you think the difference in incomes between rich people and poor people in the United States today is larger, smaller, or about the same as it was 20 years ago?" *Source:* 2002, 2004 and 2008 American National Election Studies.

income inequality as worries about the economy plummeted, but in how other factors come into play in shaping both kinds of beliefs. For example, political factors weigh much more heavily in perceptions of the national economy than in perceptions of income inequality. As shown in Figure 4.9, which extends the analysis into 2008, partisanship differences in assessments of the economy were narrow in 2002 and 2008 but gaping in 2004, owing presumably to a consensus on the recessions in 2002 and 2008 on the one hand, and to the partisan rancor of the presidential election in the non-recessionary year of 2004 on the other hand. In 2002, for instance, 83 percent of strong Democrats and 66 percent of strong Republicans thought the economy was worse than a year ago, a relatively narrow partisan gap and a typical ordering of perceptions during a Republican administration. This difference then explodes into a 72 versus 15 percent gap in 2004.

By contrast, there was little change in partisanship effects in 2002 and 2004 on the factual question of whether income inequality was larger than twenty years ago (the only question available in 2002, 2004, and 2008). In both years, there was a difference of only 4 to 6 percentage

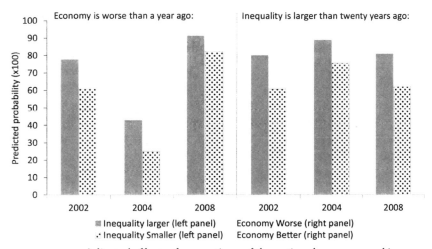

FIGURE 4.10. Adjusted effects of perceptions of the national economy and income inequality on each another. Estimates are from ordered probit regression models including education, party ideology, partisan identification, perceptions of the national economy or income inequality, and year; controls are set to midpoint values (see text for further details). See Figures 4.8 and 4.9 for the wording of the outcome questions. *Source:* 2002, 2004, and 2008 American National Election Studies.

points in the degree to which strong Democrats and strong Republicans perceived that income differences had grown larger.[48] A more substantial partisan effect appeared in 2008 but the gap was still just 14 percentage points, with the overwhelming majority of both strong Democrats and strong Republicans agreeing that income inequality was larger (84 and 70 percent, respectively). As also seen in the previous chapter, perceptions about income inequality are not as driven by partisan polarization as other issues (such as the state of the economy) appear to be.

But although distinct, and following different trajectories over time, beliefs about income inequality and broader economic conditions ultimately share a good deal in common at any given point in time. Across years, beliefs about income inequality are associated with beliefs about economic conditions. Drawing from the same models discussed above in Figure 4.9, Figure 4.10 shows that having the most negative views on the economy, relative to having the most positive views, increases the chances of thinking that income inequality has grown larger over time. This likelihood is greater for those with negative views about the economy by between 13 and 19 percentage points in 2002, 2004, and 2008. This is more than twice the size of the effect of partisanship on beliefs about income inequality in 2002 and 2004 and about the same as the partisan effect in 2008.

Similarly, believing that income inequality grew larger increased the chances of thinking that the economy grew worse over the past year by 9 to 18 percentage points. This effect is comparable to the effect of partisanship on perceptions of economic conditions in the recessionary periods of 2002 and 2008 (when consensus across parties was high). Moreover, when a range of additional controls and explanatory factors are added to these models, both effects remain strongly statistically significant. This is the most direct evidence we have that perceptions about the overall health of the economy make a strong impact on perceptions of income inequality, and vice versa.

In sum, the link between beliefs about rising tide opportunity and income inequality is consistent with the link we saw in the previous chapter. There we discovered an *expanding economy* on the heels of the 1990–1991 recession and yet *growing concerns* about income inequality, contrary to expectations of the power of the business cycle to drive economic attitudes of all kinds. Similarly, here we found increasingly positive impressions of the economy following the 2001 recession and yet slightly more widespread perceptions of growing income inequality, and qualms about it, between 2002 and 2004. Although it is true that Americans are less likely to tolerate income inequality during tough economic times, it is equally true that they will not ease up on their intolerance simply because the economy is growing. Similarly, Americans will judge the economy less favorably if they are concerned about income inequality, but they will not hide their heads in the sand or follow their partisan noses and deny that rosier economic conditions have arrived. They *will* hold out, however, for rosier times still, rosy enough to raise the bottom as well as the top. The sequence of events that we have observed suggests that although macroeconomic conditions provide an important foundation upon which to evaluate the fairness of income inequality – by providing an indication of the availability of opportunity, for example – they are not a *sufficient* explanation of those judgments. Americans care not only about a rising tide but about a rising tide that lifts all boats, including, as we saw in the previous section, fair rates of pay.

Group-Based Equal Treatment Opportunity

In this last empirical section, I examine what is perhaps the most well-known and certainly the most general set of questions about equality of opportunity available: the six questions on equal opportunities, chances, rights, and treatment that comprise the "egalitarianism" scale in the

ANES. These questions were introduced in 1984 and have been replicated in most of the ANES surveys up to 2008. Like the ANES questions on economic conditions, this time series of questions can be used to determine whether concerns about equality of opportunity arose at the same time that concerns about income inequality did, as well as whether they motivate concerns about income inequality at any given point in time. We will then be able to determine how useful this widely used set of questions on egalitarianism is for understanding beliefs specifically about *income* inequality.

As part of this investigation, I also examine whether beliefs about income inequality are motivated by concerns about violations of equal treatment based on the legally protected categories of race and gender. Such violations are sanctioned by antidiscrimination laws and are commonly associated with the term "equal opportunity" (e.g., as in equal employment opportunity). Given this association, it is possible that the egalitarian scale reflects beliefs about this particular view of equal opportunity (i.e., for protected groups) more than it reflects beliefs about class inequality. I therefore supplement my analysis of the egalitarianism scale with an analysis of questions that ask specifically about racial and gender inequality. My purpose is the same: to determine how they have changed over time as well as how they are associated with egalitarian beliefs in general and beliefs about income inequality in particular. Based on the partial interdependence of beliefs about equality of opportunity and equality of outcomes demonstrated throughout this chapter, we should expect to find at least some overlap among those who care about each of these dimensions of inequality. Once again, however, our interest is in refining our understanding of beliefs about income inequality as both related to and distinct from beliefs about opportunity.

The six questions in the ANES egalitarianism scale are shown in Table 4.6. All but one contain explicit references to equal opportunity, chances, treatment, or rights, but none contain explicit references to particular social groups. Table 4.6 indicates a wide range of support for these general egalitarian values, with the highest share of respondents (88 percent on average over the 1984-to-2008 time period) strongly agreeing or agreeing somewhat that "our society should do whatever is necessary to make sure that everyone has an equal opportunity to succeed." Although not nearly as high, support is also above 50 percent for the other two questions worded such that agreement is an expression of support for egalitarianism. For example, 67 percent agree that "if people were treated more equally in this country we would have many fewer problems." Support for greater egalitarianism is lower for the three questions in which

TABLE 4.6. *Support for Equal Opportunity, Rights, Chances, and Treatment, 1984 to 2008*

	Average Agreement/ Disagreement, 1984–2008	
	Somewhat	Strongly
Question wording, dis/agreement response, and range of dis/agreement over time:		
Our society should do whatever is necessary to make sure that everyone has an equal opportunity to succeed (agreement). Range: 82 to 91 percent.	61.6	26.8
If people were treated more equally in this country we would have many fewer problems (agreement). Range: 61 to 83 percent.	31.8	33.9
One of the big problems in this country is that we don't give everyone an equal chance (agreement). Range: 47 to 64 percent.	23.2	29.7
It is not really that big a problem if some people have more of a chance in life than others (disagreement). Range: 45 to 53 percent.	20.9	28.6
We have gone too far in pushing equal rights in this country (disagreement). Range: 32 to 47 percent.	19.1	20.7
This country would be better off if we worried less about how equal people are (disagreement). Range: 31 to 43 percent.	15.9	20.8

Note: Percentages presented are for agreement to the first three questions and disagreement to the last three questions.
Source: 1984–2008 Cumulative File of the American National Election Studies (weighted).

disagreement rather than agreement signals support. For instance, only 37 percent somewhat or strongly disagree that "this country would be better off if we worried less about how equal people are." Taken together, these responses are surprisingly tepid. Support for equality of opportunity is not as rock solid as is often assumed. In fact, in a 1987 ANES pilot study of beliefs about inequality of outcomes, the desire for less inequality of outcomes was comparable to the desire for less inequality of opportunity. For example, 60 percent of respondents agreed that "it would be better for everyone if the distribution of wealth in this country were more equal."[49]

Support for equal opportunity also varies over time. On average, total agreement to the GSS questions varies by 14, 19, and 20 percentage points over the 1987-to-2010 time period; similarly, the range over the

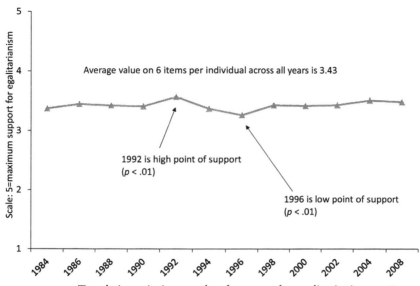

FIGURE 4.11. Trends in a six-item scale of support for egalitarianism, 1984 to 2008. See Table 4.6 for questions included in the scale. *Source:* 1948–2004 Cumulative File and 2008 American National Election Studies.

1984-to-2008 time period for the ANES questions is from 8 to 17 points. It is therefore possible that the ANES questions on egalitarianism follow the same trend as the GSS questions on income inequality, indicating an overlap in concerns about egalitarianism and income inequality. Figure 4.11 reveals that this is not the case, however. During the 1984-to-2008 period, a combined scale of support for equality of opportunity was at its highest point in 1992 and its lowest point in 1996. The scale ranges from 1 to 5 and is calculated as the average score on the six questions for each respondent (with 1 indicating lack of support and 5 indicating support). The average over the period is 3.42, falling between neutral and moderate support for equality of opportunity. The highest value for any given year is 3.57 in 1992; the lowest value is 3.26 in 1996. These patterns persist with controls for a wide range of factors. Because support for equality of opportunity fluctuated over the period in which concerns about income inequality were escalating, it is unlikely that general concerns about egalitarianism were the source of concerns about income inequality.

More obvious to lay and expert observers alike, concerns specifically about inequalities of opportunity for blacks and women were also on the wane during the period of heightened concerns over income inequality. The ANES question with the longest time series of data on views about racial inequality asks about "whether the government in Washington should make every possible effort to improve the social and economic position of blacks/Negroes and other minority groups." No question asks more simply about whether equality of opportunity for blacks and other minorities is a problem. Still, if equal treatment opportunity for blacks and other minorities was of growing concern, one might expect heightened support for government action. The long-term trend is toward *less* support for government action on behalf of blacks and minorities (except for a sharp and inexplicable blip in 1998), however. Paul Kellstedt provides a more thorough analysis of racial policy preferences and also shows that after a period of rising liberalism during the 1970s and early 1980s, racial policy preferences turned in a more conservative direction in the 1990s. Kellstedt contends that the trend toward conservatism marked a shift toward beliefs in norms of individualism and away from norms of equal opportunity, at least regarding race.[50] Finally, regarding equal opportunity for women, the best available time series is on the topic of support for women's equality, and this shows steady increases over time in such support.[51]

There is little indication, then, that a swell of opposition to violations of group-based equal opportunity arose in the 1990s and coincided with heightened opposition to income inequality. Nevertheless, at any given point in time, support for equality of opportunity and for racial and gender equality may represent different facets of a more general egalitarian ethos that includes a desire for less income inequality. We actually know remarkably little about how views about each of these dimensions of inequality are related to one another and whether and how they are constructed from views about particular social groups, such as blacks, women, the rich, and the poor.[52] This is too large a topic to tackle in any depth here, and the data are extremely sparse, but we do have a couple of years of ANES data that contain information on attitudes about egalitarianism, gender and racial inequality, a wide range of social groups (i.e., feeling thermometers about the poor, the rich, the working class, the middle class, blacks, Hispanics, immigrants, labor, and big business), and income inequality, all from the same set of respondents. With this unique combination of data, we can compare the extent to which general egalitarian views on the one hand and views about income inequality on the other are an outgrowth of views about gender inequality and racial inequality and about particular racial, ethnic, gender, and social class groups.

The results are presented in Table 4.7 and are both intriguing and puzzling. First, the egalitarianism scale is strongly and positively associated with support for women's equality and government action to

TABLE 4.7. *Estimates of the Relationship Among Beliefs About Social Groups, Social Group–Based Inequality, Egalitarianism, and Income Inequality*

Outcomes	Egalitarianism Scale (linear regression estimates)[a]	Inequality Much Larger and a Bad Thing (ordered probit marginal effects)[b]	Inequality Much Larger (ordered probit marginal effects)[b]
Variables (# of categories and coding order):			
Govt. aid to blacks (7, no to yes)	0.092 (0.017)**	0.020 (0.011)†	0.018 (0.010)†
Equal role for women (7, no to yes)	0.053 (0.021)**	−0.034 (0.011)**	0.018 (0.012)
Black	0.643 (0.081)**	−0.211 (0.062)**	−0.047 (0.049)
Hispanic	0.112 (0.100)	0.011 (0.057)	0.026 (0.048)
Female	0.073 (0.057)	−0.043 (0.030)	−0.052 (0.029)†
Feeling thermometers (0–100, negative to positive):			
Blacks	0.004 (0.002)	0.004 (0.001)**	−0.000 (0.001)
Hispanics	0.000 (0.002)	−0.004 (0.001)**	−0.002 (0.001)
Illegal immigrants	0.003 (0.002)	−0.002 (0.001)*	−0.003 (0.001)**
Rich people	−0.001 (0.002)	−0.003 (0.001)**	−0.003 (0.001)**
Big business	−0.009 (0.002)**	−0.003 (0.001)**	−0.002 (0.001)**
Egalitarianism scale	–	0.053 (0.024)*	0.070 (0.021)**
Inequality larger	0.101 (0.033)**	–	–
Select controls (# of categories and coding order):			
Party id. (7, Democrat to Republican)	−0.030 (0.019)	−0.026 (0.010)**	−0.010 (0.009)
Political views (7, liberal to conservative)	−0.145 (0.026)**	−0.020 (0.016)	−0.014 (0.014)
Economic conditions (3, better to worse)	0.054 (0.022)**	0.029 (0.010)**	0.022 (0.010)*
Year 2008	−0.118 (0.063)†	NA	0.005 (0.034)
R^2	0.39	0.12	0.07
Root MSE/Wald chi2(df)	0.82	217(24)	159(25)
N	1254	642	1254

Note: [a]See Figure 4.11 for the definition of the Egalitarianism Scale and Table 4.6 for the wording of the questions in the scale. For this analysis, the scale is standarized. [b]Estimates from ordered probit regression models are average marginal effects on the outcome category listed in the column title (i.e., "inequality is much larger and a bad thing" and "inequality is much larger" for the second and third columns, respectively). See Figure 4.9 and the text for the complete wording of the three questions that comprise these variables. **$p \leq 0.01$; *$p \leq 0.05$; †$p \leq 0.10$.

Source: 2004 and 2008 American National Election Studies.

improve the condition of blacks and minorities. The values of these coefficients remain virtually unaltered from baseline models when no other factors are controlled for in the equation. Racial identity also has a robust effect on egalitarian views, with blacks much more likely than all other racial groups to endorse egalitarian principles. By contrast, concerns about racial and gender issues seem to be less pressing in the minds of individuals who are troubled by income inequality. Those who support government action to improve the condition of blacks and minorities are more likely to be concerned about income inequality, but the effect is weakened by controls. More perplexing, support for women's equality *reduces* concerns about income inequality, as does being black (i.e., whites are disproportionately likely to be concerned about income inequality). In addition, feeling less warmly toward Hispanics and illegal immigrants *increases* concerns about income inequality, suggesting that Latino immigrants may be scapegoats for inequality.[53]

In all, the tenor of the results regarding beliefs about income inequality differs substantially from that for the egalitarianism scale. On the one hand, egalitarian values are strongly influenced by concerns about gender, racial, and ethnic inequalities, identities, and/or sympathies. On the other hand, concerns about income inequality are either not influenced by such factors to the same degree or are associated with views that are hostile toward minorities, women, and/or immigrants.

Given this conclusion, one might expect to find a similar divergence between the two outcomes in their relationship to views about social class distinctions. But although we do find one important difference, we also find a number of similarities. First, the feeling thermometers for "big business" and the "rich" are both strongly and consistently associated with views about income inequality. Negative feelings toward big business and the rich are each independently significant in raising concerns about income inequality. In a separate analysis shown in the third column of results in Table 4.7, negative views toward the rich and big business also increase the likelihood of correctly answering the factual question about income inequality, that is, that income differences have grown much larger over the last twenty years. For those who support egalitarian views, however, it is only negative views about big business that matter and not negative views about the rich.

Second, and surprisingly, sentiments about all other social-class groups – the poor, the middle class, the working class, labor, and welfare recipients – have no impact whatsoever for any of the outcomes once other factors are taken into account (results not shown). Similarly, other factors tend to weaken the effect of egalitarian values on views about income inequality and vice versa, even though they remain significant. This relationship, between general beliefs about equality of opportunity and inequality of outcomes, is mediated by more fundamental beliefs about politics and especially economics: liberal party identification or political views and pessimism about the economic outlook of the past year each raises egalitarian sentiments and concerns about income inequality. Amid these many similarities, then, the differences that stand out are that knowledge of and concerns about income inequality are aligned with distaste for the rich and big business and surprisingly little consolation, if not outright disinterest and disdain, for issues of racial, ethnic, or gender inequalities.

It does not appear, in sum, that it would be useful to infer beliefs about income inequality from general egalitarian views about group-based equality of opportunity or vice versa. Egalitarian values of this sort tap more into sympathies for inequalities based on race, ethnicity, and gender than for those based on income and social class distinctions. Beliefs about income inequality are in turn unique in their implication of the rich. This is consistent with findings from the GSS on the role of the rich in maintaining income inequality and the role of executive/worker pay disparities in shaping perceptions of economic prosperity. Particularly provocative is the finding in this section that feelings toward the rich affect both *factual* and *normative* judgments about the trend in income inequality. Because of the accuracy of the factual judgment (i.e., that income inequality has increased), it does not make sense to interpret negative feelings toward the rich as a form of bias that leads to misperceptions of the trend in income inequality. Although we cannot definitively test causal directions, we do know that the public perceives the rich as unfair beneficiaries of income inequality at best and causal agents of excessive and pernicious levels of income inequality at worst.[54] Neither the fact nor the importance of these associations between the rich and income inequality has been recognized in past research, nor are they compatible with the common assumption that Americans do not resent the rich.

The Connection between Opportunity and Inequality

Large numbers of Americans believe that hard work is the key to economic success. This belief has changed little over time according to the widely used question from the General Social Survey asking whether people get ahead more by "their own hard work" or by "lucky breaks or help from other people." The creed of hard work remains strong even when a larger portion of the population thinks their chances for upward mobility are limited; the economy is deteriorating; the rich make more than they should and the working class less; and inequality is too large, continues to exist to benefit the rich and powerful, and is unnecessary for prosperity. Remarkably, the hard work response to this particular question in the GSS is popular even when hard work responses to similar but more nuanced questions are not. For example, in various years from 2001 until 2012, Gallup asked whether individuals were satisfied with "the opportunity for a person to get ahead by working hard" and found that satisfaction (including those who were very or somewhat satisfied) plummeted from 76 to 53 percent over this period (as shown in Figure 4.1). Thus the fact that Americans have faith in the possibility of hard work to transform rags into riches – according to a single question, no less – is not an indication of their tolerance for income inequality, or even of their steadfast adherence to dominant ideologies of equal opportunity.

But because American acceptance of income inequality *is* typically inferred from their optimism about hard work in getting ahead, exactly how Americans reconcile what appear on the surface to be contradictory views about opportunity and inequality is crucial to decipher. The conclusion that emerges from exploring this question is that although Americans extol their country as the land of opportunity in principle, many believe it fails to live up to this promise in practice. This depiction of American beliefs about opportunity is hardly surprising, yet it is rarely acknowledged. More surprising, perhaps, is the belief that barriers to greater opportunity are bound up with barriers to greater equality. How exactly the two are bound together depends on how each is conceptualized. I distinguished the dominant "bootstraps" notion of opportunity, which emphasizes the role of hard work in getting ahead, from several other notions of opportunity redolent in American culture. I highlighted the roles of (1) equitable growth in providing a "rising tide that lifts all boats"; (2) fair pay in ensuring that workers and executives receive their "just deserts"; and (3) "equal treatment" in guaranteeing that the chances for upward mobility are severed from the influence of class background and social connections.

Americans custom tailor their beliefs about these different dimensions of opportunity – "rising tide," "just deserts," and "equal treatment" opportunity – to their beliefs about inequality. They coherently match particular violations of equal opportunity to corresponding problems with excessive inequality. Beliefs about inequality are distinctive and multidimensional in their own right while at the same time demonstrating strong affinities with perceptions of opportunity other than the "bootstraps" variety, which had *little to no impact* on beliefs about income inequality. In closing, I summarize three examples of such affinities.

The first example concerns the matching of beliefs about the importance of social advantages in getting ahead, and especially "knowing the right people," to beliefs about the role of the rich and powerful in perpetuating income inequality. Every violation of "equal treatment" opportunity (e.g., advantages stemming from social and family connections) is significantly associated with this particular rendering of income inequality as an instrument of the rich and powerful. By contrast, *none* of the violations of equal treatment opportunity are associated with the view of income inequality as an instrument of economic growth or decline. Americans appear to have an astute awareness of how social advantages are passed down from one generation to the next, restricting opportunity and reproducing existing inequalities at one and the same time. Yet they do not seem to believe that this particular violation of equality of opportunity is especially detrimental to economic growth and prosperity. Consistent with social psychological theories of system justification, perhaps, Americans may surmise that a certain degree of intergenerational reproduction is both inevitable and, as consequences of inequality go, relatively innocuous.

In the second example, Americans draw a tighter connection between violations of equal opportunity and economic prosperity. When opportunity is defined as fair pay according to performance and contribution, or "just deserts" opportunity, violations of equal opportunity norms seem to register as more flagrant than in other realms, with almost two-thirds of Americans asserting that low-end workers are underpaid and high-end workers overpaid. Furthermore, when perceptions of existing pay disparities exceed desired pay disparities, as they almost invariably do, Americans are more likely to strongly agree that income differences are too large, continue to exist to benefit the rich and powerful, and are unnecessary for prosperity. We also uncovered an equally strong and consistent association between violations of fair pay for executives (and not unskilled workers) and concerns about each aspect of income inequality.

Although it would seem that perceptions of pay disparities and beliefs about income inequality are one and the same thing (one about pay inequality and the other about income inequality), preordaining these results, the two follow similar but not the same trajectories over time. Higher and more accurate perceptions of the degree of pay inequality between executives and unskilled workers, taken as a factual indicator of awareness of inequality, grew steeply over time but were less important in capturing expressions of opposition to income inequality than measures of desired levels of pay and pay inequality relative to perceived levels of pay and pay inequality (these, by contrast, followed the same nonlinear trend over time in beliefs about income inequality found in the previous chapter). This suggests that the issue of fair pay is not only about abstract principles of fairness, derived from factual knowledge about levels of inequality, but about practical consequences as well, such as the potential thwarting of broader economic opportunities by unfair pay practices at the top.[55]

The third example is closely related to the second and concerns the more general relationship between income inequality and economic prosperity, or what I call "rising tide" opportunity. Here again is compelling evidence that Americans are discerning in their views about opportunity and inequality. As discussed in detail in the last chapter and replicated in this chapter with data from the ANES, American views about income inequality do not track the business cycle in a straightforward fashion, becoming more intolerant as the economy turns sour and less so as the economy rebounds. Instead, in the two instances in which we have data immediately following a recession and a few years later (1992/1996 in the GSS and 2002/2004 in the ANES), Americans expressed *greater* concern about inequality as both the economy and their perceptions of the economy improved. In the GSS data, for which we have a longer time series, it was not until 2000 that concerns subsided, presumably in conjunction with a rising tide that finally "lifted all boats."

Views about the economy and income inequality are intertwined, to be sure, but they cannot be reduced to one another. Ultimately, Americans care about equitable growth rather than growth per se. Demands for greater equality may be especially strong not when the economy is contracting but when it is expanding, and doing so only for those at the top and not for most Americans. This was the situation in the mid-1990s, as we saw in the last chapter. It also seems to characterize the past couple of years, when the Occupy Wall Street movement erupted as the anemic recovery from the Great Recession and financial crisis was well underway.

The primary goal of this chapter was to expand our ideas of what Americans think opportunity means well beyond the prototypical idea of pulling oneself up by one's bootstraps through hard work and perseverance. I went so far as to conceptualize inequality in outcomes as itself a perceived barrier to opportunity. In the next chapter, I examine the implications of recasting beliefs about income inequality as a matter of opportunity for understanding how Americans think their concerns about inequality and opportunity should be addressed in the policy arena.

Appendix

TABLE A4.1. *Adjusted Marginal Effects of Beliefs About Bootstraps and Equal Treatment Opportunity on Three Questions About Beliefs Regarding Income Inequality, 1987 to 2010*

Strong Agreement That...	Income Differences are Too Large	Inequality Continues to Exist to Benefit the Rich and Powerful	Large Income Differences are Unnecessary for Prosperity
Probability of strong agreement:[a]	.207	.143	.114
(1) Average marginal effects of single "get ahead" question:[b]			
Getting ahead through hard work[c]	−0.026 (0.009)**	−0.041 (0.009)**	−0.013 (0.008)†
Standard of living will improve[d]	−0.041 (0.009)**	−0.046 (0.008)**	−0.031 (0.007)**
N	3327	3285	3314
(2) Average marginal effects of separate "get ahead" questions:[b]			
Probability of strong agreement:[a]	.210	.116	.085
Importance for getting ahead in life...[e]			
Hard work	−0.001 (0.011)	−0.000 (0.008)	−0.007 (0.007)
Having a good education yourself	0.018 (0.011)	0.014 (0.008)†	0.004 (0.007)
Ambition	0.042 (0.012)**	0.018 (0.009)*	0.005 (0.008)
Natural ability	0.007 (0.011)	0.034 (0.011)**	−0.009 (0.009)
Knowing the right people	0.055 (0.009)**	0.046 (0.008)**	0.004 (0.005)
Having well-educated parents	0.052 (0.010)**	0.017 (0.007)**	−0.003 (0.006)
Coming from wealthy family	0.025 (0.007)**	0.017 (0.005)**	−0.003 (0.004)
A person's race	0.025 (0.008)**	0.024 (0.006)**	−0.007 (0.005)

Notes: [a]For a typical respondent, who is female, white, married, employed, and not living in the South; self-identifies as middle class, a Democrat or independent, and moderate; has mean age, age squared, household size, children, education, and family income; and has mean values on the year dummies. [b]Estimates are for a typical respondent from a binary logistic regression model with standard errors in parentheses. Only one focal opportunity variable is included at a time. [c]The codes for this variable are 1=luck and help from other people is most important; 2=hard work, luck equally important; 3=hard work is most important. The within-sample mean is 2.5. See Figure 4.1 for question wording and response distributions. [d]The codes for this recoded variable are 1=strongly disagree and disagree; 2=neutral; 3=agree and strongly agree. The within-sample mean is 2.5. See Figure 4.5 for question wording and response distributions. [e]The codes for these variables range from essential=5 to not at all important=1. Sample sizes vary with each variable as not all are available in the same years. See Table 4.2 for question wording and response distributions. **$p <- 0.01$; *$p <- 0.05$; †$p <- 0.10$.
Source: 1987, 1996, 2000, 2008, 2010 General Social Survey and 1992 International Social Survey Program.

5

Americans' Social Policy Preferences in the Era of Rising Inequality[1]

Although a vast industry of poll takers and scholars is in the business of tracking every contour of American policy attitudes, we know almost nothing about the impact of rising income inequality on social policy preferences. The American Political Science Association's (APSA) Task Force on Inequality and American Democracy emphasized the importance of this omission in its 2004 report. It tried to capture what we know about enduring attitudes toward inequality, opportunity, and government redistribution, but it was unable to document whether these had changed in any significant way in response to the steep rise in income inequality over the past several decades.[2] Since the publication of the report nearly a decade ago, the question remains unexplored. This is especially surprising given the growing number of scholars interested in the policy implications of rising income inequality, as well as a new emphasis on the vital role that policy attitudes play in shaping welfare-state spending.[3]

Although the APSA Task Force report identified data limitations as the primary reason for our lack of progress on this question, a claim with which we agree and will discuss in a moment, there are theoretical shortcomings at play as well, and these are at least as noteworthy as the data limitations. As described in previous chapters, there is a far richer and more nuanced literature on American views about inequality, opportunity, and redistribution than is on display in current discussions of public opinion about rising inequality. On the subject of policy preferences in particular, the lion's share of attention is devoted to only two views, and both have led to dead ends. One is that Americans do not care much about inequality of outcomes (as opposed to inequality of opportunity), and hence rising inequality should not produce a shift in preferences for government policy. The other view, identified with the most influential theoretical models of the political process, is that a rise in inequality will lead to an increase in demand for government redistribution. The case to recommend this view is rather slim, however, as we have not witnessed a spike in popular demands for higher taxes on the rich or more spending on the poor. To the contrary, welfare as an entitlement was abolished in 1996, and taxes on the rich were cut in the early 2000s, both to what appears to be public accord if not acclaim. Moreover, it has been difficult to reinstate taxes on the rich in the context of a looming budget deficit, although this is less a function of public will than legislative polarization. Based on this prima facie evidence, most observers conclude that rising inequality is of little consequence to American policy preferences.

Not fully satisfied with the status quo view that Americans are in the main undisturbed by rising inequality, proponents of two additional perspectives have entered the dialogue in recent years. Their views have contradictory implications. On the one hand, some scholars contend that Americans are either unaware of the true magnitude of disparities or uninformed about how such disparities can be curtailed by progressive taxes and social spending. In either event, Americans are unequipped to register their concerns about inequality in the conventional language of redistribution. On the other hand, a different set of scholars seizes on the well-known tendency of Americans to be "operational liberals," even if they are simultaneously "ideological conservatives," to argue that Americans are supportive of a wide array of government programs that are redistributive in effect, if not always in name or intent.[4] Support for liberal policies of all stripes is then offered as evidence that Americans are both aware of rising inequality and opposed to it. Although this view resonates with the tradition of casting Americans as ambivalent about inequality, the former view resonates with a more recent scholarly focus on the cognitive burdens of and barriers to participating in the political process and formulating coherent policy preferences, particularly in domains in which the issues are complex and overwrought with competing partisan interests.[5]

Despite their different predictions, all of the above views have one thing in common: with a single exception, they do not investigate *empirically* whether attitudes about income inequality are in fact related in any significant way to views about social policy.[6] Below, we explicitly test whether policy preferences are influenced by perceptions of income inequality in the fashion that scholars have proposed, or in the alternative ways implied by the findings of previous chapters. This is done by directly examining the relationship between beliefs about income inequality and social policy preferences, as well as changes in this relationship from the late 1980s to the present. The only data that allow such an examination for a variety of social policies and over a substantial portion of the era of rising income inequality come from the General Social Survey.[7] We supplement these data with corroborating evidence on social policy preferences from other sources, such as the American National Election Surveys (ANES) and public opinion surveys from polling organizations, such as Harris, Gallup, and Pew, among others.[8] Although we would prefer additional years of data, more detailed coverage of each policy domain, and coverage of a wider array of policy domains, the volume of data we analyze is substantial, and the overall patterns we observe allow us to draw several unexpected conclusions about the consequences of rising inequality for public policy preferences.

To guide the empirical analysis, and to pave the way for subsequent surveys that we hope will be more in tune with American beliefs about inequality, we build on earlier chapters to construct a new analytical framework for understanding Americans' beliefs about how to address issues of income inequality. A new framework is necessitated by new social conditions – the era of rising inequality – as well as the need to bring theoretical perspectives on beliefs about inequality into conversation with more recent research on social policy preference formation, such as the role of the media in shaping policy preferences and the onerous cognitive demands of deliberating over policy options. The framework encompasses social policies that scholars typically associate with direct reductions in income inequality (e.g., transfers of income from the rich to the poor) as well as social policies that they do not (e.g., education, health care, and social security). Special care is taken to specify the *mechanisms* that underlie preferences for *each* of these policy domains and not to lump all social policies into one catchall category of welfare state programs. The framework also incorporates policies that correspond to one of the main thrusts of earlier chapters: the potential of equitable growth to function as a form of labor market redistribution, in both reality and, more to the point, in the American mind. In addition to organizing the analysis and discussion here, the framework should prove useful in guiding future data collection and research on the political dimensions of rising income inequality.

After laying out the analytical framework and empirical strategy in greater detail, we begin by evaluating the two dominant views about public opinion on rising inequality: that Americans do not care much

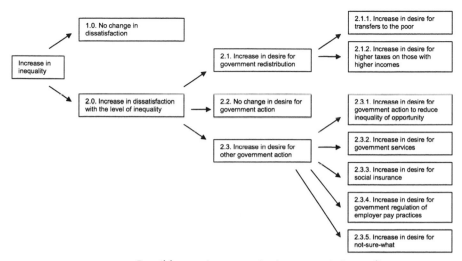

FIGURE 5.1. Possible reactions to a rise in economic inequality.

about inequality of outcomes, and that a rise in inequality will lead to an increase in demand for government redistribution. Our examination suggests little support for these views, at least for this particular period of rising inequality. Instead, Americans do increasingly object to inequality, and those who do so also believe government should act to redress it, but not necessarily via traditional redistributive programs. The evidence suggests that Americans may be unsure or uninformed about how to address rising inequality and thus are swayed by contemporaneous debates and portrayals of the issue in the media. However, we also find that Americans favor expanding education spending in response to their increasing concerns about inequality. Consistent with prior chapters, this suggests that equal opportunity in education and the labor market may be more germane than government redistribution to our understanding of the politics of inequality.

Policy Framework

Figure 5.1 outlines the analytical framework that guides the chapter. The framework consists of a series of possible responses to an increase in income inequality (the theoretical rationale for each response is discussed later when we evaluate the evidence for or against it). The first possible response is one we have already alluded to: that Americans do not care about rising inequality and therefore do not alter their policy preferences in its presence (path 1.0). The second response is that they *are* concerned about it (path 2.0), in which case we suggest three potential reactions. One is a rise in support for traditional redistributive policies (path 2.1), such as greater transfers to the poor (path 2.1.1) and higher tax rates for the rich (path 2.1.2). A second possibility is that there is no change in desire for government action; rising inequality is worrisome to Americans, but they do not think government should or can attempt to address it (path 2.2). The third is that Americans object to rising inequality and want government to do something about it, but not (or not mainly or only) via traditional redistributive strategies (path 2.3).

If Americans do not favor direct redistributive transfers of income, what type of government action do they favor? Here we distinguish five potential reactions and caution against grouping all liberal social policies into one big grab bag of government programs. First, as argued in Chapter 4, people may interpret rising inequality of outcomes as an indication of excessively unequal opportunities (path 2.3.1). This may elicit support for government action to expand opportunity, for example through greater spending on education. The second and third possible reactions follow from trends in earnings and employer-provided benefits during the era of rising inequality. For most Americans without a college degree, earnings and benefits have declined, stagnated, or grown only modestly. To keep up with the cost of living, Americans may desire greater assistance from government, through increased spending on services such as medical or child care (path 2.3.2) or increased generosity of social insurance programs such as social security and unemployment compensation (path 2.3.3). Because these programs benefit people in need but are not targeted to the poor and do not involve transfers of income without contributions, they are not typically viewed as redistribution, even though in practice they have a strong redistributive component.

Fourth, rather than programs that involve government expenditures, Americans may prefer that government impose or heighten regulations on employers, which helps to ameliorate earnings inequality and expand job opportunities in the labor market (path 2.3.4). Examples include increasing the statutory minimum wage, protecting and expanding bargaining rights, reducing immigrant employment, and limiting executive pay (or penalizing "excessive" pay). Finally, Americans may be concerned about a rise in inequality but at a loss as to what government should do in response (path 2.3.5). As a result, they may gravitate toward whatever seemingly relevant policy solution is currently at the forefront of political or media discussions.

Consistent with this framework's starting point, the empirical strategy begins with a review of the actual rise in income inequality and then determines whether any of the above responses occurred during the period when income inequality was rising, and more specifically, whether and which responses grew at the same time as income inequality did. For this we need three pieces of information: (1) attitudes about income inequality at multiple points over the period of rising income inequality, (2) policy preferences at multiple points over this period, and (3) the actual trend in income inequality over time. With these data in hand, we can develop a set of expectations that match the timing of changes in attitudes and policy preferences to the trend in income inequality.

Regarding (1) and (2), we use data from the General Social Survey and the International Social Survey Program (hereafter referred to simply as the GSS and ISSP). Although the GSS are the only data enabling us to draw inferences about the relationship over time between Americans' views of income inequality and social policy preferences, they have limitations.[9] Because replication of questions is (justifiably) prized above introduction of new ones, questions on income inequality were not introduced into the GSS until 1987, when they were included as a special module. They were then replicated in five additional years – 1992, 1996, 2000, 2008, and 2010 – as an initiative of the ISSP or GSS. Among these six years of data on attitudes about inequality, there are at least five years of data for all the relevant social policy questions in the GSS. Fortunately, all the social policy questions were asked in 1987, all but one were asked in 1996, and all but two were asked again in 2000, 2008, and 2010. The data on policy preferences therefore span two decades of rising inequality. However, several of the social policies that we identify as potentially associated by the American public with reducing inequality – such as the minimum wage, protection of wage-bargaining rights, regulation of executive pay, trade and immigration policy, and unemployment insurance – are not represented in the GSS time series at all. Nonetheless, for theoretical completeness, we maintain them in our framework and include them in our discussion.

Regarding (3), because our aim is to examine the American public's response to changes in inequality, we discuss several measures of inequality but focus on the measure people are most likely to be aware of during the period of our analysis.[10] We also review media coverage of the issue. For this information, we summarize the trends in income inequality and its media coverage that were presented in greater detail in Chapters 2 and 3 (see especially Figures 3.7 and 3.8). In Chapter 3, we relied primarily on data from the March Current Population Survey, which the Census Bureau uses to calculate the degree of income inequality among households as measured by the Gini coefficient. This would seem to be the most widely referenced measure in political discussions and debates and by journalists and scholars.[11] For trends in media coverage, we relied on Chapter 2's analysis of a random sample of media coverage in the top three newsweeklies in each year from 1980 to 2010.

Inequality according to the Census Bureau measure of the Gini coefficient increased most rapidly between the late 1970s and early 1990s, jumped between 1992 and 1993 because of a change in the Census Bureau data collection methods, and then continued to increase moderately to the end of the series in 2009. Developments from the second half of the 1990s are less straightforward than developments during the 1980s and early 1990s, as different measures followed different trajectories. On the one hand, the top continued to pull away from the middle. The ratio of hourly earnings between the 95th and 50th percentiles grew sharply and steadily from the 1980s to the 2000s (as did the share of income going to the top 1 percent of taxpayers). On the other hand, the picture brightened at times for those in the bottom half. The 50th/10th percentile ratio declined from the late 1980s to the early 2000s and then began to tick up again. Median male hourly earnings also showed signs of improvement beginning in the mid-1990s. After rising in the latter part of the 1990s, however, median male earnings reached a plateau in the 2000s, and even dipped in some years, to arrive at the end of the 2000s no higher than in 1980. On the whole, progress toward less inequality was most apparent during the economic boom of the late 1990s but was followed in the 2000s by a consolidation of high levels of inequality and stagnant income for at least the bottom half of households.

Media coverage of income inequality corresponds to some of the trend in income inequality and median male wages, but not to all of it. Media coverage marches to a different tune most notably in the early and mid-1990s, when it undergoes its first marked and sustained increase, and peaks relative to all other years in the study from 1980 to 2010. This heightened attention in the 1990s is consistent with a lagged response to the onset of rising inequality in the 1980s, as it took time for experts to recognize the trend and to come to a consensus that could be disseminated to the media. The decline in coverage after the peak in the mid-1990s, moreover, is consistent with the improvement in economic conditions in the late 1990s, the fall of some measures of inequality, and the rise in earnings for men in the middle of the distribution, all reflecting an interlude of equitable growth. The fluctuations in media coverage are also more dramatic than they are for measures of income inequality and male earnings. The drop in media coverage in the late 1990s was more pronounced than it was for these measures, for instance, and media coverage was lackluster for much of the 2000s despite historically high levels of inequality. By the end of the 2000s, coverage picks up again but does not surpass the 1990s' peaks, even during the Great Recession and financial crisis (recall, however, that our media coverage analysis ends in 2010, before the Occupy Wall Street movements brought inequality back into the limelight).

Because of this complexity, we make a few simplifying assumptions to guide our empirical approach in this chapter. First, the general trend toward rising inequality was, according to all measures, well underway by the first year of GSS public opinion data in 1987. Second, public awareness of the trend most likely grew over the 1990s, as income inequality continued to increase beyond a temporary blip and the issue became more widely acknowledged by experts and discussed by the media and politicians.[12] Accordingly, we expect the first year of data on attitudes about income inequality, 1987, to serve as a reasonable baseline against which to measure shifts in attitudes about inequality and related social policy preferences during the early and mid-1990s (i.e., at the data points of 1992 and 1996). Given the ambiguity in the trend in inequality in the second half of the 1990s, coupled with a decline in media coverage during these years, we are open regarding the likely trajectory of attitudes and preferences over the late 1990s (i.e., at the data point of 2000). However, our expectation based on the above trends in media coverage, income inequality, and median male earnings is that the reaction would be greatest in the early to mid-1990s (the data points of 1992 and 1996), lowest in the late 1990s (the data point of 2000), and somewhere in between in the late 2000s (the data points of 2008 and 2010).

Social Policy Preferences

No Change in Dissatisfaction with the Level of Inequality?
Perhaps the most commonly held view regarding American beliefs about inequality is that Americans do not care about it, or at least do not care about it very deeply. This view is often depicted in the media but is also held by a wide variety of public opinion experts and scholars. In a 2006 cover story on American inequality in *The Economist*, for example, the lead paragraph declared that "Americans do not go in for envy... The gap between the rich and poor is bigger than in any other advanced country, but most people are unconcerned."[13] This cross-national perspective

is often cited by scholars as well, who see Americans as accepting "considerable disparities of income and wealth – much more than their European counterparts do," and concerned more with equality of opportunity than equality of outcomes.[14] Regarding the particular issue of *rising* inequality, we encounter the same conclusions. For example, the coauthor of a nuanced study of American attitudes about inequality found "little evidence that rising income inequality ever captured the public's imagination."[15] Scholars have also expressed doubts based on the prima facie evidence that "no popular movement has arisen to challenge inegalitarian trends" (prior to the Occupy Wall Street movement).[16]

But even prior to the Occupy movements, changes in attitudes about inequality in the United States never squared with this hypothesis, as demonstrated in detail in Chapter 3. Trends in the share of GSS respondents agreeing with the statement that "differences in income in America are too large" indicate a substantial rise from the late 1980s to the early 1990s in the share of Americans feeling that the income gap is excessive; there is a high absolute level of agreement across time as well, ranging from 58 to 77 percent. The peak of concern is in either 1992 or 1996, depending on whether agreement and strong agreement are combined, followed in order by the late 2000s (2008 or 2010), 2000, and 1987. The GSS data include two other items that tap Americans' attitudes regarding income inequality: "Large differences are unnecessary for America's prosperity" and "Inequality continues to exist because it benefits the rich and powerful."[17] Both show even stronger trends toward intense dissatisfaction with inequality in the mid-1990s, with strong agreement and total agreement both peaking in 1996, returning to near 1987 levels in 2000, and rising once again in the late 2000s. During the high point of intense opposition in 1996, more than half of Americans strongly agreed or agreed to each of the three questions (from 58 percent to 67 percent, as compared to a range of 38 to 58 percent in 1987). The magnitude of these shifts is nontrivial compared to many other public opinion shifts.[18]

Responses to the three questions are combined into a single index to facilitate the main purpose of our analysis, which is to determine whether the shift in concern about inequality affected policy preferences.[19] To confirm that the trend for this index is robust to changes over time in compositional shifts in the population, Figure 5.2 presents the full distribution of the "attitudes about inequality index" adjusted for a variety of socio-demographic factors and political attitudes.[20] The predicted values of the index adjusted for these factors illustrate once again that dissatisfaction with inequality increased significantly between the late 1980s

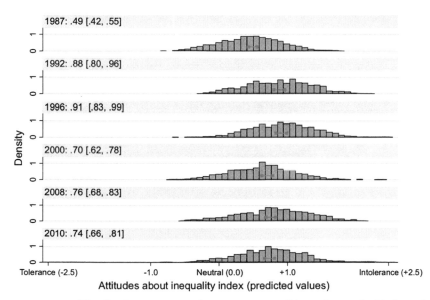

FIGURE 5.2. Distribution, mean, and 95 percent confidence interval of index of attitudes about inequality by year, 1987 to 2010. Index is an additive combination of responses to three questions about beliefs regarding income inequality; it ranges from −3 to +3. Estimates are predicted values from the linear regression model in Appendix Table A3.2. *Source:* 1987, 1996, 2000, 2008, 2010 General Social Survey and 1992 International Social Survey Program.

and the early to middle 1990s, declined in 2000, and increased modestly in the late 2000s. Still, dissatisfaction is significantly higher in all years relative to the base year of 1987.

Based on these trends, we use three criteria in assessing whether rising concerns about income inequality had an impact on social policy preferences over the same time period. First, consistent with trends in concerns about inequality, support for the particular social policy (e.g., spending on welfare) should have increased in the 1990s relative to 1987. Second, attitudes about income inequality, as measured by the index, ought to have a positive effect on support for the social policy. Third, the shift in attitudes toward inequality – in terms of either the growing number of dissatisfied individuals (a compositional shift) or a change in their policy preferences (a behavioral shift) – should account for some of the trend toward increasing support among the general public for the social policy in the 1990s.[21]

We have two additional expectations regarding these analyses. First, we expect all these patterns to occur net of the socio-demographic and political controls mentioned earlier in this section. That is, given the shift in mass public opinion that we observe in attitudes toward inequality, both here and in the more extensive analysis of Chapter 3, our objective is to gauge shifts in mass public opinion in policy preferences. Although there is growing interest in the extent to which public opinion is shaped by economic status or political ideology, our contribution is to introduce variation in policy preferences across attitudes toward inequality, controlling for other factors that are commonly singled out for subgroup analysis.[22] We leave further extensions of this kind to future research.

Second, based on the greater spread and intensity of opposition to inequality in 1992 and 1996 than in other years, and the divergence of trends in income inequality in the late 1990s, we have higher expectations for a policy preference response to rising inequality in 1992 and 1996 than in 2000. In Chapter 3, we also explored the role of a number of potentially confounding factors – including the recession of the early 1990s, the boom of the late 1990s, the Great Recession, the antiwelfare reform campaign of the mid-1990s, four presidential elections, and the actual trend in income inequality – and we concluded that the grounds for rising opposition to inequality were most fertile in 1992 and 1996. Thus given the replication of all but one of the policy preference questions in both 1987 and 1996, the 1987 to 1996 shift will be the most critical yardstick for assessing the public's policy orientation in addressing excessively high levels of income inequality. The other shifts (e.g., 1987 to 1992, 1987 to 2000, 1987 to 2008, and 1987 to 2010) will provide additional leverage.

Increase in Desire for Government Redistribution?
With both inequality and concerns about inequality on the rise, we might expect support for redistribution to have been given a boost among Americans. A long line of research considers egalitarianism to be "the value dimension that is most relevant to policy debates over social welfare."[23] Individuals with egalitarian sentiments are more likely to support government intervention in redistributive matters,[24] and it is frequently implied that support for social welfare programs is itself an indicator of the depth of egalitarian sentiment in a society.[25] In addition, median-voter models predict this type of response.[26] A higher level of market inequality implies a greater distance between mean and median (pretransfer-pretax) income, with the median farther below the mean. The lower the median relative to the mean, the more the median income person or household is likely to benefit from government redistribution, in the sense that the transfers the person receives will exceed his or her share of the tax burden and

the greater the amount of redistribution he or she will favor. This line of argument implies that increases in egalitarian sentiments should result in increases in support for conventional redistributive policies. Yet we know of no research that has analyzed these relationships over time.

The two main redistributive policies we examine involve direct transfers of income to reduce posttransfer-posttax inequality: transfers to the poor and taxation of the rich. Figure 5.3 displays trends in public opinion toward these two types of redistributive strategies using a variety of questions from the GSS. We begin with preferences regarding transfers to the poor, the type of program perhaps most widely associated with the U.S. welfare state. The GSS regularly asks whether government assistance to the poor and spending on welfare are too little, about right, or too much. Trends in the share responding that spending is too little are shown in panels (a) and (b) of Figure 5.3. Despite diametrically opposed levels of support depending on how the question is worded – with virtually no support for "welfare" and well above majority support for "assistance to the poor" – there is no indication in either case of an increase in support for these policies to mimic the rise in income inequality.[27] Instead, support declines in 1996, consistent with the passage of welfare reform at that time, and then heads north to what political scientists Joe Soss and Sanford Schram consider a steady level of support dating back several decades.[28] We observe this same pattern for other questions about helping the poor and redistributing income from the rich to the poor, shown in panels (c) and (d) of Figure 5.3.

Figure 5.4 explores these trends further and examines their connection to beliefs about income inequality. In the figure, there are two vertical lines for each of the policies in each of the years in which public opinion about the policy is available, except for the base year of 1987. The vertical lines with large squares represent the average increase or decrease in support relative to 1987 for the policy and its 95 percent confidence interval for each of the policies graphed in Figure 5.3. The policies are arrayed across the top of the figure. The estimates of average changes in policy support since 1987 are net of the various socio-demographic and political attitudinal factors noted earlier, but not net of attitudes about income inequality as measured by the index. The shift in policy support since 1987 net of attitudes about inequality is represented by the second vertical line for each policy outcome, with small squares. Recall that the index of dissatisfaction with inequality is higher in every year since 1987. If dissatisfaction with levels of income inequality results in greater support for assistance to the poor, shift in such support for the poor

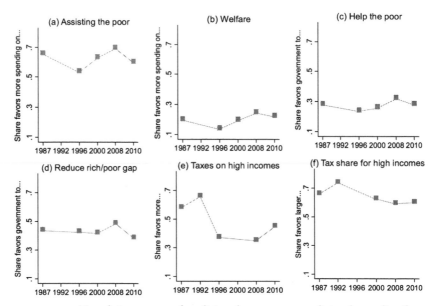

FIGURE 5.3. Trends in support of traditional government policies that redistribute income from the top and/or to the bottom, 1987 to 2010. Question wording and response categories presented in the figure are:

(a) We are faced with many problems in this country, none of which can be solved easily or inexpensively. Are we spending too much money, too little money, or about the right amount on assistance to the poor? (too little)

(b) We are faced with many problems in this country, none of which can be solved easily or inexpensively. Are we spending too much money, too little money, or about the right amount on welfare? (too little)

(c) Should the government do everything possible to improve the standard of living of all poor Americans, or should each person take care of himself? (2 categories indicating "government should")

(d) Should the government reduce income differences between rich and poor, perhaps by raising taxes of wealthy families or by giving income assistance to the poor, or should the government not concern itself with reducing differences? (3 categories indicating "government should")

(e) Generally, how would you describe taxes in America today, meaning all taxes together, including social security, income tax, sales tax, and all the rest: First for those with high incomes? (much too low and too low)

(f) Do you think that people with high incomes should pay a larger share of their incomes in taxes than those with low incomes, the same share, or a smaller share? (much larger share and larger share)

Source: 1987, 1996, 2000, 2008, 2010 General Social Survey and 1992 International Social Survey Program.

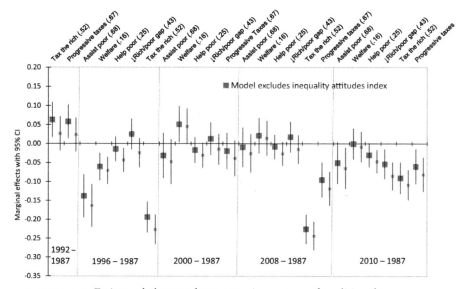

FIGURE 5.4. Estimated changes from 1987 in support of traditional government policies that redistribute income. Average marginal year effects and 95 percent confidence intervals are from ordered logistic regression models for each policy outcome pooled across years (with mean share of support across years for each policy in parentheses), with and without the index of attitudes about income inequality included in the model. See Figure 5.3 for question wording and the Appendix to Chapter 3 for a description of control variables. *Source*: 1987, 1996, 2000, 2008, 2010 General Social Survey and 1992 International Social Survey Program.

over time should be reduced when the increase in dissatisfaction with inequality (since 1987) is accounted for. As implied by median-voter and other welfare state theories, the increase in support for the policy should be a result, at least in part, of increases in dissatisfaction with inequality.

We are therefore looking for three things in Figure 5.4. First is a general increase in support for redistributive policies to correspond to the increase in dissatisfaction with inequality. This will be indicated by the vertical line with a large square located in the positive range of the figure above the horizontal line of "zero effect." Second, we look for a positive relationship between dissatisfaction with inequality and support for the social policy, although this will be represented only indirectly in the figure. Last, if a positive relationship is found, we are looking for a decline in support for redistributive policies once the increase in dissatisfaction with inequality is taken into consideration. This will be indicated by smaller squares representing a smaller number than larger squares.[29]

The first startling impression given by Figure 5.4 is that in *only one of sixteen* instances did support for improving the plight of the poor rise significantly in the two decades following 1987. Moreover, the single instance occurred in the year 2000, not a high-water mark for opposition to inequality; and it occurred for the question asking explicitly about "welfare," which garners the least support of all questions about the poor. This finding most likely reflects a rebound from the unusually negative reactions to welfare in the mid-1990s during the height of welfare reform (and welfare bashing). In all other instances, support either dropped significantly, as in 1996 and 2010, or was unperturbed. The slide in support in 1996 does not coincide with trends in concerns about income inequality, which peak at this time. However, the vertical lines with the small squares reveal that support would have been even weaker had dissatisfaction with income inequality not escalated in the 1990s and 2000s. This is a sign that those who are more likely to be dissatisfied with income inequality are also more likely to endorse polices for the poor. Despite this, we see no evidence that the population at large became more likely to support transfers to the poor in line with their growing discontent over inequality, or that those most concerned about inequality increased the intensity of their support for these policies.[30]

In the age of rising income inequality, however, it is conceivable that the taxing side of the taxing-and-spending equation better captures the ethos of redistributive policy, at least relative to spending on poverty. Does taxing the rich fare any better in the public eye than spending on the poor? To answer this, we utilize responses to questions that ask whether taxes are too low for high-income groups and whether taxes should be larger on high-income groups than on low-income groups. (We also see similar patterns in questions that ask about whether taxes are too high for middle- and low-income groups.) Figures 5.3 and 5.4 reveal that the most dramatic swings in policy sentiment occur in response to questions about taxing the rich, and these are principally in the negative direction. The pattern of support for progressive taxation fluctuates over the 1990s but shows no sustained rise for heavier taxes on the well-to-do. As shown in panel (e) of Figure 5.3, the overall level of support is quite impressive, however, attracting a majority of Americans in the late 1980s and early 1990s. Support is also amplified in 1992, but the proclivity to seek more taxes from the rich plummets in 1996 at the peak of dissatisfaction with inequality, as well as in the late 2000s during the Great Recession. The pattern is similar in panel (f) of Figure 5.3, although shifts in the consensus view that "people with high incomes should pay a larger share of their incomes in taxes than those with low incomes" are more attenuated.

When we examine more closely the relationship between trends in dissatisfaction with income inequality and tax policies, however, the picture is somewhat murkier. On the one hand, turning again to Figure 5.4, we see not only that support for both questions about taxing the rich was significantly greater in 1992 than in 1987, but that the increasing share of individuals concerned about inequality accounts for the higher level of support among the general public in 1992 (i.e., the vertical line with the small square accounts for the increase in dissatisfaction about inequality and crosses the line of "zero effect," whereas the vertical line with the large square, not controlling for attitudes about inequality, registers a positive effect). Americans less tolerant of inequality were significantly more likely to favor higher taxes on the affluent, and the increasing share of such Americans in 1992 boosted support for more progressive tax policies overall. On the other hand, there is a colossal drop in the public's inclination to favor stiffer taxation of the rich in 1996 and 2008, and a still significant but less dramatic decline in 2010. Although the progressive views of those unhappy with existing levels of inequality exert pressure in a liberal direction in all years, this pressure pales in most years in comparison to antitax sentiment.

In sum, there is some indication that concerns about inequality can be expressed as demands for higher progressive taxation to such an extent that they shift population-level preferences in a significantly positive direction, as was the case in 1992. But this appears to be more the exception than the rule. Moreover, as Larry Bartels shows in his analysis of the 2001 George W. Bush tax cuts, this may not necessarily translate into support for *actual* tax policies on the political agenda.[31] Our conclusion is much the same with regard to policies for the poor. Traditional redistributive policies are therefore not a reliable gauge of American views about income inequality or how to address it.

No Change in Desire for Government Action?

If Americans have noticed the rise in inequality and are concerned about it, but do not unequivocally favor expansion of traditional redistributive measures, perhaps they are unsure whether government should or can do anything to stem the rise. This would be consistent with a well-known countertendency to the egalitarian and pragmatic strain in American culture that we examined in the previous section, as well as counter to the self-interested behavior predicted by the median-voter model. This countertendency involves both a preference for limited government and an expectation that individuals will accept primary responsibility for securing their livelihood and that of their families. Americans look to the market system rather than to the government to deliver opportunity for upward mobility, and they believe that inequality plays a crucial role in rewarding, handsomely but appropriately, private contributions to the public good of economic growth and prosperity. This perspective goes by many names – the American dream, economic individualism, meritocracy – and has been found to be more deeply held than the norm of egalitarianism in the economic sphere.[32]

We explore the extent of support for government intervention with a simply worded question about government's responsibility to "reduce differences in income between people with high incomes and those with low incomes." This question does not mention taxation, welfare, or the poor (as does a similarly worded question that we discussed in the previous section) and therefore avoids associations with traditional redistributive policies. Given such a low bar, this question should provide a sense of whether Americans support *any* redistributive role for government *at all*. The first chart in Figure 5.5 presents trends in the share of GSS respondents strongly agreeing or agreeing with this statement. Although only about a third of Americans believe it should be the government's prerogative to reduce income differences, the share increases at the same time that trends in inequality and dissatisfaction with inequality are climbing upward.

The second chart of Figure 5.5 confirms the impression from the first chart that rising dissatisfaction with inequality is associated with an enhanced desire for government to take an initiative in reducing income gaps. When we control for compositional shifts in the population but not for attitudes about income inequality, the increase in support for a government hand in redistributing income is statistically significant and most apparent in 1996, 2000, and 2008. But this increase over time is virtually eliminated once we add the index of attitudes about inequality to the equation (i.e., the vertical lines with the small squares cross the line of zero effect). This means that increasing support among the general public for redistribution between income groups is accounted for by the increase in individuals who are dissatisfied with levels of inequality, because these individuals are more likely to support a government hand in reducing disparities.

According to these results, all three criteria for establishing a relationship between growing concerns about inequality and social policy preferences have been met: support increased over time for a reduction in inequality between income groups spearheaded by the government, those

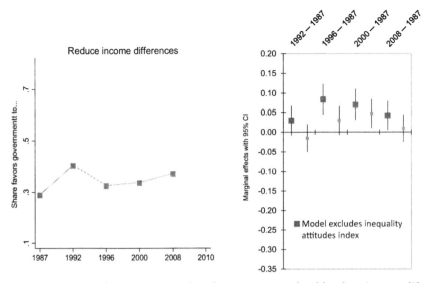

FIGURE 5.5. Trends in agreement that the government should reduce income differences, 1987 to 2010. Question wording and response categories presented in the figure are: "Do you agree or disagree that it is the responsibility of the government to reduce differences in income between people with high incomes and those with low incomes?" (strongly agree and agree). Right panel displays estimated changes from 1987 in support of the government's role in reducing income differences. Average marginal year effects and 95 percent confidence intervals are from an ordered logistic regression model pooled across years, with and without the index of attitudes about income inequality included in the model. See the Appendix to Chapter 3 for a list of control variables. *Source:* 1987, 1996, 2000, 2008, 2010 General Social Survey and 1992 International Social Survey Program.

who were concerned about inequality were more likely to support this policy orientation than those who were unconcerned, and the increase in concerns about inequality accounts for the growing popularity of this policy option. Thus rising inequality *did* appear to produce an increase in desire for some kind of government response to reduce income differences. In subsequent sections we examine whether increasing inequality and dissatisfaction with inequality may have prompted changes in preferences for specific kinds of government action other than direct transfers of income from rich to poor.

Increase in Desire to Reduce Inequality of Opportunity?

As mentioned above, although Americans tend to be ideologically conservative in the sense that in principle they prefer solutions that do not involve government, they also tend to be operationally liberal. If particular programs seem likely to work, Americans are content to endorse increased spending on them. One such program is education. Education has an ambiguous status in the menu of policy tools aimed at reducing income inequality, however. On the one hand, historically education has been viewed as a key social leveler, and it occupied a central place in Lyndon Johnson's Great Society programs.[33] Education is commonly thought to help equalize opportunity, and Americans strongly endorse equality of opportunity, as shown in Chapter 4. To take just one example, polls conducted by the American National Election Studies since the mid-1980s have consistently found more than 80 percent agreeing that "our society should do what is necessary to make sure that everyone has an equal opportunity to succeed."

On the other hand, since the Coleman Report released in the mid-1960s, many scholars and policy makers have been skeptical about the capacity of schools and school reform to make much of a dent in the life chances of children from disadvantaged families and neighborhoods.[34] And scholars of the welfare state virtually never include education as an instrument of social policy or redistributive effort.[35] As Harold Wilensky put it in 1975:

A nation's health and welfare effort is clearly and directly a contribution to absolute equality, the reduction of differences between rich and poor, young and old, minority groups and majorities; it is only a secondary contribution to equality of opportunity. In contrast, a nation's educational effort, especially at the higher levels, is chiefly a contribution to equality of opportunity – enhanced mobility for those judged to be potentially able or skilled; it is only a peripheral contribution to absolute equality.[36]

Educational opportunity enhances meritocracy, but meritocracy produces inequalities in outcomes, even if these are deemed fairer than in a less meritocratic society.

Nonetheless, as argued in previous chapters, inequality of opportunity and inequality of outcomes may be more closely intertwined than we are accustomed to thinking. Working backward from the idea that Americans "accept economic inequalities only when they are sure that everyone has an equal chance to get ahead,"[37] it may be that concerns about income inequality arose in the 1990s because of growing concerns about opportunities for upward mobility.[38] As was discussed in Chapter 4, when Americans observe rising inequality of outcomes, they may infer from this that opportunity is excessively unequal. As a consequence, they may simultaneously express heightened dissatisfaction with inequality

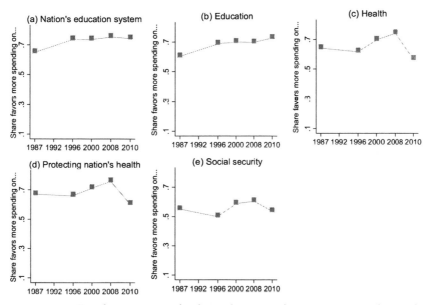

FIGURE 5.6. Trends in support of policies that expand opportunities and provide government services and social insurance, 1987 to 2010. Question wordings are: "We are faced with many problems in this country, none of which can be solved easily or inexpensively. Are we spending too much money, too little money, or about the right amount on:" (a) "improving the nation's education"; (b) "education"; (c) "health"; (d) "improving and protecting the nation's health"; and (e) "social security". Support is measured by responding that "too little money" is being spent on the programs. *Source:* 1987, 1996, 2000, 2008, 2010 General Social Survey and 1992 International Social Survey Program.

of outcomes and favor government action to expand various forms of economic opportunity. Specifically with respect to educational opportunity, analyses of growing U.S. earnings and income inequality often stress education as a key axis of division. Since the late 1970s, those with a four-year college degree or better have experienced rising real earnings, whereas those with less schooling have faced stagnation or decline. Americans seem to be aware of this "college divide."[39] Based on focus groups conducted in the mid-1990s (at the same time as we observe a peak in dissatisfaction with inequality), Stanley Greenberg argued that "it is hard to overestimate how important education and skills training are to these noncollege voters – perhaps the most important strategy for people to gain an advantage in this stagnant economy."[40]

The first two panels of Figure 5.6 chart developments over time in public opinion about government expenditures on education. There are

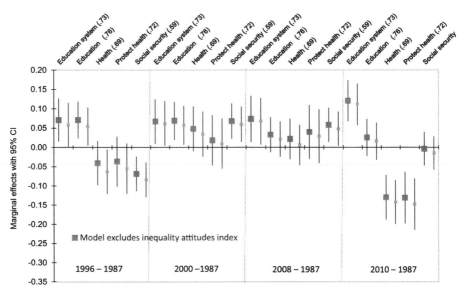

FIGURE 5.7. Estimated changes from 1987 in support of policies that expand opportunities and provide government services and social insurance. Average marginal year effects and 95 percent confidence intervals are from ordered logistic regression models for each policy outcome pooled across years (with mean share of support across years for each policy in parentheses), with and without the index of attitudes about income inequality included in the models. See Figure 5.6 for question wording and the Appendix to Chapter 3 for a list of control variables. *Source:* 1987, 1996, 2000, 2008, 2010 General Social Survey and 1992 International Social Survey Program.

two relevant GSS questions. One asks about spending on "improving the nation's education system" and the other about spending on "education." The trends for the two are similar: they indicate a small increase from the late 1980s to the 1990s in the share of Americans who favor additional spending. Although not shown here, this follows a sharper increase in support for greater spending from the late 1970s through the end of the 1980s. Over this entire period, preferences for government action on schooling correlates very closely ($r = 0.90$) with the trend in income inequality.[41] This is consistent with the hypothesis that rising inequality has prompted growing support for measures to address unequal opportunity.

This impression is, on the whole, reinforced when we delve into the relationship between beliefs about income inequality and policy preferences regarding education. Figure 5.7 provides a glimpse of how views about education policy shifted in the 1990s and 2000s, net of socio-demographic and political changes and then net of changes in attitudes about inequality (represented again by vertical lines with large and small squares, respectively). In every year since 1987, Americans are significantly more likely to say that more resources should be invested in the educational system. This is true for both forms of the education question in 1996 and 2000 and for one of the questions in 2008 and 2010. Even more fascinating from the standpoint of understanding policy preferences related to income inequality, there is *no association* between attitudes toward income inequality and educational policy preferences in 1987 for either question about education spending. Only in 1996 do we observe a robust relationship between dissatisfaction with inequality and spending on education for both questions. In other years (in the 2000s), the association is significant but only for one of the two questions.[42]

Americans who had concerns about income inequality in 1996, therefore, were more likely to connect their concerns to the educational system than those who had the same concerns in the other years.[43] This shift in preferences among those concerned about inequality is influential. Had dissatisfaction with inequality not grown, and had those who were dissatisfied not begun at the same time to entertain a stronger role for government in funding education, support for more spending on education would not have risen significantly between 1987 and 1996 (as shown by the vertical line with the small square touching the line of zero effect). Thus increasing dissatisfaction with income inequality accounts for the lion's share of increased support for education spending among the general public in 1996.

According to these results, all three criteria for establishing a significant relationship between attitudes about income inequality and policy preferences have been met for 1996: support for education spending increased over time, those who were concerned about inequality became more likely to support educational spending over time, and this shift accounts for much of the general trend in preferences for education policy. But although support for education spending remained consistently elevated throughout the 2000s, it was not as tightly bound to concerns about income inequality as in 1996. The causal path running from rising inequality to heightened dissatisfaction with inequality and a new desire for government action to equalize educational opportunity was either a random blip or more redolent during a period of transition when the two issues first became linked in public discourse, a possibility discussed further in the concluding section.

Increase in Desire for Other Government Programs?

An important component of the rise in economic inequality over the past two decades has consisted of those at the very top of the distribution pulling away from everyone else.[44] If Americans view this as the defining characteristic of inequality, they may favor an increase in government transfers for programs that tend to benefit not only the poor but also the middle class. Alternatively, or in addition, Americans may have seen their real earnings fall, stagnate, or grow at a slow pace and view this as the defining characteristic of the age of rising inequality. The same predicament could describe trends in health and retirement benefits, creating a more general sense of financial anxiety and insecurity.[45] This too could lead to a desire for government to provide a wide range of services that assist low-income and middle-income Americans alike. We therefore consider whether the rise in support for education spending actually reflects a more general increase in support for broad-based government assistance of many kinds, rather than a specific concern with equality of opportunity.

The most visible of such programs are social insurance programs such as social security (old-age pensions), health insurance, and unemployment compensation. Heightened spending on these programs also might be favored because recipients are viewed as more deserving, because they must pay into the system while working. (Unemployment insurance contributions are paid by employers, but it is widely assumed that this indirectly taxes employees in the sense that their wages would otherwise be higher.) On the other hand, we should note that, according to Karl Ove Moene and Michael Wallerstein, median-voter logic could predict that an increase in inequality will *reduce* support for social insurance spending.[46] Citizens are likely to conceive of public pensions and unemployment insurance as government pooling of risk rather than redistribution from rich to poor, and as programs for which they themselves have a nontrivial likelihood of becoming a beneficiary. The demand for insurance theoretically rises with income: those with more income tend to be willing to pay more to safeguard their living standards in the event of job loss, illness, old age, and so on. Hence, the higher the level of inequality, and therefore the lower the earnings or income of the median voter, the less the median voter will favor expenditures on these types of programs.

To gain a better handle on how views about inequality factor into preferences for social insurance programs, we first consider health care. Panels (c) and (d) of Figure 5.6 display trends in public support for more government spending on health as measured by two questions in the GSS. Support for more government spending of this kind appears to have increased steadily in the early 2000s, but from the 1980s to the mid-1990s it was flat, precisely when dissatisfaction with income inequality was growing. In addition, there was a backlash in 2010.[47] In Figure 5.7, it becomes apparent that the increases in the 2000s are quite weak relative to the declines. Similarly, there is a lower level of support for spending on health in 1996, but it is slight compared to the obvious low point in 2010. In terms of the relationship to attitudes about inequality, there is generally a greater likelihood of support for a larger dose of government spending on health among those who are dissatisfied with the existing level of inequality. Moreover, the increase in the share of individuals who are concerned about inequality and prefer additional spending on health accounts for some of the trend in policy preferences.[48] Yet despite this suggestive evidence, these data do not allow us to conclude that heightened concern about inequality in the mid-1990s and again in the late 2000s led to greater demands by the public at large for government to alleviate the costs of health care.

The GSS does not have a question on preferences about unemployment insurance, but it does ask about government expenditures on social security. Panel (e) in Figure 5.6 displays the share of Americans who thought that spending was "too little" on social security. Very much akin to the trend in preferences for health policy, the trend for social security does not correspond particularly well to that of beliefs about inequality. Most noticeably, the share preferring a boost in spending for social security fell from the late 1980s to the mid-1990s, and then rose in the 2000s before falling again in 2010. By 2010 the share was no higher than it had been in 1987. Figure 5.7 demonstrates that those who are more concerned about inequality are also more likely to favor additional government spending on social security, yet this more positive view about social security was less common in the population as a whole in 1996 than in any other year.

In sum, although support for greater spending on health and social security is generally very high (from half to three-quarters of Americans), it does not appear that Americans were seeking assistance of this kind – and thus government services more generally (beyond education) – as an antidote to their growing dissatisfaction with inequality in American society in the 1990s and 2000s.[49]

Increase in Desire for Regulation of Employer Pay Practices?
Rather than action that involves higher taxes or greater government spending, Americans may want government to respond to rising inequality by changing what it mandates of private employers. There may, for example, be increased support for raising the statutory minimum wage,

protecting wage bargaining agreements and institutions, or restricting the pay of those at the top of the distribution. These impulses follow naturally from what we know about how the decline in the real value of the minimum wage and the fall in union membership contributed to the erosion of real wages in the bottom half of the distribution, while soaring pay at the top catapulted the affluent into a new class all their own (the top one percenters).[50] The media study in Chapter 2 confirmed that these were newsworthy developments, punctuated by heightened scrutiny of executive pay, the rich, and the declining middle class, particularly during the recession and slow recovery of the early and mid-1990s.[51] As earlier studies of inequality have noted, Americans may favor market regulation rather than government redistribution in rectifying market inequalities that are viewed as unfair in the sense of restricting opportunities for obtaining good jobs with fair pay.[52] As discussed in Chapters 1 and 4, I refer to this as a preference for labor market redistribution in the private sector.

Unfortunately, the GSS does not have questions that can assess the impact of rising concern about inequality on public attitudes toward regulation of employer pay practices. We therefore turn to data gathered from polling organizations to supplement the impressions we are able to glean from the GSS questions on occupational pay discussed in the previous chapter. Regarding compensation at the bottom of the pay scale, Gallup has asked a semi-regular question since the late 1980s on whether Congress and the president should raise the minimum wage. The share supporting a higher minimum wage increased between the late 1980s and the mid-to-late 1990s, but the amount of the increase was small given already high levels of support approaching the 80 percent mark. According to the evidence presented in Chapter 4, the degree to which workers in unskilled occupations are perceived as being shortchanged has grown modestly since the late 1980s, whereas the share of Americans advocating a steep cut in executive pay is substantially higher today than it was two decades ago.[53]

To our knowledge there are no data over time on attitudes about policies that would restrict maximum compensation levels. In Table 5.1, we instead show similarly worded questions dating to the 1970s about executive pay and more recent questions on the pay of Wall Street bankers, the pay of mid-level occupations for comparison, and policies related to pay and profits. The polls reveal surprisingly consistent opposition to pay practices at the top by at least a 70 to 30 percent margin. By contrast, only 42 and 7 percent of Americans think that public

TABLE 5.1. *Public Opinion Polls Regarding Top-End Pay and Policies to Regulate High-Paying Industries*

---

(1) Top-End Pay

(Roper Poll): Now here is a list of people in different kinds of occupations . . . tell me whether it is your impression that [they] are generally overpaid, or underpaid, or paid about right for what they do: Presidents of major business corporations.
  1976, overpaid: 73%

(*Business Week*/Harris Poll): Do you think top corporate executives are worth what they are paid, or are they overpaid?
  1984, overpaid: 76%

(*Washington Post* Poll): Do you think that top corporate executives in this country are paid too much, too little, or about the right amount?
  1992, overpaid: 74%

(*TIME*/CNN/Harris Poll; *LA Times*/Bloomberg): In your opinion, are most CEO's of major American corporations paid too much, about right, or not enough?
  2007, too much: 86%

(CNN): Please tell me whether you think each of the following descriptions apply or do not apply to Wall Street bankers and brokers . . . Overpaid.
  2011, applies: 77%

(2) Comparison to Mid-Level Pay

(Quinnepac University Polling Institute): In general, do you think public employees are paid too much, too little or about right?
  2011, too much: 42%

(Associated Press/Stanford University): Do you think public school teachers get paid too little for the work they do, too much for the work they do, or about the right amount?
  2010, too much: 7%

(3) Policies Regulating Top-End Pay and Profits

(NBC News/*Wall Street Journal*): Would you favor or oppose a law limiting the tax deductibility of corporate executive salaries that are more than 25 times higher than the salaries of their company's lowest-paid workers?
  1992, favor: 64%

(Fox News/Opinion Dynamics Poll): Some people say government involvement in setting executive salaries at companies that received bailout money may lead to the government trying to set executive salaries for other non-bailout businesses. Do you think that would be a good idea or a bad idea?
  2009, bad idea: 67%

(*continued*)

TABLE 5.1 (*continued*)

(Democracy Corp/Campaign for America's Future Poll): Now I'd like to read you a list of proposals to help close the federal budget deficit. After I read each item, please tell me whether you favor or oppose that proposal.... Create a tax on excessive profits made by Wall Street banks.	2010, favor: 65%
(NBC News/*Wall Street Journal*): When it comes to each of the following groups and industries do you think we need – more or less – federal government regulation, or about the same amount as there is now? Wall Street firms.	2010, more: 57%

employees and teachers, supposedly much maligned occupations, are paid too much, respectively. This is consistent with the research of Joel Rogers and Richard Freeman showing that Americans are more supportive of worker associations than many would think, and with the majority of Americans who sided with public workers against Wisconsin governor Scott Walker's fight to curtail their bargaining rights and benefits.[54]

Polls on regulating pay and profits, as opposed to regulating industries, are few and far between, but they indicate a cautious willingness to tread a fine line of intervention. For instance, a limit on the tax deductibility of executive salaries above twenty-five times "the salaries of their company's lowest-paid workers" was backed by almost two-thirds of Americans when the proposal was floated in 1992. In 2010, the same share of Americans favored "a tax on excessive profits made by Wall Street banks" to "help close the federal budget deficit." A year earlier, however, roughly two-thirds said that it would not be a "good idea" if government tried to "set executive salaries for other non-bailout businesses," although they favored such a policy for bailed-out businesses. These are the kinds of questions on regulations regarding pay that desperately need to be incorporated into the menu of questions in our best social surveys about policy preferences so that we can get a better handle on how Americans view the regulation of labor market and pay-setting practices.

In terms of other kinds of interventions in the private economy that would enhance labor market opportunities, much attention has focused on immigration and international trade. There is a large volume of research on this subject by economists showing that increasing immigration and international trade have reduced the relative wages of unskilled workers, but these factors are generally agreed to have "not been the major force driving wage [inequality] movements."[55] Kenneth Scheve and Matthew Slaughter have examined public opinion on these matters in detail. They find that "though people acknowledge benefits, both economic and otherwise, they appear to worry more about costs – especially labor market costs – such that they opt for policies of less immigration [and less trade]."[56] Low-skilled workers are especially opposed to immigration and trade, implying that they are aware of their unique exposure to the costs in lost jobs and lower wages of economic integration. Scheve and Slaughter suggest that this should lead to greater support for social insurance and redistributive spending (although they do not analyze this proposition empirically). We do not find such an increase over the time period of our study among the general public, but there may have been one among individuals concerned about immigration and trade (these questions are not available over time in the GSS). Based on our results, we find it more plausible that concerned Americans would support targeted protections for dislocated workers (e.g., retraining grants) and funding for new industries to replace declining industries, rather than traditional social insurance and redistribution.[57]

Increase in Desire for Not-Sure-What?

A final possibility worth considering is that Americans have grown increasingly dissatisfied with the level of inequality and would like government to do something about it, but are unsure as to what type of action they favor. In this view, there is limited desire for traditional redistributive methods as the front-runner among potential responses, but preferences for other options to alleviate this new set of concerns are underdeveloped or simply unknown. Aside from a minority of individuals who are politically knowledgeable and consistent in their ideological views (perhaps to a fault in that they ignore dispositive information contrary to their views), plenty of evidence can be found that Americans' policy preferences are ill formed and based on unreliable information and misconstrued interests.[58] This depiction tends to hold especially for those who are most likely to benefit from redistributive policies of all kinds: less-educated and lower-income Americans.[59] When coupled with the fabled complexity of the issue, it is no wonder that some conclude that Americans are simply too ignorant to express an authentic voice on the topic of rising inequality (as is discussed in Chapter 1).

Not helping matters are the various groups residing on the other side of the ledger from the mass public, such as politicians, parties, the media, large social organizations, and so on, who constitute the elite public sphere. Until very recently, when the Occupy Wall Street movement percolated up from below, these groups failed to transmit a coherent message about rising economic inequality and what should be done about it. A thorough analysis of media coverage is provided in Chapter 2, and our tentative hypothesis following from that analysis, which focused less on coverage of policy content than on coverage of inequality itself, is that to the extent that inequality has been politicized as a labor market issue, the populist and policy solutions put forward have been defined in primarily two ways: first, as the need for higher education and technical skills to compete successfully in the new "knowledge" economy, and second, as the need for greater protections from foreign competition, in the form of trade barriers and curbs on immigration, as we discussed above.[60]

These frames and policy options represent a relatively narrow scope of the solutions that could come into play in reducing inequality of various forms, crowding out alternatives that might enjoy some measure of popular support. Progressive taxation, for example, is a contentious subject not because the majority of Americans oppose it, but because it tends to be upstaged by antigovernment rhetoric against higher taxes *tout court*, for which there is sympathy.[61] The spare and targeted tax initiative in Oregon, for instance, that raised taxes only on households with income above $250,000, and was injected into the political discourse as a substitute for cutting needed government services (i.e., education, health care, and public safety), passed muster from an electorate historically hostile to progressive referenda.[62] Thus, the menu of policy options available to the public is both circumscribed and inchoate, creating significant noise in policy preferences.[63] In fact, this could help to explain the inability of the Occupy movements to formulate a concise list of familiar policy demands.

As a consequence of this vacuum in elite political culture, the responses we have cataloged could reflect episodic reactions to current events, a tendency that can be more pronounced among the large share of Americans without strong ideological leanings and valid information.[64] This interpretation is consistent with the dip in support for more government spending on health that coincided with controversies over healthcare reform in the mid-1990s and again in the 2010 congressional election season. It could also help account for patterns of support for government assistance to the poor and spending on welfare, which also declined in the mid-1990s. Arguably, this development was spawned by the aggressive Republican campaign prior to and after the Republicans' success in the

1994 congressional elections to prioritize welfare reform and hold President Clinton to his 1992 campaign pledge to "end welfare as we know it."[65] Related, antitax rhetoric appears to have risen over the course of the 1990s, which coincides with the decline observed in 1996 in support for high taxes on the rich.[66]

That the intensity of dissatisfaction with income inequality peaked at this same time, when antiwelfare, antitax, and antigovernment rhetoric of all kinds (e.g., on health care and social security) reached a crescendo, reassures us that concerns about inequality are not a figment of our imagination. It also persuades us that these concerns are (or at least can be) distinct from preferences for a core group of social welfare policies traditionally associated with egalitarian, humanitarian, and pragmatic norms, or with self-interest (at least regarding income redistribution by the government). We are less certain whether the strong but transitional shift in support for more education spending, particularly among those dissatisfied with inequality, was a genuinely new response to concerns about income inequality in the mid-1990s or one that predated our survey data. This could reflect a historically novel coupling of inequality of outcomes (the problem) with equality of opportunities in the labor market (the solution). Alternatively, it could reflect the policy preferences of visible and vocal elites at that time for solutions emphasizing individual initiative and educational achievement. These elite preferences may have trickled down to the attentive public – or the attentive public may have been more receptive to them – at a time of heightened anxiety over rising inequality during the mid-1990s, and then fanned out to the rest of the population in the 2000s. Which of these two explanations is the more accurate one is a critical question for future researchers to examine.

Broadening the Policy Discussion on Inequality

Rising inequality is a signature characteristic of the past generation, and yet what effect, if any, this has had on Americans' policy preferences seems to have escaped direct scrutiny. Certainly data limitations have impeded our understanding of this question, but data of high quality do exist, combining information on attitudes toward income inequality and social policy preferences at multiple time points during the recent era of rising inequality. To better interpret such data, we have theoretically identified a wide range of conventional and unconventional perspectives on American views of inequality. We draw two conclusions regarding conventional explanations from our analysis and then discuss two potential implications of our findings that are consistent with the results from previous chapters, and which ought to inform future research on the politics of rising income inequality.

Our two conclusions address the two views that currently dominate thinking about responses to rising inequality. The first view is that rising income inequality is likely to have no impact at all because Americans are tolerant of income inequality in general and of rising income inequality in particular. In our examination of questions that ask directly about income inequality, in this chapter and in previous chapters, we found that Americans *did* become increasingly concerned about income disparities, with a peak in concern occurring during the early and mid-1990s and another, smaller flourish in the late 2000s. Moreover, there is a high degree of dissatisfaction with inequality at any given point in time, in addition to the significant fluctuation over time. Our understanding of this process in the future will depend crucially on the availability of more and better time-series data on views specifically about income inequality.

The second view that dominates thinking about responses to rising inequality is that it is likely to produce an increase in support for traditional redistributive policies that transfer income from the rich to the poor, making the posttransfer-posttax income distribution more equal. Although we find that Americans have become increasingly concerned about inequality, and that their support for government action to address rose modestly, the action Americans have tended to favor is not traditional redistributive programs. For a variety of reasons explored by other scholars, dissatisfaction with assistance to the poor and with higher taxes on the rich was especially strong in the mid-1990s during the peak of antiinequality sentiment. A surge of concern about income inequality had little impact relative to the strength of antipoverty and antitax sentiments. Although those who are concerned about income inequality are more likely to support progressive taxation and assistance to the poor at any given point in time – something we think extremely important to keep in mind with respect to progressive taxation in particular, which has received limited scholarly attention – this is not a formula that seems to have had political traction in the era of rising inequality that we study.[67]

If the GSS data suggest that neither of the dominant views is correct for the contemporary United States, what do they suggest as an alternative? We see two possibilities that ought to be pursued in future research. The first is that rising income inequality has prompted greater concern about inequality of opportunity, which in turn has prompted greater demand for increased spending on education, and in a more speculative vein, regulations that curb executive pay practices and restrain labor market inequality. Regarding expanded educational opportunities, in contrast to the widespread antispending sentiment apparent in the mid-1990s, Americans who were concerned about inequality became more likely to support education spending. This increased likelihood accounted for most of the increasing support among Americans in general for spending on education. This shift is all the more notable given the lack of any connection between views on income inequality and education spending in our baseline year (1987), a pattern consistent with the long-standing absence of education in political models of social welfare spending. Furthermore, we observe similar increases in support for spending on education in the mid-1990s in the ANES (in contrast to spending on child care, social security, and health), and a strong correlation between the trend in actual inequality and support for education spending over the longer term.

These shifts suggest the need for new research that bridges the study of inequality of educational opportunity and inequality of outcomes, both in terms of how Americans perceive the connection between the two and in terms of how policies that are meant to expand opportunities – in education as well as in the labor market – operate to foster or mitigate *actual* inequalities.

The second possibility raised by our findings is that Americans favor some sort of government action but are uncertain about exactly what that action should be (as opposed to what it should *not* be). One reason for this uncertainty may be that the issues involved are complicated and likely need to be attacked on multiple fronts. Even many scholars and policy makers are uncertain how to best address the increase in income inequality. Indeed, researchers are sharply divided about the causes and consequences of this development. As a relatively new "social problem," and one that receives only episodic media and political attention, it is not surprising that both attitudes toward inequality and corresponding policy preferences (to the extent that we have captured them in the limited array of available survey questions) would be sensitive to contemporaneous debates, including those that may have emphasized education or restraints on executive pay and Wall Street banks (as in the Occupy Wall Street movement) as a cure, instead of traditional redistributive policies. This possibility is all the more likely given the ambivalence that at times characterizes public attitudes about inequality and a wide array of other political issues, and thus the need for public elites to lead the way.[68]

Having said this, however, we do not think our findings imply that the complexities are insurmountable, leaving no room whatsoever for Americans to make rational connections between income inequality and the social policies that might address it. In fact, at any given point in time, dissatisfaction with inequality is almost uniformly associated with significantly greater support for all of the equalizing social policies that we examined, after controlling for socio-demographic characteristics and political partisanship and ideology. And although broad-based support for a wide array of spending programs was down in 1996 (except for education), it was up in the 2000s for a variety of government services – education, health, social security, and even welfare. If our surveys contained questions about other kinds of policies that would make a dent in labor market inequality through redistribution in the private sector, such as government regulation of employer pay practices (e.g., via the minimum wage or limits on executive pay) or trade (e.g., to keep "good" jobs in America), we might have found additional avenues of redress favored by those Americans most concerned about income inequality. But until the collection of data on opinion about policies related to inequality catches up with the reality of inequality, we will not know. The highest priority for future research, then, is to take American public opinion about inequality seriously enough to find out exactly how it is related to policy preferences.

Conclusion

A New Era of Beliefs about Inequality

"[At the end of World War II], the basic American promise was that if you worked hard, you could do well enough to raise a family, own a home, send your kids to college, and put a little away for retirement.... The defining issue of our time is how to keep that promise alive.... We can either settle for a country where a shrinking number of people do really well, while a growing number of Americans barely get by. Or we can restore an economy where everyone gets a fair shot, everyone does their fair share, and everyone plays by the same set of rules."

– President Obama, 2012 State of the Union address[1]

After opening his 2012 State of the Union address by paying tribute to the men and women in uniform, President Obama turned his attention to what he called "the defining issue of our time." Eschewing the cliché of the "American dream" in favor of what he called the "American promise," he nevertheless went on to sound the dream's key notes: if you work hard and play by the rules, you should enjoy a financially secure life and pass on an even better one to your children. As in other speeches, Obama relied on the example of his grandparents to humanize his argument. His grandfather served as a soldier in World War II, and his grandmother as a laborer on a bomber assembly line. They embodied a generation and an era that "gave rise to the largest middle class and the strongest economy that the world has ever known."[2] This was a hallowed time in American history, in which "bootstraps" and "rising tide" opportunities were in full bloom, but now they were in retreat, and a way needed to be found to restore them.

That the American "promise" was in peril was something on which most everyone could agree; it was the causes and solutions that were up for grabs. The contenders were many, and Obama pinpointed several of them in his address. The loss of jobs to global competition and technological change were highlighted, among other seemingly inevitable casualties of economic progress.

But he also inserted something out of the ordinary in his rendition of the rise and decline of the American middle class: the damage inflicted by income inequality. In his previous and longer campaign speech on the matter in Osawatomie, Kansas, he contrasted the equitable growth of the post–World War II era in which "every American shared in the pride and in the success – from those in the executive suites to those in middle management to those on the factory floor" with the erosion of this "basic bargain" over the past few decades. "Fewer and fewer of the folks who contributed to the success of our economy actually benefited from that success," he said in the Kansas speech. But "those at the very top grew wealthier from their incomes and their investments – wealthier than ever before." Perhaps most boldly, he attributed the financial crisis and Great Recession to the "breathtaking greed of a few and irresponsibility all across the system." He singled out for special blame those in the banks who "made huge bets and bonuses with other people's money" and regulators who "had looked the other way."

In his drawing of parallels across history and between the American dream and equitable growth, and in his targeting of the "undeserving rich" as a key player in these developments, President Obama could not have offered a more perfect (if at times oblique) illustration of the arguments at the center of this book. Given this similarity, it was perhaps inevitable that commentators would respond by either heralding the inequality message or, more likely, rejecting it as antithetical to the message of opportunity. Based on the mountain of polling results prompted by the speeches and the Occupy Wall Street movement, one analyst argued that "a campaign emphasizing growth and opportunity is more likely to yield a Democratic victory than is a campaign focused on inequality. While the latter will thrill the party's base, only the former can forge a majority." Another warned that "what the public wants is not a war on the rich but more politics that promote opportunity." Others applauded Obama's exorcising of the word "inequality" from his State of the Union address, a term that appeared nowhere in that speech but was brandished six times in Osawatomie the month before. The newer emphasis on "fairness rather than equality" was said to make "good political sense."[3] In much of the ensuing public discourse, opportunity was aligned with fairness and inequality with the fringe (e.g., the Occupy Wall Street movement), even among Democrats.

Was this merely a dispute over tactics and strategy, or was it more deep-seated? Although these kinds of squabbles are a quixotic element of all presidential campaigns, disagreement and confusion over what Americans think about income inequality is unfortunately all too familiar. The wedge between inequality and opportunity has long wreaked havoc in scholarly as well as political circles. And this says nothing of the complications arising once policy considerations enter the conversation. President Obama's foray into this minefield was, I can only imagine, well considered in terms of both the economics and politics of the issue. Nevertheless, the economics are a far more settled matter than the politics.

Regarding the economics, even if economists will benefit from the passage of time in deciphering the precise role (if any) of income inequality in precipitating the financial crisis and the Great Recession, historical trends in income inequality are themselves incontrovertible. The United States underwent a metamorphosis from a country in which income growth was equally distributed in the post–World War II decades to one in which growth was skewed dramatically toward the top thereafter. The negative repercussions of this in lost income for middle-class and poor families are straightforward, even if a great swath of families was able to stay afloat for a short while with the increased work of women and the accumulation of debt. Moreover, evidence is amassing that in the United States the preeminent indicator of equal opportunity, intergenerational mobility, is not only stagnant but less than in some European countries. The causes and consequences of income inequality are a perennial subject of debate, but these underlying economic trends are not.[4]

Obama played confidently on these economic themes, but not so with the political ones. Although it is impossible to divine the tea leaves of presidential campaign strategy, it is evident that the Obama administration perceived the politics of inequality as dicey. This is indicated by, among other things, the administration's earlier reticence in rescinding the George W. Bush era tax cuts on the rich and its avoidance of the term "inequality" in the State of the Union address, most likely a result of the flack it received from its own side and charges of "class warfare" from the other side in response to the frequent use of the term in the Kansas speech.

Yet, at the same time, the politics of inequality are not so taboo as to be swept entirely under the rug. Splashy graphs on rising inequality were posted side by side with a video feed of the president's remarks in the enhanced online version of the address. Moreover, doing away with the Bush tax cuts on the rich was a major plank of the speeches' policy platform. Finally, the Obama team took a page or two from the writings of labor economists' to launch a coherent narrative linking the rise in income inequality to growing restrictions in economic opportunity, broadly construed.[5]

In essence, the administration struggled to find a palatable way to convey the politics of income inequality to the public. In a similar vein, I would argue, the Occupy Wall Street movement was stifled in its attempt to craft a message about inequality, particularly on the thorny issue of "demands."[6] Both are glaring examples of political indecision concerning a central feature of American society. This indecision is understandable in light of the limited discourse on income inequality that dominates many (but by no means all) scholarly and public policy debates. Such debates are typically stuck on the question of whether Americans care about income inequality or not, leaving wide open the door of American exceptionalism, in which Americans are said to be tolerant of any degree of inequality whatsoever, simply not to care.

This book offers an alternative view that shifts the question from whether Americans care about inequality to when and why they do. It is based on an understanding of beliefs directly about income inequality, as well as beliefs about economic opportunity and redistributive policies. It is attuned to durable configurations of beliefs that nevertheless shift in content if not in theme over time, and to relationships among beliefs rather than to isolated snapshots, as is the pollster's prerogative. It incorporates the stance of a significant minority of the public as well as that of a majority. It is rooted as much in American history as is the exceptionalist view, and stems as much from traditions more recent (i.e., the modern civil rights movement) and more distant (Toqueville) than the progressivism of Teddy Roosevelt invoked by Obama in Osawatomie, Kansas.[7] In the remainder of this chapter, I provide an encapsulation of this alternative view of beliefs about income inequality, and why it needs to be understood as integral rather than antithetical to the concept of equal opportunity. I close with reflections on where it might be profitable to direct future research, given this view.

Iconic eras of American history are well known by their particular configurations of equality, whether political, economic, cultural, or racial. In the economic realm, as I argued in Chapter 1, we would be hard pressed to identify any era in which we could say that what America stood for was solely equality of opportunity and not, in addition, some measure of equality of results. This is because eras in which equal opportunity flourished were also eras in which economic growth was relatively equitable. Conversely, eras of economic turmoil and transition tended to be eras of inequitable growth. The particular tenor of the relationship between opportunity and inequality depends on the distributional nature of economic growth, rather than on growth per se.[8]

In the midst of the equitable growth of the post–World War II era, for instance, the economist John Kenneth Galbraith complained that no one cared about income inequality. This idea, whether originating with Galbraith or not, became entrenched in our most sophisticated theoretical treatises on beliefs about equality, coming as they did in the 1970s and 1980s on the heels of a shared, postwar prosperity. Our inherited theories about egalitarian beliefs were formulated precisely when income inequality was at a low point by historical standards, and thus, for all intents and purposes, invisible in our understanding of the politics of inequality at that time. Moreover, "production" in the private sector (in Galbraith's words) replaced taxing and spending by government as the default method of redistribution. This ensured that the concept of redistribution, or economic fairness generally speaking, would be associated more with expanding opportunities (in the form of equitable growth) than with taxing and spending, even as the "hidden" welfare state and other wage-setting institutions propped up the regime of equitable growth.[9]

Yet, despite equitable growth, many people were left behind, as Galbraith bemoaned in his plea to his contemporaries to address the problem of entrenched poverty, which later become a major goal of John F. Kennedy's presidency. The analogies between the demands of those left behind in the post–World War II period of abundant growth and those left behind today are instructive, and they prefigure a conceptual framework that integrates beliefs about economic opportunity and income inequality. The halcyon days of the immediate postwar era were not celebrated as such by all groups; not everyone shared equally in the prosperity. When the civil rights movement demanded that the exclusion of blacks (and later women) from the labor market be rectified, they were asking for the fulfillment of equality of opportunity for everyone. But this pitch for equal opportunity occasioned an argument about equal outcomes, for how were policy makers, lawyers, and social movement participants to comprehend and visualize what equality of opportunity meant? How were they to know when it had been eclipsed or achieved?

These questions cut directly to the practical issue of defining and measuring opportunity. In the 1960s and 1970s, one of the most common ways to do so was with measures of outcomes. Unequal outcomes for black and white children in the educational system, or unequal outcomes for black and white workers in the labor market, were deployed as measures of opportunities denied. Such measures were more readily observable than were unequal opportunities, which allude to hypothetical states of unrealized but deserved achievement (e.g., what would a black child have achieved if he or she had been given an equal opportunity?) rather than document them directly. Test score and wage gaps were thus used as a shortcut to gauge the degree of opportunity. This method was controversial and imperfect, but it was more than just expedient.[10]

Today we face analogous problems of definition and measurement. How are we to know whether opportunities are widely available or not? Opportunity, we are told, is the principal concern of Americans, and yet there is no comprehensive and accessible definition of what it means. The preferred definition among scholars is intergenerational mobility, or the extent to which an individual's income is correlated with his or her parents' income, which in Chapter 4 I call an "equal treatment" model of opportunity. But surely individuals adhere to other definitions, or have aspirations beyond intergenerational advancement alone. Indeed, we know that people measure their own status relative to that of their peers, and thus expectations for economic success must involve a contemporaneous component as well.[11] Moreover, in determining whether one's situation is better than that of one's parents, one must consider such factors as the state of the economy (what political scientists call a sociotropic consideration) and one's own job conditions and pay.

In Chapter 4, I termed these "rising tide" and "just deserts" models of opportunity. Building on Daniel Bell's notion of an "unjust meritocracy," which went beyond concerns about unequal treatment to encompass worries about distorted rewards, I suggest that a good job with pay commensurate with skills, contribution, and performance is part of a meritocratic society, part of the American promise. Understood in these terms, unequal outcomes can shape perceptions of unequal opportunities in multiple ways, from their impact on disparities in children's access to education to the unfair allocation of jobs and pay among working adults. Indeed, the unfair allocation of pay can itself appear to corrupt incentives and restrain rising tide opportunity, as forewarned by Michael Young in the *Rise of Meritocracy* and played out in some respects in the 2008 financial crisis.[12] This is the brew that spawns the undeserving rich, which characterizes the particular configuration of inequality and opportunity in our day.

Do Americans actually connect the dots in these seemingly complicated ways? Not only do they, but they do not connect them in the way the "tolerance" view expects. The tolerance view rests on a set of three inferences from Americans' disdain for welfare and their faith in the role of hard work in getting ahead: that Americans (1) view "bootstraps" opportunity as widely available, and thus (2) outcomes as fair and (3) redistribution as unnecessary. Once we test these inferences with questions that probe more deeply into beliefs about economic opportunity, income inequality, and redistribution, however, we find something quite different.

First, as shown in Chapter 4, the belief in hard work per se in getting ahead has *little to no effect* on beliefs about income inequality, and thus cannot be used as an indicator of American tolerance for income inequality. Second, if the concept of "luck" is spelled out for Americans, who do not often encounter this opaque concept in public discourse, then a significant minority of Americans (just under half) say that things such as social connections and coming from a privileged background are essential or very important factors in getting ahead. These beliefs about the restriction of opportunity *do correspond* to heightened concerns about income inequality. Third, as shown in Chapter 5, heightened concerns about income inequality do not preordain support for traditional redistributive policies such as welfare and taxes on the rich. Although expressions of opposition to income inequality are correlated in the cross-section with a wide range of progressive social policies, the trend over time in concerns about income inequality most closely corresponds with an increased preference for greater spending on education, a program associated in the public eye with expanding labor market opportunity rather than redistributing income. Thus it is just as misleading to read views about income inequality from views about the entire menu of liberal government programs as from views about traditional redistributive policies.

An in-depth contextual analysis of why beliefs about income inequality shifted over the period of rising inequality in the way that they did, modeled on methods of comparative and cultural sociology, and presented in Chapters 2 and 3, adds greater validity and texture to this alternative view. Across the nearly two and a half decades of this study, desires for less inequality and skepticism about its fairness and functionality are held by close to half or more of the population, and this is validated by newer and differently worded survey questions.[13] These desires for an equitable society intensify not gradually as income inequality rises over time, or episodically with the business or presidential election cycles, or only for those with less education or low incomes; rather, they rise for all groups during periods of inequitable growth when the fortunes of the middle class are declining as those of the rich are taking off.

This divergence in income trajectories is a touchstone of media coverage during the early and middle 1990s, when income inequality was first coming into its own as a full-fledged social issue, backed by a new economic consensus that inequality's ascendance was not simply a temporary blip.[14] Over the course of the three decades of media coverage in the top newsweeklies that I analyzed in Chapter 2, explicit attention to the issue of income inequality peaked in the early and middle 1990s. Although I show that the grounds for coverage of inequality were fertile in the early half of the 1980s, the study of income inequality was in its infancy, and the claim that inequality was accelerating was controversial. Coverage of inequality was therefore more implicit than explicit. Coverage was also less overt from the late 1990s into the 2000s, when Americans were buoyed by more equitable growth. The issue thus lost traction until the financial crisis and Great Recession hit; although, even then (up until 2010), coverage did not surpass the peaks of the 1990s.

Coverage certainly appears to have reemerged since 2010 with the Occupy Wall Street movement, which began in September 2011. The timing of the Occupy movements is consistent with the timing of the high-water mark of opposition in the mid-1990s, which coincided with the sluggish expansion from the early 1990s recession and not with the recession itself. We will be able to assess the impact of these events and media coverage of them on American views about income inequality with a new round of the General Social Survey, which fielded the same battery of questions about income inequality in 2012. As I describe in Chapter 2, journalists in the 1980s and 1990s were already implying that the American dream of opportunity was jeopardized by the rise in income inequality, something that is echoed in the Occupy movements, Obama's speeches, and in some media coverage of this period.

Americans' apparent acquiescence or indifference to inequality is thus a relic of a bygone post–World War II era when expanding opportunities and declining inequality coalesced under the redistributive rubric of equal and equitable growth. Opportunity may have received top billing, but inequality played more than a supporting role. The two are interdependent, with levels of income inequality tolerated as long as they are compatible with expanding opportunities, which may consist of equal growth or merely equitable growth. Many journalists instinctively reflect this view when they pair rather than oppose discussions of opportunity (as in the American dream) and inequality. Likewise, our everyday notions of opportunity (e.g., "rising tide," "just deserts," "equal treatment" opportunity) embed rather than reject notions of equitable outcomes. As shown in Chapter 4, these are not arcane frameworks. Many if not most Americans seem to be aware of rising inequality or extreme levels of inequality, and dissatisfaction is centered on the consequences of inequality rather than on its level. The "undeserving rich," the configuration of inequality and opportunity that has been developing over the past couple of decades, is similarly nuanced in its implication that Americans can have more than one – admiring – perception of the rich.[15]

Thus policy and political solutions will need to offer an antidote to economic inequality that expands opportunity. Rectifying *social* inequality, through redistributive taxes, for instance, will not transparently achieve greater *economic* equality in the labor market. But renewing and crafting new redistributive practices in the labor market is a more complex and uncharted course to follow, even if one of its major advantages is that it is regulative in nature and does not swallow up a large and visible chunk of the federal budget.[16] Creative and efficient interventions in the private economy that foster equitable growth are the wave of the future (as they were in the past) if public opinion is of any consequence. If, for whatever reason, a growth-based opportunity model ultimately proves unsustainable, the redistributive welfare model will need to be adapted to the American context; that is, it will have to become associated transparently with the expansion of opportunity for the majority of Americans. There are already hints of this at the state level, where ballot measures that present a straightforward equation of higher taxes on the rich with more spending on services such as education, health, and public safety receive popular support (e.g., in Oregon and California).

My methodological approach in this book has been to marry the social psychologist's attention to the fine-grained mechanisms of social thought and behavior with the political scientist's concern with real-world trends and preferences. I wanted to radically reduce the long arc of inference that hinders current understandings of beliefs about income inequality. Such beliefs about income inequality are typically derived from items on related but distinct and sometimes distant topics, such as the role of "hard work" and "luck" in getting ahead, support for traditional redistributive policies, beliefs in system-wide justice, and partisan attachments. These items may accord well with our prior theoretical models of how beliefs about income inequality ought to be formulated, but they do not necessarily fit into the landscape of beliefs employed by Americans in their everyday lives, or even into the landscape of beliefs in the historical periods that gave rise to our most sophisticated theoretical models.

Unlike the social psychologist, however, I relied on our best and longest-running social surveys, the staples of sociological and political research, to gauge public attitudes. Thankfully, these surveys, however imperfect, contained the questions I sought – multiple items on income inequality, barriers to opportunity, and a wide range of social policies – and were repeated across more than two decades worth of changes in economic, political, and social conditions. To interpret these changes over time, I relied mainly on quantitative survey analysis but was aided immeasurably by the more qualitatively oriented methods of comparative historical researchers and cultural sociologists. Perhaps inevitably, this led to the substitution of one arc of inference (though of a shorter arc length) for another.

Is there a more satisfying way forward for the growing number of scholars interested in the ways that beliefs condition social behavior and objective outcomes? Can we sharpen our measures and mechanisms at the same time that we explore the determinants of historical change and societal variation outside of laboratory settings? Research on beliefs about class and income inequality is flourishing, as is public attention to these issues. In the remainder of this book, and based on the findings therein, I suggest a number of avenues along which research on beliefs about income inequality is proceeding now and can advance further in the future, with the understanding that ultimately we will all benefit from collaborations across these venues, and across disciplinary and methodological boundaries.

First, researchers and, to a lesser extent, pollsters are already beginning to expand the scope of questions asked of the American public on topics of income inequality, economic opportunity, and economic and social policy. Regarding income inequality and economic opportunity, a long-standing question on researchers' minds is whether Americans are knowledgeable of the trend in rising inequality and declining social mobility.[17] Without questions of a factual nature that go back several decades, we have no way of assessing this in a definitive way at this moment in history, but we can begin to ask such questions going forward. Here we would want to know whether individuals who are more informed of the trends are more likely to lean in one direction or another in their normative assessments of inequality and opportunity or whether they are motivated by other factors, such as their ideological or partisan orientations, or their socioeconomic position. For example, my analysis in Chapter 4 of perceptions of actual pay inequalities revealed that perceptions of higher levels of pay disparities per se were much less important in shaping opposition to income inequality than the discrepancy between perceived and desired levels of pay disparities.[18]

In addition to the issue of factual knowledge, we can construct a much better understanding of how Americans think conceptually about inequality and opportunity by asking questions that are definitional in nature or incorporate alternative definitions of inequality. For example, beliefs about inequality may be affected by whether it is conceptualized as a relationship between the rich and poor, the rich and the middle class, the 1 percent and the 99 percent, whites and blacks, or men and women. Analogously, beliefs about opportunity may be affected by whether it is conceptualized generically as owing to luck or, alternatively, to a specific social advantage in getting ahead that presupposes luck, or as a function of employment rates and pay scales. The objective here would not necessarily be to construct psychometric scales, but to better differentiate theoretically among the various ways that these two rather abstract and wide-ranging concepts (i.e., inequality and opportunity) are defined by individuals and the consequences of such definitions for normative judgments and policy preferences.

Regarding economic and social policy, the most pressing need is for an enlarged sense of what qualifies as a policy that the public associates with reducing inequality. Theoretically, I have described equitable growth as a form of redistribution that occurs in the labor market, but this is not to say that Americans label or recognize equitable growth as a form of "redistribution" as such, rather than as a form of "rising tide" or "just deserts" opportunity in which good jobs are seen as plentiful. Nevertheless, equitable growth as a political objective potentially entails the use of any number of levers to alter employment and pay practices in the private sector, and thus the extent of earnings inequality, that the public may favor.

Economists and other social scientists refer to these as "institutional" factors. Most often, they include the minimum wage, wage-bargaining policies, other workplace regulations, and the catchall category of "social norms."[19] Under the latter, one can imagine employer-initiated practices that create more equitable compensation and training structures within and across firms, such as profit sharing, maximum pay spreads, universal within-firm benefits packages, and educational programs. I leave the details and feasibility of these kinds of policies to political economists to sort out;[20] my main objective is to identify the policy ramifications of concerns about earnings and income inequality. Even if such ramifications turn out to be ill considered from an economic standpoint, they reflect a valid and meaningful attempt on the part of Americans to translate their concerns about inequality into policy solutions.[21]

Finally, as Larry Bartels has shown, general policy preferences (e.g., for taxing the rich) may diverge from preferences regarding specific policy proposals (e.g., the Bush tax cuts).[22] We need a better account of how this divergence plays out across a variety of inequality-related policies and levels of policy implementation, such as at the state versus federal levels.[23]

Second, in addition to changes in survey questions, changes in the content and scope of research on inequality ideally will be incorporated into a wider array of methodologies that illuminate different aspects of the belief formation process. There is an obvious lacuna in the social survey literature on topics related to class, inequality, and economic policy, but it is beginning to be addressed in new surveys conducted around the world, particularly in Eastern Europe and China, where inequality rose dramatically after the postsocialist transition.[24] The theoretical framework that I propose in this book is grounded in survey research, but repeated cross-sectional surveys with a relatively small number of time points are ill-equipped to firmly establish causal relationships. This is where other methodologies could enter the stage, with many potential openings for further research on inequality and social class among cultural sociologists and anthropologists, social psychologists, historical sociologists, and political institutionalists. Two principal issues will need to be addressed in future research: the endogeneity of economic and political norms, and the causal ordering and determinants of beliefs about inequality, opportunity, and redistribution.

It is well recognized that social and economic norms are not free floating but embedded in a national culture developed over time and congealed in institutions that feed back into beliefs.[25] This is what political sociologists and scientists refer to as path dependence, where beliefs about a social policy are influenced by prior knowledge of and experience with the social policy in question. Despite this, we (and I) often speak of beliefs as if they *are* exogenous, and national culture as if it *is* given and monolithic. Anything pertaining to American dream ideology seems particularly susceptible to these tendencies.

This is why I was surprised by the difficulties I had in coding the coverage of income inequality and social class in newsweekly stories. Coverage was nothing like what one would expect in a society bowled over by American dream ideology. In fact, the complexities and challenges of deciphering the causes and consequences of income inequality, not to mention its myriad definitions, were reflected in a good deal of media coverage and consequently in what is culturally "supplied" to the public.[26] Although the content of news stories affirmed the tradition of treating American beliefs as "ambivalent" rather than "tolerant," much more can be done to capture and appreciate the critical, diverse, and inchoate nature of egalitarian beliefs in America. The ongoing research on framing effects and political culture by cultural sociologists, political and economic historians, and political institutionalists is essential to furthering this enterprise and guiding the development of appropriate survey questions.[27]

This research is also essential to the advancement of experimental research on the causal relationships between beliefs about income inequality, economic opportunity, and redistribution. Social and political psychologists are more knowledgeable than anyone else of the way Americans think about economic justice, fairness, and meritocracy.[28] It is among my biggest regrets that I was unable to engage this impressive body of scholarship more seriously. Three main obstacles to doing so stood in my way, obstacles that I see eroding now with the growing influence of psychological approaches across the social sciences.

First, my primary interest was in documenting changes in beliefs about inequality rather than enduring regularities in such beliefs, as is the principle objective of social psychology as a basic science.[29] Second, I was inspired by years of research on ambivalent attitudes about inequality in political science and sociology, which I took as the starting point for my inquiry rather than as a settled theory. This meant that the social psychological emphasis on meritocratic views reinforcing the status quo were less applicable than were other theoretical frameworks. And, finally, only recently has the social psychology of social class blossomed into a major subfield in its own right. For example, a new body of social psychological research is revealing that Americans do not unambiguously admire the rich but feel coldly toward them, and may even resent them at times (oh no!).[30] This finding is largely consistent with previous ethnographic research by sociologists and with the notion of the un/deserving rich at the center of this book, although these latter efforts present a more contextualized and varied set of perceptions of the rich.[31] Still, the study of attitudes about the rich is in its infancy, certainly as compared to the study of attitudes about the poor.

In sum, experimental research is, many would say, the wave of the future as social scientists become more attentive to the rigors of causal analysis and the micro-foundations of social behavior.[32] And experimental methods are certainly a necessary next step in testing the theoretical framework developed in this book. But my hope is that future experimental research in the burgeoning field of the social and political psychology of social class and income inequality will be sensitive to the dynamics of social change, the diversity of beliefs, the interdependence rather than opposition of inequality and opportunity, and the public's desire for multiple potential models of redistribution (i.e., an opportunity as well as a welfare state model).

The effervescence of scholarly, public, and political interest in the issue of income inequality from a wide range of disciplinary and political perspectives is gratifying if such interest hastens us along a path toward a better future. To do so, I have argued, requires an alternative framework for understanding *why* Americans care about income inequality and what they want done about it. At bottom, the discussion of income inequality must move beyond the question of whether Americans care about inequality or not, and beyond the abstract notions of fairness and self-interest embedded in welfare state models of redistribution. A new discourse of income inequality must instead be grounded in a practical consideration of how and when income inequality acts as an unfair restraint on widespread economic opportunity, in a multitude of ways. Only then will we be on our way to resuscitating and constructing alternative models of redistribution that lead to a more equitable economy and expanding opportunities for all Americans.

Notes

Introduction

1. Bell 1973: 451, 453, 454. See also Young 1958.
2. The opening sentences of a 2006 *Economist* cover story on inequality in the United States nicely distill these ideas: "the gap between the rich and poor is bigger than in any other advanced country, but most people are unconcerned. Whereas Europeans fret about the way the economic pie is divided, Americans want to join the rich, not soak them. Eight out of ten, more than anywhere else, believe that though you may start poor, if you work hard, you can make pots of money. It is a central part of the American Dream" ("The Rich, the Poor, and the Growing Gap between Them," *Economist*, June 17, 2006: 28). The 2007 *New York Times Magazine* cover article on the income gap similarly observed that "the U.S. has a pretty high tolerance for inequality. Americans care about 'fairness' more than about 'equalness.' We boo athletes suspected of taking steroids but we admire billionaires" ("The Inequality Conundrum," *NYT Magazine*, June 10, 2007: 11). As I show in Chapter 2 in my analysis of media coverage, however, there is a more nuanced coverage of inequality in the media as well.
3. Hochschild 1995 provides a thorough dissection of the contradictions inherent in American dream ideology.
4. For example, Schlozman et al. 2005: 28 conclude that "although Americans support a high level of equality among social groups and favor equality of opportunity, they appear to be less concerned about inequality in economic outcomes. For example, there is little public support for a massive redistribution of income or wealth." See also Alesina et al. 2004: 203; Ladd and Bowman 1998; Piketty 1995; Benabou and Ok 2001; Haskins and Sawhill 2009; Bartels 2008; Kelly and Enns 2010. These studies are discussed in greater detail in Chapter 1. Note that Lamont 2000 shows persuasively that Americans do not generally like or respect the rich in a moral sense, and further evidence presented in Chapter 1 shows that most Americans do not in fact think they will eventually become rich (based on poll data from Gallup).

5. For research on attitudes about these issues, see DiMaggio et al. 1996; Sears et al. 2000; Feldman and Zaller 1992; Gilens 1999. Also, the American National Election Studies (ANES) has a battery of questions on equality dating back to 1984. These questions focus mainly on equality of opportunity (e.g., equal chances to succeed and equal rights) rather than equality of outcomes. Regarding social groups, the ANES included "rich people" and "business people" (as opposed to "big business") for the first time in 2002 in its time series of feeling thermometer questions, which has included a long list of other social groups since the 1960s and 1970s, including the poor (1972), welfare recipients (1976), and big business (1964). I examine these questions in Chapter 4.

6. See especially Hochschild 1981; Kluegal and Smith 1986; McCloskey and Zaller 1984; Verba and Orren 1985.

7. Lipset 1996; Benabou and Tirole 2006; Sawhill and Morton 2007. There is also an important and growing literature in Europe on these topics (e.g., Busemeyer 2012; Duru-Bellat and Tenret 2012).

8. Jacobs and Skocpol 2005: 215, 218.

9. See Kluegal and Smith 1986; Feldman 1987; Kelley and Evans 1993; Osberg and Smeeding 2006; and analyses in Chapters 3 and 4. For public opinion polls on executive pay from the 1970s to the present, see Chapter 5. Chapter 1 also reviews public opinion data on these topics from previous studies.

10. The American National Election Studies Panel Survey asked the following question several times over the course of 2008, 2009, and 2010: "American households with incomes in the top 5% earn an average of $300,000 per year, and households with incomes in the bottom 5% earn an average of less than $10,000. Should this difference be smaller, bigger, or about what it is now?" The question was also asked with information about differences between the top and bottom 20% of incomes. There was little difference in responses to the two versions of the question, which ranged from 50 to 63 percent of respondents desiring less inequality (a great deal smaller or moderately smaller). Response categories were also randomized.

11. On median voter models, see Meltzer and Richard 1981; norms of procedural justice and fairness, see Miller 1992, Kluegal and Smith 1986, Verba and Orren 1985; the negative consequences of inequality, see Neckerman 2004; views of the rich, see Lamont 2000; norms of humanitarianism, reciprocity, and deservingness, see Hochschild 1981, Gilens 1999, Feldman and Steenbergen 2001, Fong et al. 2004; economic theories of inequality and growth, see Benabou 2000, Andrews et al. 2009, Voichovsky 2009, Roine et al. 2009, Stiglitz 2012.

12. Coleman 1966; Roemer 1998.

13. Hetherington 1996; Erikson et al. 2002.

14. Lewis-Beck and Stegmaier 2007.

15. In fact, Republicans often pitch tax cuts as necessary for increasing economic growth and tax increases as retarding economic growth (Lupia et al. 2007; Smith 2007). Similarly, journalists often pit progressive tax policies against economic growth policies: "The political consensus, therefore, has sought to pursue economic growth rather than redistribution of income, in keeping

with John Kennedy's adage that 'a rising tide lifts all boats'" (*Economist*, June 17, 2006: 28), and a Democratic pollster said that he found "little appetite for policies that would redistribute income as his party has advocated over the years.... Instead, people were looking for pro-growth policies that were neither traditionally Democratic nor Republican" ("Pockets Half Empty or Half Full," *New York Times*, September 3, 2006).

16. The *New York Times Magazine* (June 10, 2007) cover story on income inequality cited in footnote 2 implied that Americans supported redistributive policies that enhanced education ("Some redistribution is clearly good for the entire economy – providing public schooling, for instance, so that everyone gets an education. But public education aside, the U.S. has a pretty high tolerance for inequality"), but it is unclear whether Americans make such a connection between redistributive policies and spending on opportunity-enhancing programs. When ballot measures directly link the two, such as a hike in taxes on high incomes and businesses to finance education, health care, public safety, and other social services, the public can be very supportive, as indicated by their passage of Oregon Ballot Measures 66 and 67 in 2010.

17. On ambivalence, see Hochschild 1981, 1995; Kluegal and Smith 1986; Page and Jacobs 2009; Newman and Jacobs 2010. On ignorance, see Bartels 2005, 2008; Campbell 2010. On insecurity, see Hacker 2006. For a detailed discussion of these positions, see Chapter 1.

18. For a nuanced discussion of this position, see Jencks and Tach 2006.

19. Many suggest that if Americans only knew how high inequality was, they would object more vociferously, thus assuming that attitudes are based mainly on abstract fairness criteria (Osberg and Smeeding 2006; Hacker and Pierson 2010; Norton and Ariely 2011).

20. Galbraith 1958: 82, 97. On the idea of economic growth and abundance in the private sector in the United States fulfilling demands for social rights associated with the welfare state in Europe, see Strasser et al. 1998. This does not mean that the economy grew equitably for racial and gender groups, however (e.g., MacLean 2006).

21. On trends in equitable growth in the postwar period and inequitable growth in the period from 1980, see Kuznets 1955; Goldin and Katz 2008; Piketty and Saez 2003; Ellwood 2000.

22. Louis Uchitelle used the term "New Gilded Age" to describe the era of rising inequality ("Richest of the Rich: Proud of a New Gilded Age," *New York Times*, June 15, 2007). For an analogous argument on the long term embeddedness of postwar ideologies in beliefs about the welfare state, see Brooks and Manza 2007.

23. Katz 1989; Gilens 1999.

24. Bartels 2005, 2008: chapters 5, 6. But see debates in Hacker and Pierson 2005 and Lupia et al. 2007.

25. On Republican discourses of progressive taxes as antigrowth, see Zelizer 2003; Smith 2007.

26. Alesina and Glaeser 2004; Benabou and Tirole 2006.

27. Among these complications is the question of what we as commentators think counts as luck, what Americans count as luck, and which among these

are justifiable determinants of outcomes (e.g., ability) and which are not (e.g., race). I take up this discussion in Chapter 4.

28. As Lupia et al. 2007: 779 argue, "instead of characterizing people as misguided, it may be more instructive to conduct scholarship that attempts to better fit our analyses into their rationales – including the likelihood that they approach political problems from varying ideological perspectives and with different values in mind." They focus on what can appear to be reasonable rather than ignorant and irrational differences in tax policy preferences, but also demonstrate that the relationship among knowledge, awareness, and policy preferences can vary across issue domains. Druckman's 2012 review of motivated reasoning (i.e., partisan biases in information gathering and preference formation) also describes several individual and contextual factors that minimize partisan biases, such as having weak, ambivalent, and uninformed attitudes (i.e., not being a strong partisan); being exposed to competing messages over time and issues that are less contentious or are new and less likely to be aligned with prior ideological orientations; and having to account for a position on an issue.

29. Ragin 1987; Pierson 2004; Newman 1988, 1992; Lamont 1992, 2000; Young 2004.

30. In psychology, see, for example, Jost and Major 2001. In sociology, there is a related and significant literature on justice beliefs that also inspires my work in this book. See Jasso and Rossi 1977; Shepelak and Alwin 1986; Jasso 1999.

31. Page and Shapiro 1992; Erikson et al. 2002; Kelly and Enns 2010.

32. I am thus sympathetic to Lupia et al.'s 2007: 780 "constructive way forward" that "entails rethinking the relationship between the people who study social phenomena and the people who are being studied."

33. This more encompassing and radical approach to the definition and centrality of opportunity in theories of distributive justice is also consistent with the groundbreaking "capabilities" approach developed by Amartya Sen 1999, 2009.

34. I take the idea of the "cultural supply side" from Michele Lamont 1992, 2000.

35. Both Krugman 2002 and Piketty and Saez 2003 suggest that increasingly permissive social norms fostered the increase in income inequality, although it is likely that they are referring mainly to elite norms (Krugman 2007). But it is also possible that institutional conditions changed rather than social norms, even at the top (McCall and Percheski 2010; Stein 2010).

36. Page and Jacobs 2009; Newman and Jacobs 2010.

Chapter 1: Beyond the Opposition between Opportunity and Inequality

1. This is true even among economists. In their comparative book on redistributive policies in the U.S. and Europe, Alesina and Glaeser 2004: 217 write that "after exploring well-travelled economic theories based on pre-tax income inequality, openness, the efficiency of the tax structure, and social mobility,

we came out almost empty handed. Then we looked for an answer by moving to other fields, like history, political science, sociology, and even psychology, and we found greater success."

2. See McCloskey and Zaller 1984; Hochschild 1995; Lipset 1996.

3. Lane 1962; Free and Cantril 1968; Rainwater 1974; Jasso and Rossi 1977; Hochschild 1981; Halle 1984; McClosky and Zaller 1984; Verba and Orren 1985; Kluegal and Smith 1986; Shepelak and Alwin 1986; Bellah et al. 1986. Miller 1992 provides a review.

4. Page and Shapiro 1992; Feldman and Zaller 1992; Sears, Sidanius, and Bobo 2000; Fiorina 2005.

5. See Levy and Murnane 1992 for an early review. Chapter 2 discusses earlier debates and coverage of the issue in the 1980s.

6. Weir 1992; Sugrue 1996. See also Bell 1973; Bluestone and Harrison 1982; Piore and Sabel 1986; Harrison and Bluestone 1988.

7. Lipset and Schneider 1987 demonstrate that there was a decline in confidence in institutions of all kinds beginning in the middle to late 1960s, but that the decline began with sentiments toward government. Also, Free and Cantril 1967: 1 open their book with the presidential campaign of 1964 between Johnson and Goldwater, arguing that it presents a rare confrontation of "the two dominant schools of political thought in the United States" (i.e., liberals and conservatives) and thus an especially propitious time "for a study of American political beliefs, values, and attitudes as regards not only national but international issues." A decade and a half later, Verba and Orren 1985: vii open their book with the observation that "equality lies at the heart of policymaking and political struggle. The public agenda in 1984, for example, brimmed with equality issues – debates over the role of blacks and women, disagreements over who should shoulder what share of the tax burden, charges of unfairness hurled at one political party, countercharges that special interests wielded too much influence leveled at the other."

8. Free and Cantril 1967: 26, 30, 38, 39. The other three questions are: (1) "the federal government is interfering too much in state and local matters" (40 percent agree, 47 percent disagree, 13 percent do not know), (2) "the government has gone too far in regulating business and interfering with the free enterprise system" (42 percent agree, 39 percent disagree, 19 percent do not know) and (3) "social problems here in this country could be solved more effectively if the government would only keep its hands off and let people in local communities handle their own problems in their own ways" (49 percent agree, 38 percent disagree, 13 percent do not know).

9. Verba and Orren 1985: 5. For another influential theory of distributive justice across spheres, see Walzer 1983. See also Lane 1986.

10. Toqueville's *Democracy in America* is the touchstone for both casual observers and serious scholars of nineteenth-century United States. As discussed in the next section, historians continue to debate the significance of his work. For public opinion data on beliefs about the equal worth of humans and political equality, see McCloskey and Zaller 1984: Chapter 3.

11. Lane 1962, 1986.

12. Jackman and Jackman 1983: 210, 214. A recurring theme in the literature is the narrow scope of American debates about inequality, focusing on "minimal 'safety-net' issues without challenging the general economic fabric of society," and voicing "more concern with equality of opportunity than with equality in the distribution of rewards." Verba and Orren 1985: 50 go further out on a limb: "the most important reason for the persistent inequality of wealth is that the American ideal of equality does not embrace redistribution. Americans have developed a philosophy that justifies disparities of riches but not of power...Wealth on any scale is tolerated as long as it cannot be translated into political power. The American tradition of philanthropy stems from the belief that great fortunes can and should exist."

13. On this point, see the qualitative studies of Lane 1962; Halle 1984; Lamont 2000. Bellah et al. 1985 refer to talk of economic individualism and success as the "first language" of Americans, and talk of communal values as the second and much less-developed language.

14. Hochschild 1981: 183–184 writes that with regard to "welfare and social policies," her respondents "start out and remain egalitarian. They overwhelmingly support national health insurance, although some also want a private medical option. They endorse tuition subsidies, housing subsidies, higher Social Security payments, and so on. They most firmly support a guaranteed jobs program using both public and private sectors, and they at least claim that they would be willing to pay higher taxes to ensure its success." Regarding redistribution of wealth, Hochschild's conclusions are more tentative: "It is extraordinarily difficult to decide whether a respondent 'really' supports redistribution or not – and that may be the most important finding on this subject. Respondents cannot make up their minds because redistribution pulls them in equal, but opposite, directions. Viewed as an economic issue, it is wrong because it violates the principle of differentiation. Viewed as a political issue, it may be right because it satisfies the principle of equality." This tension leads to one version of the ambivalence perspective discussed later in the chapter.

15. T. H. Marshall 1950. In their survey of the "Two Hundred Years War" over equality, Verba and Orren 1985: 49 argue that "America has experienced periods of political leveling that produced little economic change." McCloskey and Zaller 1984 similarly argue that there has been greater consensus over democratic principles of equality than economic principles of equality because both welfare and laissez-faire capitalists share democratic values.

16. Free and Cantril 1967: 36–37, and chapter 2.

17. Bartels 2008: 130. Regarding opposition to strict equality of outcomes, in a survey conducted by Kluegal and Smith 1986: 112 only 3 percent of individuals supported "complete equality of incomes"; in a survey reported in McCloskey and Zaller 1984: 84, only 7 percent thought "all people would earn about the same under a fair economic system"; and the range of agreement that all earnings should be "about the same" as opposed to "based on ability" was from 0 percent (Republicans) to 17 percent (blacks) among a group of leaders surveyed by Verba and Orren 1985: 72.

18. Note that some proponents of America's individualism also acknowledge its downside, for example in higher crime rates. Lipset 1996 calls this the "double-edged sword" of American exceptionalism.

19. Haskell 2000; Kloppenberg, 2001: 472. Kloppenberg 2003: 350 argues that "although the impulse to identify an essential and enduring American ethos has persisted ever since [the arrival of English settlers in North America], the evidence of struggle has become irresistible. Designating any specific set of commitments as genuinely or distinctively 'American' no longer seems convincing." See also Toqueville 2006; Hartz 1955; Lipset 1996.

20. Both ascriptive hierarchy and the domination contract refer to racial, ethnic, national, and gender inequalities (Smith 1993, 2007; Pateman and Mills 2007; Mills 2008). On multiple traditions, see also Bellah et al. 1985. The debate over the extent to which these traditions are separate or intertwined is far from resolved (Stears 2007).

21. Smith 1993: 563. Novak 2008: 763, 771, 763 defines state power as including everything "from the first national governing institutions to the conquest of western lands; from the creation of a vast public infrastructure for the promotion of commerce to the construction of a powerful defense and military establishment; from the expansion of governmental powers of police, regulation, administration, and redistribution to the invention of new ways of policing citizens, aliens, races, morals, and gender relations in the production of national culture." Novak argues that "in an era dominated by both European states and European state theory . . . [in which] despotism was the chief problem of political thought . . . the story of an exceptional and weaker version of that state in the United States was predictable, perhaps even necessary," although he disputes the accuracy of this perspective.

22. Alesina and Glaeser 2004: 126ff, 183–185 argue that the ultimate causes of conservative political power are geography (large territory), racial/ethnic heterogeneity, and military success, which "also gave [the right] the ability to push their own distinctive way of understanding economic opportunity." From the World Values Survey, they cite the following evidence of differences in ideologies between Americans and Europeans: "In the U.S. 29 percent of respondents believe that the poor are trapped in poverty and 60 percent of respondents believe that the poor are lazy. In Europe, 60 percent of respondents believe that the poor are trapped in poverty and only 26 percent believe that the poor are lazy. In Europe, 54 percent believe that luck determines income. Only 30 percent of Americans share this view" (2004: 183–184). These attitudes are correlated with less support for redistributive policies and social spending in the United States. The authors also show the same relationship among individuals in the United States, and find that variation in other beliefs about the causes of poverty and the availability of opportunity affect attitudes about redistribution, after controlling for income (see also Fong 2001). Similarly, several political scientists in the 1980s focused on elite public opinion regarding democracy, capitalism, and egalitarianism because of its presumed influence on broader public opinion (e.g., Verba and Orren 1985; McCloskey and Zaller 1984; Jackman and Jackman 1983).

23. References are often made to descriptions of the unique American economic context as expressed by Karl Marx, John Stuart Mill, Werner Sombart, Friedrich Engels, and G. W. F. Hegel, in addition to Toqueville.

24. Long and Ferrie 2007: C66; see also Ferrie 2005: 208. The United States is less mobile in the 1950 to 1970 era than in the 1860 to 1880 era. The United States and Great Britain have similar rates of intergenerational occupational mobility in the late-nineteenth century once the occupational structure is taken into consideration.

25. Erikson and Goldthorpe 1992.

26. Long and Ferrie 2007: C68, C69. They also note that "the frontier was never the destination for more than a small fraction of US internal migrants after 1850." On the open educational system as the basis for ideologies of equal opportunity, see Goldin and Katz 2008: 287–289. For studies showing that mobility was not substantially greater in the United States than other European countries, see Alesina and Glaeser 2004: 65–68.

27. Ferrie 2005: 200–201.

28. Piketty 1995: 552.

29. Alesina and Glaeser 2004: 130 write that "the reason for the permanence of [conservative] American institutions is American success in suppressing attempts to force change through violence. America's counter-revolutionary success itself is the result of its large size and its isolation."

30. Benabou and Tirole 2006: 723, 725, 726, 700, also citing Max Weber's *The Protestant Ethic*. A growing body of economic research connects religious beliefs to economic behavior (e.g., McCleary and Barro 2006).

31. Psychological theories of beliefs in a just world and "system justification" have considerable empirical support. But although such beliefs are considered fundamental to psychological functioning, psychologists also study individual variation in these beliefs, linking stronger versions to authoritarianism, political conservativism, and free market ideologies. See Jost et al. 2003, Jost and Major 2001. Unfortunately, these theories are rarely applied to changing historical and social conditions in the United States and focus largely on system justification. For a new focus on the potential for system-changing as well as system-justifying beliefs, see Johnson and Fujita 2012.

32. These endogenous wealth effects also incline individuals to oppose redistribution as inequality rises (because income rises as well) in another of Benabou's models (Benabou 2000; Kelly and Enns 2010).

33. Alesina and Glaeser 2004: 191.

34. In a review of Alesina and Glaeser 2004, Pontusson 2006: 324 argues that their "approach may be adequate for the purpose of explaining the exceptional nature of the American case, but it becomes problematic from a broader comparative perspective, for there is a lot of reshuffling of country rankings on the dependent variable that happens in the intervening period." However, he also uses the United States as an example of such reshuffling: "The U.S. was a laggard in 1930 and 1990, but less obviously so in 1960." One of the reasons that changes may have been more substantial in Europe than the United States is that European countries were transformed from monarchies to parliaments in the twentieth century.

35. Benabou and Tirole 2006: 723. For the role of shocks in affecting beliefs about the economy and redistribution, see also Giuliano and Spilimbergo 2009.
36. Verba and Orren 1985: 18–19.
37. Respondents were asked whether they agreed with the following statement: "more equality of incomes would allow my family to live better" (Kluegal and Smith 1986: 106–107, 110).
38. Kluegal and Smith 1986: 112.
39. Feldman 1987.
40. McCloskey and Zaller 1984: 84.
41. Kluegal and Smith 1986: 77. For the top three reasons, about two-thirds of respondents rated each reason as very important. For the next two, nearly half of respondents rated each reason as very important. Regarding political influence, McCloskey and Zaller 1984: 176 found that two-thirds of the general public believe that "corporations and people with money really run the country," as opposed to "have less influence on the politics of this country than many people think" (15 percent).
42. Kluegal and Smith 1986: 120.
43. Verba and Orren 1985: 251.
44. Lamont 2000: chapter 3. Social pyschologists are coming to similar conclusions (e.g., Fiske 2011).
45. For a summary, see, for example, Fiske 2011: chapter 1.
46. Bell 1973: 451, 453. A just meritocracy is "made up of those who have earned their authority." I discuss the idea of an unjust meritocracy in greater detail in Chapter 4.
47. Young 1958; Hochschild 1981: 69. For the rise in inequality in the late-nineteenth century, see also Goldin and Katz 2008: 287–289, and for evidence of lower levels of inequality in the United States relative to other countries in the early part of the 19th century, see Lindert and Williamson 2011. Even conservative depictions of late-nineteenth century capitalism were critical of excessive wealth and degrading poverty (Nackenoff 1992).
48. They argue that the "prevalence and stability of belief in the dominant ideology, in the face of enduring objective features of the stratification system and changing beliefs and attitudes in some areas related to inequality, produces the inconsistency, fluctuation, and seeming contradiction in the attitudes toward inequality and related policy found in the American public" (Kluegal and Smith 1986: 6–7). Additional evidence of the "context dependence of beliefs about justice" can be found in experimental studies of small groups and vignette studies (Miller 1992: 589; see also Jasso and Rossi 1977; Shepelak and Alwin 1986).
49. See also Hochschild 1981, 1995; Jackman and Jackman 1983; Verba and Orren 1985; McCloskey and Zaller 1984;. The latter two books examine beliefs among leaders with similar economic backgrounds but with different ideological orientations, which also prompt different kinds of challenges to the dominant ideology.
50. Hochschild 1981: 15.
51. Bellah et al. 1985: 295.

52. McCloskey and Zaller 1984: 134. Also in the mid-1970s, Americans were concerned about big business holding "too much power" and trusted big business the least among a group of twenty-four institutions. Additional evidence comes from Gamson 1992, who selected "troubled industries" as one of four political issues about which Americans would have formed an opinion from personal experience or media coverage in the 1980s (the others were nuclear power, affirmative action, and the Arab–Israeli conflict). He identified critical points of coverage as the Lockheed loan request in 1971, Carter's six-point plan for the steel industry in 1977, and the Chrysler bailout debate in 1979. His analysis (Gamson 1992: 145) of conversations among working people about "troubled industry" also found a "recurrent bit of popular wisdom . . . that whatever happens, the rich somehow manage to get richer and the poor people are hurt. Overall, some version of this sentiment was expressed on this issue in more than half of the total groups and in more than 70 percent of the black groups."

53. Lipset and Schneider 1987 find that confidence in the relatively scandal-free financial sector (at that time) was high whereas confidence in oil, chemical, and nuclear industries was low.

54. McCloskey and Zaller 1984: 300.

55. Strasser, McGovern, and Judt 1998; Judt 2005.

56. Howard 1997.

57. Lichtenstein 1989; Jacoby 1997; Cohen 2003; Klein 2004; Jacobs 2004.

58. Galbraith 1958: 77. See also Kochan, Katz, and McKersie 1986.

59. Cohen 2003: 127 (emphasis added). Other historical research emphasizes the explicitly redistributive nature of labor and consumer strategies in the 1930s and 1940s to raise wages, reduce prices, and universalize benefits (Klein 2004; Jacobs 2003, 2005).

60. By contrast, these norms were associated with the public welfare state in Europe (DeGrazia 1998). McCloskey and Zaller 1984 provide evidence of public support for the private enterprise system as "generally fair and efficient" and giving "everyone a fair chance" (134). Lane 1986: 393–396 cites McCloskey and Zaller 1984 and other studies to argue that there is a "harmony of interests" between workers and capitalists because Americans view profits as legitimate rewards and "the source of 'good times' and future income" (394). In this positive sum game, "harmony of interest takes the place of justice, and claims of justice will be muted" (Lane 1986: 395–396). John Kenneth Galbraith cast his net more broadly, decrying this as the "truce on inequality," in which "increasing aggregate output is an alternative to redistribution or even to the reduction of inequality" (1958: 262, 97, and chapter 7 more generally).

61. This is not to exaggerate the degree of consensus, particularly given legitimate criticisms of public opinion surveys for minimizing expressions of conflict (Fantasia 1988). Rather, although struggles continued, nearly everyone agrees that these struggles had run their most radical course by the late 1950s. To take just one example, Jacobs 2003, 2004 once saw consumer movements as redistributive movements when middle-class consumers united with labor to press for price controls in the 1930s and 1940s. But she argues that the middle class then split with labor around the issue of rising inflation in the

1950s, which employers successfully pinned on labor and their collective bargaining power.

62. Nancy MacLean 2006 argues that affirmative action came to be seen as a middle-class and bureaucratically imposed movement only after deindustrialization limited the potential for integration of blue-collar jobs. In fact, attempts at integration occurred very early on in the construction and manufacturing sectors. This suggests that civil rights activists were not fully aware of the gathering macroeconomic and industrial shifts that would constrain the drive toward integration and equal pay in working-class occupations.

63. Ellwood 2000. Note that economic growth is a necessary but not sufficient condition for equitable growth. Thus my approach builds on but also refines accounts that focus on the benefits of growth alone (e.g., Friedman 2005).

64. Lipset and Schnedier 1987: 238. See also McCloskey and Zaller 1984: chapter 5.

65. Because of antistatist sentiments present even during the 1950s and 1960s, Zelizer 2003 argues that federal policy makers employed a set of tools to support popular social reforms without raising taxes. Business regulation was one such tool, in addition to deficit spending, earmarked taxes, tax expenditures, state/local taxes, and most especially government revenue from economic growth. On fiscal constraints on social spending due to liberal as well as conservative calls for limited taxes, see also Galbraith 1958.

66. See Jacobs 2003, 2004 and Rodgers 2000, who argue that the United States was less exceptional in its social policy development relative to Europe during the period from 1900 to the end of World War II. See also O'Connor 2002.

67. Galbraith 1958: 82, 97.

68. The exception is Verba and Orren 1985, who described levels of income inequality as having changed little over the course of the previous century.

69. For a discussion of using outcomes as measures of opportunities, see Roemer 1998. In a footnote in Verba and Orren's 1985 opening chapter, the authors lament the opposition of opportunities and outcomes in the literature and discuss how the two actually form a continuum. However, they then follow tradition in citing the opposition as one of four central oppositions that structure the politics of equality in the United States (the others being politics/economics, individual/group, and ideal/reality).

70. Blank 1997; Ellwood 2000.

71. Piketty and Saez 2003; Mishel et al. 2003, 2007; DeNavas-Walt, Proctor, and Smith 2011.

72. Lipset 1996: 55–59.

73. Lipset 1996: 17.

74. For example, in a December 11, 2000 editorial in *USA Today*, Dinesh D'Souza wrote that "an excessive focus on inequality carries the presumption that the explosion of affluence we are experiencing is cause for mourning, when in fact it is cause for celebration: the United States has extended to millions of ordinary people the avenues of freedom and personal fulfillment previously available only to the aristocratic few." On trends in media coverage of inequality and social class, see Chapter 2.

75. Alesina et al. 2003: 23.

76. Ladd and Bowman 1998: 3.

77. Bowman 2000. Several prominent media stories repeat this view. For example, the *Economist* opened its cover story on U.S. inequality in a nearly identical vein: "The gap between the rich and poor is bigger than in any other advanced country, but most people are unconcerned. Whereas Europeans fret about the way the economic pie is divided, Americans want to join the rich, not soak them. Eight out of ten, more than anywhere else, believe that though you may start poor, if you work hard, you can make pots of money. It is a central part of the American Dream" (*Economist* 2006: 28).

78. See Piketty 1995; Benabou and Ok 2001; Corak 2005; Morgan, Fields, and Grusky 2006; Smeeding, Erikson, and Jantti 2011. There are those who say that an increase in intergenerational mobility matters less than an increase in absolute mobility as measured by a boost in living standards. Like Lipset, these authors broaden the definition of "opportunity." See various contributions to "Rising Wealth Inequality: Should We Care?" *New York Times* Room for Debate, March 21, 2011.

79. Page and Jacobs 2009.

80. Page and Jacobs 2009: 95–96. Newman and Jacobs 2010: 126 are less sanguine about policy attitudes and reside more firmly in the ambivalence camp, but they too argue that "as the gap between rich and poor in America yawned wider, the public became increasingly dissatisfied with the inequality they saw around them." They argue that "America is all about equality of opportunity for upward mobility, not about equality of outcomes." The underlying attitude of tolerance for inequality did not change; rather, the level of inequality became "so severe that many Americans are beyond their breaking point, and are therefore amenable to an increased role for government" (162, 146–147). Yet both books do acknowledge that the trend in public concern about income inequality is not linear during the period of rising inequality (McCall 2007; Kenworthy and McCall 2008) and do not empirically test the relationship between beliefs about inequality and social policies.

81. Bartels 2008: chapters 5 and 6.

82. For example, see Bartels 2005: 19 in which he argues that "[t]aken as a whole, the data from the 2002 NES survey reveal very little popular enthusiasm for economic inequality."

83. Different personality types and social dispositions may be more oriented toward system justification than others, but, like Kluegal and Smith's dominant ideology, the strongest underlying tendency of Americans is to believe in the justice of existing economic relations (e.g., Jost et al. 2003).

84. Bartels 2008: chapter 9 presents evidence on the different and unequally represented policy preferences of low-income and high-income constituents. See also Gilens 2012 and McCall and Manza 2011 on policy preference differences by income and class on a broad spectrum of issues. Despite such evidence, Bartels 2008: 289 concludes that the correlation between income and policy preferences is not "so substantial that support for egalitarian policies is limited to 'those mired in poverty.'" Furthermore, in countering arguments by Hacker and Pierson 2005 that Americans did not firmly support the Bush tax cuts when given a choice between the cuts and spending on popular social programs, Bartels argues that "detailed probing would almost certainly reveal

a good deal of ambivalence, uncertainly, and outright contradiction in the views of individual citizens regarding the various provisions of any specific plan... Thus the appealing-seeming option of popular sovereignty is both psychologically unrealistic and logically incoherent" (Bartels 2008: 175). Similarly, he (2008: 293) later argues that partisan control of government is much more determinative of policy outcomes than "public mood," even in the analyses conducted by those (i.e., Erickson, MacKuen and Stimson 2002) who emphasize the important influence of public opinion (293). For another alternative view on the rational responses of voters to the Bush tax cuts, see Lupia et al. 2007.

85. Norton and Ariely 2011: 12. Verba and Orren 1985, Kluegal and Smith 1986, and Osberg and Smeeding 2006 also showed that estimates of occupational earnings disparities were smaller than actual disparities.

86. Norton and Ariely 2011. Hacker and Pierson 2010: 151–155 worry about lack of information as well, focusing on vast underestimates of CEO pay, but also cite evidence that Americans know and care about rising inequality (e.g., Kenworthy and McCall 2008).

87. Consistent with Page and Shapiro's *The Rational Public* (1992), for instance, Page and Jacobs 2009: 100 conclude from their research that "the general accuracy of the public's perceptions is remarkable, given the complexity of government policy, deliberate efforts to sow confusion, and the wide range of topics there are to think about."

88. Hacker and Pierson 2010.

89. Kelly and Enns 2010.

90. The exceptions are Bartels 2005 and McCall and Kenworthy 2009.

91. See discussion earlier in the chapter (e.g., Galbraith 1958, Cohen 2003, Zelizer 2003).

92. The claim that preferences regarding income inequality and redistribution are rooted in the social, political, and economic institutions of the postwar period and are relatively impervious to change is consistent with Brooks and Manza's 2007: chapter 5 theory of "why welfare states persist" amid significant short- and long-term economic change. They counter their sociological model to economic models that predict swings in public opinion based on reactions to existing policies and economic cycles (e.g., Erikson et al. 2002). My approach also differs from both models in that I specify the conditions for both stability and change in attitudes about income inequality and related issues, and these conditions are particular to the issue of income inequality rather than bundled with broader liberal and conservative swings in public mood.

93. I define this broader and more popular notion of opportunity in greater detail in Chapter 4. See also Jencks 1992 on the "opportunity" orientation of the Great Society era programs.

94. See discussion earlier in the chapter (Kluegal and Smith 1986; Roemer 1998; Bell 1973) and in Chapter 4.

95. McCormick 2011: 5 describes the centrality of a zero-sum dynamic in his interpretation of the class politics of Machiavelli. He writes that "the people do not naturally resent the great for possessing material advantages but rather

for using such advantages against themselves, that is, to abuse less wealthy citizens." The economic relationship between inequality and opportunity, as opposed to the perception of that relationship, is hotly debated and receiving greater attention among economists (e.g., Reich 2010; Stiglitz 2012).

96. Although they are mainly proponents of the tolerance perspective, Ladd and Bowman 1998: 114 end their study with this cautionary note: "The free enterprise system functions best when it encourages accumulation and restraint. The latter quality seems noticeably absent in many areas of life today, a development that could make people more sensitive to economic inequality." See also Page and Jacobs 2009: 36 for evidence on this point culled from various newspaper stories.

97. In the most in-depth study of middle-class beliefs about the affluent available, Michele Lamont 2000 finds little evidence that Americans respect the rich in a moral sense but neither does she find that they resent them (as they do in France). Bartels 2008:136–142 likewise shows that the rich rank far down on the feeling thermometer, and Ladd and Bowman 1998: 114–115 testify to the modesty of popular aspirations for becoming rich some day. As Lane 1962: 79 aptly put it, Americans "need only chances (preferably with unknown odds) for a slightly better life than they now have." On the obligations of the rich to the public good, see McCormick 2011.

98. Thus an equitable-growth strategy is not simply an economic-growth strategy, something that the media and political analysts often pose as the "political consensus" over income redistribution (*Economist* 2006: 28). For instance, a Democratic pollster said that he found "little appetite for policies that would redistribute income as his party has advocated over the years. Instead, people were looking for pro-growth policies that were neither traditionally Democratic nor Republican" (Leonhardt 2006: 12). But the point is not growth per se.

Chapter 2: The Emergence of a New Social Issue

1. Gilens 2001; MacKuen et al. 2002; Enns and Kellstedt 2008. Even the economy is open to framing effects, however (Hetherington 1996).

2. Jackman and Jackman 1983; Page and Jacobs 2009; Hacker and Pierson 2010.

3. For a review of the relationship among information, values, and policy views, see Hochschild 2001, Sides and Citrin 2007. In some instances, survey questions attempt to adjust for misinformation. For example, a battery of questions in the General Social Survey begins with a factual statement ("on the average, Blacks have worse jobs, income, and housing than white people") before asking respondents about the causes of racial disparities. The ANES fielded a similar battery of questions about race, gender, and income disparities in 2002 and income disparities in the 2008–2009 Panel Study.

4. There is a tendency to be more pessimistic about others and society than about oneself, and this pessimism about society may be the default perspective in the context of low information (Hochschild 2001).

5. Bartels 2005.

6. There are other questions of a factual nature asked in the 1980s and 1990s, but they do not have the same wording repeated over time and reveal no consistent trend (Ladd and Bowman 1998).

7. The puzzle of income inequality even made its way onto the virtual pages of Salon.com in a ten-part series that reviewed competing economic and political explanations of income inequality (Noah 2010).

8. Ladd and Bowman 1998: 3 (emphasis in original). This is presumably why survey questions about inequality ask about "differences" or "gaps" between groups defined as the "rich" and "poor" or "haves" and "have-nots," which limits the definition of income inequality available in surveys of this kind.

9. In trying to define class for a series in the *New York Times* on the subject in 2005, one reporter found it frustrating that there was no agreed-upon definition among academics (Scott 2008).

10. Under 10 percent desire "almost no differences" between income groups (Jackman and Jackman 1983: 208).

11. Studies have long shown that Americans underestimate the degree of income inequality and yet still prefer less inequality than they think exists (Kluegal and Smith 1986; Verba and Orren 1985; Kelley and Evans 1993; Osberg and Smeeding 2006). Although it is tempting to assume that opposition would be even greater if the real figures were known (Page and Jacobs 2009; Norton and Ariely 2011; Krugman 2007), Gilens 2001 shows that the influence of issue-specific factual information on policy preferences varies across issues and levels of prior political information and knowledge. The strongest effects occur for those with high levels of general knowledge on topics in which misinformation is great. On the economy, information effects are small because knowledge is relatively accurate. Partisanship and motivated reasoning can also bias the reception of knowledge (Bartels 2008; Druckman 2012).

12. Bourdieu 1984; Lamont 1992, 2000; Young 2004. Young shows that awareness of class and racial hierarchies varies inversely with social isolation. Jackman and Jackman 1983 show that members of lower classes have more finely attuned perceptions of class distinctions and interests than members of upper classes.

13. Hodge 2008: 359. Another journalist wrote that "the public has a very finely tuned calibration about how it assigns class location" (Suarez 2008: 362).

14. Hauser and Warren 1997; Kelley and Evans 1993.

15. Lamont 1992: 7, 135–136; Lamont and Volnar 2002: 171. There is no assumption that the cultural supply side either determines or reflects social perceptions in a straightforward fashion. To show how the two interact is the challenge of research in this area as well as in the large literature on framing effects in which "frames in communication" (i.e., messages in the media) are compared to "frames in thought" (i.e., individual perceptions). See Chong and Druckman 2007 for a review of framing effects. Subsequent chapters discuss how public opinion on income inequality accords with the media analysis presented in this chapter.

16. Gamson 2006; Griswold 1987. The study of framing and the more general sociology of culture (e.g., Griswold 1987) are both relevant here, although they often use different conceptual frameworks. I draw from both, but the

conceptual tool kit of cultural sociology is a better fit with my interest in the public discourses of both broad social structures and specific political issues, encompassing political and non-political frames as well as factual information about the social world.

17. Hochschild 1995; Lipset 1996.

18. See Alesina and Glaeser 2004 and Benabou and Tirole 2006 for models in which beliefs about inequality and redistribution are endogenous to formal political ideologies and institutions of redistribution. See also Brooks and Manza 2007 for a theory of the embeddedness of beliefs about social welfare spending within national and historical contexts.

19. It would also be useful to systematically examine the role of political rhetoric and institutions in shaping views about income inequality over time. In his historical analysis of party platforms, Gerring argues that the "spectacular increase in social inequality from the 1970s to the 1990s occasioned little comment from Democratic orators, [whereas] it is difficult to imagine Bryan, Wilson, Rossevelt or Truman remaining silent on such matters" (1998: 236). Regarding the role of politics in shaping issues and policies other than income inequality, such as health care, social spending, and taxes, see Jacobs and Shapiro 2000, Mettler and Soss 2004, and Hacker and Pierson 2005.

20. See Gilens 1999; Jacoby 2000; Jacobs and Shapiro 2000; Baumol, Blinder, and Wolff 2003; Ferree, Gamson, Gerhards, and Rucht 2002.

21. On the presumed low salience of the issue, see Campbell 2010. On media coverage of income inequality, Jeff Madrick 2003:257 lamented that "America is now more unequal than at any time since the 1920s, and it has happened with hardly any discussion." As we will see, there are periodic waves of coverage, and during these times, scholars often speculate that the issue is gaining greater attention (e.g., Murphy 1997; Saez 2009).

22. Personal experience and social networks can convey political information at odds with elite framing and even cancel out the effects of elite framing on public opinion (Druckman and Nelson 2003). I do not rule out this possibility, but it is beyond the scope of this study. It should be noted that information conveyed in social networks more often reiterates elite frames than challenges them.

23. Chong and Druckman 2009: 8 distinguish new issues as those with an "absence of general agreement among elites and the public about how to construe them." Opinion is expected to be more malleable at this stage of the issue-attention cycle.

24. Gamson 2006: 462 refers to the "the level of analysis issue" as the "most difficult, still unresolved problem confronting the analysis of framing contests." He regards the problem as "most messy at the meta-issue level, and it is especially important because often we want to connect issue-level frames with this higher or deeper level."

25. Lamont 1992, 2000 emphasizes the role of contextual changes in shaping perceptions of social class, including shifts in structural conditions. She focuses on differences across national contexts whereas I emphasize changes over time in the cultural supply side itself (e.g., Lamont 2000: 248–249). Political scientists and sociologists also emphasize the role of context in shaping ideas

and social change (Pierson 2004; Brooks and Manza 2007), but there is considerable debate as to which aspects of the context are most consequential for shaping public opinion (e.g., Sides and Citrin 2007).

26. Kluegal and Smith 1986; Kelley and Evans 1993.
27. Suarez 2008: 364.
28. See Morris and Western 1999 and McCall and Percheski 2010 for a review of these debates.
29. Piketty and Saez 2003. Reliable information about income at the extreme right tail of the distribution is not available from conventional sources such as the Census Bureau because of top coding to maintain confidentiality.
30. There were, however, several influential analyses of family and income inequality in the 1990s (e.g., Danziger and Gottschalk 1994).
31. These distinctions were developed through both deductive and inductive methods. Coverage of income inequality could be considered a "genre" that scholars seek to make comprehensible deductively based on our expert knowledge of the topic (Griswold 1987). Inductive methods are used to incorporate subject knowledge and aspects of the genre discovered in the process of analyzing cultural artifacts (e.g., frames in news articles). For a description of inductive methods in media analyses, see Chong and Druckman 2009.
32. This includes unionization, the minimum wage, corporate governance and restructuring, and equity norms within firms.
33. Bluestone and Harrison 1982; Harrison and Bluestone 1988; Kuttner 1983; Edsall 1984, 1988; Levy and Michel 1986; Levy 1987; Newman 1988; Katz 1989; Phillips 1990.
34. The study of inequality within and between occupations and occupational groups, however, has gained more interest lately (Autor 2010; Kim and Sakamoto 2008; Mouw and Kalleberg 2010).
35. McLanahan and Percheski 2008; Kenworthy 2005.
36. Newman 1988, 1993.
37. Gilens 1999; Kellstedt 2000. Due to a less straightforward subject matter, however, our method deviated from that of Gilens and Kellstedt, who were able to obtain their target population of articles with only a few keywords, such as "race" and "welfare."
38. Irrelevant articles here and in subsequent searches were on the following topics: racial or gender inequality, gay rights, inequality in other countries, individuals whose names are part of a subject term (e.g., Marc Rich), references to popular culture that include part of a subject term (e.g., a movie named "Big Business"), clearly personal affairs about a single individual, noneconomic elites (e.g., in art or religion), and social class as a predictor of noneconomic phenomenon (e.g., health, drug use). A total of 19 articles were excluded (5 for "wage differentials," 6 for "income inequality," 6 for "equality," and 2 for "meritocracy").
39. Edsall 1984, 1988.
40. "Dreams, Myths and Realities," *USNWR*, July 25, 1988. The article ends with the following: "What the times demand and the American public seeks in a new leader is a supreme pragmatist – a practical man of competence and integrity who can attract talent and deal with the increasing complexities and

competition in a world economy. This is the test by which to judge Michael Dukakis and George Bush... [I]n this election, the crucial judgment is who can reverse the trends toward inequality and bring more of our people closer to the American dream."

41. This last article appeared in 1981 with the subject term "equality" and was written as an editorial by Thomas Sowell ("We're Not Really 'Equal'," *Newsweek*, September 7, 1981). Although conceived as a philosophical rumination on the nature of gender and racial inequality, it was not initially screened out because it made allusions to general theories of inequality. Still, it failed to discuss inequality according to any of the criteria listed in Table 2.1, and thus the article was eventually deemed irrelevant during coding.

42. "Is the Middle Class Really Doomed to Shrivel Away?," *USNWR*, August 20, 1984; "Two-Tier Pay Stirs Backlash among Workers, *USNWR*, September 23, 1985.

43. The journalist Robert Kuttner published a piece titled "The Declining Middle" in the July, 1983, issue of *Atlantic Monthly*, quoting Bluestone and Harrison's *The Deindustrialization of America* (1982) and several Census Bureau and Bureau of Labor Statistics reports. By the time James Fallows wrote on the same topic in the same magazine in July, 1985, evidence had shifted against the declining–middle-class thesis. Fallows mentions a media circus around an earlier *Fortune* magazine article ("The Mass Market is Splitting Apart," November 28, 1983) based on a Census Bureau study of the declining middle class that was later debunked. See also Levy and Michel's 1986 study, which was commissioned by the Joint Economic Committee. Diana Kendall 2005: chapter 6 provides evidence that the specter of middle-class decline has haunted media discourse for over a hundred years.

44. Hacker 2006: 19 cites data from a private firm showing that, over the 1979 to 2005 time period, feelings of job insecurity peaked in the mid-1990s, with 45 percent of respondents saying they were "frequently concerned about being laid off."

45. Gilens 1999.

46. I report counts of articles but the overall number of articles (the base) has remained relatively constant over time and, if anything, has declined slightly. Thus using share measures does not alter these results.

47. "Income Gap Is Issue No. 1, Debaters Agree," *Washington Post*, December 7, 1995.

48. Jacoby 1997: 262. The abstract of one article says this about Buchanan: he "decries the 'stagnant wages of an alienated working class' and lambastes overpaid CEOs, is going beyond standard Republican indictments of the 'intellectual elite' to attack the financial elite. He also implicates much of the world's non-Caucasian population. Buchanan says that low-wage immigrants and low-wage foreign workers compete with native-born Americans to drive down wages" ("Who's Really to Blame?", *TIME*, November 6, 1995).

49. The quotation about media coverage is from Ladd and Bowman 1998: 1–2, 114.

50. "The Rich Get Richer," *USNWR*, February 21, 2000.
51. "Indifferent to Inequality," *Newsweek*, May 7, 2001.
52. *USA Today*, December 11, 2000 (emphasis added).
53. Celebrity CEOs were often given credit for the bull market and booming economy of the late 1990s (Khurana 2002).
54. Somewhat consistent with the lack of emphasis on inequality that I find, Kendall 2005: chapter 4 argues that corporate malfeasance during the early 2000s was covered as a matter of individual pathology rather than structural design.
55. Other journalists appearing at this time as well as in the 1980s include Robert Samuelson of *Newsweek* and Donald Bartlett and James Steele of the *Philadelphia Inquirer*, then writing for *Time*.
56. "Trickle-Up Economics," *Newsweek*, October 2, 2006 (emphasis added). The full quote is: "Although Americans do not regard rich people with much envy, they believe that wealth should be broad-based, and trickle-up economics, with most benefits flowing to the top, seems un-American . . . no one should be happy with today's growing economic inequality. It threatens America's social compact, which depends on a shared sense of well-being." The information in the article is based on "the government's recent release of household income and poverty figures for 2005 [which] has sharpened the debate" (showing lower median household income and higher poverty since the last business cycle peak in 2000, but higher concentrations of income at the top).
57. "The Quagmire of Inequality," *Newsweek*, June 11, 2007. Samuelson goes on to say that "Whether the debate becomes an empty exercise in class warfare or a genuine search for ways to reconcile economic justice and economic growth is an open question."
58. "Rich Man, Poor Man," *USNWR*, June 12, 2006 (emphasis added).
59. On the concentration of income at the top, Gross references the work of Emmanuel Saez at the University of California, Berkeley (emphasis added).
60. "The End of Upward Mobility?," *Newsweek*, January 26, 2009, and "We Are Not in This Together," *Newsweek*, April 20, 2009.
61. See the first two panels of Figure 2.2 and the first panel of Figure 2.1. Many "explicit" mentions of income inequality, moreover, are one-liners, as are mentions of stagnant or declining median family income (e.g., "America's Bull Run," *USNWR*, January 14, 2008; "Upper East Sliders," *Newsweek*, October 20, 2008; and "Spread the Wealth?" *Newsweek*, November 10, 2008). Another article pinpoints rising inequality at the top as just one of several causes of economic anxiety and focuses on the problems of the upper classes trying to keep up with the super rich ("Welcome to Elsewhere," *Newsweek*, January 26, 2009).
62. "The American Dream Goes On," *USNWR*, June 23, 2008.
63. Chong and Druckman 2009 followed the same inductive procedure in their analysis of over a dozen political issues in the media.
64. This was perhaps to be expected given the upper- and middle-class focus of the mainstream media as described by Gans 2004.

65. After removing duplicates and unrelated articles, the population of articles from the three newsweeklies with these subject terms numbered 417 over the thirty-one–year period without including "labor," and 956 when including "labor."

66. On this bias, see Gans 2004.

67. Looking at the top two subjects of top-end groups, coverage of executive salaries was highest in 1991–1992, followed by 2002–2004, whereas coverage of the rich was highest in 1997, 2003 and 2007, followed by 1999, 2009, 2010, and 1995. Coverage of the middle classes peaks with fifteen articles in 1994 and 1995, followed by the early 1990s and late 2000s (ten articles in 1991 and 1992, and again in 2008 and 2009).

68. Kuhnen and Niessen 2012: 7.

69. "Pressure to Perform," *USNWR*, April 6, 1992. Other articles make more direct connections between income inequality and economic turmoil: "With rich Americans controlling so much money, it is understandable that consumer confidence is now at an almost unprecedented low and that most consumers are worried about their economic futures. *The massive income disparity may have already contributed to the United States' recent productivity losses...*" ("A Very Rich Dessert," *USNWR*, March 23, 1992, emphasis added).

70. As Kevin J. Murphy, an economist and expert on executive compensation, writes: "Although the US business press had followed CEO pay for decades, the CEO pay debate achieved international prominence in the early 1990s. The controversy heightened with the November 1991 introduction of Graef Crystal's expose on CEO pay, *In Search of Excess*, and exploded following President Bush's ill-timed pilgrimage to Japan in January 1992, accompanied by an entourage of highly paid US executives. What was meant to be a plea for Japanese trade concessions dissolved into accusations that *US competitiveness was hindered by its excessive executive compensation practices* as attention focused on the 'huge pay disparities between top executives in the two countries'" (Murphy 1997: 417–418, emphasis added).

71. See again Murphy 1997 on the issue of partisanship: "Consistent with *TIME* magazines's labeling of CEO pay as the 'populist issue that no politician can resist,' high CEO salaries emerged as a bipartisan campaign issue among the leading candidates in the 1992 presidential election," citing the *Wall Street Journal* (January 21, 1992 and January 15, 1992) and *TIME* (May 5, 1992). On negativity bias, see Chong and Druckman 2009.

72. "Double-Talk about 'Class'," *TIME*, March 2, 1992; "Back to Class War?," *Newsweek*, February 12, 1996 (emphasis added).

73. See Dinardo, Lemieux, and Fortin 1996.

74. Baumol, Blinder, and Wolff 2003: 36.

75. Indeed, it appears that the *Readers' Guide* has recently substituted "income distribution" for its subject term "income inequality."

76. See Gilens 1999, Dyck and Hussey 2008, and Kellstedt 2000 for approaches that retain all articles from the search as relevant and then either code pictures only or use computerized methods to identify frames. See Appendix A for further details on our hand coding process.

77. The confidence intervals shown in panel 2 of Figure 2.2 confirm the significance of the shifts over time in media coverage. The intervals are estimated from a saturated Poisson regression model with total number of articles regressed on year dummies and with 1987 as the excluded category. Results do not change when rates of coverage rather than numbers of articles are used as the outcome.

78. The content coding in Appendix C shows high levels of coverage of taxes, the rich, and the poor in the early 1980s. Subject terms occurring frequently during this period include: United States/economic conditions and economic policy, income taxes/taxation, the budget, unemployment, labor, and inflation.

79. "The Key Voting Blocks," *USNWR*, August 29, 1988.

80. Tellingly, in the acknowledgements section of Harrison and Bluestone's *The Great U-Turn* (1988: xxix), the authors write that "first, we are grateful to those who helped pay our research bills during a period when this sort of iconoclastic investigation was generally out of fashion. In Washington, the U.S. Congressional Joint Economic Committee and the Economic Policy Institute were there when we needed them... Second,... a number of mainstream and conservative economists, journalists, and public officials relentlessly challenged us to reexamine our methods and strengthen our arguments." Much of the debate over growing polarization between good jobs and bad jobs is covered in Newman's *Falling from Grace* (1988), which investigates the middle- class experience of downward mobility, including executives downsized from major corporations and air traffic controllers displaced from well-paying union jobs. See also Michael Katz's *The Undeserving Poor* (1989) on growing poverty, and Kevin Phillips' *The Politics of Rich and Poor: Wealth and the American Electorate in the Reagan Aftermath* (1990). Whereas Newman argues that episodes of downward mobility are hidden (PATCO being an exception, though she argues there was little sympathy for the workers), Phillips repeatedly claims that average Americans know about rising inequality and are angry about it.

81. George H. W. Bush is infamous for raising taxes as part of a 1990 budget agreement after issuing a campaign promise that he would not. Bill Clinton's major pieces of tax legislation came in 1993 (Omnibus Budget Reconciliation Act) and 1997 (Taxpayer Relief Act).

82. This is consistent with Katherine Newman's observation in 1993 that "news of economic disaster has dominated the media for the past four years, gathering strength as the election season of 1992 neared" (p. ix) and with Hetherington 1996. It is also consistent with responses to a question from the Survey of Consumer Finances about government economic policy, which are more negative in 1992 than in any other year from 1970 (when the series begins) to 2008.

83. NAFTA, Patrick Buchanan, and Ross Perot reflect this shift.

84. "First Things First, Mr. President," *Newseek*, December 8, 2008. By social reform, Samuelson does not even mention income inequality explicitly; instead he mentions health care reform.

85. "How the Next President Should Fix the Economy," *TIME*, May 26, 2008, citing many academics, such as Bartels 2008, Hacker 2006, and Piketty and Saez 2003.

86. See discussion earlier in the chapter and, for example, Zaller 1992; Ferree et al. 2002; Saris and Sniderman 2004; Campbell 2004: chapter 4; Chong and Druckman 2007; Lamont 2000.

87. As Page and Shapiro 1992: 319 write: "[P]olitical information and interpretations conveyed to the public have become highly unified... Practically all Americans are exposed to the same facts and ideas, through network television news and the wire service reports that dominate daily newspapers and provide the grist for discussion by friends and neighbors." I do not assume that the sources I examined are widely read by the general public, however, only that they reflect topics of national concern arising from objective societal conditions as well as from segments of society, potentially including many Americans themselves. Other studies examine media coverage as a reflection of public opinion and show how media coverage affects corporate behavior. See, for example, a study of the effect of negative media coverage of CEO pay on corporate compensation practices (Kuhnen and Niessen 2012).

88. On the declining representation of redistributive issues in social organizations, see Skocpol 2007.

89. Our preliminary analysis of coverage as a function of levels of income inequality, unemployment, growth, and political engagement suggests that these have little predictive power. This is especially the case for levels of income inequality.

90. The residual categories once again were those that only mentioned employment or economic conditions or those that only mentioned a single group's financial circumstances. These were very difficult to separate from one another, because most articles focusing on the economy made some reference to average incomes or some other income group, even if only in passing. Thus we do not analyze those data any further here.

Chapter 3: American Beliefs about Income Inequality

1. Permissive social norms are often a residual explanation cited by economists after accounting for the role of economic factors in causing the increase in inequality (Krugman 2002; Piketty and Saez 2003). For a view that loosened social norms among executives enabled the rise of executive compensation, see Bebchuck and Fried 2003. Scholarship that focuses on beliefs about opportunity and redistribution includes, among others, Alesina and Glaeser 2004; Benabou and Tirole 2006; and Haskins and Sawhill 2009.

2. Recent scholarship documenting that Americans care about income inequality, but from a variety of viewpoints, includes Bartels 2005, 2008; McCall and Kenworthy 2009; Page and Jacobs 2009; and Newman and Jacobs 2010. Chapter 1 provides a fuller discussion.

3. On the growth of incomes at the top, see Piketty and Saez 2003.

4. On the economic relationship between economic growth and income inequality, see Benabou 2000; Voichovsky 2009.

5. McCloskey and Zaller 1984; Kluegal and Smith 1986; Lane 1986. This type of question is being analyzed in the Chinese context, however (White 2010; Xie et al. 2011).

6. Page and Jacobs 2009 and Newman and Jacobs 2010 argue that concerns have increased with rising inequality, although they also note the finding of a more complicated, nonlinear trend (McCall and Kenworthy 2009). This analysis is extended later on in the chapter. Those who argue that Americans are largely ignorant of the scale of income inequality, and that this leads to their political acquiescence, include Norton and Ariely 2011 and Hacker and Pierson 2010. Bartels 2008 argues that Americans are uninformed of the policy implications of income inequality.

7. On increasing partisan polarization, see McCarty, Poole, and Rosenthal 2006 and Gelman 2008; on the effect of partisan polarization on policy preferences, see Bartels 2008.

8. The Appendix provides information about the GSS/ISSP and the samples used in this analysis.

9. The ISSP and GSS also include questions about the actual and preferred pay of a select group of occupations, and these data have been used to analyze attitudes about inequality. However, these questions are not as suitable for time series analysis for two reasons: (1) they are not available in as many years (1996 and 2008 are missing), and (2) the selection of occupations varies substantially across the available years. For different purposes, I examine these data in the following chapter. Other questions on inequality in the American National Election Studies ask about equal rights, equal opportunities, and equal chances without referring to any particular type of inequality, allowing respondents to answer with different forms of inequality in mind (i.e., racial or gender inequality). See the Appendix for further discussion of survey question bias.

10. Ladd and Bowman 1998.

11. See Bartels 2005 for factual questions added to the 2002 ANES, which were then replicated in 2004 and 2008. I discuss these in greater detail in the next chapter. They show that most people think that income inequality increased over time: 74 percent in 2002, 81 percent in 2004, and 79 percent in 2008 said that "differences in income between rich people and poor people in the United States today is larger than 20 years ago" (as opposed to "smaller" or "stayed the same"). As discussed in the previous chapter, these response levels resemble those of the longest-running question that is factual in nature. The question is a Harris poll about whether the rich are getting richer and the poor are getting poorer. Agreement to this question shot up from less than a majority (45 percent) in 1966 to well over a majority (61 percent) in 1972. Thereafter, agreement fluctuated from 65 to 83 percent, with peak levels of agreement occurring in the early 1990s. The marked rise in the 1960s and 1970s predates the rise in income inequality, so it is unclear why this occurred; perhaps it was because of the greater visibility of the poor rather than the rich at that time. Subsequently, both questions seem to indicate that Americans consider rising inequality to be a natural or normal state of affairs *at all times*. Nevertheless, to the extent a trend for the Harris question can

be isolated, it is consistent with the nonlinear trend in the GSS data shown later on in the chapter.

12. These conclusions are confirmed by statistical analyses. See the Appendix section on "statistical tests of descriptive trends" for further details.

13. Although I focus on the "strongly agree" outcome throughout the rest of this chapter and the book, I tested many other specifications, and they were consistent with the results presented below. Where relevant, I will refer to some of these other specifications, such as ordinal and variance logistic regressions. See the Appendix section on "analytic models" for further details.

14. Lipset 1996; McClosky and Zaller 1985; Hochschild 1995.

15. As discussed in Chapter 1, McClosky and Zaller 1984, Kluegal and Smith 1986, Hochschild 1981, 1995 all speculated that beliefs could shift as a result of social and economic transformations. Lipset 1996 denies that there were ever any serious structural challenges brought on by rising inequality. Lane 1962 argues that Americans expect only a small chance for upward mobility, but wrote during a period of robust and equitable economic growth.

16. For a description of regression equations and variables, see Appendix sections "analytic models" and "variable definitions." Descriptive statistics are provided in Appendix Table A3.3.

17. It is also possible that people have changed their understandings of what inequality means, which is plausible given the high degree of abstraction inherent in the term. However, it is still unlikely that large numbers of Americans changed their levels of tolerance *systematically* because of changes in their *individual* conceptions of what inequality means. A more likely scenario is that individuals were subject to similar information that shifted the meaning of inequality in similar ways.

18. Lemieux 2008.

19. Median-voter models (Meltzer and Richard 1981) predict that the median voter would be better off supporting redistributive programs when median income falls below mean income (as it does in times of rising inequality), implying that voters with income at the median or lower level should be more likely to oppose increasing levels of inequality. For a variety of reasons, this dynamic may apply more to those falling in the bottom third than in the middle of the income distribution (Pontusson and Rueda 2010). As discussed in Chapter 1, a revealing experiment by Kluegal and Smith 1986: 110 showed that more than a majority of Americans believed that greater equality was in their material interest, with 62 percent agreeing that "more equality of incomes would allow my family to live better." However, self-interested opposition to inequality fell to 42 percent among those who first responded to questions about the fairness and functionality of inequality in principle. Material self-interest is therefore a potentially important factor in determining responses to growing income inequality, as long as it is not dampened by the view that rising inequality is beneficial for overall economic growth and innovation.

20. In fact, many economists argue that income inequality has grown mainly as a result of changes in the supply and demand for skills as measured by the premium in wages that college-educated workers earn relative to

non–college-educated workers (Goldin and Katz 2008). See also Teixiera and Rogers 2000 and Frank 2005 for political analyses that define the working class as the non–college-educated.

21. On the role of education in liberalizing and informing beliefs, see Kluegal and Smith 1986, Zaller 1992. The hegemonic claim is that rising inequality is an inevitable consequence of technological change, whereas the empirical evidence casts some doubt on this relationship (Voichovsky 2009).

22. On the role of elite politics in shaping policy preferences and attitudes about inequality, see Bartels 2008, and a more detailed discussion of Bartels's findings in Chapter 1. In their descriptive analysis, Page and Jacobs 2009 find more partisan agreement than disagreement on issues related to income inequality. Neither examines trends over time.

23. For debates on the realignment of low income and education voters from liberal to independent and conservative positions, see, for example, Bartels 2008: chapter 3; Campbell 2007.

24. The most consequential demographic shifts included the aging and grow-ing racial diversity of the population, both resulting in more opposition to inequality in the late 2000s than in 1987. In their analysis of data up to 2000 Newman and Jacobs 2010 show that cohort effects do not affect trends in responses to whether income differences are too large.

25. The composition is fixed with median or modal values for categorical vari-ables and means for ordinal variables: female, white, married, employed, not living in the South, self-identified as middle class, a Democrat or independent, moderate, with one or more children, and mean age, age squared, household size, education, and family income.

26. Appendix Table A3.4 provides additional information on the effect of each compositional shift on the year coefficients as they are entered sequentially in nested models. In this table, only two inequality outcomes are shown for illustrative purposes, as the trends are similar for all questions. As Appendix Table A3.4 makes apparent, there was little change in the year coefficients as each subsequent set of compositional factors was entered into the model, even in the linear regression models with the index of all three questions as the outcome and in the y-standardized binary logistic regressions. In other logistic equations, coefficients are inflated by the change in scale of the latent dependent variable as explained variance increases with additional explana-tory variables, which makes real changes in effects due to compositional shifts more difficult to identify.

27. This is consistent with much previous research (Verba and Orren 1985; Kluegal and Smith 1986; Gilens 1999) but also might be the result of common method and endogeneity bias among the attitudinal variables, something I examine further later on in the chapter.

28. Part of this effect could be attributed to response bias. Recall that in the original wording of this question, agreement indicates support for inequal-ity. Opposition to inequality would therefore have to be registered by dis-agreement with the original wording. Because agreement bias tends to be greater for those with less education, the strong positive effect of education could reflect this bias (i.e., among those who were opposed to inequality, the

educated were more likely to respond with disagreement than the less educated) (Zaller 1992).

29. The top is defined as the 88th percentile (because of the top coding of family income as described in the Appendix), the middle as the 50th percentile, and the bottom as the 10th percentile of family income within the analysis sample.

30. To determine whether the composition of moderates changed significantly in a liberal direction from 1987 to 1996, explaining the increase in intense opposition among them, I examined the party identification of moderates and found that moderates actually became significantly more conservative in their party identification (moving toward the Republican end of the scale).

31. Schlozman et al. 2005: 23. However, there is no research that tests this proposition. Gilens 1999 finds support for this proposition, but he examines attitudes toward welfare instead of inequality.

32. On policy mood, see Erikson, MacKuen, and Stimson 2002; on awareness of basic economic indicators among the least educated, see Enns and Kellstedt 2008; on parallel movements across groups, see Page and Shapiro 1992.

33. There are actually several GSS questions that are potentially relevant here but they are not available in all years (e.g., about job insecurity, financial satisfaction, and intergenerational mobility). However, they were uneven and much weaker indicators of beliefs about inequality in cross-sectional analyses than the question about improving one's standard of living that I use here.

34. Warren and Tyagi 2004 and Frank 2007 discuss the increasing cost of major consumption items such as health care, housing, and a college education. Frank argues that rising costs are in part a function of rising income inequality, in which the rich favor privatization of services and drive up the costs of quality for everyone else.

35. Piketty 1995; Benabou and Ok 2001; Alesina et al. 2004.

36. The correlation of errors from a bivariate probit regression equation in which responses to both questions are outcomes provides a measure of the strength of this relationship and tests for endogeneity. The mobility question should be considered endogenous if it is correlated with the same omitted macro-level explanatory factors that potentially affect opposition to inequality – such as macroeconomic conditions and levels of inequality, which I will examine shortly – or if it is closely intertwined in people's minds with the fairness of income inequality such that the two are simultaneously determined. There is a significant correlation of errors (*rho*) between perceptions of inequality and mobility, but the correlation is relatively low and uneven, in the .14 to .32 range. Because endogeneity produces inconsistent coefficients for the endogenous variable as well as for explanatory variables, such as the time trend, I use the bivariate probit equations to provide consistent estimates of the equation's full parameters, and find that the time trend in opposition to inequality is robust (Wooldridge 2002: 472–478; Baum et al. 2003).

37. The GSS is typically fielded across the spring months of the year. In order to measure unemployment and consumer sentiment over the twelve months preceding the survey, I define it as the average monthly rate from April of the

previous year to March of the survey year. Note also that unemployment and growth rates do not overlap exactly. I use unemployment rates because the public is more likely to be aware of these, but the conclusions drawn from these series do not change if growth rates are used instead of unemployment rates. The index of consumer sentiment is available on a monthly basis from the Survey of Consumers at the University of Michigan. The unemployment rate is from the Bureau of Labor Statistics.

38. See the discussion in Chapters 1 and 4. There are a variety of potential reasons, ranging from violations of norms of fairness to concerns about its broader social consequences. Examples of the former include perceptions that levels of inequality exceed some ideal (but imprecise) level; that very high incomes at the top and/or very low ones at the bottom are unduly influenced by luck, greed, or personal connections and are not commensurate with contributions to society; or that inequalities are the result of discrimination or otherwise represent an unfair restriction of opportunity. Examples of the latter include perceptions that inequality results in high rates of crime, underfunded public institutions, lack of access to higher education, large disparities in health outcomes, residential and social segregation, and/or undue political influence by the wealthy.

39. It is in fact now commonplace in lists that include technological change, globalization, immigration, and other factors to cite social norms as one of the explanations of rising inequality (McCall and Percheski 2010).

40. See Bartels 2005 and Campbell 2010 for skepticism about the salience and transparency of the issue to Americans given their inability to connect their beliefs about income inequality to their views about progressive taxation. Bartels analyzes data at a single point in time in the early 2000s, however. Page and Jacobs 2009 argue that Americans are mostly informed and aware of rising income inequality, as do Newman and Jacobs 2010, but provide no direct evidence of awareness. See Chapter 1 for a fuller discussion.

41. The data come from the March Current Population Survey (CPS). These income data do not take into account noncash transfers; they do not subtract taxes; and they undercount very high incomes (due to topcoding). But they are widely used.

42. The now widely reported measure of income held by the top percentiles and fractiles of the income distribution using tax data was not available until the early 2000s (Piketty and Saez 2003), after a good portion of the period of our study. Note also that academic and expert knowledge of rising earnings and income inequality did not spread widely until the early 1990s (Levy and Murnane 1992), even though there were several commentaries on the phenomenon in the 1980s and it was covered by the media at that time as well (e.g., Harrison and Bluestone 1988; Phillips 1990). Topics related to income inequality, such as taxing and spending and labor disputes, were covered by the media as well, as discussed in Chapter 2 and apparent in Figure 3.8.

43. See especially Gottschalk and Danziger 2005, Mishel, Bernstein, and Allegreto 2007, and the review in McCall and Percheski 2010.

44. Page and Shapiro 1992; Zaller 1992.

45. I used the *Readers Guide to Periodical Abstracts* to search for articles in the three major American newsweeklies (*Newsweek, Time,* and *USNWR*) with keywords related to income inequality. A random sample of articles in each year was selected (N=1,179) and hand coded for content related to income inequality. For further details and other methods of content analysis consistent with the results presented here, see Chapter 2.

46. In addition to the media analysis presented in the previous chapter, several scholars writing about the early and mid-1990s mention the negative media coverage of inequality at the time (e.g., Newman 1993; Jacoby 1997; Ladd and Bowman 1998; see also Morin and Berry 1996). For example, Jacoby 1997: 262 wrote of Patrick Buchanan's visibility in the Republican primaries of 1996 and his focus on issues of inequality, aiming "his rhetoric at top executives such as Robert E. Allen, the head of AT&T, who receive huge salaries while laying off thousands of workers." Ladd and Bowman 1998: 1–2, 114 also described a "media bombardment of stories about fabulous salaries and extravagant lifestyles" in the mid-1990s. Murphy 1997 describes the importance of the issue of excessive executive pay in the presidential campaign of 1992 and Hetherington 1996 of the unrealistically negative media coverage of the economy during that election.

47. When articles are restricted to those that discuss the trend in *rising* inequality, the spike in coverage in the calendar year 2000 is not as high as the peak in the mid-1990s. That is, the discussion of *rising* inequality was greater in the 1990s than in 2000.

48. The confidence intervals shown in Figure 3.8 confirm the significance of the shifts over time in media coverage. The intervals are estimated from a saturated Poisson regression model with total number of articles regressed on year dummies and with 1987 as the excluded category. Results do not change when rates of coverage rather than numbers of articles are used as the outcome.

49. Studies of policy mood also show relatively low levels of liberalism in the mid-1990s as compared to the late 1980s and the late 2000s (Stimson 2009; Kellstedt 2000). For example, conservative welfare reform was enacted in the mid-1990s. In addition, the popular vote in the presidential elections of 1992, 1996, 2000, and 2008 all went to a Democratic candidate despite variation in levels of concern about income inequality across those years. Thus the presidential election cycle is not consistent with the trend either.

50. Mainstream opposition accords well with Zaller's 2004: 204 argument that "low information" voters tend to be more centrist and labile in their attitude formation and thus more apt to respond critically when "societal problems arise," and Althaus's 2003 contention that information bias is mitigated when information is more widely available, as when an issue is receiving heightened media attention.

51. This interpretation is partially consistent with Hetherington's 1996: 392 observation that periods "when growth is positive but not dramatic" could raise the influence of media coverage of the economy on political outcomes (as he showed was the case in 1992). However, I am arguing that both media and public perceptions could be focused on the *distributional* consequences

of economic growth rather than on economic growth per se. I provide further evidence in the next chapter that American views of the economy became more positive in the mid-1990s along with actual levels of growth even though their levels of economic anxiety about the future and their opposition to inequality remained high.

52. Krueger and Solow 2001; Khurana 2002.
53. Nearly a quarter of Americans still strongly maintained that income differences were too large, but the share of strong agreement to the other two questions dropped to 9 and 13 percent.

Chapter 4: Why Do Americans Care about Income Inequality?

1. Jencks and Tach 2006: 25 report that "[a]lmost all adults in West Germany, Britain, and the United States agree that economic inequality is fair, 'but only if there are equal opportunities,'" citing data from the International Social Justice Project. Japan, however, shows a much lower level of agreement.
2. Sawhill and Morton 2007: 5 provide evidence from the same sources as I do (i.e., the ISSP) that Americans "have tended to be far more optimistic about their ability to control their own economic destinies through hard work, less likely to believe that coming from a wealthy family is important to getting ahead, less likely to think that differences in income within their country are too large, and less likely to favor the government's taking responsibility to reduce those differences." Similarly, although Haskins and Sawhill 2009: 1–2, 5 regard rising income inequality as both important and connected to opportunity, they say that they "focus more on opportunity than on inequality and poverty [because] Americans... are far more interested in equal opportunity than in equal results."
3. Research in experimental social psychology examines variation among Americans in their beliefs about the legitimacy of group hierarchies but does not expand much on the analytical distinction between beliefs about opportunities and outcomes or on how the context of income inequality affects such beliefs (e.g., Jost and Major 2001).
4. Roemer 1998: 24.
5. See, for example, Hochschild 1995; Kluegal and Smith 1986; Lamont 2000; Young 2004.
6. When asked what they "think is more important for this country: to reduce inequality or to ensure everyone has a fair chance of improving their economic standing," 71 percent select the latter (Economic Mobility Project 2009: 18).
7. Questions that ask about this possibility are rare. One that did revealed an overwhelming majority of respondents (71 percent) agreeing that "greater economic inequality means that it is more difficult for those at the bottom of the income leader to move up the ladder" (Economic Mobility Project 2009: 18). Similarly, Sawhill and Morton 2007: 7 hint that "the nation is ill at ease and seems to be wondering whether increasing inequality is affecting one's ability to get ahead." And Kluegal and Smith 1986 found that 62 percent of respondents thought that "more equality of incomes would allow my family

to live better." Aside from beliefs, studies of the relationship between income inequality and intergenerational income mobility find a negative correlation between the two and suggest that inequality inhibits mobility (e.g., Esping-Anderson 2007; Bjorklund and Jantti 2009). More generally, the original rationale for equalizing opportunity was in fact to eliminate the effect of differences in social class background on the educational and economic opportunities and outcomes of children (e.g., Young 1958). For a full discussion of previous research on opportunity and inequality, see Chapter 1.

8. Bell 1973: 426.

9. Perhaps the most contentious issue is whether ability and effort (and other relevant heritable characteristics) are considered accidents of birth and therefore undeserving of disproportionate rewards, in which case true equality of opportunity is impossible and equality of results is the default principle of distributive justice, or whether such characteristics are considered a fair basis for inequalities in rewards as long as opportunities along other dimensions (e.g., family background, race, gender) are equal. See debates in Bell 1973; Jencks et al. 1972; and Roemer 1998.

10. For example, in introducing affirmative action as a policy to level the playing field between racial groups, President Johnson used the metaphor of a race between a shackled (black) and unshackled (white) runner (Bell 1973: 429). Roemer's 1998 preferred definition of equal opportunity is also that of the level playing field, especially when applied to education.

11. Bartels 2005: 18 shows that education is considered the most important cause of income disparities (see Chapter 5 for further discussion).

12. Robert Lane 1962: 79 argues that Americans expect *some* but not *a lot* of opportunity.

13. The "the state of the economy" is considered essential or very important in determining economic mobility by 62 percent of Americans. This share is less than for factors such as hard work, ambition, education, health, and a stable family, but considerably more than for knowing the right people, having educated parents, coming from a wealthy family, luck (21 percent), gender and race (Economic Mobility Project 2009: 15). Eighty-one percent of Americans also see "keeping jobs in America" as a very effective way for government to improve economic mobility, a higher share than all other policies, including "making college more affordable" (Economic Mobility Project 2009: 17). Regarding information about the economy, Enns and Kellstedt 2008: 438, 450 argue that "the economy is a relatively easy cue or heuristic to use to update political attitudes [because] economic news is pervasive" and find that "[e]ven the least sophisticated receive and respond to objective economic indicators." With regard to perceptions of general economic trends, then, there is more "signal" than "noise" among nearly all Americans even though at times economic news and reporting can be distorted and these distortions can have political consequences (Hetherington 1996).

14. Erikson, MacKuen, and Stimson 2002; Gilens 1999.

15. However, "the near-universal support for abstract principles of racial equality" must be contrasted to "lackluster support for policies" (Kryson 2000:

140). Women are also seen to be more legitimate victims of discrimination than are blacks (Kluegal and Smith 1986).

16. Some social scientists infer racial and gender discrimination from unequal outcomes (e.g., earnings) among equally qualified men and women and whites and minorities, whereas others argue that unobservable job-related characteristics and preferences explain unequal racial and gender outcomes. Similarly, in a study of intergenerational mobility, Nathan Grawe 2004: 61 states that "implicit in this approach is the recognition that earnings combine both opportunity and preferences." He also makes the analogy that unequal earnings among otherwise similarly qualified individuals who come from different social class backgrounds is evidence of unequal opportunities by class (see also Jonsson et al. 2011: 144). Grawe draws from Roemer 1998: 13, who goes further (at least in education) and *defines* equal opportunity as the distribution of resources that equalizes outcomes such as "educational achievements or future earnings" among those who exert equivalent levels of effort (relative to their social backgrounds). Similarly, Bell criticizes Coleman (in the Coleman Report) for having "redefined equality of opportunity from *equal access to equally well-endowed schools (inputs) to equal performance on standardized achievement tests (equality of outcomes)*" (Bell 1973: 431) (emphasis in original). That is, equal outcomes became the measure of equal opportunity. In law, unequal outcomes among otherwise equally qualified individuals has been used as evidence of "disparate impact" discrimination, indicating bias in seemingly neutral and nondiscriminatory procedures (for a review, see Pager and Shepherd 2008).

17. MacLean 2006: 107; Dobbin 2009: 14. The line between equal treatment and equal outcomes is further blurred by the wide discretion permitted to workplaces and courts in defining the meaning of discrimination and antidiscrimination because the law itself is so vague (Dobbin 2009: chapter 1).

18. Sen 2000: 9, 13 writes that "if paying a person more induces him or her to produce more desirable results, then an incentive argument may exist for that person's pay being greater. This is an instrumental and contingent justification [or merit] (related to results) – it does not assert that the person intrinsically 'deserves' to get more" simply by virtue of the position he or she inhabits.

19. Such distortions and inefficiencies can be introduced by excessive pay compression as well. Bell 1973: 453, 454, an otherwise enthusiastic supporter of meritocracy, describes the possibility of an "unjust meritocracy" in which distinctions of merit are "invidious and demean those below" and "those at the top convert their authority positions into large, discrepant material and social advantages over others." Bell 1973: 451 advocates policy supports for the disadvantaged but also a fair distribution of rewards based on achievement ("one of the most vexing questions in a post-industrial society"). The unappealing side of meritocracy was also "counter-argument" to Michael Young's "argument" for meritocracy in his influential and satirical book coining the term, *The Rise of Meritocracy* (1958). In "Meritocracy Revisited," Young 1994: 88–89 worries both about the corrupting power of technocratic elites, who could be "ruthless in pursuing their own advantage,"

and the potential demoralization of the less favored, who could be "damaged in their own self-esteem." See Chapter 1 for a fuller discussion.

20. MacLean 2006: 336.

21. The greater emphasis on merit defined as intelligence (especially via intelligence tests), talent, ability, and "cleverness" rather than effort is clear in early descriptions of meritocracy, such as Young 1958 and Bell 1973. One of the main objectives of meritocracy was to increase national competitiveness by harnessing the previously untapped *talent* of the lower classes.

22. For both ideological and psychological reasons, beliefs in a just world are common in unjust societies, fostering both social legitimacy and pro-social behavior (e.g., Hochschild 1995; Jost and Major 2001). However, these beliefs vary across nations as well as across individuals, with beliefs in fairness appearing to be higher in more unequal societies but lower among minority groups (e.g., Benabou and Tirole 2006, Fong 2001, O'Brien and Major 2005, Svallfors 2006).

23. Fong 2001; Alesina and Glaser 2004; Benabou and Tirole 2006.

24. The exact wording of the question is: "Some people say that people get ahead by their own hard work; others say that lucky breaks or help from other people are more important. Which do you think is most important?" The response categories are "hard work is most important," "hard work, luck equally important," and "luck or help from other people most important."

25. As discussed in Chapter 3, the three questions on income inequality that serve as outcomes in this chapter are Likert items (with strong agreement, agreement, neither, disagreement, and strong disagreement as response categories) and ask about whether "differences in income in America are too large," "inequality continues to exist because it benefits the rich and powerful," and "large differences in income are unnecessary for America's prosperity." The models on which Figure 4.2 is based are provided in the first panel of Appendix Table A4.1, and are calculated for the typical respondent after controlling for the wide range of factors discussed in Chapter 3. See the Appendix to Chapter 3 for further details on the methods used to analyze the General Social Survey data.

26. This average marginal effect (0.046) is also larger than the marginal effect of the forced-choice "get ahead" question (0.041) on beliefs about the rich and powerful despite having more categories (five versus three categories).

27. Bartels 2008; Lamont 2000; Fisk 2011.

28. This conclusion is based on separate year-by-year bivariate probit models, with the first outcome defined as strong agreement to the "benefits the rich" question and the second outcome defined as *not* thinking that hard work alone is the most important factor in getting ahead (i.e., selecting luck/help from others or both luck/help from others and hard work). As a measure of endogeneity, the correlation of errors of these two outcomes is relatively low and not as high as in a separate bivariate probit regression with mobility pessimism as the second outcome. Moreover, the correlation of errors is highest in 1987 (.207)**, followed by 2008 (.181)*, 1996 (.165)**, and 2000 (.104). The forced-choice "get ahead" question is not asked in 1992, but the more detailed questions about getting ahead are. The only factors

that are endogenous with the "benefits" question are "knowing the right people" and "coming from a wealthy family." The correlation of errors for these factors as the second outcome is higher in 1992 than in 1987 and 2000 (the only other years of data for these questions).

29. There is little change in the coefficients for the year variables when the "get ahead" variables are included in regressions in which strong agreement to the inequality questions are the outcomes.

30. This may seem like an unlikely combination of trends, but several studies argue that Americans respond to economic hardship not by demanding government intervention but by resorting to their own devices, which suggests a greater emphasis on the necessity of hard work during difficult times (e.g., Feldman 1982; Greenberg 1996).

31. Again, see Greenberg 1996; Feldman 1982.

32. In three of the four years, five occupations are available: executives, cabinet ministers, doctors, skilled workers, and unskilled workers. Unfortunately, in 2010, skilled workers were excluded from the survey, leaving three high-level and only one low-level occupation in all four years. Therefore, I focus on only the two occupations at the top and bottom that are available in all four years. Analyses with the five occupations in three years are consistent with these results.

33. The figures here are based on the actual amounts reported by respondents for executives, unskilled workers, and doctors, some of which were not disclosed in the public-use sample of the GSS that contains only a single top-coded category of one million dollars or more. The raw data were then top coded to eliminate outliers: the top .2 percent of cases for unskilled workers, the top .3 percent for doctors, the top .4 percent for the desired pay of executives, and the top .7 percent for the perceived pay of executives.

34. Across all years, 64 percent of Americans believed unskilled workers deserved more than they earned, and the same percent believed that executives deserved less than they earned.

35. My results may differ because I use the actual values above the top-coded category for executives (cf. Osberg and Smeeding 2006).

36. See Osberg and Smeeding 2006 on the gap between actual executive pay and that estimated by respondents.

37. Many other variations on this basic measure were tested as well with similar results (Jasso 1999; Osberg and Smeeding 2006; Kelley and Evans 1993).

38. As shown in the second panel of Table 4.5, the average marginal increase in strong agreement to the "prosperity" question from 1987 to 1992 is reduced from 0.076 to 0.063 points (or by $(1-(0.063/0.076))*100 = 17$ percent) when preferences for less pay inequality are taken into account. This obtains for y-standardized coefficients as well.

39. Note that strong agreement to the question about the benefits of income inequality for the rich is significantly higher, after controls, only in 1996, which is why the year dummies in the second panel of Table 4.5 for that outcome are not significant.

40. Individuals who estimate a higher level of inequality may be more sensitive to and disapproving of inequality, exaggerating the degree of inequality to

correspond with more egalitarian norms, in which case we would expect a strong association with beliefs about income inequality. Like the other models in this section, these models control for partisanship, ideology, education, income, and other related factors.

41. This was true when the perceived pay disparities variable was entered alone and when it was entered together with the measure of just deserts opportunity.

42. It is possible, however, that preferences regarding pay at the top are well represented by preferences about executive pay, whereas preferences regarding pay at the bottom, or in the middle, are not well represented by preferences about the pay of unskilled factory workers. Thus this analysis should be replicated with a more representative set of occupations, especially at the bottom and middle of the distribution.

43. Enns and Kellstedt 2008; Lewis-Beck and Stegmaier 2007.

44. The first follow-up question asks about whether the difference in income was much or somewhat smaller or larger ("Would you say the difference in incomes is much (larger/smaller) or somewhat (larger/smaller)?" The second follow-up asks "Do you think this is a good thing, a bad thing, or haven't you thought about it?"

45. The recession lasted from March to November 2001 (Business Cycle Reporting Committee, National Bureau of Economic Research, http://www.nber.org/cycles/july2003.html).

46. Across the two years of 2002 and 2004, we can only compare perceptions of national economic conditions and not personal finances. Respondents are asked explicitly whether their financial situation is the "same" in 2002 but not in 2004 (the wording in 2004 is the more typical). Fortunately, perceptions of national economic conditions have a much stronger effect on beliefs about economic inequality than do perceptions of personal finances.

47. These are weighted percentages derived from responses to three questions about whether income inequality is larger/smaller/about the same than twenty years ago, how much larger/smaller, and whether this is a good thing/bad thing/have not thought about it (see also note 44). The joint distribution is measured as: 5=much larger and bad thing; 4=somewhat larger and a bad thing, or somewhat smaller/much smaller and a good thing; 3=unsure of trend, or declined and no opinion; 2=larger and no opinion; 1=larger and good thing or smaller and bad thing. The percentages reported in the text include categories 4 and 5 but exclude those who thought income inequality fell. The mean of the joint variable rose as well, from 3.33 in 2002 to 3.46 in 2004. The scale is adapted from Bartels 2008: 146.

48. These results are predicted probabilities derived from two separate ordered probit regressions in which perceptions of national economic conditions and income inequality are the outcomes, respectively. The regression for national economic conditions included variables for political views, party identification, education, year dummies for 2004 and 2008, an interaction between the 2004 dummy and party identification, and views about whether income inequality changed. The regression for income inequality included variables for political views, party identification, education, year dummies,

an interaction between the 2008 dummy and party identification, and views about the national economy. Control variables were set to the midpoints on their scales to derive predicted probabilities.

49. Feldman 1987.

50. Kellstedt 2000. In separate analyses, I found trends to be similar for comparable questions in the GSS (HLPBLK, NATRACEY, and NATRACE), which also have no effect on the time trend of the three questions about beliefs regarding income inequality.

51. The exact wording of the question is: "Recently there has been a lot of talk about women's rights. Some people feel that women should have an equal role with men in running business, industry and government. Others feel that a women's place is in the home. And of course, some people have opinions somewhere in between. Where would you place yourself on this scale or haven't you thought much about this?" This question measures support for women's equality rather than concerns about the lack of equality between men and women. The latter type of question is not available in either the ANES or the GSS. Thus we must infer that concerns about gender inequality would not have grown at the same time as support for gender equality.

52. One thing we know is that Americans are much more likely to attribute gender inequality to discrimination than they are to attribute racial inequality to discrimination (Kluegal and Smith 1986). In an analysis of the 2002 ANES special modules on explanations of gender, racial, and income inequalities, "discrimination holds women back" garnered the largest share of respondents saying that it was "very important" (41 percent) in explaining gender inequality in jobs and incomes (among six explanations offered). This was followed in order of importance by two other "structural" explanations: "government policies help men more" (25 percent) and "women don't get a chance to get a good education" (22 percent). By contrast, only 20 percent said discrimination was a "very important" explanation of racial disparities. The most important explanation of both racial disparities and disparities between high- and low-income groups was a structural explanation as well, however: the lack of a "chance to get a good education" (28 percent thought this was a very important explanation of racial disparities and 56 percent of income disparities).

53. However, warm feelings toward blacks result in greater concerns about inequality.

54. That is, either the rich are especially unpopular when income inequality is seen as particularly objectionable, or the rich are maligned for their negligent stewardship of the economy (i.e., for delivering inequitable rather than equitable growth).

55. It is possible that unfair pay for other occupations at the bottom or in the middle (besides unskilled workers) would affect attitudes toward inequality as well, but these are not available in the complete time series.

Chapter 5: Americans' Social Policy Preferences in the Era of Rising Inequality

1. This chapter extends the analysis in McCall and Kenworthy 2009.

2. Jacobs and Skocpol 2005: 217–218 concluded that the study of "changes in political behavior and public opinion [will be] essential to evaluate the impact of rising economic inequality. This will require assembling over-time data on a comprehensive set of critical indicators – from public opinion and political behavior to trends in economic distribution and organizational activity."

3. Jacobs and Skocpol 2005; Brooks and Manza 2007.

4. On the distinction between operational liberals and ideological conservatives, see Free and Cantril 1967.

5. For example, see Bartels 2005, 2008 on the "ignorance" view (as discussed in greater detail in Chapter 1) and Page and Jacobs 2009 on the "ambivalence" view.

6. Bartels 2005 examined the relationship between attitudes about rising income inequality and the George W. Bush tax cuts.

7. Studies over time of changes in attitudes about income inequality and social policy preferences in recent decades have focused on societies undergoing rapid social change, such as Eastern Europe (e.g., Kluegal, Mason, and Wegener 1995), whereas recent empirical research on this topic in the United States has focused on a single point in time (e.g., Bartels 2005, 2008).

8. More information on social policy preferences from public opinion organizations is provided in McCall and Kenworthy 2009. In this chapter, we focus on data from the GSS during the period in which attitudinal data on income inequality are available (i.e., 1987 to 2010).

9. The ANES times series of six questions on egalitarianism (examined in Chapter 4) cannot be used because they are skewed toward beliefs about equality of opportunity (e.g., equal chances) and formal equality (e.g., equal rights and treatment) and not equality of outcomes (e.g., income disparities). Substitutions proposed in a 1987 Pilot Study would have moved the scale "away from equality of opportunity [and] toward equality of outcomes" with questions that mentioned "the distribution of wealth" and "economic differences," but the changes were not adopted (Feldman 1987: 3). Feldman provides a psychometric evaluation of the pilot questions that raises potentially important empirical and conceptual differences between equality of opportunity and outcomes. By contrast to the ANES questions on egalitarianism, the GSS questions mention "differences in income," "large differences in income," and "inequality" that benefits the "rich and powerful."

10. Note, for example, that the now widely reported measure of income held by the top percentiles and fractiles of the income distribution using income tax return data was not available until the early 2000s, well after the starting point of our study (Piketty and Saez 2003).

11. This is because this information is disseminated by the Census Bureau in its annual Current Population Report on *Income, Poverty, and Health Insurance*, which is widely read by journalists covering economic issues. The Gini coefficient is the portion of total household income that would need to be redistributed from high-income households to low-income ones in order to have a completely equal distribution.

12. This issue is explored in detail in earlier chapters. There are three indications of greater awareness of rising inequality in the 1990s as compared to the 1980s. First, consensus among academics and experts that rising inequality

was more than just a temporary phenomenon probably did not emerge until the early 1990s (e.g., Levy and Murnane 1992; Katz and Murphy 1992). Second, the media analysis of articles on inequality-related subjects in Chapter 2 showed that coverage was concentrated in the early 1980s and again in the early and mid-1990s. Third, several books by scholars during the mid-1990s noted the rise in negative media coverage of inequality in the United States, including Lipset 1996, Jacoby 1997, and Ladd and Bowman 1998.

13. *Economist* 2006, 28. In the aftermath of the Occupy Wall Street movement, however, another Economist issue on inequality in 2012 (October 13, 2012) said little about American views.

14. APSA Task Force 2004, 654. See also Alesina, Di Tella, and MacCulloch 2004.

15. Bowman 2000.

16. Mead 2004: 671.

17. To be consistent across questions, we inverted the responses to the "prosperity" question so that a positive score indicates a less tolerant position on inequality. The original wording is that inequality is *necessary* for prosperity. Note also that this indicates some variation in the direction of question wording among the three questions, with two questions worded in a positive direction (so that agreement indicates support for greater equality) and one worded in a negative direction. See the Appendix to Chapter 3 for further information about these questions.

18. Page and Shapiro 1992.

19. The index is a simple addition of the responses on each question for cases with responses to all three questions (and the resulting scale ranges from -3 to 3, as the items were scaled for analysis to range from -1 to 1). Given the small number of items and the reversed direction of one item (i.e., the "prosperity" question), the alpha reliability coefficient is 0.46 with corrected item-total correlations of 0.43 (for the "too large" question), 0.29 (for the "benefits" question), and 0.16 (for the "prosperity" question). We could improve the alpha reliability to 0.56 if we removed the prosperity item, but given the similarity of mean trends over time in these questions and the conceptual importance of this dimension of inequality of outcomes, we retained the item. We have analyzed these data extensively with individual items, a two-item index, and the three-item index, and we do not find differences in our results.

20. The full set of variables used to control for compositional shifts over time includes age, gender, race, region of the country, size of place, employment status, marital status, household size, presence of children, years of education, family income, subjective class position, subjective chances for upward mobility, political ideology, and political party identification. See the Appendix to Chapter 3 for further information about these variables.

21. We use ordered logistic regression for these analyses given the categorical nature of the outcome variables. We pool the data across years for our main analyses but also run separate regressions for each year. The first criterion is met if the coefficients on dummy variables for each year of data after 1987 (i.e., 1987 is the excluded category) are positive and significant in the pooled regressions. The second criterion is met if the coefficient on the inequality

attitudes index is positive and significant in the pooled regressions and in the year-by-year regressions in the 1990s and 2000s. We further test for whether policy preferences among those concerned with inequality *shifted* over the 1990s, which is indicated by the year-by-year coefficients and an interaction term between the index and the year dummies in the pooled regressions. The third criterion is met if the general trend over time toward increasing support/spending is affected by the shifts occurring in the number of individuals concerned about inequality (a compositional effect) or in their policy preferences (a behavioral shift). See McCall and Kenworthy 2009 for further details on these models for the period up to 2000.

22. On growing partisan polarization, see McCarty, Poole, and Rosenthal 2006; Gelman 2008; Bartels 2008. Regarding our data, in Chapter 3 we did not find a strong effect of either income, education, or broad occupational category on views of income inequality, although more detailed measures may reveal a greater impact (e.g., Scheve and Slaughter 2006 use detailed occupational wages from census data to identify unskilled and skilled workers and their attitudes about immigration policy).

23. Feldman and Zaller 1992: 288.

24. There have been many extensive studies of the relationship between egalitarian norms (or humanitarian and pragmatic concerns) and policy preferences, with most exploring the conflicts and ambivalence that egalitarian sentiments produce within a culture that emphasizes individual responsibility (Hochschild 1981; McCloskey and Zaller 1984; Verba and Orren 1985; Kluegal and Smith 1986; Feldman 1988; Feldman and Zaller 1992; Feldman and Steenbergen 2001). For evidence of little ambivalence on a scale measuring support for social welfare policies, see Steenbergen and Brewer 2004.

25. Tolerance for inequality of outcomes, in particular, is often inferred from lack of support for redistributive policies: "To recapitulate, although most Americans support a high level of equality among social groups and favor equality of opportunity, they appear to be less concerned about inequality in economic outcomes. For example, there is little public support for a massive redistribution of income or wealth" (Schlozman et al. 2005: 28).

26. Meltzer and Richard 1981. See also Kenworthy and Pontusson 2005; Kenworthy and McCall 2008.

27. It is well-known that Americans are particularly hostile to "welfare" (Katz 1989; Gilens 1999).

28. Soss and Schram 2007.

29. We also confirmed these results using y-standardized coefficients.

30. Indeed, the evidence points toward a smaller positive effect of inequality attitudes on support for *every* traditional redistributive policy (i.e., a smaller coefficient on the index in year-by-year equations not shown here). Although these are not always significantly smaller in 1996, the uniformity of the results is striking. Note that the sample sizes are relatively small given the split-ballot design of the GSS for the policy questions ($N \approx 350$), so the standard errors of the estimates are larger.

31. Bartels 2005.

32. In addition to the citations in endnote 24, see Lane 1986 and Hochschild 1995.
33. Matusow 1984; Goldin and Katz 2008. Many economists also assume that "social programs such as job training and college tuition subsidies are central features of the modern welfare state" (Cunha, Heckman, and Navarro 2006: 295).
34. Bowles and Gintis 1976; Jencks et al. 1972; Wolff 2006.
35. Korpi 1983; Hicks 1999; Huber and Stephens 2001.
36. Wilensky 1975: 6.
37. APSA Task Force 2004: 654.
38. As shown in Chapter 3, pessimism about upward mobility did increase from 1987 to 1992, 1996, 2008, and 2010 (from 10.5 percent of respondents in 1987 strongly disagreeing or disagreeing that "people like me and my family have a good chance of improving our standard of living" to roughly a quarter or more in the early and mid-1990s and the late 2000s).
39. Teixeira and Rogers 2000.
40. Greenberg 1996. In a somewhat similar vein, in trying to explain why self-interest is only weakly connected to political outcomes, Stanley Feldman argues that "the vast majority of Americans believe that economic mobility is in fact a function of personal initiative" rather than political action (Feldman 1982: 464). Feldman finds that Americans do not fault social conditions for their personal situation, whereas Greenberg argues that Americans fault social conditions but do not expect them to change and are therefore left to their own devices. In the 2002 ANES, there is support for both views. The most common explanation for income differences was that "some people don't have a chance to get a good education" (55 percent), above "some people just don't work hard" (45 percent) (Bartels 2005: 18). The third and fourth most common explanations were "discrimination" and government policies that "helped high income workers more" (25 percent each).
41. McCall and Kenworthy 2009.
42. When the responses to the two differently worded questions on spending on education are combined into a single pooled analysis, the increases in support are significant in the 2000s as well.
43. For both questions about education spending, the coefficient on the inequality attitudes index is not significant in 1987 and is significant in 1996 in separate regressions for each year. The interaction term (between the 1996 dummy and the inequality attitudes index) is significant for one of the questions on education spending. For further discussion of these interaction effects, see McCall and Kenworthy 2009.
44. Piketty and Saez 2007.
45. Hacker 2006.
46. Moene and Wallerstein 2001.
47. Going farther back, support increased more substantially in the late 1980s, pushing the long-term trend in the upward direction (and the correlation with the Gini coefficient is 0.73) (McCall and Kenworthy 2009).
48. For one of the questions, the year dummy for 1996 becomes significantly negative when the inequality attitudes index is added to the equations,

indicating that the growing number of individuals concerned about inequality stemmed a significant decline in support for health-care spending in 1996.

49. Data from the 1948–2008 Cumulative ANES support these diverging trends on education and other government services during this period. Using 1988 as the excluded category, to correspond with the base year of 1987 in our analysis of GSS data, we found that support for increased spending on public schools (VCF0890) and financial aid for college students (VCF0891) was significantly greater from the mid-1990s on (from 1994 to 2008) for the former and in 1992 and 1996 for the latter (which was not replicated in later surveys). In contrast, support for increased spending on government services "such as health and education" (VCF0839), child care (VCF0887), and social security (VCF9049) was either the same or significantly lower in the early and mid-1990s. Support for government health insurance (VCF0806) was significantly greater in 1992 but significantly lower or the same in 1994 and 1996, relative to 1988. No other controls were included in these regression equations. See also Schneider and Jacoby 2005, who describe the unusual dip in support for government policies in 1996.

50. Dinardo, Fortin, and Lemieux 1996; Piketty and Saez 2003.

51. For example, looking back at the early 1990s, Kevin J. Murphy, an economist and expert on executive compensation, argued that "consistent with *Time* Magazines's labeling of CEO pay as the 'populist issue that no politician can resist,' high CEO salaries emerged as a bipartisan campaign issue among the leading candidates in the 1992 presidential election"' (Murphy 1997: 418).

52. McCloskey and Zaller 1984; Lipset and Schneider 1983.

53. GSS respondents in the 1987, 1992, 2000, and 2010 were asked how much unskilled workers and chairmen of large national corporations were paid and how much they should be paid. The median ratio of "should" pay to perceived pay for unskilled workers grew from 1987 (1.11) to 2010 (1.20). The median ratio for chairmen of national corporations declined from 1987 (.70) to 2010 (.40). These calculations use the actual survey responses rather than the top-coded values available in the public use files of the GSS. See Chapter 4 for further details and analyses of these data.

54. Freeman and Rogers 1999; "Another Poll Brings Bad News for Wisconsin Governor Scott Walker," US News Blog, March 7, 2011.

55. Scheve and Slaughter 2006: 227.

56. Scheve and Slaughter 2006: 224.

57. Data from the 1948–2008 Cumulative ANES show some weak support for government guarantees of "a job and a good standard of living" (VCF0809) in the 1990s, relative to 1988 (for further details of the ANES analysis, see footnote 49).

58. See Saris and Sniderman 2004 for a review and collection of relevant essays. On misconstrued interests related to the George W. Bush tax cuts, see Bartels 2005.

59. Berensky 2002.

60. Regarding the issues of immigration and trade, Scheve and Slaughter 2006: 251 note that "only limited attention has been paid to the role of information

and elites in influencing how individuals evaluate policy alternatives and their interests."

61. Morgan 2005; Campbell 2007. But see Bartels 2005, who argues that expressed support for higher taxes on the rich does not result in support for specific policies that propose to do so (or opposition to policies that cut taxes on the rich).

62. Oregon Measure 66 was passed in 2010, as was Oregon Measure 67, which raised taxes on businesses and corporations. Similar measures have been passed in other states, most recently in 2012 in California. However, one such measure was rejected in Washington in 2011.

63. Sniderman and Bullock 2004.

64. Zaller 1992, 2004.

65. Schneider and Jacoby 2005. Mettler 2007 argues that there was a material basis for public opposition to programs such as AFDC, Food Stamps, and unemployment compensation as well: their benefit and coverage levels had been declining since the 1970s, reducing the constituency of supportive beneficiaries.

66. Campbell 2007: 16, 29.

67. Beyond a general rise in antiwelfare and antitax sentiment during the time period of our study, we have not sought to theoretically explain why rising inequality would *not* result in rising support for traditional redistributive policies, *contra* median-voter theories. Moffitt, Ribar, and Wilhelm 1998: 429 offer an alternative median-voter model based on median-voter responses to a drop in unskilled wages (an aspect of rising inequality). They argue that support for welfare state benefits will fall if "(i) falling wages induce greater caseloads and hence drive up the cost of a marginal increase in benefits; (ii) associated with the increase in caseload is an increase in work disincentives, which voters may dislike; and (iii) falling wages may create a gap between welfare and non-welfare working poor which voters may wish to reduce by benefit reductions."

68. Newman and Jacobs 2010.

Conclusion

1. See http://www.whitehouse.gov/the-press-office/2012/01/24/remarks-president-state-union-address.

2. This particular quotation comes from President Obama's speech on the economy in Osawatamie, Kansas, delivered on December 6, 2011. See http://www.whitehouse.gov/the-press-office/2011/12/06/remarks-president-economy-osawatomie-kansas.

3. William Galston, "Why Obama's New Populism May Sink His Campaign,", December 17, 2011, *The New Republic*, http://www.tnr.com; Andrew Kohut, "Don't Mind the Gap,", January 27, 2012, *New York Times*, http://campaignstops.blogs.nytimes.com; Stanley Fish, "Fair Is Fair," January 26, 2012, *New York Times*, http://campaignstops.blogs.nytimes.com.

4. Ellwood 2000; Piketty and Saez 2003; Neckerman 2004; Ermisch, Jantti, and Smeeding 2012. In addition, consistent with the argument in this book,

several prominent economists are now making the case in public and political venues that income inequality has curtailed opportunity, broadly construed to include equal access to education, intergenerational mobility, and economic growth. President Obama's Chief of Economic Advisors, Alan Krueger, delivered a well-publicized speech at the Center for American Progress directly on this topic a few weeks in advance of the 2012 State of the Union address. See also Joseph Stiglitz, "Of the 1%, by the 1%, for the 1%," May 2011, *Vanity Fair*, written prior to the Occupy movement; Reich 2010. The economic details of these claims are far from settled, however (e.g., Voichovsky 2009).

5. Reich 2010; Stiglitz 2011, 2012; Krueger 2012.

6. Even if the movement declared that demands were not part of its mission, and the media unfairly criticized the movement for not unifying around a set of concrete political and economic demands, there certainly were a wide range of problems and potential solutions aired by movement members, signaling the vast scope and complexity of the issue and the inability of a single demand or a few demands to address it. For example, some focused on money in politics while others focused on school and mortgage debt, without necessarily referring to income inequality per se.

7. Obama compared his desire to reduce inequality to Teddy Roosevelt's progressive attack on the excesses of industrial capitalism, which Roosevelt launched in a speech in Osawatamie, Kansas, in 1910. I discuss this and other eras in American history in Chapter 1.

8. See also Goldin and Katz 2008, Friedman 2005.

9. Galbraith 1958. The landmark theories developed at this time include Hochschild 1981, Kluegal and Smith 1986, Verba and Orren 1985, and McCloskey and Zaller 1984. On the hidden welfare state, see Howard 1997. On the role that growth played in generating revenues and financing the welfare state, Zelizer 2003. On the conditions and institutions that generated wage compression during World War II and in the 1950s, see Goldin and Margo 1992 and Lichtenstein 1989. Chapter 1 offers a fuller discussion.

10. Coleman 1966; Roemer 1998.

11. Kelley and Zagorski 2004.

12. Bell 1973: 453; Young 1958.

13. In the ANES 2008–2010 Panel Survey, for example, the range of responses across four waves and two different wordings of a question about whether income differences should be smaller or bigger was 55 to 62 percent in favor of a smaller difference. (See also note 18.)

14. Levy and Murnane 1992.

15. On critical as well as admiring perceptions of the rich, see also Lamont 2000.

16. On regulatory policies to reduce labor market insecurity and inequality, see Kalleberg 2011, Bernhardt 2012.

17. Bartels 2005, 2008; Norton and Ariely 2011; Osberg and Smeeding 2006.

18. In addition, regarding the role of knowledge of the level of income inequality, in the 2008–2010 ANES Panel Study, there appears to be little effect of identifying the exact difference in incomes between the top and bottom 5 percent or 20 percent on preferences about whether the income difference

should be bigger or smaller. Responses to these questions (in terms of the degree of opposition to inequality) were very similar to responses to the GSS questions that did not include factual information about the level of inequality.

19. Dinardo et al. 1996; Piketty and Saez 2003; Krugman 2002; McCall and Percheski 2010 provide a review.

20. Freeman and Rogers 1999; Rogers 2012; Krueger 2012.

21. For a similar impulse in understanding beliefs about policy preferences among the general public, see Lupia et al. 2007.

22. Bartels 2005.

23. For example, straightforward state referenda may be more effective in garnering support for redistributive policies than complex federal tax policies (as in Oregon Measures 66 and 67).

24. Whyte 2010; Kluegel et al. 1995; Xie et al. 2011.

25. Brooks and Manza 2007; Alesina and Glaeser 2004; Benabou and Tirole 2006; Pierson 2004.

26. Lamont 1992.

27. Lichtenstein 1989; Lamont 1992, 2000; Cohen 2003; Jacobs 2004; Zelizer 2003; Ferrie 2005; Hacker and Pierson 2005.

28. This is a large literature (e.g., Jost et al. 2003; Jost and Major 2001). For an important example of a related literature in sociology, see Jasso 1999. For recent research more along the lines of the arguments in this book, in which both system-challenging and system-justifying beliefs are examined, see Johnson and Fujita 2012.

29. Social psychologists typically study the effect of real world societal or contextual change in cross-national and comparative studies rather than in studies of changes in attitudes over time.

30. Recent examples include, Fiske 2011, Fiske and Markus 2012.

31. Lamont 2000.

32. Morgan and Winship 2007; Druckman et al. 2011.

References

Alesina, Alberto, Rafael Di Tella, and Robert MacCulloch. 2004. "Inequality and Happiness: Are Europeans and Americans Different?" *Journal of Public Economics* 88: 2009–2042.

Alesina, Alberto and Edward L. Glaeser. 2004. *Fighting Poverty in the US and Europe: A World of Difference*. New York: Oxford University Press.

Althaus, Scott. 2003. *Collective Preferences in Democratic Politics*. New York: Cambridge University Press.

Andrews, Daniel, Christopher Jencks, and Andrew Leigh. 2009. "Do Rising Top Incomes Lift All Boats?" Harvard University Kennedy School of Government Faculty Research Working Paper Series 09–018.

Autor, David. 2010. "The Polarization of Job Opportunities in the U.S. Labor Market." Washington, DC: The Hamilton Project.

Bartels, Larry M. 2005. "Homer Gets a Tax Cut: Inequality and Public Policy in the American Mind." *Perspectives on Politics* 3(1): 15–31.

Bartels, Larry M. 2008. *Unequal Democracy*. Princeton, NJ: Princeton University Press.

Baum, Christopher F., Mark E. Schaffer, and Steven Stillman. 2003. "Instrumental Variables and GMM: Estimation and Testing." Working Paper No. 545, Department of Economics, Boston College.

Baumol, William J., Alan S. Blinder, and Edward N. Wolfe. 2003. *Downsizing in America: Reality, Causes, and Consequences*. New York: Russell Sage Foundation.

Bebchuk, Lucian A. and Jesse M. Fried. 2003. "Executive Compensation as an Agency Problem." *Journal of Economic Perspectives* 17(3): 71–92.

Bell, Daniel. 1973. *The Coming of Post-Industrial Society: A Venture in Social Forecasting*. New York: Basic Books.

Bellah, Robert, Richard Madsen, William Sullivan, Ann Swidler, and Steven Tipton. 1985. *Habits of the Heart: Individuals and Commitment in American Life*. New York: Harper and Row.

Benabou, Roland. 2000. "Unequal Societies: Income Distribution and the Social Contract." *American Economic Review* 90(1): 96–129.

Benabou, Roland and Efe A. Ok. 2001. "Social Mobility and the Demand for Redistribution: The POUM Hypothesis." *Quarterly Journal of Economics* 16: 447–487.

Benabou, Roland and Jean Tirole. 2006. "Belief in a Just World and Redistributive Politics." *Quarterly Journal of Economics* May: 699–746.

Berensky, Adam J. 2002. "Silent Voices: Social Welfare Policy Opinions and Political Equality in America." *American Journal of Political Science* 46: 276–287.

Bernhardt, Annette. 2012. "The Role of Labor Market Regulations in Rebuilding Employment Opportunity in the U.S." *Work and Occupations* 39(4): 354–375.

Blank, Rebecca. 1997. *It Takes a Nation: A New Agenda for Fighting Poverty.* New York: Russell Sage Foundation, and Princeton, NJ: Princeton University Press.

Bluestone, Barry and Bennett Harrison. 1982. *The Deindustrialization of America.* New York: Basic Books.

Borklund, Anders and Markus Jantti. 2009. "Intergenerational Income Mobility and the Role of Family Background." Pp. 491–520 in W. Salverda, B. Nolan, and T. Smeeding, eds., *The Oxford Handbook of Economic Inequality.* New York: Oxford University Press.

Bowles, Samuel and Herbert Gintis. 1976. *Schooling in Capitalist America.* New York: Basic Books.

Bourdieu, Pierre. 1984. *Distinction.* Cambridge, MA: Harvard University Press.

Bowman, Karlyn H. 2000. "No Din over Dollar Divide." *Chicago Sun-Times,* July 31: 31.

Brooks, Clem and Jeff Manza. 2007. *Why Welfare States Persist.* Chicago: University of Chicago Press.

Busemeyer, Marius R. 2012. "Inequality and the Political Economy of Education: An Analysis of Individual Preferences in OECD Countries." *Journal of European Social Policy* 22(3): 219–240.

Campbell, Andrea L. 2007. "Parties, Electoral Participation, and Shifting Voting Blocs." Pp. 68–102 in P. Pierson and T. Skocpol, eds., *The Transformation of American Politics.* Princeton, NJ: Princeton University Press.

Campbell, Andrea L. 2010. "The Public's Role in Winner-Take-All Politics." *Politics & Society* 38(2): 227–232.

Campbell, John L. 2004. *Institutional Change and Globalization.* Princeton, NJ: Princeton University Press.

Chong, Dennis and James N. Druckman. 2007. "Framing Theory." *Annual Review of Political Science* 10: 102–126.

Chong, Dennis and James N. Druckman. 2009. "Identifying Frames in Political News." Pp. 238–267 in E. P. Bucy and R. L. Holbert, eds., *Sourcebook for Political Communication Research: Methods, Measures, and Analytical Techniques.* New York: Routledge.

Coleman, James. 1966. *Equality of Educational Opportunity.* Washington, DC: National Center for Educational Statistics.

Cohen, Lisabeth. 2003. *A Consumers' Republic: The Politics of Mass Consumption in Postwar America.* New York: Alfred A. Knopf.

Corak, Miles, ed. 2004. *Generational Income Mobility in North America and Europe.* New York: Cambridge University Press.

Cunha, Flavio, James Heckman, and Salvador Navarro. 2006. "Counterfactual Analysis of Inequality and Social Mobility." Pp. 290–346 in S. Morgan, D. Grusky, and G. Fields, eds., *Mobility and Inequality*. Palo Alto, CA: Stanford University Press.

Danziger, Sheldon and Peter Gottschalk, eds. 1994. *Uneven Tides*. New York: Russell Sage Foundation.

DeGrazia, Victoria. 1998. "Changing Consumption Regimes in Europe, 1930–1970: Comparative Perspectives on the Distribution Problem." Pp. 59–83 in S. Strasser, C. McGovern, and M. Judt, eds., *Getting and Spending*. New York: Cambridge University Press.

DeNavas-Walt, Carmen, Bernadette D. Proctor, and Jessica C. Smith. 2011. *Income, Poverty, and Health Insurance Coverage in the United States: 2010. Current Population Reports*, P60-239. Washington, DC: U.S. Government Printing Office.

DiMaggio, Paul, John Evans, and Bethany Bryson. 1996. "Have Americans' Social Attitudes Become More Polarized?" *American Journal of Sociology* 102(3): 690–755.

DiNardo, John, Nicole M. Fortin, and Thomas Lemieux. 1996. "Labor Market Institutions and the Distribution of Wages, 1973–1992: A Semiparametric Approach." *Econometrica* 64: 1001–1044.

Dobbin, Frank. 2009. *Inventing Equal Opportunity*. Princeton, NJ: Princeton University Press.

Druckman, James N. 2012. "The Politics of Motivation." *Critical Review* 24: 199–216.

Druckman, James N. and Kjerston Nelson. 2003. "Framing and Deliberation." *American Journal of Political Science* 47: 728–744.

Druckman, James N., Donald P. Green, James H. Kuklinski, and Arthur Lupia, eds. 2011. *Cambridge Handbook of Experimental Political Science*. New York: Cambridge University Press.

D'Souza, Dinesh. 2000. "Celebrate, Don't Mourn, Nation's Mass Affluence." *USA Today*, December 11: 29A.

Duru-Bellat, Marie and Elise Tenret. 2012. "Who's for Meritocracy? Individual and Contextual Variations in the Faith." *Comparative Education Review* 56(2): 223–247.

Dyck, Joshua and Laura Hussey. 2008. "The End of Welfare as We Know It? Durable Attitudes in a Changing Information Environment." *Public Opinion Quarterly* 72(4): 589–618.

Economic Mobility Project. 2009. "Findings from a National Survey & Focus Groups on Economic Mobility." Washington, DC: Pew Charitable Trusts.

Economist. 2006. "Inequality and the American Dream." June 17–23: 28–30.

Edsall, Thomas. 1984. *The New Politics of Inequality*. New York: W. W. Norton & Company.

Edsall, Thomas. 1988. "The Return of Inequality." *Atlantic Monthly*, 261 (June): 86.

Ellwood, David T. 2000. "Winners and Losers in America: Taking the Measure of the New Economic Realities." Pp. 1–41 in D. Ellwood, R. M. Blank, J. Blasi, D. Kruse, W. Niskanen, and K. Lynn-Dyson, eds., *A Working Nation*. New York: Russell Sage Foundation.

Enns, Peter and Paul M. Kellstedt. 2008. "Policy Mood and Political Sophistication: Why Everybody Moves Mood." *British Journal of Political Science* 38: 433–454.

Erikson, Robert S., Michael MacKuen, and James Stimson. 2002. *The Macropolity*. New York: Cambridge University Press.

Erikson, Robert and John H. Goldthorpe. 1992. *Constant Flux: Comparative Analysis of Social Mobility in Industrial Nations*. Oxford: Clarendon Press.

Ermisch, John, Markus Jantti, and Timothy Smeeding, eds. 2012. *From Parents to Children: The Intergenerational Transmission of Advantage*. New York: Russell Sage Foundation.

Esping-Andersen, Gosta. 2007. "Equal Opportunities and the Welfare State." *Contexts* 6(3): 23–28.

Fallows, James. 1985. "America's Changing Economic Landscape." *Atlantic Monthly* 255(March): 47–65.

Fantasia, Rick. 1988. *Cultures of Solidarity: Consciousness, Action, and Contemporary American Workers*. Berkeley: University of California Press.

Feldman, Stanley. 1982. "Economic Self-Interest and Political Behavior." *American Journal of Political Science* 26: 446–466.

Feldman, Stanley. 1987. "Evaluation of New Inequality Items." 1987 NES Pilot Study Report.

Feldman, Stanley. 1988. "Structure and Consistency in Public Opinion: The Role of Core Beliefs and Values." *American Journal of Political Science* 32: 416–440.

Feldman, Stanley, and Marco Steenbergen. 2001. "Social Welfare Attitudes and the Humanitarian Sensibility." Pp. 366–400 in J. H. Kuklinski, ed., *Citizens and Politics: Perspectives from Political Psychology*. New York: Cambridge University Press.

Feldman, Stanley and John Zaller. 1992. "The Political Culture of Ambivalence: Ideological Responses to the Welfare State." *American Journal of Political Science* 36: 268–307.

Ferree, Myra Marx, William Anthony Gamson, Jurgen Gerhards, and Dieter Rucht. 2002. *Shaping Abortion Discourse: Democracy and the Public Sphere in Germany and the United States*. New York: Cambridge University Press.

Ferrie, Joseph. 2005. "History Lessons: The End of American Exceptionalism? Mobility in the United States since 1850." *Journal of Economic Perspectives* 19(3): 199–215.

Fiorina, Morris. 2005. *Culture War? The Myth of a Polarized America*. Boston, MA: Pearson Longman.

Fiske, Susan T. 2011. *Envy Up, Scorn Down: How Status Divides Us*. New York: Russell Sage Foundation.

Fiske, Susan T. and Hazel Rose Markus, eds. 2012. *Facing Social Class: How Societal Rank Influences Interaction*. New York: Russell Sage Foundation.

Fong, Christina M., Samuel Bowles, and Herbert Gintis. 2006. "Strong Reciprocity and the Welfare State." Pp. 1439–1464 in S. Kolm and J. M. Ythier, eds., *Handbook of the Economics of Giving, Altruism, and Reciprocity: Volume 2*. Amsterdam: Elsevier B. V.

Fong, Christina M. 2001. "Social Preferences, Self-Interest, and the Demand for Redistribution." *Journal of Public Economics* 82(2): 225–246.

Frank, Robert H. 2007. *Falling Behind: How Rising Inequality Harms the Middle Class.* Berkeley: University of California Press.

Frank, Thomas. 2005. *What's the Matter with Kansas?* New York: Metropolitan Books.

Free, Lloyd, and Hadley Cantril. 1967. *The Political Beliefs of Americans.* New York: Simon & Schuster.

Freeman, Richard B., and Joel Rogers. 1999. *What Workers Want.* Ithaca, NY: Cornell University Press and the Russell Sage Foundation.

Friedman, Benjamin. 2005. *The Moral Consequences of Growth.* New York: Vintage Books.

Galbraith, John Kenneth. 1958. *The Affluent Society.* Cambridge, MA: Houghton Mifflin.

Gamson, William. 1992. *Talking Politics.* New York: Cambridge University Press.

Gamson, William. 2006. "A Review of Frames of Protest and Framing American Politics." *Political Communication* 23: 461–463.

Gans, Herbert. 2004. *Deciding What's News.* Evanston, IL: Northwestern University Press.

Gelman, Andrew. 2008. *Red State, Blue State, Rich State,* Poor State: *Why Americans Vote the Way They Do.* Princeton, NJ: Princeton University Press.

Gerring, John. 1998. *Party Ideologies in America, 1828–1996.* New York: Cambridge University Press.

Gilens, Martin. 1999. *Why Americans Hate Welfare: Race, Media, and the Politics of Antipoverty Policy.* Chicago: University of Chicago Press.

Gilens, Martin. 2001. "Political Ignorance and Collective Policy Preferences." *American Political Science Review* 95(2): 379–396.

Gilens, Martin. 2012. *Affluence & Influence: Economic Inequality and Political Power.* Princeton, NJ: Princeton University Press.

Giuliano, Paola and Antonio Spilimbergo. 2009. "Growing Up in a Recession: Beliefs and the Macroeconomy." Discussion Paper No. 4365. Bonn, Germany: Institute for the Study of Labor.

Goldin, Claudia and Lawrence Katz. 2008. *The Race between Education and Technology.* Cambridge, MA: Harvard University Press.

Goldin, Claudia and Robert Margo. 1992. "The Great Compression: The Wage Structure in the U.S. at Mid-Century." *Quarterly Journal of Economics* 107(Feb.): 1–34.

Gottschalk, Peter, and Sheldon Danziger. 2005. "Inequality of Wage Rates, Earnings, and Family Income in the United States, 1975–2002." *Review of Income and Wealth* 51: 231–224.

Grawe, Nathan D. 2004. "Intergenerational Mobility for Whom? The Experience of High- and Low-earning Sons in International Perspective." Pp. 58–89 in M. Corak, ed., *Generational Income Mobility in North America and Europe.* New York: Cambridge University Press.

Greenberg, Stanley B. 1996. "Private Heroism and Public Purpose." *The American Prospect* 7(28): 34–40.

Griswold, Wendy. 1987. "A Methodological Framework for the Sociology of Culture." *Sociological Methodology* 17: 1–35.

Hacker, Jacob. 2006. *The Great Risk Shift.* New York: Oxford University Press.

Hacker, Jacob and Paul Pierson. 2005. "Abandoning the Middle: The Bush Tax Cuts and the Limits of Democratic Control." *Perspectives on Politics* 3(1): 33–53.

Hacker, Jacob and Paul Pierson. 2010. *Winner-Take-All Politics*. New York: Simon & Schuster.

Halle, David. 1984. *America's Working Man: Work, Home, and Politics among Blue-Collar Property Owners*. Chicago: University of Chicago Press.

Harrison, Bennett and Barry Bluestone. 1988. *The Great U-Turn*. New York: Basic Books.

Hartz, Louis. 1955. *The Liberal Tradition in America*. New York: Harcourt Brace Jovanovich.

Haskell, Thomas. 1996. "Taking Exception to Exceptionalism." *Reviews in American History* 28(1): 151–166.

Haskins, Ron and Isabel Sawhill. 2009. *Creating an Opportunity Society*. Washington, DC: Brookings Institution.

Hauser, Robert M. and John Robert Warren. 1997. "Socioeconomic Indexes for Occupations: A Review, Update, and Critique." *Sociological Methodology* 27: 177–298.

Hetherington, Marc J. 1996. "The Media's Role in Forming Voters' National Economic Evaluations in 1992." *American Journal of Political Science* 40(2): 372–395.

Hicks, Alexander. 1999. *Social Democracy and Welfare Capitalism*. Ithaca, NY: Cornell University Press.

Hochschild, Jennifer. 1981. *What's Fair? American Beliefs about Distributive Justice*. Cambridge, MA: Harvard University Press.

Hochschild, Jennifer. 1995. *Facing up to the American Dream*. Princeton, NJ: Princeton University Press.

Hochschild, Jennifer. 2001. "Where You Stand Depends on What You See: Connections Among Values, Perceptions of Fact, and Political Prescriptions." Pp. 313–340 in J. H. Kuklinski, ed., *Citizens and Politics: Perspectives from Political Psychology*. New York: Cambridge University Press.

Hodge, Roger. 2008. "Class Notes." Pp. 359–360 in A. Lareau and D. Conley, eds., *Social Class: How Does It Work?* New York: Russell Sage Foundation.

Howard, Christopher. 1997. *The Hidden Welfare State: Tax Expenditures and Social Policy in the United States*. Princeton, NJ: Princeton University Press.

Huber, Evelyne, and John D. Stephens. 2001. *Development and Crisis of the Welfare State*. Chicago: University of Chicago Press.

Jackman, Mary R. and Robert W. Jackman. 1983. *Class Awareness in the United States*. Berkeley: University of California Press.

Jacobs, Lawrence R., and Robert Shapiro. 2000. *Politicians Don't Pander: Political Manipulation and the Loss of Democratic Responsiveness*. Chicago: University of Chicago Press.

Jacobs, Lawrence, and Theda Skocpol. 2005. *Inequality and American Democracy: What We Know and What We Need to Learn*. New York: Russell Sage Foundation.

Jacobs, Meg. 2003. "Pocketbook Politics: Democracy and the Market in Twentieth-Century America." Pp. 250–275 in M. Jacobs, W. Novak, and J. Zelizer, eds., *The Democratic Experiment*. Princeton, NJ: Princeton University Press.

Jacobs, Meg. 2004. *Pocketbook Politics*. Princeton, NJ: Princeton University Press.

Jacoby, Sanford. 1997. *Modern Manors: Welfare Capitalism since the New Deal*. Princeton, NJ: Princeton University Press.

Jacoby, William G. 2000. "Issue Framing and Public Opinion on Government Spending." *American Journal of Political Science* 44(4): 750–767.

Jasso, Guillermina. 1999. "How Much Injustice Is There in the World? Two New Justice Indexes." *American Sociological Review* 64(1): 133–168.

Jasso, Guillermina and Peter Rossi. 1977. "Distributive Justice and Earned Income." *American Sociological Review* 42(2): 639–651.

Jencks, Christopher. 1992. *Rethinking Social Policy*. Cambridge, MA: Harvard University Press.

Jencks, Christopher, Marshall Smith, Henry Acland, Mary Jo Bane, David Cohen, Herbert Gintis, Barbara Heyns, Stephan Michelson. 1972. *Inequality: A Reassessment of the Role of Family and Schooling in America*. New York: Basic Books.

Jencks, Christopher and Laura Tach. 2006. "Would Equal Opportunity Mean More Mobility?" Pp. 23–58 in S. Morgan, G. Fields, and D. Grusky, eds., *Mobility and Inequality*. Palo Alto, CA: Stanford University Press.

Johnson, India R. and Kentaro Fujita. 2012. "Change We Can Believe In: Using Perceptions of Changeability to Promote System-Change Motives over System-Justification Motives in Information Search." *Psychological Science* 23(2): 144–150.

Jonsson, Jan O., David B. Grusky, Reinhard Pollak, Matthew Di Carlo, and Carina Mood. 2011. "Occupations and Social Mobility: Gradational, Big-Class, and Micro-Class Reproduction in Comparative Perspective." Pp. 138–172 in T. M. Smeeding, R. Erikson, and M. Jantti, eds., *Persistence, Privilege, and Parenting: The Comparative Stuidy of Intergenerational Mobility*. New York: Russell Sage Foundation.

Jost, John, Sally Blunt, Jeffrey Pfeffer, and Gyorgy Hunyady. 2003. "Fair Market Ideology: Its Cognitive-Motivational Underpinnings." *Research in Organizational Behavior* 25: 53–91.

Jost, John and Brenda Major, eds. 2001. *The Psychology of Legitimacy: Emerging Perspectives on Ideology, Justice, and Intergroup Relations*. New York: Cambridge University Press.

Judt, Tony. 2005. *Postwar: A History of Europe since 1945*. New York: Penguin Books.

Kalleberg, Arne. 2011. *Good Jobs, Bad Jobs: The Rise of Precarious and Polarized Employment Systems in the United States*. New York: Russell Sage Foundation.

Katz, Michael. 1989. *The Undeserving Poor: From the War on Poverty to the War on Welfare*. New York: Pantheon Books.

Katz, Lawrence F. and Kevin M. Murphy. 1992. "Changes in Relative Wages, 19673–87: Supply and Demand Factors." *Quarterly Journal of Economics* 107(February): 35–78.

Kelley, Jonathan and M. D. R. Evans. 1993. "The Legitimation of Inequality: Occupational Earnings in Nine Nations." *American Journal of Sociology* 99: 175–225.

Kelley, Jonathan and Krzysztof Zagorski. 2004. "Subjective Social Location: Data from 21 Nations." *International Journal of Public Opinion Research* 16(1): 3–38.

Kellstedt, Paul M. 2000. "Media Framing and the Dynamics of Racial Policy Preferences." *American Journal of Political Science* 44(2): 239–255.

Kelly, Nathan and Peter Enns. 2010. "Inequality and the Dynamics of Public Opinion: The Self-Reinforcing Link between Economic Inequality and Mass Preferences." *American Journal of Political Science* 54(4): 855–870.

Kendall, Diana. 2005. *Framing Class: Media Representations of Wealth and Poverty in America*. Lanham, MD: Rowman & Littlefield.

Kenworthy, Lane. 2005. *Egalitarian Capitalism? Jobs, Incomes, and Equality in Affluent Countries*. New York: Russell Sage Foundation.

Kenworthy, Lane and Leslie McCall. 2008. "Inequality, Public Opinion, and Redistribution." *Socio-Economic Review* 6: 35–68.

Kenworthy, Lane, and Jonas Pontusson. 2005. "Rising Inequality and the Politics of Redistribution in Affluent Countries." *Perspectives on Politics* 3(3): 449–471.

Khurana, Rakesh. 2002. *Searching for a Corporate Savior: The Irrational Quest for Charismatic CEOs*. Princeton, NJ: Princeton University Press.

Kim, ChangHwan and Arthur Sakamoto. 2008. "The Rise of Intra-Occupational Wage Inequality in the United States, 1983–2002." *American Sociological Review* 73(Feb.): 129–157.

Klein, Jennifer. 2004. "The Politics of Economic Security: Employee Benefits and the Privatization of New Deal Liberalism." *Journal of Policy History* 16(1): 34–65.

Kloppenberg, James T. 2001. "In Retrospect: Louis Hartz's 'The Liberal Tradition in America'." *Reviews in American History* 29(3): 460–478.

Kloppenberg, James T. 2003. "From Hartz to Tockqueville: Shifting the Focus from Liberalism to Democracy in America." Pp. 350–380 in M. Jacobs, W. J. Novak, and J. E. Zelizer, eds., *The Democratic Experiment*. Princeton, NJ: Princeton University Press.

Kluegal, James R., and Eliot R. Smith. 1986. *Beliefs about Inequality: Americans' Views about What Is and What Ought to Be*. New York: Aldine De Gruyter.

Kluegal, James R., David S. Mason, and Bernd Wegener, eds. 1995. *Social Justice and Political Change: Public Opinion in Capitalist and Post-Communist States*. New York: Aldine De Gruyter.

Kochan, Thomas, Harry Katz, and Robert McKersie. 1986. *The Transformation of American Industrial Relations*. Ithaca, NY: Cornell University Press.

Korpi, Walter. 1983. *The Democratic Class Struggle*. London: Routledge and Kegan Paul.

Krueger, Alan. 2012. "The Rise and Consequences of Inequality in the United States." Washington, DC: Center for American Progress.

Krueger, Alan and Robert Solow, eds. 2001. *The Roaring Nineties*. New York: Russell Sage Foundation.

Krugman, Paul. 2002. "For Richer." *New York Times Magazine*, October 20: 62–142.

Krugman, Paul. 2007. *The Conscience of a Liberal*. New York: W. W. Norton & Company.

Kryson, Maria. 2000. "Prejuduce, Politics, and Public Opinion: Understanding the Sources of Racial Policy Attitudes." *Annual Review of Sociology* 26: 135–168.

Kuhnen, Camelia and Alexandra Niessen. 2012. "Public Opinion and Executive Compensation." *Management Science* Articles in Advance: 1–24.

Kuttner, Robert. 1983. "The Declining Middle." *Atlantic Monthly*, 252(July): 60.

Kuznets, Simon. 1955. "Economic Growth and Income Inequality." *American Economic Review* 45: 1–28.

Ladd, Carll Everett and Karlyn H. Bowman. 1998. *Attitudes toward Economic Inequality*. Washington, DC: American Enterprise Institute.

Lamont, Michele. 1992. *Money, Morals, and Manners: The Culture of the French and American Upper-Middle Class*. Chicago: University of Chicago Press.

Lamont, Michele. 2000. *The Dignity of Working Men: Morality and the Boundaries of Race, Class, and Immigration*. Boston, MA: Harvard University Press and Russell Sage Foundation.

Lamont, Michele and Virag Molnar. 2002. "The Study of Boundaries in the Social Sciences." *Annual Review of Sociology* 28: 167–195.

Lane, Robert E. 1962. *Political Ideology: Why the American Common Man Believes What He Does*. New York: Free Press.

Lane, Robert E. 1986. "Market Justice, Political Justice." *American Political Science Review* 80: 383–402.

Lareau, Annette and Dalton Conley, eds. 2008. *Social Class: How Does It Work?* New York: Russell Sage Foundation.

Lemieux, Thomas. 2008. "The Changing Nature of Wage Inequality." *Journal of Population Economics* 21: 21–48.

Leonhardt, David. 2006. "Pockets Half Empty, or Half Full." *New York Times*, September 3, 2006: 1, 12.

Levy, Frank. 1987. *Dollars and Dreams*. New York: Russell Sage Foundation.

Levy, Frank and Richard Michel. 1986. "An Economic Bust for the Baby Boom." *Challenge* March/April: 33–39.

Levy, Frank and Richard Murnane. 1992. "U.S. Earnings Levels and Earnings Inequality: A Review of Recent Trends and Proposed Explanations." *Journal of Economic Literature* 30: 1333–1381.

Lewis-Beck, Michael and Mary Stegmaier. 2007. "Economic Models of Voting." Pp. 518–537 in R. Dalton and H. Klingemann, eds., *Oxford Handbook of Political Behavior*. New York: Oxford University Press.

Lichtenstein, Nelson. 1989. "From Corporatism to Collective Bargaining: Organized Labor and the Eclipse of Social Democracy in the Postwar Era."

Pp. 122–152 in S. Fraser and G. Gerstle, eds., *The Rise and Fall of the New Deal Order*. New York: Princeton University Press.

Lindert, Peter H. and Jeffrey G. Williamson. 2011. "American Incomes Before and After the Revolution." National Bureau of Economic Research Working Paper 17211.

Lipset, Seymour Martin. 1996. *American Exceptionalism: A Double Edged Sword*. New York: W. W. Norton & Company.

Lipset, Seymour Martin and William Schneider. 1987. *The Confidence Gap: Business, Labor, and Government in the Public Mind*. Baltimore, MD: Johns Hopkins University Press.

Long, Jason and Joseph Ferrie. 2007. "The Path to Convergence: Intergenerational Occupational Mobility in Britain and the United States in Three Eras." *Economic Journal* 117: C61–71.

Long, J. Scott and Jeremy Freese. 2003. *Regression Models for Categorical Dependent Variables Using Stata*. College Station, TX: Stata Press.

Lupia, Arthur, Adam Seth Levine, Jesse Menning, and Gisela Sin. 2007. "Were Bush Tax Cut Supporters 'Simply Ignorant?' A Second Look at Conservatives and Liberals in 'Homer Gets a Tax Cut.'" *Perspectives on Politics* 5(4): 773–784.

MacLean, Nancy. 2006. *Freedom Is Not Enough: The Opening of the American Workplace*. Cambridge, MA: Harvard University Press and Russell Sage Foundation.

Madrick, Jeff. 2003. "Inequality and Democracy." Pp. 241–265 in G. Packer, ed., *The Fight is for Democracy*. New York: HarperCollins.

Marshall, Thomas H. 1950. *Citizenship and Social Class, and Other Essays*. Cambridge: Cambridge University Press.

Matusow, Allen J. 1984. *The Unraveling of America: A History of Liberalism in the 1960s*. New York: Harper & Row.

McCall, Leslie. 2005. "Do They Know and Do They Care? Americans' Awareness of Rising Inequality." Unpublished manuscript, Northwestern University and Russell Sage Foundation.

McCall, Leslie. 2007. "The Undeserving Rich: Beliefs about Inequality in the Era of Rising Inequality." Unpublished manuscript, Department of Sociology, Northwestern University.

McCall, Leslie and Kenworthy, Lane. 2009. "Americans' Social Policy Preferences in the Era of Rising Inequality." *Perspectives on Politics* 7(3): 459–484.

McCall, Leslie and Jeff Manza. 2011. "Class Differences in Political and Social Attitudes." Pp. 552–570 in R. Y. Shapiro and L. R. Jacobs, eds., *The Oxford Handbook of American Public Opinion and the Media*. New York: Oxford University Press.

McCall, Leslie and Christine Percheski. 2010. "Income Inequality: New Trends and Research Directions." *Annual Review of Sociology* 36: 329–347.

McCarty, Nolan, Keith Poole, and Howard Rosenthal. 2006. *Polarized America*. Cambridge, MA: MIT Press.

McCleary, Rachel M. and Robert J. Barro. 2006. "Religion and Economy." *Journal of Economic Perspectives* 20(2): 49–72.

McClosky, Herbert and John Zaller. 1984. *The American Ethos: Public Attitudes toward Capitalism and Democracy*. Cambridge, MA: Harvard University Press.

McCormick, John P. 2011. *Machiavellian Democracy*. New York: Cambridge University Press.

McLahanan, Sarah and Christine Percheski. 2008. "Family Structure and the Reproduction of Inequalities." *Annual Review of Sociology* 34: 257–276.

Mead, Lawrence M. 2004. "The Great Passivity." *Perspectives on Politics* 2: 671–675.

Meltzer, Allan H. and Scott F. Richard. 1981. "A Rational Theory of the Size of Government." *Journal of Political Economy* 89: 914–927.

Mettler, Suzanne. 2007. "The Transformed Welfare State and the Redistribution of Political Voice." Pp. 191–222 in P. Pierson and T. Skocpol, eds, *The Transformation of American Politics*. Princeton, NJ: Princeton University Press.

Mettler, Suzanne and Joe Soss. 2004. "The Consequences of Public Policy for Democratic Citizenship: Bridging Policy Studies and Mass Politics." *Perspectives on Politics* 2(1): 55–73.

Miller, David. 1992. "Distributive Justice: What the People Think." *Ethics* 102: 555–593.

Mills, Charles. 2008. "Racial Liberalism." *Publication of the Modern Language Association* 123(5): 1380–1397.

Mishel, Lawrence, Jared Bernstein, and Heather Boushey. 2003. *The State of Working America, 2002/2003*. Ithaca, NY: ILR Press.

Mishel, Lawrence, Jared Bernstein, and Sylvia Allegretto. 2007. *The State of Working America, 2006/2007*. Ithaca, NY: ILR Press.

Moene, Karl Ove, and Michael Wallerstein. 2001. "Inequality, Social Insurance, and Redistribution." *American Political Science Review* 95(4): 859–874.

Moffitt, Robert, David Ribar, and Mark Wilhelm. 1998. "The Decline of Welfare Benefits in the U.S.: The Role of Wage Inequality." *Journal of Public Economics* 68: 421–452.

Morgan, Kimberly J. 2005. "Financing the Welfare State: US Tax Politics in Comparative Perspective." Unpublished manuscript, Department of Political Science, George Washington University.

Morgan, Stephen, Gary Fields and David Grusky, eds. 2006. *Mobility and Inequality: Frontiers of Research from Sociology and Economics*. Palo Alto, CA: Stanford University Press.

Morgan, Stephen and Christopher Winship. 2007. *Counterfactuals and Causal Inference*. New York: Cambridge University Press.

Morin, Richard and John Berry. 1996. "A Nation That Poor-Mouths Its Good Times." *Washington Post*, October 13, A1.

Morris, Martina and Bruce Western. 1999. "U.S. Earnings Inequality at the Close of the 20th Century." *Annual Review of Sociology* 25: 623–657.

Mouw, Ted and Arne Kalleberg. 2010. "Occupations and the Structure of Wage Inequality in the United States, 1980s to 2000s." *American Sociological Review* 75(3): 402–431.

Murphy, Kevin J. 1997. "Executive Compensation and Modern Industrial Revolution." *International Journal of Industrial Organization* 15: 417–425.

Nackenoff, Carol. 1992. "Of Factories and Failures: Exploring the Invisible Factory Gates of Horatio Alger, Jr." *Journal of Public Culture* 25(4): 63–80.

Neckerman, Katherine, ed. 2004. *Social Inequality.* New York: Russell Sage Foundation.

Nelson, Thomas E. and Donald R. Kinder. 1996. "Issue Frames and Group-Centrism in American Public Opinion." *Journal of Politics* 58(4): 1055–1078.

Newman, Katherine. 1988. *Falling from Grace: The Experience of Downward Mobility in the American Middle Class.* New York: Free Press.

Newman, Katherine. 1993. *Declining Fortunes: The Withering of the American Dream.* New York: Basic Books.

Newman, Katherine and Elisabeth Jacobs. 2010. *Who Cares? Public Ambivalence and Government Activism from the New Deal to the Second Gilded Age.* Princeton, NJ: Princeton University Press.

Noah, Timothy. 2010. "The Great Divergence." *Slate.com.*

Norton, Michael and Daniel Ariely. 2011. "Building a Better America – One Wealth Quintile at a Time." *Perspectives on Psychological Science* 6(1): 9–12.

Novak, William J. 2008. "The Myth of the 'Weak' American State." *American Historical Review* 113(3): 752–772.

O'Brien, Laura and Brenda Major. 2005. "System Justifying Beliefs and Psychological Well-Being: The Roles of Group Status and Identity." *Personality and Social Psychology Bulletin* 31(12): 1718–1729.

O'Connor, Alice. 2002. *Poverty Knowledge: Social Science, Social Policy, and the Poor in U.S. History.* Princeton, NJ: Princeton University Press.

Osberg, Lars and Timothy Smeeding. 2006. "'Fair' Inequality? Attitudes toward Pay Differentials: The United States in Comparative Perspective." *American Sociological Review* 71: 450–473.

Page, Benjamin I., and Lawrence R. Jacobs. 2009. *Class War: What Americans Really Think about Class War.* Chicago: University of Chicago Press.

Page, Benjamin I. and Robert Y. Shapiro. 1992. *The Rational Public: Fifty Years of Trends in Americans' Policy Preferences.* Chicago: University of Chicago Press.

Pager, Devah and Hana Shepherd. 2008. "The Sociology of Discrimination: Racial Discrimination in Employment, Housing, Credit and Consumer Markets." *Annual Review of Sociology* 34: 181–209.

Pateman, Carole and Charles Mills. 2007. *Contract and Domination.* Malden, MA: Polity.

Perlstein, Steven. 1995. "Debaters Agree: Politicians, Financiers, Analysts at Capital Hill Forum Differ Sharply on What Can Be Done." *Washington Post,* December 7: B11.

Pew Research Center. 2007. "Trends in Political Values and Core Attitudes: 1987–2007." Available at: www.people-press.org.

Phillips, Kevin. 1990. *The Politics of Rich and Poor.* New York: Random House.

Pierson, Paul. 2004. *Politics in Time: History, Institutions, and Social Analysis.* Princeton, NJ: Princeton University Press.

Piketty, Thomas. 1995. "Social Mobility and Redistributive Politics." *Quarterly Journal of Economics* 110: 551–584.

Piketty, Thomas and Emmanuel Saez. 2003. "Income Inequality in the United States, 1913–1998." *Quarterly Journal of Economics* 118(1): 1–39.

Piketty, Thomas and Emmanuel Saez. 2007. "Income and Wage Inequality in the United States, 1913–2002." Pp. 141–225 in A. B. Atkinson and T. Piketty, eds., *Top Incomes over the Twentieth Century*. Oxford: Oxford University Press.

Pontusson, Jonas. 2006. "The American Welfare State in Comparative Perspective: Reflections on Alberto Alesina and Edward L. Glaeser, Fighting Poverty in the US and Europe." *Perspectives on Politics* 4(2): 315–326.

Pontusson, Jonas and David Rueda. 2010. "The Politics of Inequality: Voter Mobilization and Left Parties in Advanced Industrial States." *Comparative Political Studies* 43(6): 675–705.

Ragin, Charles C. 1987. *The Comparative Method: Moving beyond Qualitative and Quantitative Strategies*. Berkeley: University of California Press.

Rainwater, Lee. 1974. *What Money Buys: Inequality and the Social Meanings of Income*. New York: Basic Books.

Reich, Robert. 2010. *Aftershock: The Next Economy and America's Future*. New York: Knopf.

Rodgers, Daniel T. 2000. *Atlantic Crossings: Social Politics in a Progressive Age*. Cambridge, MA: Harvard University Press.

Roine Jesper, Jonas Vlachos, and Daniel Waldenström. 2009. "The Long-Run Determinants of Inequality: What Can We Learn from Top Income Data?" *Journal of Public Economics* 93(7–8): 974–988.

Roemer, John E. 1998. *Equality of Opportunity*. Cambridge, MA: Harvard University Press.

Rogers, Joel. 2012. "Productive Democracy." Pp. 171–188 in K. MacDonald, S. Marshall, and S. Pinto, eds., *New Visions of Market Governance*. New York, NY: Routledge.

Saez, Emmanel. 2009. "Striking It Richer: The Evolution of Top Incomes in the United States (update with 2007 estimates)." Unpublished manuscript, Department of Economics, University of California, Berkeley.

Saris, Willem E. and Paul M. Sniderman, eds. 2004. *Studies in Public Opinion: Attitudes, Nonattitudes, Measurement Error, and Change*. Princeton, NJ: Princeton University Press.

Sawhill, Isabel and John Morton. 2007. *Economic Mobility: Is the American Dream Alive and Well?* Washington, DC: Pew Charitable Trusts.

Scheve, Kenneth and Matthew Slaughter. 2006. "Public Opinion, International Economic Integration, and the Welfare State." Pp. 217–260 in. S. Bowles, P. Bardhan, and M. Wallerstein, eds., *Globalization and Egalitarian Redistribution*. Princeton, NJ: Princeton University Press.

Schlozman, Kay L., Benjamin I. Page, Sidney Verba, and Morris Fiorina. 2005. "Inequalities of Political Voice." Pp. 18–87 in L. Jacobs and T. Skocpol, eds., *Inequality and American Democracy: What We Know and What We Need to Learn*. New York: Russell Sage Foundation.

Schneider, Sandra K. and William G. Jacoby. 2005. "Elite Discourse and American Public Opinion: The Case of Welfare Spending." *Political Research Quarterly* 58(1): 367–379.

Scott, Janny. 2008. "Reflection on 'Class Matters'." Pp. 354–358 in A. Lareau and D. Conley, eds., *Social Class: How Does It Work?* New York: Russell Sage Foundation.

Sears, Donald O., James Sidanius, and Lawrence Bobo, eds. 2000. *Racialized Politics: The Debate about Racism in America*. Chicago: University of Chicago Press.

Sen, Amartya. 1999. *Development as Freedom*. New York: Oxford University Press.

Sen, Amartya. 2000. "Merit and Justice." Pp. 5–16 in K. Arrow, S. Bowles, and S. Durlauf, eds., *Meritocracy and Economic Inequality*. Princeton, NJ: Princeton University Press.

Sen, Amartya. 2009. *The Idea of Justice*. Cambridge, MA: Harvard University Press.

Shepelak, Norma J. and Duane F. Alwin. 1986. "Beliefs about Inequality and Perceptions of Distributive Justice." *American Sociological Review* 51(1): 30–46.

Sides, John and Jack Citrin. 2007. "European Attitudes toward Immigration: The Role of Interests, Identities, and Information." *British Journal of Political Science* 37(3): 477–504.

Skocpol, Theda. 2007. "Government Activism and the Reorganization of American Civic Democracy." Pp. 39–67 in P. Pierson and T. Skocpol, eds., *The Transformation of American Politics*. Princeton, NJ: Princeton University Press.

Smeeding, Timothy M., Robert Erikson, and Markus Jantti, eds. 2011. *Persistence, Privilege, and Parenting: The Comparative Study of Intergenerational Mobility*. New York: Russell Sage Foundation.

Smith, Rogers M. 1993. "Beyond Tocqueville, Myrdal, and Hartz: the Multiple Traditions in America." *American Review of Political Science* 87: 549–566.

Smith, Rogers M. 1997. *Civic Ideals: Conflicting Visions of Citizenship in U.S. History*. New Haven, CT: Yale University Press.

Smith, Mark A. 2007. "Economic Security, Party Reputations, and the Republican Ascendance." Pp. 135–159 in P. Pierson and T. Skocpol, eds., *The Transformation of American Politics*. Princeton, NJ: Princeton University Press.

Soss, Joe, and Sanford F. Schram. 2007. "A Public Transformed? Welfare Reform as Policy Feedback." *American Political Science Review* 101(1): 111–127.

Sniderman, Paul M. and John Bullock. 2004. "A Consistency Theory of Public Opinion and Political Change: The Hypothesis of Menu Dependence." Pp. 337–358 in W. Saris and P. Sniderman, eds., *Studies in Public Opinion*. Princeton, NJ: Princeton University Press.

Stears, Marc. 2007. "The Liberal Tradition and the Politics of Exclusion." *Annual Review of Political Science* 10: 85–101.

Steenbergen, Marco R. and Paul R. Brewer. 2004. "The Not-so-Ambivalent Public: Policy Attitudes in the Political Culture of Ambivalence." Pp. 93–130 in W. Saris and P. Sniderman, eds., *Studies in Public Opinion*. Princeton, NJ: Princeton University Press.

Stein, Judith. 2010. *Pivotal Decade: How the United States Traded Factories for Finance in the Seventies*. New Haven, CT: Yale University Press.

Stiglitz, Joseph E. 2011. "Of the 1%, by the 1%, for the 1%." *Vanity Fair*. May 5, 2011.

Stiglitz, Joseph E. 2012. *The Price of Inequality: How Today's Divided Society Endangers Our Future*. New York: W. W. Norton & Company.

Stimson, John A. 2009. "Updated from James A. Stimson. 1999. *Public Opinion in America: Moods, Cycles, and Swings*, 2nd Ed. Boulder, CO: Westview Press." http://www.unc.edu/~jstimson/Data.html.

Strasser, Susan, Charles McGovern, and Matthias Judt, eds. 1998. *Getting and Spending: European and American Consumer Society in the Twentieth Century*. New York: Cambridge University Press.

Suarez, Ray. 2008. "Holding Up a Mirror to a Classless Society." Pp. 361–364 in A. Lareau and D. Conley, eds., *Social Class: How Does It Work?* New York: Russell Sage Foundation.

Sugrue, Thomas. 1996. *Origins of the Urban Crisis: Race and Inequality in Postwar Detroit*. Princeton, NJ: Princeton University Press.

Svallfors, Stefan. 2006. *The Moral Economy of Class*. Palo Alto, CA: Stanford University Press.

Toqueville, Alexis de. 2006 [1835, 1840]. *Democracy in America*. New York: HarperPerrenial Modern Classics.

Teixeira, Ruy and Joel Rogers. 2000. *America's Forgotten Majority: Why the White Working Class Still Matters*. New York: Basic Books.

Verba, Sidney and Gary Orren. 1985. *Equality in America: The View from the Top*. Cambridge, MA: Harvard University Press.

Voichovsky, Sarah. 2009. "Inequality and Economic Growth." Pp. 549–574 in W. Salverda, B. Nolan, and T. Smeeding, eds., *The Oxford Handbook of Economic Inequality*. New York: Oxford University Press.

Walzer, Michael. 1983. *Spheres of Justice: A Defense of Pluralism and Equality*. New York: Basic Books.

Warren, Elizabeth and Amelia Warren Tyagi. 2004. *The Two-Income Trap: Why Middle-Class Parents Are Going Broke*. New York: Basic Books.

Weir, Margaret. 1992. *Politics and Jobs: The Boundaries of Employment Policy in the United States*. Princeton, NJ: Princeton University Press.

Whyte, Martin King. 2010. *Myth of the Social Volcano: Perceptions of Inequality and Distributive Injustice in Contemporary China*. Palo Alto, CA: Stanford University Press.

Wilensky, Harold. 1975. *The Welfare State and Equality: Structural and Ideological Roots of Public Expenditures*. Berkeley: University of California Press.

Williams, Richard. 2006. "Generalized Ordered Logit/Partial Proportional Odds Models for Ordinal Dependent Variables." *The Stata Journal* 6(1): 58–82.

Wolff, Edward N. 2006. *Does Education Really Help?* Oxford: Oxford University Press.

Wooldridge, Jeffrey. 2002. *Econometric Analysis of Cross-Sectional and Panel Data*. Cambridge, MA: MIT Press.

Xie, Yu, Arland Thornton, Guangzhou Wang, and Qing Lai. 2011. "Societal Projection: Beliefs Concerning the Relationship between Development and

Inequality in China." Unpublished manuscript, University of Michigan Department of Sociology.

Young, Alford. 2004. *The Minds of Marginalized Black Men: Making Sense of Mobility, Opportunity, and Future Life Changes*. Princeton, NJ: Princeton University Press.

Young, Michael. 1958. *The Rise of Meritocracy 1870–2033: An Essay on Education and Equality*. London: Thames and Hudson.

Young, Michael. 1994. "Meritocracy Revisited." *Society* 31(6): 87–89.

Zaller, John R. 1992. *The Nature and Origins of Mass Opinion*. New York: Cambridge University Press.

Zelizer, Julian. 2003. "The Uneasy Relationship: Democracy, Taxation, and State Building since the New Deal." Pp. 276–300 in M. Jacobs, W. Novak, and J. Zelizer, eds., *The Democratic Experiment*. Princeton, NJ: Princeton University Press.

Zaller, John R. 2004. "Floating Voters in U.S. Presidential Elections, 1948–2000." Pp. 166–212 in W. Saris and P. Sniderman, eds., *Studies in Public Opinion*. Princeton, NJ: Princeton University Press.

Index

CPSIA information can be obtained at www.ICGtesting.com
Printed in the USA
LVOW12s1214060214

372589LV00005B/6/P

9 781107 699823